To Lisa

Keep 'em
growing

J. C.
Jeannie Cheatham

"O.K.
I will"

"Being an admitted, although recovering, racist and sexist when it comes to playing blues and jazz, I have [become] further educated and much less prejudiced after reading Jeannie Cheatham's book *Meet Me with Your Black Drawers On*. Jeannie's book drives home the fact that we who embrace music as a profession share common joys and common miseries. Having played with Jeannie I will never again say 'plays good for a woman.' I can't say she's 'one of the boys,' but she is definitely one of the musicians. Thanks, Jeannie, for a wonderful book from another point of view."

—FRED WESLEY, James Brown's former music director
and author of *Hit Me, Fred: Recollections of a Sideman*

"Jeannie, I never got a chance to thank you for writing the song 'Meet Me with Your Black Drawers On,' so let me do that [now]. Touring with the *Some of My Best Friends Are the Blues* revue gave me a chance to perform your song in twenty-one cities, and the audience response to it was great. You know you got the audience when they start slapping their knees. I know you've written a book [of the same name]; accept my best wishes on the success of it."

—DELLA REESE, singer, television and
movie actress, author, and minister

"The truth is alive and well in *Meet Me with Your Black Drawers On!* I know, because I've been the legendary Bo Diddley's band leader and bass player for twenty years. Prior to that, I got to spend two incredible years playing with Jeannie Cheatham. She taught me where 'the pocket' is. This book is right in 'the pocket.'"

—DEBBY HASTINGS, highly acclaimed bass player
for Bo Diddley and many other artists

"Behind the mesmerizing sound of Jeannie and Jimmy Cheatham's Sweet Baby Blues Band, there is the mesmerizing life of Jeannie Cheatham, which she chronicles in this captivating biography. *Meet Me with Your Black Drawers On* reads better than fiction. It has all the elements of a page-turner—a hardscrabble upbringing, race and gender discrimination, a love for music, a young girl's life on the road. There's more—this book is jazz history, love story, family triumph and tribulation, and a whole lot of adventure. Stitched together with lyrics, this is a fascinating saga of a life mostly spent on the road, and the sacrifices and rewards Jeannie Cheatham faced as she followed her muse. I laughed and I gasped as I read this book. It's a great read!"

—JULIANNE MALVEAUX, PH.D., economist and syndicated columnist
who writes for more than twenty national newspapers, including
USA Today, Los Angeles Times, Detroit News, and *San Francisco Examiner*

Meet Me with Your Black Drawers On

Meet Me with Your Black Drawers On

MY LIFE IN MUSIC

by Jeannie Cheatham

University of Texas Press   Austin

Requests for permission to reproduce material from
this work should be sent to:
Permissions
University of Texas Press
P.O. Box 7819
Austin, TX 78713-7819
www.utexas.edu/utpress/about/bpermission.html

♾ The paper used in this book meets the minimum requirements of
ANSI/NISO Z39.48-1992 (R1997) (Permanence of Paper).

Library of Congress Cataloging-in-Publication Data
Cheatham, Jeannie.
Meet me with your black drawers on : my life in music / by Jeannie Cheatham. — 1st ed.
p.   cm.
ISBN 0-292-71293-6 (cl. : alk. paper)
1. Cheatham, Jeannie.   2. Singers—United States—Biography.   I. Title.
ML420.C4705A3   2006
781.65′092—dc22
2005019192

DEDICATION

I dedicate this memoir to M'Ma, Elizabeth Evans;
to my babies, Shirley and Jonathan;
to my family, Rick, Dave, and Jo-Anne;
to my mentor and dearest friend, Mariam Kirby,
whose stern admonition to "Finish the damn book!"
spurred me onward;
and to my loving man,
who patiently read every word as I wrote them,
Jimmy Cheatham.

Contents

. . . .

Acknowledgments

. . . .

To *Monica Spilker*, cheerleader and guidance counselor;
Eve Shaw, *Danah Fayman*, and *Joannie Mosher*,
for their encouragement;
Glenn Barrows, president of Concord Records,
for his generosity;
Jere Hilton, *Tamara Rand*, *Gail Jacobson*, and *Louticia Grier*,
who lent me their shoulders to cry on;
Nansy Phleger, *Dickie Motherwell*, and *Lawrence Zaidman*,
for their spiritual support;
Cynthia Sesso,
for her invaluable input;
Carroll Parrott Blue,
for her wonderful assistance and unselfish contributions;

and to all the Cats and Griots,
given the gift of the soul of music,
who gathered no moss, carried the message, and dedicated
themselves to the spirit of the Sweet Baby Blues Band.

Bless them all.

Prologue
BRAND-NEW BLUES

. . . .

I tried on a brand new blues this morning;
'Cause my old blues don't fit no mo' . . .

The words of the blues song lodged inside my soul like static in an old radio—the dial set somewhere between stations.

My Great Gramma's words got all tangled up in that static. She always said, "Jeannie, you gotta know when to fight and when to run away. It takes a wise soul to know the difference."

Well, I don't know how wise a decision I had made, but I think I was running away so I *could* fight.

Early that morning, at the crack of dawn, I'd arrived at the Greyhound bus station and said hello to the jackbooted policeman on duty. His job was to stop and question all arrivals as they descended the bus steps. The city of Akron did not tolerate drifters. You had to show the cop your money or a letter about a job, or he would send you to the ticket agent, who would hand you a one-way ticket right back to wherever you had come from.

The policeman said, "Going out again, Miz Evans?"

I nodded yes. He was used to seeing me and the musicians I performed with, or M'Ma's gospel choir, or just me alone, going to play somewhere in the tristate area—Youngstown and Cleveland, Ohio; Erie, Pennsylvania; West Virginia; and all the little places in between. This morning's journey was different.

Got to change the way I'm living
Ain't nothing like it was before . . .

The lyrics were pounding in my head. A new song crying out to be born crept unbidden into my brain. My head began to ache. I rubbed my temples and thought, maybe someday I'll finish it.

I looked at my watch. There was still some time before the bus pulled out, so I headed to the restroom.

The room was spotless and deserted, too early in the morning to find an attendant on duty. The silent space felt like a sanctuary for those few moments. I took a deep breath and let it out slow. I was ready for change, but that didn't mean I felt confident about what I was doing.

Then my reflection flashing out at me from the restroom's mirrors caught my eye. Dark brown skin clear. Big eyes dark blue-brown. Lips thin, with Max Factor cherry red lipstick carefully applied. I pressed them together again to even out the color. One quick turn so that the long, full grey wool skirt flared out from my hips. I put my hands on my waist. The matching jacket was princess style—nipped in, with six self-covered buttons marching to the top of the neat little Peter Pan collar.

"I'm just a little too skinny," I said out loud to the empty stalls. I weighed ninety-eight pounds, with a size 0 bra. Well, really size 30, with rolled-up stockings stuffed inside to fill the cups.

After one quick pat of my freshly curled coal black hair, I took a nickel out of my big ol' purse and said, "Okay! Heads or tails—Cleveland or Columbus?"

Up! Up! The coin twisted and turned in the air. I caught it with my right hand and quickly clapped it onto the back of my left. "Tails—Cleveland! Heads—Columbus!"

I peeked under my hand. "Heads it is! Columbus, here I come!"

Turning on my high-heeled grey pumps, I wriggled my toes so that I could feel the hundred-dollar bill stashed in my right shoe and marched out of the restroom straight to the ticket window. I bought a ticket to Columbus and boarded the Greyhound bus, headed south from Akron.

I was eighteen years old, it was 1945, and the whole world was in flames.

I seated myself halfway between the driver and the john. The Greyhound started filling up, so I put my pocketbook on the seat next to me to ward off obnoxious characters. Most of the time the ploy worked superbly. Most men hated to ask you to move something from the seat so that they could sit in it. Besides, men had a short pipeline to their bladders and preferred sitting back by the john. Women didn't mind asking at all.

Sure enough, a tall skinny spraddle-legged white woman, her dishwater blonde hair swinging over her right eye, climbed into the bus, looked up and down the aisle, then indicated that she'd like to sit down beside me. I looked her over to see if she was a lonely soul who might talk me to death, or one who would just nod and smile and quickly fall asleep. Checking out the circles under her eyes, I decided that she was younger than she looked and had been hanging out all night long. She'd probably "kak" out as soon as the wheels started turning. So I shoved my big ol' pocketbook under the seat between my feet.

"Well, this is a great day for a long ride," she said hoarsely.

With the lyrics still loud in my head, I wouldn't meet her eyes, and said to myself, Damn! Did I read this wrong? Is she gonna talk all the way to Columbus?

But no, thank God, she promptly leaned her head back on the clean white square of cloth the Greyhound people supplied, and immediately fell sound asleep.

I breathed a sigh of relief and stared out the window as the bus lumbered out of the station, leaving a cloud of black smoke behind. Almost at once, practically everybody on the bus lit up a cigarette. It didn't really matter to me, 'cause the night before I had played piano all night long for a comic, two shake dancers, and the band finale in a crowded smoke-filled nightclub.

The bus rumbled through Akron, shifting gears, lurching through sudden stops and starts before finally hitting the two-lane highway due south. Tall buildings and bridges soon gave way to homes with backyards and swings made of old automobile tires. As the sun climbed in the sky over patchy gardens and giant sunflowers I knew I was on my way. Somewhere.

I was thinking that my life up until then had been just like that Greyhound bus: shifting gears, sudden stops and starts, clouds of smoke, and now a journey into the unknown.

"Lordy!" I sighed and tilted my head back, shifting, turning, trying to find a comfortable space for my neck, so stiff and tense I thought the bones might snap. Back and forth, back and forth I rolled my head, until finally some of the static in my mind started to clear.

I thought, I'm through with all of them! I had been a "good little girl"—going along to get along—working my fool head off trying to get somewhere in this world!

It seemed like all sorts of folks wanted to get in my way. The policeman who patrolled a small village between Cleveland and Akron came to mind. He was white and we weren't. That meant he could position himself so that he could stop us on our way home after performing Saturday nights, and force us to unload all our instruments by the side of the road. Then he would ask, "How much money y'all got?" And he'd hold out his hand. We'd have to fork over money so he would let us repack our stuff and go home.

Once we tried to outsmart him and said we'd played but hadn't gotten paid. He smiled with his lips—not with his ice blue eyes. "Well," he drawled, "y'all get that junk back into yo' automobile and y'all follow me back to the jail!"

We exchanged anxious glances and hurriedly reloaded everything, then jumped in the car and did exactly as he ordered. We were sweating, our hearts beating wildly, but nobody said anything.

We followed the police car, its siren wailing, back, back into the lonely woods on a narrow bumpy road. Finally we stopped in front of a little dark house. The lights and siren died, and he climbed out of the police car and walked back to our car. "Git out!" he barked. Malicious, he added, "Welcome to my home."

We felt anything but welcome. He hustled us up the worn wooden front steps, unlatched the door, and turned on the light inside. There wasn't much furniture: a scarred dark red leather sofa with the stuffing coming out, two spindly chairs, one leaning left, one leaning right.

Behind a wooden desk, O Lordy! stood a cage-like structure with bars on the front. "What y'all think of my jail?" he asked with a little sneer. "One of you is gonna stay here as ransom while the rest of you go home and git me some money."

My knees were shaking, but I wouldn't let on how frightened I was. The drummer, my cousin Charles, was a big guy—in stature and in spirit. He wanted to be a minister. He spoke up in no uncertain voice, "I'll stay here. You guys go on home and get the money." We knew what he meant. *Get goin' and get back!*

We did. We drove a ways and waited the time it would take to drive to Akron and return. Then we made our way back through the shadowy woods to the little jailhouse home, paid the money, and Charles was a free man. Glory!

We had a conference on the way home. Since there was no way to get to and from our gig without driving through that village, we decided to quit that good job for fear he would kill us one dreary night for resisting arrest, or some other redneck lie.

The bus lurched, and something bitter came up in my throat. I swallowed fast to keep it down and blinked even faster to hold back unwanted tears.

College? A lost opportunity! Working three jobs—running the elevator part-time at the YWCA, teaching piano to young people, and playing jazz with bands at night—never brought in enough money to allow me to continue college past the second year.

Art school? An impossible dream! I'd won a scholarship with my portraits and still lifes. But when the white officials had found out that I was colored, suddenly I wasn't qualified for *anything* but a token $50 worth of clothes. I wanted to kill them all! I had forced my tears back and stomped out without taking the money.

Now, I looked around at the other riders on the bus and took a deep breath. In my mind, angry thoughts twisted one upon another. Nobody's gonna make me cry! Nobody and nothin'! No more bending over backward—no bitter tears for me!

My whole body burned with fury, and the powerful words of the new blues song fueled my rage.

> *I'm gonna buy me a hatchet!*
> *Cut down my weepin' willow tree . . .*

"Aw, foot!" I muttered to myself. "I'd sure like to take all the fools that used me and abused me and shoot 'em in the face with a shit pistol!"

A roaring sound filled my ears. I shook my head, closed my eyes, and sat very still. After a while a cold calm descended over me, and I knew I had to settle down. Keep this up, I told myself, and you won't be worth a dime when you get to Columbus.

But the painful memories would not be denied, and my rage returned with a vengeance. I opened my eyes and stared down at my clenched fists, thumbs turned in like a little child's. "I'm gonna show them all!" I whispered.

There was only one thing certain. I was headed someplace, somewhere, somebody needed a good musician. As long as I kept my spirits high and my soul intact, I figured my ten fingers and the eighty-eight keys on a piano would take me anywhere I wanted to go.

"I don't need none of them!" My tone was fierce, my voice pitched low, it did not disturb my sleeping seatmate.

I felt a delicious stir of freedom and, at the same time, a shiver of fear and, way down deep inside, a shadow of sadness.

Nobody had bothered to say goodbye.

Meet Me with Your Black Drawers On

Back to the 'Hood

. . . .

I was born on a sultry August afternoon in 1927, in a small red house built by Greek immigrants down by the clear blue waters of Summit Lake in Akron, Ohio.

M'Ma was very young—so was M'Da. Since I was the first child of either, it took them quite awhile to notice that though I was born healthy and lively, for some unknown reason nothing was going in and, worst of all, nothing was coming out. Pretty soon it became apparent that I was becoming very uncomfortable.

The family doctor was completely mystified and could suggest nothing to relieve my condition, so Hattie was called in.

Hattie was M'Ma's mama, a tiny copper-colored woman with blue-gray eyes. Mac, my grandpa, nicknamed her "Fing" because, he said, "Her waist was so small, you could slip a finger ring around it." The child of a six-foot-four-inch Blackfoot Indian woman and a five-foot-four-inch Irishman, Hattie became a Christian Scientist in the South in the 1920s, and, being of very independent mind and spirit, she was sought after by everyone for her wise input and sage medical advice. She ministered to both animals and humans.

Hattie came to my cradle and peered down at my still, little brown body. Then she said, "Looks like nothin's goin' in and nothin's comin' out!"

Everyone nodded in solemn agreement.

"Give me that child!" she said quietly. "We'll see if she really wants to stay here with us or not!"

She took me home with her to her farm out in Springfield Township. She owned sixty-two acres that she'd acquired by buying up land that was in foreclosure. She worked as a maid and did husbandry for an old white man who was a real estate salesman and developer. They had enjoyed a long and fruitful friendship.

The farm was a fairyland, filled with fields of corn both sweet and seed, green grassy fields surrounded by one-hundred-year-old oaks, tall pines, and wildflowers in every color of the rainbow. Singing birds, bobolinks, redbirds, robins, whip-poor-wills, cardinals, and, every once in a while, a chicken hawk would come freewheeling in the blue sky. Hattie would grab the old gun stashed behind the kitchen door and take a shot—Boom! Boom!

"That'll learn you," she'd shout. "Go get yo' own farm!"

Near the farmhouse nestled Blue Pond, full of eating fish. Grandpa Mac would help us catch them, but we had to throw most of them back. "There's plenty of food at the house—we won't need the fish," he would say. "If you catch more than you can eat, you'll surely starve someday. Everything balances out," he'd chuckle. "Now, let me touch the hem of your garment." He always referred to that portion of the Bible when he hung out with us.

Everything on Hattie's farm was white—the ducks, the geese, the chickens, the dog, the cats, the goat, the house—even the outhouse.

Hattie used to say, "I got power and dominion over all these white things. Only God got power over me!" (Which is why she and Grandpa Mac got divorced in a real court of law—none of that reverse broom-jumpin' stuff for her.)

When we arrived at the farm she carefully checked me out and administered hot mineral oil to my swollen belly and gently massaged my little brown body—and lo—pretty soon—a miracle! Stuff came out, making room for stuff to go in, and thus began my odyssey on the earth.

Hattie said, "Well, that's that. The way this child holds on to everything, she either gonna go to jail or she gonna be famous."

She was right—I did both.

* * *

Life was sweet on the farm. Every evening Gramma Hattie would play the pump organ and Uncle Richard (M'Ma's youngest brother) would wind up the Victrola or play his trumpet. Big bands and Bessie Smith and Jay McShann—I was too little to know the difference, but Gramma had saved my life.

Finally, I was taken back to M'Ma and M'Da, just in time to be moved from the little red house to the little brown house on Bina Avenue in Akron. My sister, Charlotte, and my brother, Jerry, were born soon after.

Bina Avenue rose steeply from Summit Lake at the bottom to Manchester Road at the top. We lived a half block from the lake, and it was heaven to wake up early in the morning and breathe in air nobody else had breathed. On the right was a lovely piece of land covered with peach trees and with grapevines bending over with luscious dark purple fruit. You could look beyond the tall ancient oaks and rest your eyes on the grassy knoll that swept down to Summit Lake. This land belonged to Great-Aunt Catherine and Uncle Sid.

At the top of Bina Avenue lived an Italian family—Grampa Mac called them Eye-talyins—with two children who were our playmates, Jovie and Eddie.

Then came the home of Aunt Bessie (M'Ma's sister), Uncle James, and my three boy cousins, Junior, Charles, and Bobby.

At the bottom of the hill, on a corner lot, lived a couple of the "Caucasian persuasion"; they had moved to Bina Avenue all the way from Georgia. They were quiet people. Oh, they'd say, "How do?" when you passed their house, but they would get up off their porch swing and go into the house to avoid having much contact with us. Every once in a while the woman would cross the street, march halfway up Bina Avenue, pass the Reverend Frank's big house, and come down the walk leading back to our little brown house.

The woman knew that my little brother, Jerry, could be found sitting on the bottom step of the porch in his little white suit, swinging his feet in his little high-top white shoes, waiting for M'Ma to come home from work. Every once in a while he would look around and then say in his deep voice, "Ah want . . . my . . . Mama! Ah want . . . my . . . Mama!" He had a funny voice for a baby. For almost two years he didn't say anything. But once he started speaking, everything came out in a bass voice. It really startled grown-ups, but we were used to it.

The woman would walk up to our porch and sidle up to Jerry and say, "Hello there, little one. May I pick you up and hold you?"

He'd look up at her with his solemn little face and then look at us—Charlotte and me—then back to the woman and nod yes. She'd stoop over, pick him up, and hug him, all the time making little clucking noises. Then she'd kiss him on his round brown cheek, put him back down on the steps, say, "Goodbye, little sweet boy," and walk slowly back to her house.

M'Ma said, "Well, she doesn't have any children, and I guess her arms are hungry and empty for someone to love." M'Ma smiled at us and said, "You-all did the right thing, reporting her, though. Very good!" M'Da shifted his Red Man tobacco to the other side of his mouth and declared, "Yeah . . . one of her arms is probably hungry all right, but the other arm realize that the cute little brown baby surely gonna grow up to be a six-foot Negro one of these days!"

On our side of Bina Avenue, at the very top of the hill, lived the China-

Man and his invalid wife. He wasn't really Chinese; he was an Irishman who had a beet-red face and hair to match. His arms were red. His neck was red. We expected he was red all over, but we didn't dare tell M'Ma and M'Da about that. We called him the China-Man because we had never seen anybody else who looked that strange. We reasoned he had to be a China-Man.

He would get really drunk every week and beat his poor invalid wife. We'd hear her crying in a high weird whine, "Stop! Oh, Red, please stop!" So M'Ma and Uncle Sid would go up to his house and stop him from torturing that poor pale slip of a woman. Then he would start to cry and cling to them and plead, "Take me to the Reverend Uncle Frank. I want him to baptize me so I can be forgiven of me sins." Then he'd pass out. Everybody would return to their own homes and thank God it was finally quiet.

The next house belonged to Great-Aunt Ouida and the Reverend Uncle Frank. Named for a river in Africa, Ouida was Grandpa Mac's sister. She was the mother of my girl cousin, Edna, who was born twenty days after I came to earth. Edna was considered a miracle baby because Great-Aunt Ouida was fifty-four when Edna was born. Edna practically lived at our house since her brothers were so much older.

The house at the bottom of the hill was occupied by a Hungarian family —a big tall hairy father, a little plump pleasant mother, and two little girls, Minka and Evie. They practically lived at our house, also.

It turned out that the social life of the neighborhood swung between two focal points. During the daytime, all the kids hung out at our house: three boy cousins, two Hungarians, one girl cousin, two Eye-talyins, me, Charlotte, and Jerry. Now, we weren't allowed to let anybody into the house while M'Ma and M'Da worked: strict orders that were scrupulously obeyed. My aunts would check on us throughout the day, and we all had a wonderful time playing football, baseball, kick the can, and hide-and-seek. The field and our big old yard gave us plenty of room for plenty of fun.

After work, the grown people ate dinner, washed their dishes, and in the soft light of the evening, gradually gathered at Great-Aunt Catherine and Uncle Sid's house to listen to their big floor-length Philco radio. They'd talk politics—about the Rooshans and Mussolini and Roosyvelt—and listen to *Amos 'n' Andy* and *Wings Over Jordan*, filling up with pride when Joe Louis would wallop somebody.

That's also when we'd have dessert.

Someone, mostly M'Ma, would bake a 1-2-3-4 cake or some cookies, or my Aunt Bessie would bake a pie. Aunt Catherine supplied lemonade in summer on the porch, and coffee or hot chocolate in the parlor in winter. Fireflies flickered and streetlights came on. Then someone, usually the Reverend Uncle Frank, would stand up and stretch and say, "I guess we better call it a night and get a head start on tomorrow." One by one everybody said "Good night" and slowly walked to their homes.

* * *

All the big events were celebrated at Aunt Catherine and Uncle Sid's home. The first automobile on Bina Avenue was delivered brand-new to Uncle Sid. The whole neighborhood gathered around to exclaim and admire.

"How shiny!"

"Look at the wheels!"

"Wow! There's running boards!"

The men all looked solemn. The China-Man said, "This calls for a celebration." Of course, they all ignored him, since he was always looking for any excuse to celebrate.

Then at last, the Reverend Uncle Frank said, "Well, Sid, why don't you give her a spin?"

We all exclaimed, "Yes! Yes! Give her a spin, Uncle Sid."

That automobile was delivered right from the factory. The man brought it, parked it, and left in another car driven by his sales partner. Now, Uncle Sid was rather impulsive and barked a lot instead of talking. But he didn't fool us. We knew he was a kind and gentle soul who blustered and sputtered to cover it up.

"What's the hurry?" he said. "What's the hurry?" Crossing his arms over his chest, he added, "It took them a long time to make this car in Detroit City. It took a long time to deliver it here, right in front of my house. I guess I can do a few more minutes of admiration before I crank her up."

M'Ma said later that Uncle Sid was really trying to reestablish his credibility on Bina Avenue because the week before he had been caught red-handed down in Kenmore with another woman. We children heard the whispers and watched lips disappear into thin straight lines on the faces of Aunt Catherine, Aunt Bessie, Aunt Ouida, and M'Ma.

That fateful day, Uncle Sid told Aunt Catherine that he was going out. She said, "OUT? When will you be back?"

"When I get good and ready," he barked and out he went.

Well, Aunt Catherine rounded up M'Ma, Aunt Bessie, and Aunt Ouida.

Armed with a broom handle, mop handle, a flatiron, and a galvanized iron bucket, the four of them marched down Bina Avenue, turned right on Summit Lake Boulevard, tromped the six blocks into Kenmore, and knocked on the scarlet woman's front door.

When she answered the door and saw the Bible brigade, she flung the door wide open and stepped aside. They marched in, weapons at the ready, and cornered Uncle Sid. They gave him a "Mississippi Camp Beating" while he tried to retrieve his clothes. They gave the woman "what for" also, but had a little mercy on her because she wasn't married to Aunt Catherine—Uncle Sid was.

Then, full of righteousness and the sweet smell of victory, they marched my uncle back down Summit Lake Boulevard, back up Bina Avenue. After that, each marched to her own home to lie down and sleep the sleep of the just.

So, Uncle Sid was understandably a little cautious about everything after that episode—even the new car. He opened the door of the new Buick, looked around grandly, cranked her up, and took off.

We all cheered, "Hooray, Uncle Sid! Hooray!"

He drove down the hill, turned right, and continued around the block. When he came back into view again, he drove to where we were all cheering wildly, stopped the car, got out, and took a deep bow. The China-Man ran back to his house to start celebrating. The Hungarian picked Uncle Sid up in a giant bear hug and said something that nobody understood, but sounded complimentary.

My Uncle Sid felt good all over. He turned to Aunt Catherine and said, "You get in and I'm going to show you how to drive."

She threw out her hands. "No! No! I don't wanna drive."

"Just like a woman," he retorted. "When you want them to do something, they say no. When you don't want them to do something, they say yeah."

Aunt Catherine could not resist the challenge. With a toss of her head, she got behind the wheel of the shiny new Buick, cranked her up, and stepped on the gas. The Buick lurched forward and started speeding down the hill. Intending to make a right turn on Summit Lake Boulevard, she stepped on the gas instead of the brake and drove that new Buick straight into Summit Lake.

We all—grown folks and little children—stood stunned. Nobody spoke a word. Then my Uncle Sid exploded into a paroxysm of curses and blasphemies as he ran down to the lake. Fortunately, the Buick had stalled on a sandbar with lots of cattails growing on it, so that only the front of the car was partially submerged.

My aunt jumped out of the car on one side, and my uncle jumped in on the other. He cranked her up, and with the help of the men of Bina Avenue, he backed out of Summit Lake, all the time calling on all that was holy to strike all the women down dead. He backed all the way up the street as the whole neighborhood—men, women and children—watched. He stopped the Buick, leaped out the door, and ran up to Aunt Catherine, who was soaking wet from the knees down. "Fool!" he roared. "Fool woman!"

Now, he was a short man, and my Aunt Catherine was taller than he. She caught him in midair as he hurtled toward her, and began hammering on him as if he were a tenpenny nail.

"Don't you use that kind of language around here," she shouted. "We're ladies!" Then she began mopping up the sidewalk with his short body. It took Uncle James, M'Da, the Reverend Uncle Frank, and the Hungarian to pull her off him.

My aunt stomped haughtily up onto her porch, then turned, unable to resist one last aside. "I guess that'll teach you. When a lady says no, a lady means no!" With that, she strode into her house and slammed the door.

Well, nobody ever forgot that day, but nobody talked about it either. At least not in front of Great-Aunt Catherine or Uncle Sid.

I think Uncle Sid had had his belly full of fornication and blue phrases. He opted for running numbers instead. That's when you bet on three numbers—in this case, each number represented the number of a horse in three successive races in New York. You paid twenty-five cents, or some such, for your numbers, and if your horses won, you got paid one dollar for every penny you bet.

His territory grew quite wide, and since the odds of hitting the numbers straight were less than a rat's chance in a cat contest, he did quite well. He tried to convince Aunt Catherine of his fidelity and civility by buying her a new floor-length Philco radio and, wonder of wonders—the piano.

The Piano

· · · · · · · · · · · · · · · · · · · ·

*E*ight little brown legs swung on the front steps of the Reverend Uncle Frank's house. Forty sticky fingers popped Walnettos caramel candy in and out of four sticky mouths. My cousin Edna, Charlotte, Jerry, and I.

It was late Saturday afternoon. The sun had begun its slide down toward the west over the waters of Summit Lake, and the whole neighborhood was beginning to quiet down after a day of hard work that began at sunrise. Every Saturday was hectic on Bina Avenue. It began with hot oatmeal and milk and sugar in a bowl for kids and grown-ups alike. Then the dishes were washed and put away and the day began.

First, beds were stripped and the laundry was loaded into machines, and while the washing was being done, out came scrub buckets, mops, brooms, and dust cloths. Sheets and pillowcases were changed; clean towels were put up on the racks. Furniture was polished with Watkins furniture polish brought personally by the Watkins man, who also sold liniments for aching bones and vanilla—real vanilla extract for the cakes that were baked on Saturday for Sunday dinner. Parker House rolls were made up and set aside to rise under a white muslin cloth.

After the clothes were washed, they were hung out on the line to dry. We all helped, whatever age group we fell into—even my baby brother, Jerry, could hand you clothespins as needed.

In the background, underpinning all the activity, was the radio. We listened to the Golden Gate Quartet, with their lush harmonies, and the Wings Over Jordan choir, guaranteed to get your soul ready for Sunday. Bill Kenny and the Ink Spots keened "If I Didn't Care" on every radio except the China-Man's. He sang in his yard at the top of his lungs in a really beautiful tenor voice—"My Bonnie Lies over the Ocean" or "Mother McCree."

Saturday's air carried the scents of our kitchens. Navy beans simmered on the backs of every stove and range on Bina Avenue, except for Jovie's mama's house. There the pungent smell of spicy tomato sauce for spaghetti wafted from the open windows. Even the China-Man cooked corn beef and cabbage while he liberally laced himself with Irish whiskey—getting himself worked up for his usual Saturday-night rampage.

Saturday brought the milkman with his horse and buggy. He sold bread, too, and hot cross buns at Easter time. Mr. Mendel, the ragman, came with his horse and buggy to take away discards, old metal and paper and such, then hung around to swap a few stories with the men. But the most important outsider, who came early on Saturday morning, was the iceman. He delivered the ice to keep the weekend chickens and Jell-O intact for Sunday dinner.

Gramma Hattie brought the chickens live from her farm, along with sweet corn, greens, and juicy red tomatoes. She also sold chickens, ducks, geese, and fresh vegetables to people all up and down the line on the journey from Springfield to Akron and back.

There seemed to be a real knack to killing chickens. M'Da and Grampa Mac would take one to the back of the house so we wouldn't see (we peeked anyway). Then M'Da scooped up a chicken, grabbed it by the neck, and with a single snap—the deed was done. Grampa Mac would say, "It's all in the wrist. Yeah, it's all in the wrist!" M'Da would echo, "Yeah, it's all in the wrist, all right!"

Then they would drop the chickens into a tub of very hot water; doing this made it easier to pull off the feathers. M'Ma called it "dressing the chickens," but it was more like undressing them. Once all their feathers were off, M'Ma cleaned the chickens and put them on ice. By Sunday they were on their way into our old roasting pan to become Alabama smothered chickens in their own gravy. In the middle of the Great Depression, it was literally us or the chickens.

M'Da and Grampa Mac liked doing chores together. M'Da agreed with Mac on most things. Except one. He did not approve of it when Mac, after a hard day's work at the 20th Century Foundry, would come to visit, lie down on the floor, and wait for Jerry to ask him, "Grampa, you need a shave?" Mac would answer, "Yeah, I do believe I do."

So Jerry would climb up on the clothes hamper in the bathroom, fetch M'Da's straight razor, fill his shaving mug with water, return to the body stretched out on the floor, and proceed to shave him while Mac, arms across his chest, slept blissfully.

To his credit, Jerry never, ever cut Grampa Mac. Mac's philosophy was that children were the smartest they were ever going to be in the years before they went to school and got tampered with by the system.

After the shave, Jerry would say, "Wake up, Grampa! Yo' face is smooth now!"

Grampa would wake up, sit up, run his big gnarled hands over his face, and say, "Boy, you are the best barber I ever *did* see!" Jerry would smile, skip back to the bathroom, climb onto the hamper, and put everything carefully away. Then he'd go sit on the bottom step of the porch.

When M'Da warned, "Mac, one of these days you gonna wake up dead, or worse," Mac would only smile in his own sweet way, as if he knew a secret.

He always brought us treats hidden in his many pockets—sometimes pennies, sometimes a piece of the garlic sausage that always hung between the sticky flypaper in his Hungarian friend's restaurant. This particular Saturday, he'd given us Walnettos.

The Walnettos were almost finished when down Bina Avenue hill rumbled a large gray truck. Two men peered out the windows of the truck as if they were looking for the correct address. We watched intently as they finally stopped smack in front of Aunt Catherine and Uncle Sid's house. The men opened the rear doors and began to tug at a large object covered in a gray cloth. By this time, everyone on the street had come out to see what was going on. "What is it? Can we help?" Questions were flying back and forth as we stood back and the men took over.

We heard Uncle Sid saying to Aunt Catherine, "You always said you wanted a piano. . . . Well, here it is!" He pulled off the gray cloth, and, indeed, there it was—black and beautiful and gleaming in the sun. Brand-new, off the floor of the piano company. Uncle Sid really knew how to impress.

Aunt Catherine threw up her hands, making little sounds like "Ummm" and "Oh!!" and "Glory!" As she smiled wider and wider, we all did too. The only piano we had ever seen was the gap-toothed heavy-legged monster at the St. Paul Baptist Church.

After everyone had a chance to touch it, the men went into a long dialogue on what place of honor the piano should occupy in the house. The China-Man suggested, "I think it should be in the basement. That way if we do a wee bit of partyin' and we have a wee drink, it won't disturb anyone."

Nobody even answered him. All the men said, "How about the living room?" They liked that location 'cause it was the first room you entered when you opened the front door—requiring not too much lifting or straining or pushing or pulling.

But all the women—M'Ma, Aunt Bessie, Aunt Ouida, Joey's mama, and, of course, Aunt Catherine—said, "Oh no. It belongs in the parlor."

And so that's where it went.

All black and shiny, with white and black keys that looked as if they were smiling, and down below, three pedals, gold and gleaming. And smack in the middle of the front panel was its name written in gold—Story and Clark.

That piano changed life as we knew it on Bina Avenue. Glory!

Three Visitors

....

 he brand-new piano seemed to have magic powers. It drew three people from three different lifestyles and three different points in the universe to our little community on Bina Avenue.

First came my Great-Gramma Lizzie from Birmingham, Alabama. She lived with Gramma Hattie, her daughter, but Uncle Sid drove out to Springfield in his big black Buick early Sunday morning and brought her and her old carpetbag to our house. She would stay with us a couple of days. Uncle Sid would take her back to Springfield around midweek.

She was always glad to see us and gave big hugs, smelling of homemade sachet, mostly roses and lilies. Her long ankle-length skirts swirled and crackled from her starched petticoats trimmed with tatted and crocheted lace. Her go-to-meeting suit was a black two-piece outfit, tailor-made because she was so tall and could not buy her clothes in a regular ladies store.

She went to our church, St. Paul's Baptist, more for the social setting than for the religious bounty it offered. A staunch, down-the-decades Methodist, she sniffed at the exuberant amens and the speaking in tongues and the fierce, fiery sermons offered up by members of our congregation. Especially those by Mr. "L," who would come to church about every three months, fling open the double doors, drop to his knees, and start praying in a loud voice as he crawled all the way from the front door to the foot of the pulpit, beseeching and imploring the Heavenly Father to save his rascally soul and his whole rascally family. He'd always pause at the pew where all of us little ones were sitting, frozen and clutching one another. Casting his rheumy red eyes up at us, he'd cry, "Suffer!" We would flatten our little bodies against the back of the pew. "Suffer, little children!" He'd cry out again in an ominous tone, "Suffer little children to come unto thee, O Lord!"

Then he'd move on down the aisle.

When at last he got to the foot of the pulpit, he would prostrate himself, fling out his arms, and cry, "And Father, when we come"—gasp—"to our dying day"—gasp—"and stand before you at the foot of yo' throne"—gasp—"I pray that you will take me to yo' bosom"—gasp—"and let me walk around heaven all day. Amen!"

The church would be in an uproar, with amens all around.

On the way home from the service, we would walk sedately past Summit Lake, where Great-Gramma Lizzie would always draw up all six feet four inches of her Methodist majesty and declare, "You know, some Baptists think God Almighty is deaf."

Nobody argued with her, because she was so big and a hundred years old and still as strong as any man. She really claimed "elder" status on Bina Avenue.

She made us girls sit with our knees together and our dresses pulled down over them because, she said, "Nobody wants to see Possible"—whatever that was. She made us walk around with books on our heads and taught us to curtsy. Every lunchtime we had to set the table with a tablecloth, and all the glasses and silverware had to be in the correct places.

She was a tough old bird, but she had one redeeming quality. Her presence in our house released me from the interminable babysitting that I had to do while M'Ma and M'Da were working. My baby sister, Charlotte, and baby brother, Jerry, were my wards, and I fiercely guarded them from the various cousins (from my dad's side of the family) who supposedly came to care for us, but instead invaded our home, pulled out the drawers, meddled in M'Ma's things, laughed loudly, cursed, farted, and refused to change Jerry's diapers until just before M'Ma came home. They tried to threaten me for telling on them, but I was always "The Warrior," and my cousins quickly understood that they would have to kill me to keep me quiet. So Great-Gramma Lizzie was called to the rescue.

I would flee over to Aunt Catherine's house with my papers and crayons and steep myself in the stillness of the darkened parlor, where all the curtains and drapes had been drawn so the rugs and upholstery wouldn't fade. The peace seemed like heaven to me.

Almost five years old, I really needed some space and some time alone in which to draw and color and think and grow.

I offered to polish Aunt Catherine's furniture, so I was always welcome. She would say when I knocked on her door, "I know who's there. A little girl with a pretty smile come to help me clean my house." I wiggled with pleasure at the compliment. After dusting everything I could reach, I sat under the piano, back against the soundboard, and drew and colored while Aunt Catherine tried to play. At times she stumbled so bad that I pressed the soft pedal. She never noticed. She never used the pedals anyway.

I stayed until Uncle Sid came home from work, and then reluctantly I gathered my drawings and got ready to cross the street to my house. I figured that by now the little ones would be napping anyway. At this time of day Great-Gramma Lizzie always smoked a pipeful of homegrown "yarbs" (herbs) that she had dried; the "yarbs" kept her eyes clear and prevented asthma. Whatever the "yarbs" were, they made our heads go round and round and caused the babies to take long naps.

The Sunday after the piano was delivered to Aunt Catherine, we went to church as always, opened the double doors (they were never locked), and when we had filed in, heard a voice come out of the stillness: "I'm a stranger in a strange land, and I come to worship with you-all and perhaps break bread with you brethren."

He stood there quietly with his hat in his right hand: a tall gentleman, coppery colored, amazing straight black hair hanging on his forehead. M'Da, all the uncles, and the other deacons shook hands with him. As the church started filling up, he introduced himself as "a stranger in a strange land." He kept one hand in his pocket, put his hat under his left arm, and then shook hands with his right hand. Everyone said, "Howdy, you're most welcome to take service with us."

We children really kept our eyes on him. We kept turning around so often to watch him that M'Ma hissed at us. That meant "do right or you'll catch it later!"

After church, Aunt Catherine and Uncle Sid invited the man to have Sunday dinner at their house. We were all very excited because we knew if we hurried our dinner, we could all go over and listen to the tales from the stranger.

And so it was.

After dinner we all gathered in the parlor and out on the porch to see and hear what the stranger had to offer. I stowed myself under the piano where I wouldn't be noticed and wouldn't be distracted by the little ones. But all of a sudden the stranger pulled out the piano stool and sat down. When M'Ma saw this, she said, "Jeannie, maybe you'd better move out of the way."

The stranger peered down and smiled. "She's no bother at all."

I said to myself, Hope I don't have to push down the soft pedal.

Wonder of wonders! The stranger put his left foot on the soft pedal and his right foot on the loud pedal. Then a ripple of sound came out of the piano. It was as if the sun had come up over Summit Lake.

The stranger started softly, then cascades of sound came out like Niagara Falls—spilling, tumbling, dancing; he wove a tapestry that showed where he had come from and, O Lawd! where he was going. I knew that I'd never heard anything like it before. I knew I was in the presence of a being infused with the soul of music. I crawled out from under the piano and stood at his left hand with my eyes, mouth, and heart wide open.

And wonder of wonders, the man had no left hand! He used the nub that stood in place of a hand to play what I now know was stride piano. His left flashed to and fro over the black keys. *And* the white keys.

His right hand darted up and down the piano, from the words "Story and Clark" to the very highest note and back again. I thought my heart would come out of my narrow little chest. I thought if he didn't stop, I would die. I thought if he *did* stop I would die.

At that moment, I knew my soul's destiny. I looked at the stranger, and on his face was a light that I'd never seen before, a kind of shine. His eyes were closed, his lips were smiling. The music came to a crashing end and he stopped playing. Then he started again. Quietly, as soft as a whisper, he played "Amazing Grace." I had never heard anyone play this song on the piano. In church it was sung in a call-and-response manner without any piano at all, just folks singing all by themselves.

It was so quiet in the parlor and on the porch that it felt like a fairy world. Tears were on cheeks, glistening in the evening sun. It made my stomach hurt. It made me feel that I was no longer a little girl. There was a knowing—a feeling that I was my great-gramma as she used to be. It was like a flash, and then, as he finished the hymn, it was gone. My soul came back into my body, and I turned and ran out of the house, down the steps, across the street, and into my own room. I put on my jammies and crept into bed.

Mr. Arthur Reginald Riley

. . . .

It rained hard the next couple of days—you could barely see the line between the sky and Summit Lake. I stood on the porch of our little house, peering through the weeping willow trees. All you could see was the color gray.

Great-gramma finally let me go over to Aunt Catherine's house. I felt as if I had been in jail for two whole days. I ran across the street as fast as I could, carefully wiped my feet on the mat outside the door, then entered the quiet, dark parlor. "Hi, Aunt Catherine," I called, "I'm here."

She came out of the kitchen, wiping her hands on a towel. Her copper-colored face wore no smile that day. The dimples on her cheeks had disappeared. "Well, you know where the furniture polish and dust cloths are," she said, turning to go back into the kitchen.

Uncle Sid came thundering down the stairs. "Well, hello there, Jeannie. Come to keep yo' auntie company, eh?"

I nodded yes.

"Catherine," he called loudly, "I'm going out. I'll be back in one hour."

Aunt Catherine came out the kitchen again. Sternly, she warned, "Don't forget to wear yo' rubbers. You don't wanna get wet feet."

He grinned and replied, "I like wet feet!" And away he went, leaving Aunt Catherine scowling and fuming.

The piano lid was closed. The dust was so plentiful you could write your name in it. This surprised me, since Aunt Catherine usually played, or tried to play, every day and always kept the piano shiny and clean. I hadn't been there for a while, so I asked her, "Aunt Catherine, don't you want to play today?"

She shook her head and said sadly, "You know, child, I haven't touched that piano since the stranger played last Sunday." She looked deep into my eyes. "It don't seem right."

I nodded. I really understood and I felt a little sad.

One hour later we heard Uncle Sid's big old Buick in the driveway. I ran to open the door, and up the porch steps came Uncle Sid and a man I had never seen before. A slightly built white man, he wore a gray coat and pants, a light blue shirt, and a black tie and hat. They both wiped their feet carefully before coming into the parlor.

Uncle Sid announced in his most important voice, "This is Arthur Reginald Riley, and he came all the way from London, England. I brought him here to teach you how to play that piano, Catherine."

Aunt Catherine's eyes opened wide. "Howdy," she said shyly, taking a step back.

" 'Ow do you do?" Mr. Riley said.

Uncle Sid said loudly, "After the show the one-hand stranger put on, we really got a good fix on how that piano supposed to sound."

Mr. Riley looked a bit puzzled, but he smiled, and his blue eyes sparkled. His frail body leaned a little to the right.

M'Ma told us later that it was because he had kidney trouble from drinking so much English tea. She said all English people drink a lot of tea. We wondered if they all leaned to the right, but were too polite to ask.

When Uncle Sid asked him to play something for us, he quietly said, "Of course. It will be my pleasure." He sat down on the piano stool, hands in his lap, eyes closed, his breathing deep and steady. Then he raised both hands and placed them on the keys, opened his bright blue eyes, and began playing a beautiful song, as different from the one-hand stranger as day is from night, but it made your insides ebb and swell with the story the music told. When he finished he was very still. He turned to us and said, "That was the 'Rustle of Spring' by Christian Sinding—a Nordic composer."

We all smiled and nodded.

Uncle Sid cleared his throat. "All right, Riley," he said, "she's all yours. I'm going out, and I'll be back in one hour to take you home."

Aunt Catherine and I were left in the capable hands of the Englishman, who took a red book from his valise and placed it on the piano. He gestured for Aunt Catherine to sit on the piano stool.

Just as she put her hands on the keys, he admonished her, "You must address the piano! Do not touch the keys!"

I sat on the couch, watching and listening intently. How is she going to learn to play with her hands in her lap, I wondered.

"You must let the music come to you," he continued. "Close your eyes and sit up straight!"

Wow, I thought, nobody had ever talked to Aunt Catherine like that before. I was immediately, completely impressed with Arthur Reginald Riley.

Aunt Catherine meekly obeyed. He reached in his pocket and pulled out two pennies, placing them on the backs of Auntie's hands. He then took her elbow and gently guided her up the five keys starting with C. She did it. The pennies didn't move. Then she was told to come down the five notes. As she maneuvered her unruly fingers downward, off flew the pennies.

Auntie struggled for an hour: up—fine, down—disaster.

Mr. Riley never budged.

"All right, Riley," Uncle Sid said when he came back, "how much do I owe you?"

"Fifty cents, Mr. Cox," Mr. Riley sighed. He then put on his coat and hat and said to Auntie, "You must practice every day. I'll be back next week at the same time." With that, he and Uncle Sid went out into the rain and drove away in the Buick.

As soon as they left the driveway, I whispered almost to myself, "I can do that."

My aunt said, "You can?"

"Yes," I said.

"Show me," she said.

And show her I did. I addressed the piano. I called on the music. Then up and down the five notes I went, and the pennies did not fall off.

And so it began.

Every week Mr. Riley came. Every week I would sit on the couch and absorb everything he did. I'd wait until he left the house, then do everything he had done. Then I'd teach Aunt Catherine all week long.

I found out that if you half close your eyes when you're going to draw a picture of a tree or the lake, your body gets out of the way and you can draw anything you want. So I tested this out with the music. Whenever I listened to Old Man Riley play, I half closed my eyes, and the music went past my body and into my heart and later came out my fingers exactly the way he had played it. Lovely! And since M'Da taught us all to read, write, and do simple math before we went to school, reading the instructions in the red book was very easy.

After about two months, Aunt Catherine still struggled. It was as if her fingers were both blind and deaf, though Mr. Riley was still patient and didn't budge.

But the day came when he finally told my Uncle Sid, "Mr. Cox, I cannot take your money another week. I won't be coming back anymore."

There was utter silence in the parlor. My heart started beating wildly in my chest. "But," I cried, "but you must! You *must* come back!"

Surprised, Aunt Catherine and Uncle Sid sputtered, "Well, what's this?"

"I wanna play the piano!" I cried. "I wanna learn how to play like the one-hand stranger!"

Mr. Riley said, "Well, I don't know . . ." But Uncle Sid interrupted him. He was a man of action, he was. "You have to ask yo' mama if it's all right."

I sensed that it was now or never. I hopped up on the piano stool and played all Aunt Catherine's lessons—with pennies! Mr. Riley's mouth flew open as he listened carefully. Then he started turning pages in the red book, and I played until I had to stop. Quietly, his blue eyes sparkling, he said, "Go ask your mother. I'll wait right here until you return."

I raced across the street as fast as my little brown legs could take me. Breathlessly, I told M'Ma that I wanted to play the piano, that I would be a good girl forever and wouldn't get mad never and would even thread Great-Gramma's needles for her quilts without one frown. It seemed like a lifetime before M'Ma smiled and said, "Well, we need a piano player for the church, so I guess it'll be all right."

"I guess" always meant "yes"!

I had found my life's work. Aunt Catherine gave me the shiny black piano. It was a glorious day when the men of Bina Avenue moved it into our little house.

M'Ma paid Mr. Arthur Reginald Riley fifty cents a lesson for six years, then a dollar a lesson for seven more years: thirteen years in all. Chopin, Beethoven, Hanon's virtuoso studies, Bach's Two- and Three-Part Inventions, and Mr. Riley became my major focus.

Mr. Riley took me all over Ohio (with M'Ma, of course) to play recitals and weddings, teas and socials. Rounding out my musical activities, I played for St. Paul's Baptist Church. I also discovered Thomas A. Dorsey's music, which was a lot more modern than some of the older folks liked. There was a whole hullabaloo in church between the folks who wanted no change from spirituals like "Swing Low, Sweet Chariot" and those who wanted gospels like "When I've Done the Best I Can" and "Does Anybody Here Know My Jesus?" But I played there every Sunday and sometimes even on Saturday—funeral day.

Funerals

· · · · · · · · · · · · · · · · · ·

One fall day, one of the church members who lived near the end of Summit Lake, down where the cattails grew tall and thick, past the old stone bridge, close to the streetcar tracks, in one of the row houses that stood like old gray tombstones leaning into each other, came to Bina Avenue to talk to the Reverend Uncle Frank. He tearfully rendered an account of how a young relative playing on the tracks had gotten run over by a streetcar.

My sister, Charlotte, had a clear, beautiful voice, and we did duets for funerals. Naturally, we had to play for this one. My heart squeezed a little, and skipped a couple of beats. We had always played for old dead people before, not a child of seven years. But that Saturday we mustered up our courage to go to St. Paul's and pushed open the creaky old doors. Inside it was so still you could hear a fly buzzing in the corner of the stained-glass window near the front pews. We went up to the choir stand and spoke softly about the songs we would sing and play.

Soon, the funeral directors came into the church, pushing the little casket on wheels, bumping down the center aisle. They were white—there weren't as yet any colored funeral directors to serve the community—and they really didn't know how to prepare black people for the great beyond. They had a general idea about eyes and noses and mouths, but they had a very theatrical idea about color. And they were not sensitive to the reason for closed caskets versus open caskets.

The mourners streamed in, covered with black veils and all kinds of funeral finery. Everything went well. The Reverend Uncle Frank spoke about being cut down before your time and we sang "Mercy, Lord" and the people started a slow procession to view the body. Now we were singing softly as the people approached the casket for one last view.

Blood-curdling screams came from their throats! It was as if lightning had struck all the mourners simultaneously. Somebody screamed, "Look at his face! Oh my Gawd!" As the mourners piled on each other to get a look, the casket was accidentally pulled from its stand. Over went the casket and out rolled the body.

Charlotte started crying. "Stop," she begged me, "stop playing!" But I figured the only order in the place was the measured beauty of the music, so I didn't stop.

The funeral directors, their faces red and perspiring, joined the melee. Somehow they managed to put the body back into the casket, yelling, "Everybody out! Everybody out!" One heavyset woman had fainted, and two deacons pushed and pulled until she was on her feet. Out they all rushed, out the doors, and down the steps to the waiting hearse. Not until the church emptied did I stop playing. Then I went to see what all the fuss was about.

I couldn't believe my eyes. The funeral directors had painted the poor little child's cheeks bright red, eyebrows black, and heavy lines over the closed eyes. The lips were also bright red. But most bizarrely of all, the tracks of the streetcar had been left imprinted on the still, grease-painted face.

Charlotte shrieked, "Let's go, Jean, let's get out of here!"

We did, as fast as our legs could carry us.

* * *

That day I learned to put a shield around myself to keep out the grief of the people the deceased had left behind, but Charlotte was so tenderhearted that she tried to beg off sometimes during the services. I'd whisper, "You wanna get paid, don't you?"

It was good to know that I could use this shield whenever I needed, especially when dealing with too much grief and too many blues and too many people who breathed more than their fair share of air.

Like the Reverend Uncle Frank.

The Reverend Uncle Frank, Lessons on Men, and Finding Jesus

· · · · · · · · · · · · · · · · · · ·

The Reverend Uncle Frank had a big shiny face, round like a full moon. It glowed. Unlike most folks who aren't as skilled, he knew how to rest his glasses low on his nose. Those glasses never slipped, even as sweat trickled down his forehead when he preached the gospel on those steamy summer Sundays back in our old neighborhood in Akron, Ohio.

The Reverend Uncle Frank had a convincing way about him. He was a born preacher, a man of the Lord. He sold religion and had plenty of buyers. He was as filled with exuberance as the young Fats Waller, who played piano, wrote songs like "Honeysuckle Rose," and could consume three whole chickens at one sitting.

The Reverend Uncle Frank had a booming voice. He knew just how to inflate words to get the most mileage from them, like "Ahhhhhmeeen." He knew when to whisper and when to yell. He could really do fire and brimstone.

It didn't matter what day or month it was, he always wore a white shirt and a black tie. His slacks stayed creased, no matter what. Those creases didn't dare ask for a day off. To finish it off, he wore black high-topped hook-and-eye boots, like the kind men wore back in the early 1900s. He was still wearing them in the 1930s. I just figured he had a secret source: he wore them for another twenty years, and they always looked spanking new.

His favorite name for anyone suspected of chicanery in spirit or mind was "scutter": "That scutter is completely full of skee-go-dee." That meant the person who was the object of his scrutiny was surely on the slippery slope headed straight to perdition or hell or maybe even worse. And as sure as can be, a lot of the time he was right.

The Reverend Uncle Frank owned a big gray two-story house with a wide front porch and the little house in the rear, which he rented to us. His address was 515 Bina Avenue; our address was 515 F½ Bina. A large piece of land separated the two dwellings—our playground, our fairyland, a kingdom where imagination ruled.

The Reverend Uncle Frank might have been working for the Lord, but he was out for himself, too. So when he started a candy store in his enclosed front porch, we weren't all that surprised. By midsummer one year he realized just how many times the neighborhood kids went up the street to Mr. Muckley's store for candy. Though a Caucasian, Mr. Muckley knew how to cater to our sweeter instincts.

Not that the Reverend Uncle Frank needed the money—he just didn't like it when any money got past him. So he bought bulk candies for a penny a pound and tried to sell them to us for a penny apiece. Since we could all read, write, and figure, we ignored his store altogether. With heads high and eyes front, we marched right past that porch of his, climbed the hill to Mr. Muckley's store, and plunked down a penny for an afternoon's worth of sugar. Did we hear "Scutters!" coming from that big front porch? We didn't turn to find out.

When the Reverend Uncle Frank had a problem, he took it to the Lord. The very next Sunday came a sermon on our behavior; scutters that we were, we had to listen then. I still remember him saying, "I don't think the Lord would take too kindly to people that ignored Moses *after* their bid for freedom. Even in these modern days of iniquity and sin, there has to be some loyalty in people of color toward their own kin, 'specially their own flesh and blood."

Then he belted out the hymns: "There is power, power, wondrous working power / In the precious blood of the Lamb." He had a wondrous voice and all, but he sure didn't make us change our minds about where we wanted to spend our money. But the candy did pose a sticky problem because we couldn't afford to make him angry with us. M'Ma and M'Da rented our home from him. We played on his property, and he was our reverend and our relative.

M'Ma never failed to give good advice, and as always she knew just what to say. She told us, "Look, everybody needs grease to live—some more than others." We knew what she meant. The Reverend Uncle Frank was a sucker for flattery, so we greased him good. The very next Sunday as we walked down the aisle after church, we each shook his hand and said, "That was a great sermon, Reverend Uncle Frank. Nobody could do it better."

"It's not me speaking, folks!" he said. "It's the Loooorrrd!"

M'Ma smiled sweetly and replied, "Well, the Lord sure knows whose voice to choose. Amen!" And five little ones following M'Ma piped up, "Amen!"

Now the reason I'm talking about the Reverend Uncle Frank is that I learned a lot about life and men from him. He was a perfect example of most of the older club owners—white, black, and otherwise—who I've had to deal with my entire musical life. The Reverend Uncle Frank, like the club owners, was a good man at heart. But he had to eat a little bit off your plate before he would hand it to you. You know what I mean. So we learned to grease him and let him think he had the best of us. But we continued to make our own decisions.

I learned another lesson about life from the Reverend Uncle Frank. Since I was the chief musician in the church and M'Ma was the leader of the children's choir, I found out early on that the Reverend Uncle Frank, like so many club owners, might be the car, but I was the engine.

Oh, my uncle was good. He knew how to go from the first of the chord to the third to the fifth and then bring them on home on the seventh. But he couldn't make 'em come to Jesus without me. I think he knew this, yet I didn't let him know that I knew it too. I kept it way down in my heart, like a little bitty bluebird, and I wouldn't bring out the big guns unless I really had to. I knew that he needed me more than I needed him—just as I always knew that the club owners and the vocalists needed me. And knowing that helps balance a relationship.

Speaking of coming to Jesus, on the first Sunday of every month our white clapboard church, walking distance from the little house on Bina Avenue, would serve communion. On that day we'd find soda crackers and Mogen David grape juice on the altar.

The Reverend Uncle Frank would preach until the perspiration lapped under his chin. There were twelve of us in the choir, all under the age of twelve. The Reverend Uncle Frank really wanted all the choir members to accept Jesus as our personal savior and go on to adulthood. But he held fast to the notion that he alone would baptize us. That's why, sometimes, he'd preach directly at us children. I can still hear the sound of his booming voice throbbing in my ears.

The thought of being baptized by the Reverend Uncle Frank produced plenty of chatter in our group. The older kids delighted in scaring the be-jeezus out of the little ones. Yet we all continued to resist him as if he were the devil himself. If we succumbed, we knew what would happen, and the thought of that scared us more than the thought of not having our mortal souls saved. It had everything to do with the Reverend Uncle Frank and the cold clear waters of Summit Lake.

Those of us older than eight had seen the Reverend Uncle Frank try to baptize this sister who was on the portly side. When he got to "I baptize thee in the name of the . . ." he didn't get a chance to go any further. As he bent the sister backward into the water, her chubby hands folded across her ample bosom, something happened. She disappeared. It was as if the lake had swallowed her up. One guzzle—she was gone.

The Reverend Uncle Frank rippled the waves a bit with his broad fingers, and for the first time in my life, I saw him speechless. He could not find her. Thanks to two deacons who rushed to the poor woman's aid, her plump frame was pulled from the lake bottom. Like a choking whale, she coughed and spit, and the baptism continued. Years later Mama told me that we nearly had to change hymns that day: we almost had a funeral right in Summit Lake.

So you can see why we didn't want the Reverend Uncle Frank to save us, neither our souls nor our bodies. Mama understood and didn't pressure us kids. She mostly let us make our own decisions and counted on us to make the right ones.

It took a traveling preacher woman from Kansas City, the Reverend Mary, who was visiting churches in Ohio, to move our sinful souls to Jesus. She came up to the pulpit, faced the choir directly, and asked, "What's your favorite hymn, children?" It was "Does Anybody Here Know My Jesus?" We really showed off. The music reverberated through every person in the congregation. Boy, did we get amens!

Then ever so quietly she asked, "Children, do you really believe what you just sang?"

We looked at each other. We were stunned. Nobody had ever laid all that responsibility on us before. But she didn't stop there. "Children, do you know that your mamas and daddies have charge of your body and soul until you come of a certain age, but from then on, you're on your own? Do you want to grow old with the Lord as your new caretaker, or do you want to try it all alone?"

I could feel my eyes getting wider. I had never thought about going it alone before. I stepped forward. "Uh, Reverend Mary," I said softly at first, then managed to find my voice. "Reverend Mary, are you going to baptize us?"

She seemed startled, but said, "It would be my pleasure, child."

Relief flooded the children's choir. One by one, we all marched from the choir area straight down to the pulpit amid mighty amens. And there was a lot of "Thank you, Jesus!" coming from the parents, too. If we had known about praying for divine intervention, we would have been certain that the Lord had just answered our prayers.

The Reverend Mary's face was streaming tears as she knelt with us. She began singing the softest, most heavenly version of "Amazing Grace" I had ever heard, like angels were whispering the chorus. I looked out and saw M'Ma crying. I had made her proud, and I knew that I would be fine in the hands of the Reverend Mary and Jesus.

The following Sunday all of us were dressed in white as we went down to Summit Lake and committed ourselves to do the right thing for the rest of our lives. And the Reverend Mary didn't drown any of us in the cold clear waters of Summit Lake on that sweet summer's day.

The Coming of the Cold

. . . .

It was hard as hell trying to be holy all the time!

My sister broke out in hives, and my cousin Junior threw a rock across the street, a throw that was a wonder to behold!

It flew out of his hand and made a magnificent turn halfway across and sped straight into my cousin Edna's face. Her mother, Aunt Ouida, got heartless mad at Junior, marched across the street after stanching the blood flowing down poor Edna's face, and gave Junior "what for"!

M'Ma was philosophical about our struggle. She said it was like riding a racehorse down the glory road. If you fall off, you get up, check yourself out, and get right back on.

Great-Gramma Lizzie said quietly, "It's not where you goin', it's how you get there that counts!" She must have been listening to somebody: not long after, on her 107th birthday, she asked M'Ma and Gramma Hattie to help her pack her grips (bags), and then she got on the L&N (Louisville & Nashville) train back to Alabama.

She visited her other relatives, talked about how she had hid in the root cellar with the ol' master's children and the silverware when the damn Yankees came during the Civil War! "A rascally bunch!" she recalled. When the ol' master died, he left two drunken sons, who somehow left the deed to all their land to Great-Gramma Lizzie and her kin. This was the source of the pension that she received every single month of her life.

One evening, she went into the bedroom of the home of old Aunt Munch, lay down, and died quietly in her sleep. She was born a slave, but she sure didn't die a slave! Her mind was made up and her heart was set.

M'Ma said, "Great-Gramma went to glory just in time."

The Reverend Uncle Frank preached on the next few Sundays about the "snake" that had entered our little Garden of Eden on Bina Avenue.

The snake's name was "sit-down strike"!" All the tire and rubber workers in Ohio had decided that they wanted shorter hours, shorter weeks, and more money. "Let me hear an amen!" thundered the Reverend. "Amen!" the whole congregation cried out.

Some say that the sit-down strike was invented in Ohio; some argue that it was invented in Michigan. But the outcome was the same: no money, not funny!

Goodrich, Goodyear, Firestone—all were shut down, and the men of Bina Avenue did not work for three years! Three long years! The only man who worked full-time was Grampa Mac, and that was because he worked at 20th Century Foundry. The rest of the men did odd jobs—we asked M'Da what an odd job was. He said with a snort, "Anything legal that paid a few dollars." He was a wonderfully talented a carpenter, but was not allowed to join the carpenters' union on account of his skin color. So he had to take jobs that nobody else wanted—or that paid very little.

Then the sit-down strike forced every woman except the China-Man's wife, who was still bedridden, to do what they called "day's work." This meant being a maid, cook, window washer, wall washer, laundry woman, and whatever else the wealthy white women required.

Nobody in the neighborhood could remember a colder winter. It came right on the heels of the sit-down strike. Summit Lake froze over, and the snow came down so fast that the drifts of cold white powder came up over our heads. Tunnels were shoveled so folks could walk. We all had to climb up Bina Avenue hill on our hands and knees to go to school, to work, and to get groceries.

M'Ma put rolled-up rugs down at the front door to keep the snow from blowing in. The windows were also stuffed with rolled-up rags to keep out the fierce wind.

Uncle Sid said, "Boys! It's colder than a well digger's bee-hind out there!" Aunt Catherine pursed her lips, but didn't say anything. In fact, most of the women tried very hard to keep the atmosphere in the homes sweet and gentle because the men started getting kind of quick to fire up, and would say prickly and mean things.

Gramma Hattie said, "Well, I tell you what. You ask a man who he is and he'll tell you that he works at this place or that place. He can't separate who he is from what he does!" All the women nodded their heads in agreement, sadly sipped their hot tea, and made little crumbs out of their 1-2-3-4 cake.

Aunt Catherine bristled, "Well, they gonna have to settle this strike soon, or I'm gonna have to put Sid out in the street!" They all tittered nervously at this statement because nobody wanted to be a "grass widow" during these hard times. A grass widow was a woman who was separated, but not divorced, from her husband.

Even so, M'Da disappeared for longer and more frequent weekends to Cleveland and Pittsburgh, and he and M'Ma quarreled a lot. They must have been in their late twenties, the youngest couple in the neighborhood. The Reverend Uncle Frank sometimes would counsel them about "everybody getting along together," and I guess they took his advice, since a new little sister was born in October of that year. M'Ma named her Jo-Anne.

In those days, a woman would spend ten days in the hospital after having a baby, her stomach would be bound tightly with bands of cloth, and she would be guided in the care and feeding of the child. M'Ma said that was why we could almost stand on her stomach. The muscles would grow back where they belonged. And I guess that was why it was so easy for her to go right back to work.

Since we were in school, Jo-Anne was cared for primarily by Aunt Catherine and M'Da, when he wasn't doing odd jobs or visiting Cleveland or Pittsburgh.

M'Ma tried to hide her unhappiness, but I missed her playfulness. And we all missed M'Da taking us to the library to draw out our own books, and the giant geography jigsaw puzzles he would buy and place on the card table by the door. We would stop and push in a piece or two on our way in or out the house.

I would ask M'Ma, "Can I help? What do you want me to do?"

I practiced the piano diligently every morning and every evening. It was my special place to hide from everyone and everything.

Charlotte and I would have the table set when M'Ma came home from work. We'd peel potatoes and do simple cooking and heat up food she had prepared the night before.

M'Da was a good cook too, so we had no problem eating plenty of good food. Especially since M'Ma and the women of the neighborhood had canned so much food all last fall. Tomatoes, tomato juice, peaches, pear conserves, green beans, applesauce, and apple jelly in Mason jars were stored in each basement.

After supper, if M'Da was away, M'Ma would sometimes go into her bedroom, open the lower dresser drawer, and take out a tissue-covered package. In the worn paper was her pride and joy—a red silk velvet dress cut on the bias to show off a tiny figure! She would let us feel the smooth rich material and tell us the story of the red dress.

"I wore this dress and orange-blossom perfume," she would begin softly. Her head would tilt to one side and her eyes would go all moist and soft. "My girlfriend and I arrived at the Duke Ellington concert at the Akron Armory real early." She would draw her small frame up proudly. "Heads turned when we came in! We made our way up to the front of the band and stood in front of the trombone player!"

Now, we had heard this story many times, but we held our breath in anticipation. "There he was!" M'Ma would whisper. "So elegant and so handsome; his gold trombone sounded like a woman crying!" We waited, barely moving. "His hair was shiny like patent leather shoes, and he caught my eye and waggled his slide at me!"

"Oooo!" Charlotte, cousin Edna, and I breathed. "He waggled his slide!" we repeated.

M'Ma waited for full effect.

"Go on! Go on!" we cried.

"When the intermission came," M'Ma continued, "he came off the bandstand and said, 'Hello, ladies! Are you enjoying the music? My name is Lawrence Brown. What's yours?'"

M'Ma would always stop there, slowly fold the red silk velvet dress into a neat little square, place it tenderly back into the white tissue paper, and put it back into the lower dresser drawer. Then she would sigh, her brown hands smoothing her apron and her head fallen forward. She would stand there with her back to us; finally she'd turn and face us and declare, "Well, just think! If I had married Mr. Brown, we might have had a house of our own, and maybe had Mr. Duke Ellington himself to dinner—and maybe you-all would have had hair as shiny and black as patent leather shoes!" She drew her shoulders up and smiled, "Well, let's not waste time wishing. Let's make some oatmeal cookies!"

She was our M'Ma again.

The harsh winter weather did not let up. Everyone faced the blasts of cold arctic wind and made the best of things.

Even the Reverend Uncle Frank took a job at a very wealthy white woman's estate, shoveling snow, washing walls, painting and wallpapering walls, and doing all the heavy lifting.

Every day the woman would open a can of Campbell's tomato soup, put in five cans of water, heat it up, put some in a bowl, put the bowl on a table out on the porch, and then call out, "Frank! Oh, Frank! Your lunch is ready!"

Uncle Frank would wash his hands in the basement, come up to the porch, put on his coat and his scarf and his hat, and eat the soup.

After two days of this treatment, he rebelled. "Ouidy," he told my aunt, "I do think that white woman is insane! I cannot and will not do all this heavy work without proper nourishment! I want you to fix me a proper lunch, namely, fried chicken, corn bread, and sweet potato pie, and fix me a Mason jar of sweet tea."

Aunt Ouida did just that.

When he went back to work and lunchtime came, he spread out his lunch on the table on a tablecloth he brought from home and proceeded to devour the "sumptuous repast," as he called it. The woman came out on the porch with her usual watery offering and said, "Why, Frank! What have we here?"

Uncle Frank replied in his most solemn "come to Jesus" voice. "Madame! *We* don't have *nothing* here! *I* have something here! It is called my lunch. You take yo' soup and keep it for yourself. It is obvious to me that you need it more than I do!" With that he bit into the crunchy fried chicken leg and proceeded to eat his lunch. Needless to say, he demanded his money for a half day's work and went home—never to return.

That Sunday he was truly inspired! He spoke so eloquently that he saved three people! The topic of his sermon was "What good is it to possess the whole world and lose your soul?"

Amen.

Summer Heat

. . . .

Spring finally came to Bina Avenue. And it came late, around May. Gramma Hattie was worried. "I think we better all hunker down; spring so late and all—that does not look good for planting seeds." She was right. Spring lasted about a week, and then summer came blasting in. It became so hot that people and animals were panting and sweating and heat devils danced on the sidewalks. The women were getting leaner and the men were getting meaner.

Aunt Bessie and M'Ma said, "Let's have a church picnic!" They were inspired. "We'll go to Summit Beach Park and have some fun time!"

M'Da and Grampa Mac shook their heads. "Not Summit Beach Park. Maybe we can get on the excursion to Cleveland near Lake Erie. The union is trying to do something for families 'cause we been on strike so long." We all danced around and cheered, "Yay!"

Everyone helped make potato salad and fried chicken and ham and pickles and chocolate cake and melons on ice and plenty of Mason jars full of Alabama lemonade.

We caught the excursion train about five a.m. one hot morning, and, oh, what a journey! People were singing gospel and "Polly Wolly Doodle," and kids were everywhere, their eyes popping out at the movement of the train, watching the houses and yards flash by as the train picked up speed.

The Reverend Uncle Frank was jubilant, always happy to be in a crowd and on the move. M'Ma was angry with him because he did not want to help pay for an extra electrical outlet for our house. M'Ma and M'Da wanted to install a newfangled electric stove to replace the old kerosene stove we had used for so many years.

M'Ma had been doing day's work for a Mr. Mason, who ran an Ohio Edison store. Since the streetcar she took to work ran right past the Ohio

Edison store, M'Ma saw a sign in the window that said "Free cooking lessons—Learn to cook foods served to the Crowned Heads of Europe."

She got off the streetcar and went in; she took lessons for eighteen months. As she explained later, "They taught us all kinds of cheffing and cooking for large groups and banquets—with all the proper wines!" She was truly excited. And so were we because she would try out all the goodies on us: charlotte russe—chocolaty and rich with whipping cream—and orange duck and petits fours.

"I am not going to work for these rich women and be at their mercy! I am going to be a chef—and cater their parties!" she declared. "And I'm going to get one of those new electric ranges!"

Mr. Mason told her he would help her and M'Da get a range with no down payment, since it was such a new product—and he hoped that they would tell everyone else on Bina Avenue so he could make lots of sales.

M'Ma always knew a good deal when she saw one, but she had to figure how to get the reverend to fork over the forty-five dollars to pay for the electric line to the street. He was adamant about the line and suspicious of the new range. He really thought lightning would strike it and everybody who had anything to do with it.

But the Lord works in mysterious ways! Somebody gave M'Da a boy's brand-new Red Rover wagon as payment for making a new screen door. M'Da brought the pretty Red Rover wagon home for my little brother, Jerry. Jerry was delighted in his own quiet way. He pulled the wagon up to the Reverend Uncle Frank's house and parked it at the front steps. When the Reverend Uncle Frank came out, he saw the Red Rover wagon and stopped short. "Hey!" he shouted. "Boy! Where did you get that pretty Red Rover wagon?"

Jerry looked up at him and replied "M'Da." He never said much. He always spoke in little short sentences. And he always spoke softly.

The Reverend Uncle Frank put his hands up to his big round face. "Boy! I ain't never had no red wagon! I ain't never rode in no red wagon!" He walked all around it, and then he said, "Boy! Let me ride yo' Red Rover wagon!" Now, the reverend weighed at least two hundred pounds. He took that wagon to the top of Bina Avenue and hoisted his big wide behind onto the little red wagon.

By then, Uncle Sid had come out his house because Jerry had started bawling in his bass voice. "What's the matter, Jerry?" Jerry pointed up the hill. Sid took one look and started running up the hill. We all ran to the front to see what all the fuss was about.

All we saw was a blur! A large human being on a child's Red Rover wagon, hurtling down the hill! The Reverend Uncle Frank was laughing wildly and holding on for dear life. All the wheels came off the Red Rover wagon at the same time! It skidded to a screeching stop! Sparks flew!

The Reverend Uncle Frank got off the wagon, slapped his leg, and sheepishly said to all of us, "I ain't never had a Red Rover wagon." He dragged what was left of the wagon back to the tearful Jerry, lifted him up, and declared, "Boy! You got a good wagon there!" Then he put Jerry down and went in his house.

Jerry looked like he was in shock. He didn't cry anymore. He just stood there. So did we. Uncle Sid cleared his throat and said, "I'll help you fix your wagon, Jerry. Don't you worry 'bout a thing." He went into his house, brought some tools, and tried to straighten out the axles and put the wheels back on, but it was no use. The wagon always leaned, and the wheels had a mind of their own. Jerry never touched that Red Rover wagon again. We never knew what he thought about it, either.

But when M'Ma got home and found out, she was "heartless mad." She went to the reverend's house after dinner, in spite of M'Da's objections. She said in a steely voice, "Frank, you really don't have to worry about Jerry's new Red Rover wagon." We looked surprised. "I do believe that the money for the new electric line will just about cover everything nicely!"

Now, the reverend could not let himself look cheap in front of the whole neighborhood, so he blustered, "Arump! Arump! So it will, Lizzie, so it will!"

And it was done. We got the first electric range in the neighborhood.

At the picnic in Cleveland, on Lake Erie, we rode the merry-go-round and the ponies, and we ate until our tummies almost burst. In the late summer afternoon, the little ones took naps and the grown-ups told stories and jokes. It was a good day.

The ride home seemed long. And when we finally arrived home, some people from down in Kenmore were standing in front of the Reverend Uncle Frank's house. They were crying and holding one another. "What on earth is the matter? What's wrong?" Uncle Sid pushed his way into the center of the little crowd.

One of the men from Kenmore gasped, "Reverend Williams, you must come, and Sid and Earnest, you must come also!" He paused and looked at M'Ma. "Ma'am, maybe you could come, too?"

He stood still, and then, drawing a deep breath, he said, "You know, it's a good thing you-all did not go to Summit Beach Park today. As you-all well know, some of the white workers at the rubber plants want to stop the strike and go back to work. Their women don't have day's work like ours. The rich white women won't hire poor white women, so they are really having a rough time of it! They blame the black workers for holding out for shorter weeks and hours and better pay. They think we are to blame for their hunger and lack of jobs. Some are too proud to go to the union food banks, and never took part in the common gardens."

His voice broke.

"So when we went over to Summit Beach Park today, there was a gang of these white men from West Virginia, and when we got in line to get tickets for the rides, they started yelling. 'Niggers! You stop us from working! We don't want you standin' in the same line, and you niggers ain't gonna ride no roly-coaster today!' With that, they pulled Mabel White out of the line, and one of those peckerwoods kicked her in her stomach!"

"No!" everyone breathed. "Is she gonna be all right? She's only a teen-ager! She's so pretty! Why would anybody wanna hurt her?" The questions came thick and fast.

Now, Mabel White was one of Uncle Sid's near and dear relatives, and he snarled, "Come on! Let's not stand here talking! Let's go down to Mabel's house!" They piled into the cars and took M'Ma because she was used to nursing people back to health.

Late that night we could hear car doors slamming and voices pitched low, and I got up and went to the door and opened it for M'Ma. M'Da was still in Kenmore with Uncle Sid and the Reverend Uncle Frank. She came in and went straight to the bathroom and washed her face and hands. When she came out, she said, "Are the kids all asleep?" I said, "Oh yes! I made some tea for you."

M'Ma sat down heavily and said, "That's a good girl. Thanks." Then she took a sip and put down the cup. "What is it that makes people so wicked? Why don't they ever jump on the people that are the guilty ones? The people that own the rubber companies? The men that lay people off just when you getting on your feet? They are all home in their big houses, sleeping in the beds we made up! On laundry we washed! Eating the food we cooked! Safe behind big iron gates, all out of harm's way!"

I sat on the floor next to her chair in the dark and waited. "Your Dad and Grampa knew trouble was brewing with those people at Summit Beach Park. That's why they suggested the picnic at Lake Erie!" She made a sound in her throat. "Mabel White died tonight!"

Wrong Direction

. . . .

You lookin' in the wrong direction
If you think I'm gonna change my mind
My bag's all packed, I gonna
Leave yo' butt behind!

I think the sudden appearance of my period galvanized M'Ma into action.

It came early in my life, like a bad dream that doesn't disappear when you open your eyes. I woke up in the middle of the night with a start, terrorized by the sight of blood. My whole body felt like broken piano pedals stomped on by some barrelhouse boozehound.

I ran into M'Ma and M'Da's bedroom. "Ma! Ma, wake up," I whispered. "Something's happening. Oh, something's happening!"

M'Da, who slept on the front as "The Protector," woke first, took one look at me standing in the moonlight in my long, blood-stained nightgown, shook M'Ma, and said, "Liz, wake up! Jeannie needs you."

M'Ma sat up, frowned at the stains on my nightgown, and asked, "Why in the world did this happen to you so early in life and in the middle of the night?" I didn't have any kind of answer to that and just stood there trembling. Crawling over M'Da, she grabbed my shaking hand and pulled me down the hall, back to the room I shared with my two sisters. They were still sound asleep.

"How did all this blood get on your pillow?" M'Ma demanded.

I didn't know—I thought it all came out my ear.

M'Ma's lips disappeared. She introduced me to the ungainly apparatus of the time, showing me how to wear the dreaded belt and clumsy pad. After we cleaned up the mess in my bed, she turned to me and said, "Listen and listen good! This is all natural. Tomorrow when you get up, you do everything you been doing. Make the bed, make the oatmeal, wash dishes, and since it's Saturday, it's your turn to scrub the kitchen. I don't want to see frowns or grimaces or hear any groans. I don't want anybody in this house to feel that you have a problem, 'cause you don't. And when you go to school, get a job, and get married, you are not to let anybody know if you have cramps or pain, even if you do. This is a natural event, and you gonna do this once a month till you're fifty years old at least. So you might as well make up your mind to include it in your schedule."

I didn't sleep the rest of the night. When the sun splayed a rosy fan of color across the morning sky, I got up and quietly got dressed so I wouldn't wake my two sisters. I walked on tippy-toes to the kitchen, put on the big old pot of oatmeal, turned it down to warm on the new electric stove, and went outside. I walked down to Summit Lake, where I stood on the shore taking long deep breaths, letting the serenity of the blue water, colored pink in places where it reflected the sky, wash over my battered spirit. I thought, wow, I don't wanna be a grown woman, or even a lady. I don't wanna be nobody's wife and have a husband who makes you mad an' you barely ever talk about him if you my Great-Gramma Lizzie and he's an Irishman. Or get a divorce from him if you my Gramma Hattie an' you like to farm and own lots an' lots of land an' he wants to stay in town an' work in the foundry an' hang out with his Hungarian friends an' drink. Or be unhappy like M'Ma sometimes 'cause M'Da hangs out in Cleveland or Pittsburgh an' thinks the Reverend Uncle Frank speaks the *only* truth.

I picked up a rock, observing its shape. "Hey, this is a great rock," I said to myself. It was skinny and flat and had sharp edges. I threw it sidearmed across the surface of the lake, and, wonder of wonders! it skipped *four* times. Even my boy cousins could make a stone skip only *three* times.

"Wow, I'm gonna be just like a four-time skipping rock! Ain't nobody gonna squeeze me into no miserable little space with miserable people, miserable oatmeal, and, most of all, miserable monthly periods. NOBODY!"

I took one last look at the lake, then turned and marched back up through the tree-filled vacant lot, up to the little house, and started doing my chores with a vengeance. M'Ma just smiled.

That evening after all the Saturday work was done and the kids were all fed and washed and ready for bed, I told M'Ma, "I am not gonna play for the St. Paul's Baptist Church again—ever—for nothing! I deserve to be paid just like every other church organist and pianist in this town. I've played for them since I was barely past five years old, and now I want some money!" The words rushed from my mouth like a waterfall.

M'Ma and M'Da looked startled, then looked at each other. M'Da cleared his throat. "Um . . . you know the Reverend Uncle Frank says we workin' on our soul salvation and each of our gifts belong to the Lawd."

"The Lawd own everything," I said, clenching my fist. "He really don't need money—I do. I wanna save money for when I grow up."

M'Da took a few deep breaths, shaking his head from side to side. "See how you raise these kids? *You* talk to her—I'm going to bed." And he did.

M'Ma said quietly, "Well, if you made up your mind, decide on a price and tomorrow we'll present it to the deacon board."

Suddenly I felt frightened. But there was no turning back now. "All right, M'Ma. I think I'll go to bed, too." I hugged myself. "Good night."

"Wait!" M'Ma said. "I'm gonna tell you something important. When it comes to money, always ask for more than you think you're gonna get. Then, when they come down to your *real* price, nobody feels bad. Everybody wins. All right?"

I nodded. We grinned at each other. It really felt good sharing this quiet moment alone with M'Ma.

* * *

Bird and fish can fall in love,
Give all that they can give—
But O my brother—O my sister—
Where are they gonna live?

"Dad bop it!" The words exploded out of M'Da's mouth, along with crumbs from the biscuit he had been chewing. "Dad bop it!" he roared. This time it was accompanied by his big brown fist pounding the kitchen table. "I'm not gonna speak to the deacon board about no money for Jean to play the piano in church. It's her God-given duty! And I'm not gonna move—nowhere! We're safe here. When I'm on strike and can't pay the rent, Uncle Frank lets us stay here. I ain't gonna buy no house, only to have to give it back to the white folks when I can't pay the mortgage!" He lost his speech and started jabbing his finger in the air for emphasis. "I . . . ! I . . . !" he stammered, marking time.

While he was thinking of what else he wanted to say, M'Ma dove into the breach like a hummingbird, so fast you couldn't see her wings moving. "*I* ain't what *is!*" she said, her long eyes flattening out and her lips disappearing. "*I* don't mean a *thing*. The operative word is *we! Us!* My girls and boy are not sharecroppers for Uncle Frank! They can speak up for what they want in *this* life! And they are growing up fast—faster than either of us realize. *And* they'll soon graduate from Margaret Park Grade School."

Her voice became even more intense. "They and their cousins are the only Negroes in the school. They get all As and Bs and take part on an equal footing in *all* the activities. Ernest, they are not gonna go to Kenmore High School with a bunch of low-life people, black or white, who only concentrate on what's below their belts. We movin' to the west side so they can go to a good high school and maybe college—so they can be somebody in this world!"

She took a deep breath. We were all rooted to our chairs. The Sunday morning breakfast—homemade biscuits, gravy, grits, ham, salmon croquettes, and a big old bowl of fresh cut-up fruit—was being ignored altogether. M'Ma and M'Da seldom had words, but when they did, it was a *doozy*. It felt like Beethoven and boogie-woogie were crashing together in our little kitchen.

"I'm not going anyplace!" M'Da had found his voice. "No where! With nobody!" With that he stood up, the kitchen chair crashing behind him, grabbed a biscuit and a big slice of ham, slapped them together, and left the house, slamming the screen door behind him. "DAD BOP IT!"

M'Ma set the fallen chair upright. She shook her head and sighed. "All right kids, let's get ready for church. We mustn't be late." Her copper-colored face suddenly looked thinner. "Sometimes I think your Dad and I are like a bird and a fish who fall in love and don't know where to live." She patted my shoulder. "C'mon, Jean. Let's go meet the deacon board."

The New House

· · · · · · · · · · · · · · · · · · ·

M'Ma did buy a house.

Glory!

The ever-enterprising Great-Uncle Sid came by one day and said, "Lizzie, I *do* feel lucky! In fact I feel so full of luck that it's getting ready to spill all over onto you. I got a good number for you!"

M'Ma laughed. "Sid, go on! You know I'm trying to save money for the down payment on a house. I can't spare one thin dime for your numbers games."

But Uncle Sid persisted. He did some tall persuading to get her to play the gambling game, since she was a Bible-reading Baptist lady and it made her leery of which side of "sin street" she was stepping on. But he was right. She hit that number straight. In fact, she won so much that, when added to her savings, it was enough for the down payment on the house.

We sang a song sometimes that included the lines "He may not come when you call Him, / But He *always* come on time." And he came on time. The previous Sunday M'Ma had approached the deacon board about paying me a salary for pounding the piano *all day* every Sunday—Sunday school, prayer service, church service, and back at night for the Baptist Young People's Union. The Reverend Uncle Frank and six deacons sat in a circle and made little cathedrals out of their fingers while they pondered our request. They hemmed and they hawed, and then hawed and hemmed because they knew that *we* knew they had the money in the treasury.

Our timing could not have been better. The church had just enjoyed a visit from the white politicians who came to our church only at election time, and sat stiff as trees in the back row in their three-piece suits with gold watches hanging from thick gold chains and their high white collars that were so tight their faces turned as red as fire when they said loud amens. When the politicians came to call, the Reverend Uncle Frank always preached about the rich men who could more easily go through the eye of a needle than they could get into heaven.

After the sermon, following an invitation from the reverend, they came up to the front of the congregation to speak on things political. And they always left a very generous amount of money in the collection plate. "Greenbacks!" Grandpa Mac would say. "Greenbacks to fatten up the treasury."

And so we stood in front of the deacon board and waited for what seemed like a week. Finally, the head deacon cleared his throat, rubbed his hand over his shiny bald head, and said in his most unctuous tones, "We have, er . . . ah, er . . . ah! What I mean to say is, we have decided that we cannot answer your request, Miz Evans. Er . . . ah . . . we are dedicated to saving the monies in the treasury for an old-colored-folks home so we can have a refuge in our dotage."

"What's dotage?" I asked.

M'Ma clapped her hand over my mouth.

The head deacon looked up at the ceiling and pronounced each word as if it caused him pain, "Dotage means old age . . ." He paused. "Er . . . ah . . ."

M'Ma's lips disappeared. "Who? Just *who* is gonna take care of *you?* If you had any sense at all, you'd give that money in scholarships to the young people so they can be doctors and nurses and *really* care for you." She made a fist. "Since you have no vision," she said, soft spoken and all the more impressive because she hadn't raised her voice, "as for me and mine, we resign."

And we did! And we never went back!

* * *

M'Ma went into action. She started asking all the people she and M'Da worked for if they knew of any houses for sale on the west side of Akron. Even Gramma Hattie's old real estate partner had suggestions. Finally, a white man whose parents had died and left an empty house on a quiet tree-lined street came up with a proposal. He accepted as a down payment the money that M'Ma had, and the papers were drawn up by his and her law-yers. The Evans Bank (no relation) took the mortgage.

The white man had one request. "You will be the only Negro family on the block. I'm leaving town and don't want any trouble. I don't want the neighbors to know that you bought the property. Don't go into the house in the daytime till I'm gone," he said.

So Uncle Sid drove M'Ma by the house and said, "Well, Liz, these houses on this street are all solid built and in good shape. Give me the key, and I'll put on my overalls and go round the back as if I'm the handyman. I'll check the foundation. Then I'll go in and check the furnace." He did and everything was fine. A brand new furnace!

As soon as the white man left town, we got busy. We moved the new electric stove, all the home-canned Mason jars of food, Great-Gramma's quilts, all our clothes, the brooms and buckets for cleaning, and flower cuttings carefully wrapped up in damp paper and cloths. Mr. Riley, that faithful old piano teacher, helped supervise the moving of the piano. We even moved brother Jerry's big black cat.

But we did not take the rickety old beds or the couch or the old living-room furniture.

We also did not take M'Da. He refused to move with us. He had no faith in the move, and he sure didn't want to anger the Reverend Uncle Frank.

Inside, the new house was truly wonderful. We ran up and down the stairs, poking into closets and—oh wow!—bedrooms upstairs and bedrooms downstairs, a large living room and big old dining room, an eat-in-sit-down kitchen, and a really big backyard bordering a huge vacant lot that went all the way to the next street behind the house. A backyard tailor-made for both garden and games.

And wonder of wonders . . . a great big basement with a large coal room full of *hard* coal for the furnace. This discovery delighted M'Ma, since soft coal was cheap, but always smoked up the whole house.

"A wringer washing machine!" she exclaimed. It had two rollers to wring out the clothes and clotheslines already in place to dry them.

We had only one bathroom, but we were used to that.

And we had one other new thing we had never had before. M'Ma got a gun. Not a blunderbuss like Great-Gramma Lizzie's or a shotgun like Gramma Hattie's. It was a dainty little silver .22-caliber pistol. She showed us older kids how to clean it, oil it, and load it up. Moving to the new neighborhood had its joys, but we no longer had the luxury of the protection of Uncle Sid, the Hungarian, the Reverend Uncle Frank, or even the China-Man. Since M'Da wasn't living with us, we were on our own, with Midnight, the cat that thought he was an attack dog.

Gramma Hattie often said, "An egg is dedicated, but a chicken is committed." We were really committed as a family to that house.

Nobody ever locked their doors at night, so M'Ma told us, "Anybody try to come in here at night uninvited, we shoot first, drag him *into* the house, *then* call the cops." Her lips disappeared, so we knew she really meant business.

That night we slept on the floor in our bedrooms on pallets made of blankets and Great-Gramma's quilts. We all said our prayers with M'Ma: "Our Father who art in heaven . . ." And we all thought about M'Da.

And in the dark, in the middle of the night, I lay awake—body stiff, hands clenched with my thumbs tucked in, legs crossed at the ankles—anxious and full of fear, hoping M'Da would soon come back to help M'Ma. I knew that in the morning I would get up and try to do everything perfect to help around the house and strain my little body to the last inch to make M'Ma smile. I'd try hard to fill the big hole left in the shaky foundation of our family by M'Da choosing to leave us all alone.

Then I got heartless mad.

I whispered to myself, "I wish Our Father in Heaven would take a long green willow switch to our father on earth, and *make* him do the right thing and come home to live with us in the New House."

The little house on Bina Avenue, Akron, Ohio. I lived there from 1927 to 1939.

The cool blue waters of Summit Lake, less than half a block from the little house. Excellent for fishing and baptisms.

M'Ma (Elizabeth Smart Evans). Five feet of fierce determination.

Grandma Hattie (Hattie Daniels Smart). Five feet three of cool calculation.

Great-Grandma Lizzie (Elizabeth Jordan Daniels). Six feet two of sheer survival.

Me at sixteen. Graduation photo from West High School, Akron, Ohio, 1943.

It's an Ill Wind That Don't Blow Somebody *Some* Good

. . . .

M'Da was working the midnight shift at Firestone, so we were all alone. Oh, yes! M'Da had come back like a thief in the night. We woke up one morning, and there he was in the kitchen, making pan-fried potatoes and onions and fresh sausage and toast and fresh fruit cut up in a big old bowl.

"It's M'Da!" we exclaimed. "You're back!" We had smiles all around. Shy glances at M'Ma, who was standing in front of the cupboard in her pink chenille robe, looking rosy and pleased.

"Wash up so you-all can eat." M'Da was majestic. "You don't wanna be late for school." He turned back to the stove and started humming "My Bonnie Lies over the Ocean." It was his favorite song.

We all looked at M'Ma for the go-ahead. She nodded and we were galvanized into action.

A small shadow came over M'Da's face. I was watching him intently, and knew what he was thinking. But *truth is the light!* He had been gone so long that he had kind of lost his place in the pecking order. Then he noticed that I was standing there watching him. "You too," he said. "Go on! Do what I say!" His voice was gruff.

I hurried up the stairs and sat on my bed, trying to make sense of what was happening. "Whoa!" I muttered. "Whoa!" I had been M'Ma's right-hand person for a long, long time, it seemed to me. "Oh, well," I said to myself, "we shall see what we shall see." I got dressed and rushed downstairs.

I guess it was all right. We soon fell into the rhythm of a new routine that included M'Da. It must have been all right with M'Ma 'cause we got a new refrigerator and a new brother, Richard, named for our jazz-playing uncle.

The windows in our little world began to open wider and wider. In fact, the windows all blew out and the roof of our new house blew two streets over when Ohio's worst tornado struck in April.

M'Ma had just come home from the hospital with David, our new baby brother, when the rains poured into the house through the huge gaping hole left by the missing roof. It rained on David and Richard, who was almost two years older, and on all the rest of us—Charlotte, Jerry, Jo-Anne, and me.

The nearly hundred-mile-an-hour winds pushed the electric stove through the kitchen door and into the dining room, and boards from the garage went through the kitchen walls like straws through butter. All the lights went out.

We ran downstairs, screaming in terror, and jumped into bed with M'Ma and the two littlest and newest members of the family, just as all the air was sucked out of the house. It sounded like a freight train was roaring around railroad tracks in the heavens.

* * *

As the old saying goes: "It's an ill wind that don't blow somebody some good." The movie *Gone with the Wind* blew into town, and the crowds were so large and the lines so long that the theaters on Main Street abandoned the usual practice of sending Negroes to the balcony and white folks to the mezzanine. All the theater manager could see was greenback dollar bills. He forgot all about black, and he sure forgot about white.

That was the end of segregation on Main Street in Akron, Ohio.

* * *

When the winds of war came in '41, Grampa Mac and Uncle Sid and the Reverend Uncle Frank discussed strategy. "Well, I don't think we should be goin' over to Yurrup [Europe] mindin' ev'rybody else's business!" The Reverend Uncle Frank was fixed in his opinion.

We stayed with Aunt Catherine and Uncle Sid while our house was all torn up from the tornado—it took six months for the government to help with repairs. Uncle Sid would drive us to school and pick us up. After school, we would sit around and listen, just like the old days. Nobody mentioned M'Ma becoming a Methodist after leaving St. Paul's Baptist.

"Look, mark my words!" Grampa Mac would say, taking his Bowles cigar out of his mouth, "These men, Roosy-velt, Hitler, Hiro-heeta, and that English bird, Winston Chu-chill, are the four horsemen in the Bible. And that Rooshin is drivin' the chariot they all hooked up to. They busy bringin' in Armageddon!" Everyone would nod and look solemn.

I don't know if they were bringing in Armageddon or not, but they sure pulled almost all of the Negro boys out of West High School and left almost all of the white boys behind. The white boys were going to college to be doctors and lawyers, and so were exempt from the draft. Most of the Negro boys were slated for the rubber factories (since there was a serious lack of money and scholarships), so they were drafted and sent away to keep America free.

There was no prom for us Negro girls at high school graduation. There weren't enough Negro boys to go around.

My mother's younger brothers were drafted. They came home on leave, handsome and impressive in their crisp uniforms, complaining bitterly about not being able to fight the enemy. "We don't do nothin' but carry caskets and dead soldiers. We wanna fight like white men. We're just as brave as they are!"

In the midst of the ruckus, Grampa Mac's question came soft as a whisper. "So you stay behind, pickin' up dead folks, ay?" My uncles nodded, twisting their soldier caps around and around in their brawny hands.

"Well," Grampa looked grim, "better *carryin'* those caskets than *ridin'* in them!" He slapped his leg and chortled. "Now, let me touch the hem of yo' garment!"

And that was that.

* * *

The winds of change touched every point in our city. Because of the war, the factories and steel mills were going full blast and the city smelled awful. The rubber smell permeated the atmosphere day and night, and was joined by pungent smells from the Quaker Oats Company. Sometimes we could hardly breathe, but we got used to it.

Most of the best young musicians were drafted also. They marched off to war, and the ill wind that blew them overseas blew all of us who were left behind into good positions. We were hired to play the *best* jobs. We quickly moved into the breach. With the help of the really old musicians and the 4-Fs (those excluded from military service for medical, psychological, or family-support reasons), we absorbed the repertoire of the times, and also reveled in the new music called bebop and rhythm and blues.

Glory! I was accepted at the University of Akron in 1944.

"A college woman!" I hugged myself. "I'm really here." I strode all over the small campus, went to class, studied in the library, played bridge in the card room, took the bus home when it rained, and walked home when it didn't. I took a nap, dressed in my music clothes, played all night in the different clubs, rushed home to sleep a few hours, then up and back to school.

Meanwhile, M'Da's whole personality had been changing. O Lordy! He startled me one day when he came home from work and announced, "Jean, I'm not buyin' you no more clothes! I'm not buyin' you no more shoes! And I'm surely not sendin' you to college next year!" I stood there stunned. My heart squeezed until I could hardly breathe. He turned and went into his bedroom and slammed the double doors.

I knew M'Da, who had been one of the stalwart deacons of St. Paul's Baptist Church, had never drunk liquor or beer—only "sweet-nin" water and Alabama lemonade. But lately he had been stopping at a bar near the Firestone plant. He had made friends with a large sleepy-eyed dark-skinned man M'Ma called Kingfish, after the character in *Amos 'n' Andy*. It was as if he had put a spell on M'Da.

"He's stopped bringing home his paycheck!" M'Ma was livid. She got dressed up and went somewhere and talked to somebody, and the next thing we knew, there was a huge argument, and then M'Da yelled, "DAD BOP IT!" and slammed out of the house. He and Kingfish went to Cleveland for the whole weekend.

"Jeannic," M'Ma said that evening as I was getting dressed to go play music in a club on Main Street, "I have only enough money for one more semester at Akron U., but we'll see what happens." I swallowed hard. I knew she wanted me to be a teacher like my Aunt Helen, M'Ma's younger sister.

She whispered, "I straightened out your dad's money. I went to Firestone and talked to people over there, and they helped me fix it so your dad's paycheck goes straight from them into the Firestone Bank." She paused and smiled grimly. "I got the bank book in *my name only.*" I stared at her, trying to absorb the news. "Kingfish will spend no more of the Evanses' money!" M'Ma had declared war.

* * *

I sold some to a policeman!
I sold some to a judge!
I would have sold some to the mayor
But the mayor had a grudge

Here we were—cousin Gene on drums, George on sax, and me on the big-legged gap-toothed piano—playing on a stage at a bar called The Bucket of Blood.

It was a rugged roadhouse in Barberton, Ohio, and M'Ma would have had a *fit* had she known what kind of place it *really* was. But I was determined to earn money for college, and The Bucket of Blood paid top dollar.

Every Saturday night there was a woman who would show up in a shiny red dress, her stocking seams going straight up the back of her legs. We were amazed at this because she was always so drunk that she would open the door of the club and fall in. She had not a hair out of place. Her two upper front teeth were solid gold!

"I been drinkin'," she would sing in a hoarse voice. "Lawd, I been drinkin'—an' when I *git* home, babe—*please*—let me lay down an' rest!"

We played the blues for this woman as if she were a queen. The people would dance closer than close. They called it "dancin' on a dime." A woman put both her arms around a man's neck, and the man would put both his hands on her behind, and away they would go. The lights were turned way down low, and the smoke would curl and swirl toward the ceiling's dark wooden beams.

The bar was made up of a long plank set on barrels, and would be full of barflies sitting on tall rickety stools. The bare wooden tables would be covered with drinks—beer, wine, and illegal white lightning. Gold jewelry and gold teeth flashed and glittered in the half-light.

"Turn out all the lights an' call the law!" somebody would shout, and Gene would lay a heavy backbeat on the drums. The sax would growl, and I would tickle the high notes on the old piano.

Barbequed pig-ear sandwiches were available with coleslaw to help feed the bad, bad whiskey. There was no bathroom in the bar. But away out back, leaning against some tall oak trees at the edge of a clearing, was the outhouse. My cousin said, "Don't drink water after three o'clock in the afternoon so you won't have to go out in the dark to that outhouse!" And we didn't.

The men who drank at The Bucket of Blood were mostly field-workers, and the women were camp followers and fruit and vegetable pickers. The men carried razors covered with big handkerchiefs or bandanas in their back pockets. Sometimes they pulled out the kerchief and cut somebody's face. Those razors were kept so well honed that the victim often was not aware that he had been cut until he saw blood running down his shirtfront.

There was a big window right behind the stage. We used it to escape from fights and arguments that sometimes started as quick as a flash.

My man got somethin'
He keeps it hid—
But I got somethin'
I can find it wid'

That woman could really sing the blues, and the screams of laughter from the crowd egged her on. But, alas, her husband would arrive around midnight to try to make her come home.

Crash! The door would open, and in he would come, red eyes glaring, and yell, "Virginia, it's time for you to come on home!" Then he'd take out a .44 and shoot at the ceiling. Bang! Bang!

Everybody headed for cover under the tables. And we, with our hearts racing wildly, more afraid of our folks' hearing about the dangers we faced every Saturday night than of getting shot, headed out the window with the sax and as many drums as we could grab. The party would halt temporarily until the wild and woolly couple left the roadhouse. Then back in the window we would climb and start playing again.

We always got paid well. And we made sure we got paid *early!*

* * *

Running the elevator every afternoon at the YMCA was a pleasant, quiet task after the high drama of the roadhouse. My second job, it was ideal because I could practice all my old classical music on the lovely old Steinway piano that stood in the corner of one of the meeting rooms during my supper break.

Oh, I also had playing time at the University of Akron, accompanying occasional class instrumentalists and vocalists. But I really valued playing time *alone*. Me, myself, and I! It was a "soul refreshment."

My third job was teaching piano to young children in their homes. Saturday mornings, I would hop buses and go from one student to another. It was my least favorite job. Their mothers never made them practice. I would go quietly berserk because they all sounded like just Aunt Catherine, *week* after *week*.

* * *

"Bend over!"

The nurse held the white cotton ball to the bottle of alcohol and sterilized the spot. The doctor held the needle in the air ready to plunge it into my behind. The syringe was full of B vitamins. "You're really run down," he said, blue eyes glinting behind his eyeglasses. "What do you do all week?"

"Well . . ." I rearranged my clothes while the nurse smiled sympathetically. Then I ran down my schedule, making sure I included everything. The doctor shook his head.

"You're doing too much," he admonished. "You have to take these shots twice a week till your system's back to normal."

"Yes, Doctor, but I'm tryin' to . . ."

"No buts!" He shook his finger at me and scolded. "Your mother told me you've been going to sleep on the bus and riding to the end of the line!" I hung my head. Gee, why did she have to tell him that? I asked myself.

When I looked up, the doctor's eyes had softened. "Look, I understand, I had to work my way through med school with no sleep. Believe me, I understand. But you're a little small to take on so many jobs. Better to concentrate on *one* job that pays *well!*"

"Yes, Doctor." But I didn't. I was determined.

* * *

The days and nights went by like a whirlwind. M'Ma tried. I tried. But we couldn't come up with enough greenbacks for a second year at the university.

"Okay," I steeled my resolve, "if I can't continue college, I'll go to art school and become an art teacher." So I added this to my already hectic schedule. My former art teacher at West High submitted some of my artwork to the Akron Art Institute, and—have mercy!—I won a scholarship.

"You got a letter. It's from the art people!" Charlotte was excited. She dropped the mail on the table.

"Really? Let me see." I ripped open the letter. I never could wait to open anything properly, and now I was more impatient than usual. I took a deep breath. "Wow! I won! I won!"

I read the letter a second time. "It says I won a first-prize scholarship at an art school in New York and would I call M. O'Neil's department store for further details."

"New York." Charlotte grinned. She was planning to join the air force in a few weeks. "Maybe I'll change my mind and go with you!"

"Yeah, sure!"

Well, the day came for me to meet with the other winners at M. O'Neil's conference room, and when I walked in the whole committee stopped talking and stared. "Who are you?" One of them finally spoke up.

"I'm Jean Evans. The first-prize winner." I spoke up proudly.

"What?" Stammering, they withdrew into a corner of the room and whispered and waved their arms around.

Finally one of the women walked briskly over to me, her arms folded across her chest. "Well, well! So glad to meet you, but I'm afraid that there has been a *big* mistake. An error, as it were." Her lips smiled, but her blue eyes were steely. "Your scholarship was a mix-up. Your real prize is this: you can pick any outfit in the store for, er, uh, up to $50. This salesperson will take you downstairs right now, to begin choosing. Now, isn't that nice?" She turned and walked over to the other prizewinners, second and third place, both white.

The saleswoman came up, nervous, her face scarlet, and said in a squeaky, high-pitched voice, "This way, come right this way."

I turned and walked out of the conference room, out of the store, and all the way home, perspiration staining the underarms of my pale blue two-piece suit, beading up on my forehead, running down into my eyes, and mingling with the salt of the tears pooling there.

Temporarily blinded, I wiped my eyes with the little white linen handkerchief that was nestled in my left breast pocket, stepped in a crack in the sidewalk, and broke the heel on my new patent-leather shoe. I stopped. Then leaned over and pulled the broken heel out of the crack, took off both shoes, and walked in my stocking feet all the rest of the way home.

When I got to our front door, I looked at the new roof, the new front windows, the new paint the government had supplied to *all* the victims of the tornado. They fixed up our house. But they *could not* fix up our *home*.

* * *

Dealing with M'Da was like drinking a cup of hot lard. We couldn't figure out what was eating him. My sister Charlotte, tall, willowy, with an ever-ready smile, was getting ready to leave for the air force. And brother Jerry, who grew to six feet almost overnight and who was playing excellent bass fiddle by now, stayed away from home as much as possible.

So did I. I threw myself wholeheartedly into playing music. I loved the approval of the older, seasoned musicians. They taught me the tricks of the trade—how to read an audience, how to accompany vocalists. "Always carry yo' drink with you," they advised. "If you leave it, buy a new one! Always keep yo' union dues paid up—the better clubs are union—an' get yo'self an agent."

They gave me a couple names, and I rushed to their offices. We checked each other out, and they started getting me work. "Get some cards made with your name on them—and be sure to have *raised letters* on them." The agents were really helpful. "You must have photos made." I did. They called them "lobbies."

These people were a gold mine of lifesaving information:

"Always make friends with the bartender an' the chef!"

"Never hang out and drink in the club where you work!"

"Ev'ry shut eye ain't 'sleep!" Smirks all around.

"If you been out on the road a long time, always call first before you show up at home!" Knowing laughter from *all* the cats.

* * *

When we lived on Bina Avenue, time seemed to go by oh so slowly. But now the seasons seemed to fly by, piling on top of one another—winter, spring, summer, fall.

The winters especially seemed warmer and shorter, which was a real boon for all us at Easter time. When Negroes buy their Easter finery, neither wind, rain, nor snow up to their hips stops them from showing off. Women who heralded spring by wearing hats ringed around with artificial flowers, shiny new shoes, and robin's-egg blue silk—or pink linen dresses and pale green coats—hopped over snowdrifts to get to Easter services.

And that night they came, finery and all, to the Akron Armory, where they would jump and sway to the Sultans of Rhythm and stars like Al Hibbler, who was a great baritone vocalist for Duke Ellington's band and who just happened to be blind. I sat proudly on the bandstand with thirteen old men and 4Fs in tuxedos. I wore a white one-shouldered Grecian-style gown with a thin gold belt and gold sandals. The trumpets, trombones, and saxophones were shiny and golden also. The music filled the armory to the brim with great rhythms and gorgeous sounds.

"She looks like a fly in the buttermilk!" The mother of a young man who had a crush on me gave her opinion of my appearance. And he trotted right over after the show to let me know what she said.

"What?" I stared at him. I knew that report was pure envy and spite. His mother wanted him to marry a light-skinned girl, so he could "up the race." I didn't want to marry anybody. Besides, I knew I looked great. Al Hibbler said so, although he was stone blind. He said he could tell by my walk.

"Ugly women drag their feet!" Hibbler chortled. "That's how I can tell!" The whole band laughed and started telling lies. It was great fun.

* * *

Our beloved Grampa Mac was found dead under the bridge that crossed over the clear blue waters of Summit Lake.

That's one funeral I did not play.

M'Ma said, "I want you all to remember him laughing and playing 'Under the Double Eagle' on his harmonica." I knew she'd said that because she didn't want us to see her cry.

Yellow Cab to the Red-Light District

. . . .

I took a yellow cab down to the red-light district. It was 4:30 in the afternoon and the sun was sinking in the west. The cab traveled over to Bowery Street, went down the hill, and made a left turn on Main Street, past M. O'Neil's department store and its bitter memories of racism and deception. On the right was the hill that I had climbed to get the bus to the University of Akron—more memories and a lesson about what the lack of greenbacks can do to your life. We passed the theater that had finally let Negroes sit downstairs, then made a left turn down Mill Street to Howard Street. A quick right past the drugstore—the official headquarters of Max Factor theatrical makeup, powders to put a hex on *any*body, St. John the Conqueror root, and candles of all colors for spells and incantations.

And there we were on the street of dreams: whiskey and wild women, numbers men, drugs (mostly marijuana and heroin), hunchbacks and homosexuals, jazz at Benny Rivers's club, the Sugar Bowl (where the junky partners could get ice cream to cool their flaming insides), gangsters from Cleveland and New York hiding out in plain sight, Tim McCoy's relatives' hotel (where *nobody* stayed all night), and finally Booker Brooks's Cosmopolitan Club.

"Let me out here."

The cab driver pulled over, jumped out, ran around, and opened my door. "You sure you wanna get out here?"

I didn't answer. I lifted my chin a little, paid him his fare with a tip, and walked across the sidewalk, pausing in front of a narrow door. I turned and looked up and down the street. Some of the night people were out and about, squinting up at the setting sun, hands cupped over eyes made sensitive by smoke and alcohol. Some of the men covered their conked or curled hair with stocking caps made from cut-off nylon hose. Everybody was smoking cigarettes.

Directly across the street, in front of his shoeshine parlor, sat a huge brown-skinned man, four hundred pounds of him stuffed into a tan suit. He wore a big white hat and a white shirt with loosened black tie. He grinned, waved his short fat arm, and smacked his lips.

"In your dreams!" I said to myself as I shifted the pale green strapless gown I was carrying to my other arm and jerked the door open. I peered up the steep dark stairway and grabbed the rail with my free hand, using it as a guide as I crept to the top, feeling my way with my toes.

As I entered the barroom, my nose filled with the smell of stale beer and cigarettes. The room was dark and quiet, and I waited while my eyes adjusted to the change from fading daylight to hardly any light. Finally, I could see that the bar ran the length of the room on the right-hand side, just beyond the open door, not too far from the stairs.

"Lookin' for somebody?"

There was a lone figure sitting at the bar and smoking a cigarillo, a woman wearing a black cocktail dress and a little black cocktail hat, legs crossed at the ankles, heels hooked on the middle rung of the tall barstool. She was of a high-brown color and had an open, friendly face. Her smile revealed even white teeth with a gap in the middle.

I nodded. "I'm the new piano player. I'm supposed to meet the rest of the musicians here to rehearse the show."

"You're early." From under thin, penciled eyebrows, her black eyes, ringed with lashes thick with mascara, looked me up and down. "They don't usually start till 'round 5:30. My name is Connie." She halted and gave me the once-over once again. "Ain't you a little young to be in a place like this?"

I laughed. "I'm older than I look." I was still about five feet two inches tall. I kept growing well into my twenties, finally arriving at five feet four inches. I weighed ninety-five pounds soaking wet.

"Well, Booker not gonna let you sit at the bar, you know—he don't wanna get his place shut down!"

"I know. He explained all the rules to the agent. The agent explained the rules to us." I liked her. She was "straight life."

"You gotta agent?"

"Yes."

"You smart!" She took another drag on her cigarillo.

"It's worth the ten percent." I continued, "I don't have to hustle so much, and they know club owners I can't get to. I only hope I like the other musicians the agent picked. They *have* to be able to cut the show!"

"Well, each to his own. I cut the middleman out of my life years ago." I looked a little puzzled. She covered her smile with her hand. "Go on in — the dressing room for vocalists and dancers is off the main showroom. If I were you, I'd change now 'cause those chicks really stake their claim when they come in. You won't wanna be in there with their catty ways and loud perfume. Their perfume fight World War Three *ev'ry* night!"

She giggled. I knew she knew what she was talking about.

"Thanks." I went into the showroom and looked around. The chairs were crowded close to little round tables. Every inch of space was used so the club could get the most dollars for each show, which included a cover charge *and* a minimum drink charge. The dance floor did double duty as the space for the floor show. Dark velvet curtains covered the windows and draped across the back wall directly behind the small bandstand.

"Boy, you really have to get along to play on this stage!" I said to myself as I slid onto the piano bench and opened the piano lid. "Do all the keys work?" I ran some scales all the way up and all the way down. "Okay." I slid off the bench and headed for the dressing room.

It was small, with a counter running along one wall under large mirrors complete with bright lights all around. I changed clothes quickly, fixed my hair, and touched up my makeup. It would have to last all night. I never drank water after four p.m. so that I wouldn't have to go to the bathroom. Bathrooms were always congested with customers standing in line. Besides, it was too hard to take care of business in such a long dress. Finally, I rolled up two nylon stockings and stuffed them in my bra. Then I pushed and pulled until I had a little cleavage. I needed all the help I could get. A few more minor adjustments, and I was satisfied with the girl I saw reflected in all those shiny mirrors.

"Where *is* ever'body?" Voices were coming from the showroom. "Where is all the show folks? Let's get this show on the road!"

Laughing, I sidled out of the dressing room. The rest of the group had arrived — sax, bass, and drummer.

"Hey, cats!" I was glad to see them and relieved that everyone was early. "Hey, Doodie!" they replied. "You ready?" I asked. "Ready for Freddy!" they rejoined.

They introduced themselves: Bob, Bilroy, Cecil. Then they set up their instruments and cracked jokes while the sax began running passages, the bass bowed G–D–A–E over and over, and the drummer made a mighty racket, flams and paradiddles and cymbal crashes.

"Who's on the show?" The bass player shouted in my ear.

"Don't know!" I shrugged. We never knew. Sometimes they had music, sometimes they didn't. Vocalists would say, "I left my music on the bus . . . let me hum a song to you . . ." Or they would say offhand, "Just play something fast here, something slow there, and then when you see me lean over, you know it's near the end, but not quite the end—you know. Just follow me!" They had an attitude because they knew they were in the wrong. They covered themselves with casual and used bluster as armor.

Lord, Lord, Lord!

It was our job to make them look and sound good—there was no one to complain to—and the task called upon all our creativity, improvisational skills, and just plain old bravado. Not knowing exactly what was going to happen really was heady! We felt in complete control because, in a funny way, we were the engine. We were running things. Shades of the Reverend Uncle Frank.

They came in together—the MC, or master of ceremonies, the vocalist, and the dancer. We rehearsed each one of them, and then it was almost showtime.

The club filled up fast, every seat taken long before the first show. The hum and buzz, the clink of glasses, the waiters and waitresses gliding effortlessly between the white-tableclothed tables, the lights low and sensual, fueling and heightening the sense of anticipation of a night at the "Cosmo."

The clientele was made up mostly of bald-headed white men, some with girlfriends, some alone. I spotted Connie sitting at tables with various men. They would talk awhile, he'd buy her a drink, then they'd disappear together. A little while later, she would come back, still wearing that little black hat, and sit with another gentleman. It slowly dawned on me what Connie's business *really* was.

The MC was Tim McCoy, a sly fellow, funny and congenial, and an easy act to play for. He said, "Good ev'nin' ladies and what came with you!" And the show began.

He was a tall drink of water, with twinkling brown eyes and a ready smile. Boy, did he know the art of pantomime! While we played "Tea For Two" softly behind him, he pretended he was a woman taking a bath. His act was pretty graphic and had the audience in stitches; at the end he would pretend to jump out of the tub and start doing a slide dance. We played louder and louder until he made his last flourish and took his bows to thunderous applause.

Then the lights dimmed and Tim whispered, "Ladies and gentlemen, I'd like to present to you, for your pleasure, the divine Miz Green. She's gonna sing straight to your hearts! Miz . . . Annie . . . Green!"

He turned stage right and held out his hand. A beautiful voice came from the darkness: "Let's . . . build . . . a . . . stairway to the stars . . ." She started walking toward the stage in a sleek silvery dress. The spotlight followed her every move, and her voice was silky, pure and warm. A big-boned woman, she moved with grace, and when she reached the front of the stage, she took the mike off its stand, closed her eyes, and finished the beautiful ballad.

The cats in the band were instantly in love with her. So was the audience. Her whole performance was one of the classiest acts I'd ever witnessed.

If she had chosen to, she could have been a *major* star. "I love my home too much to stay away for very long," she explained to the cats in the band. "My husband takes care of the children (five of them!) while I'm away, and I'm not away often and I'm not away long!"

After her last song, she gave a deep theatrical curtsy and glided off the stage, blowing kisses to the audience and to the band.

"And now, people!" Tim McCoy grinned slyly. "All right, all you men! Keep yo' hands out yo' pockets and on the tables!" Big laughter from all the men. "I'm about to present to you the most luscious lady. A portrait of potent pulchritude . . ." He looked back at us and grinned, "*There's* a word for you!" Turning back to the audience, he put his hand over his heart. "People, this girl's body was sent down from the Elysian Fields! She built like a brick shithouse—I mean shipyard—but don't let me tease you! I'm here to please you! I'd like to present for your personal perusal . . ."—he took a deep breath—"Miz Lola Lace!"

The band struck up a fast version of "Cherokee," and from out of the darkness hurtled Lola, a high-yellow whirling dervish. She wore a long filmy coat over a sparkly bra and G-string, and sparkles glittered on the blood-red toenails of her bare feet. She wore large dazzling earrings and sparkles in her wavy, long black hair. Her pale face was skillfully made up with long false eyelashes, blood-red lipstick, and a black mole painted on her buttery-colored cheek. She twirled and she whirled, all the time spreading her arms so the filmy coat looked like gossamer wings. The perfume she wore wafted through the entire room.

Now, there are two kinds of exotic dancers, or shake dancers. Very artistic dancers perform themed acts, enhancing the theme with props like a drum, a lamppost, or fans as well as special music. Seductive, they tease and gradually disrobe, all the time promising with their eyes and lips more than they could have *ever* delivered.

Then there are the "floor" dancers, generally held in contempt by the other dancers because they are usually raunchy and leave very little to the imagination.

Lola was a floor dancer.

"Oh, oh!" The bass player leaned over and whispered, "This gonna be a long night!" We had rehearsed with Lola, but she had left out the main part of her act, as it were!

She threw her gauzy coat down near the band and hit the floor! She did a split and down she went, working her way out of her sparkly bra at the same time. This left little cups over her nipples called pasties. Her G-string was still in place, but she took a dollar out from some place—we couldn't tell where—and put it on a table near the dance floor. Then she flung one of her long yellow legs over the table, and when she danced away, the dollar bill had disappeared.

"Hey, hey!" The men roared and whistled and stomped. "Did you see that?"

Money came from wallets all over the room, twenties and hundred-dollar bills. Lola took her time. First from the floor, then from the tables, the money disappeared—and it was not like she folded up the greenbacks and pocketed them. There *were* no pockets. Finally, up she popped and whirled around (not one greenback did she drop!) and danced off the stage.

The audience went insane!

We played the last fast, furious measures of "Cherokee" while Tim, Annie, and Lola came back and took bows. We played them off stage, be-bopped and extended the ending with big chords, sax glissandos, and drumrolls, and that was the end of the first show!

* * *

Wending my way back home in a yellow cab, I hugged myself. We played the last show, and then more musicians came in from Cleveland, Youngstown, and Pittsburgh for an all-night jam session. I played my heart out, happy that I had the endurance built up from years of all-day-every-Sunday gospel playing. The cats blew the roof off the club, and the air got smokier and smokier as the night wore on. At last, as the session wound down, we played some good old down-home blues. Then we called it a night, tired but jubilant, just basking in the afterglow. "See you tomorrow." "Not if I see you first!"

I looked out the window of the yellow cab and saw the sky beginning to turn pink and gold. The sun was rising in the east. My heart was full to bursting. I'd done good—my first show at Booker's Cosmo Club—my first night jamming with world-class cats—and my first night down in the red-light district.

Let the good times roll!

* * *

"I ain't never known a woman to make that kind of money! Why, you make mo' money than I do *ev'ry* week!"

M'Da had cornered me in the upstairs hallway. I was a little groggy from playing piano all night. We had played our usual three shows at the Cosmo, but had had another burning, elegant jam session that lasted until broad daylight.

M'Da waited until M'Ma had gone to work, then came up the narrow stairs and knocked on my bedroom door. I got up and peered out the door with one eye open, one eye shut. "What is it, 'Da?"

"How much they payin' you down at Booker's?"

"What?"

"Don't tell me 'what.' Just tell me how much!"

I knew he had worked the night shift at Firestone, and it was obvious he and Kingfish had stopped at a bar and drunk their breakfast. I swallowed, then hesitated. I felt a cold dread in my middle. Then I told him how much.

He looked stunned. "How much?" He put his hand over his mouth. "You make more . . ." He halted. "Listen, you go' have to start paying to stay here. Rent or something." He struggled with his thoughts. "It ain't right a female make mo' money than a man. 'Specially when I work ten hours a night in a factory cuttin' rubber!"

"How much rent you want?" I decided that I had better hurry up and settle this. No one was home but M'Da and me. Everybody else was at school, at work, or next door with Miz Jones, who took care of the two little boys.

"The goin' rate. You live here like you in a roomin' house, you hear?"

"All right." I was really at a loss for a moment, then I dove in. I knew I had to get everything out, right then. I squared my shoulders. "I will pay rent ev'ry week."

M'Da nodded.

"Who do I give it to?"

M'Da looked at me suspiciously. "You tryin' to be smart?"

"No."

"Well, you better not. This is still *my* house." He rubbed his face. "You pay *me*, that's who!"

"Okay." I smiled. "Now, it's like paying at a roomin' house, right?"

He nodded.

"Well, then," I continued, "I'll be an official roomer. I'm not washin' and ironin' or sweepin' or scrubbin' or babysittin'. I'll buy my own food or eat at Booker's restaurant!"

M'Da glared at me. His finger started stabbing the air. "Now, now, just wait a minute! Who you think gonna do it if you don't tell the others what to do—just like you been doin'?"

"That's not my problem. Fair is fair! You really had a bargain. But now things are changed, and now I gotta get some sleep so I can go to work at the club tonight."

He stared at me, then went down the hall, down the stairs, and out the front door. I left M'Ma a note about my change of status.

The next day, all hell broke loose. Words sprayed the air like buckshot! Words like "*my* roof," "*my* rules," "be fair" (that from M'Ma), and "she's right"! It seemed as if the whole house was about to implode.

I escaped over to Gramma Hattie's farm. She listened quietly to my complaints, her blue eyes focused on a place somewhere above my head. Sometimes they were closed tight, creases radiating from both corners. I could hear my Uncle Richard's record player playing Jay McShann. Uncle Richard had come home on leave; he really loved Jay McShann. Gramma Hattie held up her right hand, and the words that were rushing out of my mouth like a waterfall dried up. She looked at me, her blue eyes like steel.

Jay McShann's words floated in the air, "Just think about our future / Forget about yo' used to be!" Gramma Hattie's soft voice was sure, "Fly away, little bird, fly away!"

I did. I left home for good.

Junkies and Jazz

. . . .

Dreamed about a reefer five foot tall
Ain't too big an'
Ain't too small . . .

*E*very single night when the sun went down behind the seven green hills that made up the city of Akron, the moon came up and shone its silvery light on all the night people: hustlers, show folks, and midnight creepers, all of whom came out in droves, dressed in all their best finery. The porkpie hat was still alive, but men, musicians and civilians alike, began adorning their heads with berets, copying Dizzy Gillespie, and their faces with goatees. Women wore beautiful cocktail dresses and long gloves that traveled all the way up past the elbows. And rhinestones, rhinestones, rhinestones!

All the hepcats and hip kitties snapped their fingers on two and four. Phrases like "zoot suit with the ape shape" described the fashion of the more adventurous males. There was a new word the cats used to describe those of the Caucasian persuasion: "ofay."

And there were words splayed in the air, whispered in groups under streetlights, passed along behind hand-covered lips. Words like "marijuana," "pot," "weed," "reefer," "grass," "roach," and "tea." Also, Benzedrine, or "bennies," as uppers were called. Drop one of those in your Coca-Cola, and you were jerked up into a world where sleep was nowhere to be found. Everything accelerated. Pulses pounded, hearts raced to dangerous levels, and it took a couple of days and nights to come down.

And then there was the big daddy of 'em all—heroin: "horse," "H," "fix," "cop," and "the Man." The Man could be the dope dealer from whom you copped your fix. Or the Man could be the narcotics agent who caught you copping your fix. If that happened, you were likely to be arrested and sent to Lexington, Kentucky, to do time for illegal drug trafficking and, horror of horrors, kick your habit *cold turkey.*

The people who were "using" spent all their energy looking for drugs, looking for money to pay for drugs, consuming drugs, then starting all over again. Scurrying back and forth, back and forth on Howard Street, mingling with the crowds, making short forays into dark alleys, greeting each other with, "Man, did you cop?"

"Yeah."

"You gonna be mean, or you gonna share some of yo' shit with yo' ace boon coon?"

"Well, man, where was you when I seen the Man?"

There were no free rides except for the very first dose given by the dealer to get the person hooked. After that it was "Root, hog, or die poor!" The monkey jumped on their backs for a long, long ride.

* * *

It was a way of life: the music, the constant movement, the madness. And the wonderful high energy was truly marvelous—but it really felt good to go home and rest. Musicians called home a "crib." My crib was a room I rented from the mama of a vocalist friend of mine named Ethel. Lucky me! We got along really well.

Ethel could sing like a bird. A very dark-complected girl, she was born with white feet. She used Max Factor's black eyebrow pencils to color her pale skin so it wouldn't show through her black mesh stockings and gold evening sandals.

Ethel's mama, big, buxom, and dark-skinned, with a mouth full of gold teeth—a Saturday-night fish-fry woman—nevertheless was very strict. "No drinkin'! No drugs! No company! Yo' mama would not like it if I was loose with you!" She spoke with a firm voice. "And," Ethel's mama added as she smiled and threw me a sly look from under her long eyes, "no hangin' out in the car when those fellas bring you home! Drive up, git out, an' come in!"

I was happy in my room, even though the wallpaper was printed with dark brown roses on squiggly vines and the lumpy mattress on the old metal bed kept rolling me into the middle of the bed. But it was a quiet refuge from the wicked world.

I was careful with my cash. I still had my little stash of money saved for college. Sometimes I imagined myself as the Little Match Girl, standing at the back door of M'Ma's new house, dressed in rags and tatters, up to my hips in cold wet snow, tears frozen on my face, begging to be taken back. The picture put a big knot in my stomach and filled my soul with dread. Perish the thought! But this bleak mental melodrama kept me from getting into the drug scene or anything else shady. I refused to insult myself, and I couldn't *stand* the idea of M'Da pointing his finger and sputtering, "See! See there! See there, Lizzie! See how you raised her!"

* * *

Marijuana was outlawed in 1933 or '34, but the older cats still used it. In fact, Daddy-O Duncan, a well-known trap drummer around town, smoked himself some reefer at intermission one night behind the nightclub where he was performing, then came inside flying high as a kite. He was a small black man, with large eyes and a ready smile, about sixty-five years old. But he was still a cat!

He sat down at his trap drums, and his band started playing, and he started singing, "Dreamed about a reefer five foot tall / Ain't too big / An' it ain't too small!" Then he went into a Gene Krupa–like drum solo and hit his snare drum so hard that his *eyes crossed!*

No doctor could tell him *why* it had happened, and no doctor could tell him *when* his eyes would uncross. But never you mind. Daddy-O kept on playing his drums *every* night. And he kept on smoking reefers—*every* night.

* * *

"That boy's music makes grown men cry!" The owner of the Golden Rail on Main Street was speaking about our saxophone player. "He's a little peculiar, but he sure fills up my club, 'n' that's all I care about."

Boy, was I relieved. We had finished our stint at Booker's club and were now breaking records on Main Street. Not only because of the large crowds every night, but also because we were the first young black group *on* Main Street and *in* this particular club.

Pop Teasley, bass player and elder statesman, and his group took over Booker's club. It was a great group: Dennis Lewis on alto sax, a hard bopper who played like the wind; pianist Rudy Black, who reminded folks of Bud Powell; and one of the best drummers I ever heard, a master, Eddie Robinson.

I felt a little nervous about appearing on Main Street, not because of our ability to please the all-white middle-class and blue-collar audience, and certainly not because of our musicianship. It was because of Bilroy. He stood tall, a good-looking cat, medium brown with pleasant mannerisms. He was a brilliant soloist and a natural showman. When he played a ballad, grown men *did* cry and women wanted to take him home with them. But Bilroy was a *stone junkie!* And Bilroy did what junkies do: he went to sleep standing up whenever he wasn't soloing. And his nose ran.

The audience was fascinated with this handsome well-dressed man who seemed to go into a trance and then come out of it when we yelled, "Bilroy! You're up!" We incorporated reviving Bilroy into our act, and sometimes the audience would join in the cry: "Bilroy! You're up!" And he would go into action and blow the roof off the club.

"I have no idea what they (the folks) think about this scene," I murmured to the bass player.

"Don't worry 'bout it," he replied. "The place stays packed, and the owner picked up our option."

"Yep!" I smiled. That meant we could play there indefinitely.

We played all the money songs done by Louis Armstrong, Duke Ellington, and Pete Johnson, *and* a parody of Patti Page's "How Much Is That Doggy in the Window," which was on the jukebox. In between each verse, which we all sang, we played wild, wild bebop. Oh, we'd tear it up! And Bilroy was a virtuoso on his tenor sax—after we woke him up!

Bilroy's wife, Dottie, was his source for heroin. A very pretty girl with golden brown skin and long, naturally curly black hair, she was a shake dancer down at Booker's club. Every night after her first show she caught a cab and raced up to the side door of our club. We heard her tap-tap-tap at the door, look around to see if the coast was clear, then let herself directly into our large dressing room.

"Hey, Dottie!"

"Hi," she replied. She seemed a little shy, and never really looked you in the eye. She slung a long black velvet cloak over her dancing gear, and she wore ballet shoes on her tiny feet. You could tell by the way she walked that she had taken ballet lessons sometime in her past. She carried a very expensive leather make-up case with gold-colored hinges and a gold lock. And in the beautiful case was Bilroy's fix. "Hurry up! Hurry up!" he would mutter, his voice hoarse. You could tell he was in some kind of pain.

"All right! Hold your horses, B. I'm going as fast as I can!" She spoke between clenched teeth; the tension of running between her job and our job was awfully hard on her.

He sat in a chair at the make-up counter, mirrors reflecting six images of him rolling up his sleeve, tying off his arm with a cord, and—thump! thump!—trying to bring up his veins so he could pump in the needle full of H. Dottie would wait patiently until he was done, then take the paraphernalia and put it all back into her cosmetic case, close it with a snap, throw her black velvet cloak over her shoulders, then toss her long black hair and say, "See you cats!"

"Take it easy, Dottie." And out she would run to her waiting cab and back down to Booker's.

"Bilroy!" We would shake him a little. "You can't nod here. It's almost time to get back on stage!" We would prod him, and he was always pleasant and laid back. He would adjust his sax strap around his neck, fix his shirt collar and tie, grab his horn, and out the door to the stage we'd go.

I held my breath every night throughout this ritual, and so did the bass player and drummer. But we were philosophical about the whole thing, knowing that nobody could cure a junkie like Bilroy. Somewhere deep within, there was a hole in his soul. And out of that hole came this gift from God, and everybody knew it, and everybody was warmed by its fire.

But one night Dottie didn't show up! Bilroy was beside himself! During the set he paced up and down the stage, and when we made it back to the dressing room, he kept saying over and over, "Where is Dottie? Where *is* that girl?" His face was covered with perspiration, and his arms were folded tightly over his stomach. "I'm gonna be sick!"

I said, "Take it easy, Bilroy! We just have one more show an' we'll make it short!"

"Okay, okay!"

We did a short show. We played "St. Louis Blues" and let the drummer do a long solo to take attention off Bilroy. The audience was pretty plastered by this time of night, so a loud drum solo really fit the bill. We brought the tune to a crashing finish, said good night, and sang our end song:

> *Be kind to yo' fine feathered friends*
> *For a duck may be somebody's mother*
> *You may think that this is the end—*
> *Well, it is, f___!*

And off we ran to the dressing room.

Several people from Booker's club were standing there. They had come in the side door. "Bilroy! Come on! Hurry! Dottie's in the hospital!"

"What?"

They rushed Bilroy out the side door and into a waiting car. "I'll put his horn away," the bass player said solemnly. "I'll take it with me. If he calls you, tell him I have his axe!"

One of the cats from Booker's club came back into the dressing room. "What's up?" We were filled with dread. "What's goin' on with Dottie?"

"Dottie's dead. She overdosed on some bad H!"

"When?"

"Well, she didn't show up for her first show, so we went next door to the hotel, an' she was dead in her room—the needle still in her arm."

"Oh God! Dottie and Bilroy have five kids!"

"Mercy!"

It was horrible. But it was all so very true.

The last time we saw Bilroy he was getting on the train for the long ride back to Illinois with his saxophone and the body of his beautiful young wife. She gave *everything* just to be with him. We never saw or heard from Bilroy again.

World War II

· · · · · · · · · · · · · · · · · · ·

Got a new disposition
Got me a new routine!
Got me a brand new washer
To keep my laundry clean!

During intermissions, all the show folks and musicians hung out at the Sugar Bowl, located right across the street from Booker's club. It was a great place to get away from the crowds and smoke.

The Sugar Bowl served milkshakes, burgers, and specialties like sardines, which the "Table Eater" enjoyed whenever he came to town. He said, "The bones in the little girls keep my teeth strong. I can pick up a table with a woman sittin' on it, and dance, and not drop either one." And it was true. He performed this feat every night.

Gathered at the Sugar Bowl, we discussed Dottie and Bilroy. Dottie's departure affected us all in different ways. Most of us were still in our late teens and early twenties, and inclined to be romantic. Some called Dottie and Bilroy the "Romeo and Juliet of the junkies." Some of the cats expressed themselves with well-worn adages. "Well, she died young and made a beautiful corpse!" Connie, the pro, took a long drag on her cigarillo and, closing one eye against the curling, acrid smoke, said, "Well, they say only the good die young. Sometimes it *pays* to be bad!"

I had played music for so many funerals at such a young age that I felt detached from the whole thing—until I thought about Dottie's five kids growing up without their mother's love.

And I felt anger, but not at Dottie for dying. I was furious with the hoofer who had arrived in Akron and weaseled his way into a gig at Booker's as a tap dancer and master of ceremonies. He couldn't tap-dance at all. The top of his body, his arms making elegant swimming motions, looked really smooth, but the bottom of him had feet that stomped the dance floor so hard that we swore he was gonna start an earthquake on Howard Street. He had very dark skin and was shaped like a penguin, with chemically straightened black hair swept straight back from a low forehead. His eyes were set suspiciously close to his broad nose. He sported three diamonds screwed into his front teeth.

One night, hanging at the edge of our crowd at the Sugar Bowl, he warbled in a singsong: "Lawd, she was so beautiful, but she had to die, someday! / I wanted some of her lovin' before she passed away!" He snickered, but nobody laughed. A piano player from one of the clubs down the street looked at his watch and announced, "Showtime, show folks!" Everybody scattered to their waiting stages and crowded clubs. Dottie had been a junkie, but she'd never been a whore.

* * *

All during the war years, America was on the move, six ways to Sunday!

Sharecroppers laid down their plows and walked away from their mules. Servicemen and servicewomen came home from all the killing and dying and took a look around. The colored service people saw the same old Jim Crow signs, freshly painted, at lunch counters, drinking fountains, and restrooms, and saw their children still using leftover and secondhand books sent over from the white schools. And they decided to "follow the drinking gourd" one more time to the top of the world, the whole Great Lakes region. Detroit, Toledo, Chicago, Akron, Youngstown, Cleveland, Erie, and Buffalo were all caught up in a frenzy of people looking for work in steel mills and rubber plants.

Every musician who even *thought* he could play was also part of this massive movement. And the music was ever changing. We were making it up as we went along, writing new music and scavenging for new tunes from the movies and Tin Pan Alley, bringing them back to jam sessions and rehearsals, and mixing them with a huge dose of bebop and blues.

Our audience hung out in droves at the clubs, looking for companionship and good times, money burning in their pockets. They cheered and yelled and stomped and made the musicians feel they could do no wrong.

Three musicians came to Akron, took me under their wings for a short time, and encouraged me when I needed it the most. Sadik Hakim, a pianist from Duluth, Minnesota, taught me new voicings for chords. Because his folks were professors and played classical music, he got a kick out of my showing him the penny trick while I played Bach's Two- and Three-Part Inventions. He said, "You have perfect fingering! You had a great teacher!" He advised, "You've got to leave here and go to New York. You'll grow there. But you gotta go alone! Don't carry no dead weight!"

Another pianist, Tadd Dameron, was very patient with my questions and gentle with his answers. He was from Cleveland, and held court in Sharon, Pennsylvania, with musicians who came from far and wide. He wrote and arranged music in a completely new fashion that made small bands sound big. He composed tunes like "Our Delight" and "Casbah," which we jumped on and immediately added to our own repertoires. He arranged music for Jimmy Lunceford's band, Billy Eckstine, Sarah Vaughan, and Dizzy Gillespie's big band. He, too, said, "Girl, go to the city! Go to New York. Go alone. And go *soon!*"

Then there was Norris Turney, also from Ohio, who played with Tiny Bradshaw and Billy Eckstine's big band, among others. He held court at the Bluebird Cafe in Youngstown, and we eagerly accepted all the musical ideas and advice he had to offer. He played all the reed instruments and showed us by doing, how to solo over driving background riffs and how to phrase our solos so we could stand out and be heard. He also said, "Get out of here! Get out of this area before you get *caught!*" He was adamant. "Go to New York!"

All three of these mentors were older and more experienced than I. They gave me contacts in New York—people who could help me get started. They had one dear thing in common. They all called me "Sis"!

*   *   *

Being on the run and having big fun can really lull a body into a feeling that the good times were rolling and were gonna keep on rolling forever. But going two weeks without a gig for the first time in a long string of triumphs put my head back where it belonged.

I was more than a little scared being without work; it gave me too much time to think and to worry. What if I don't get another good-paying job soon? Let me see: rent, food, hairdresser, cleaners, and layaway (one dollar down and one dollar a week) for my costumes. I had a small stash of money, but I'd put that aside for emergencies. Did this count as an emergency?

The cats shook their heads and lamented, "You only as good as yo' last gig!" But bet you a fist full of funny money—and the money in my purse had sunk to nearly that level—that I didn't sit in my dingy little room and brood. I went to see Tadd Dameron in Sharon, Pennsylvania, and started passing out my business card and asking around. Lots of cats were there to check out Tad's latest musical inventions. I had arrived in the right place at the right time.

I met tenor player Curt Parnell. He offered me a gig in his house band at a club in Cleveland. The gig included a paid room at a hotel and a meal at the restaurant-bar where we were to perform. *Thank God! He always come on time!*

Curt hired a bass player and a drummer from Cleveland so that he didn't have to pay for hotel rooms or food for them. They lived at home. A tall slender dark-skinned man in his late forties, with a charming gap in his front teeth and a thoughtful, furrowed brow, Curt hailed from Toledo. He had played old-style swing music for years. When the new music blasted onto the scene, he was unnerved. "I really struggled," he told me. "Lots of cats my age put their instruments away for good. They stashed them under the bed or in their closet. The end! I went into the woodshed and listened to 'Shaw 'Nuff' and 'Anthropology' and Dizzy Gillespie and others, and I didn't come out until I could play the new music. Now I mix the two styles—and keep on steppin'!"

We performed on an elevated stage behind the bar. The stars had to perform on the floor, down where the customers crowded around the little tables. Johnny Ray, a slight, graceful man with a tearjerker voice, was our first headliner. He prowled from table to table with the mike in one hand, the other covering an ear so he could hear his own voice, singing his hit songs "Cry" and "Little White Cloud." He brought tears to everyone's eyes and wrung every heart in the room. He was good, he was nice, and he was partially deaf.

We played for Billy Farrell, who went berserk if anyone even hinted that he sounded like Billy Eckstine. He needn't have worried. He had a strong, true baritone voice. But he also brought big-band arrangements to our four-piece combo. It was like bringing a gun to a knife fight. The sax player had to play the lead trumpet part to make sense out of the arrangement, and I had to almost stand on my head to make the music sound full and complete. It asked for every inch of our musicianship. I kept thinking, "Lawd, lawd, lawd!" His hit song was a great treatment of "You've Changed."

Savannah Churchill was our third headliner. She sang a heart-wrenching version of her hit song, "I Want To Be Loved." A beautiful woman with a lovely voice, beautifully dressed for success, she gave us sheet music with her picture on it.

All three headliners appeared at this little club to break in their acts before they went on to grab national and international attention.

And then I played for my first stalker!

"He got eyes for you," the bass player said.

"What?"

"Big, bulgin' eyes!" he continued. "He comes in here ev'ry night and stands along the back wall, watchin' ev'ry move you make."

"You're crazy."

"No, I'm not. You got your back to him, but I can see the whole audience. He got big, bulgin' eyes for you!"

When we finished the first show, I went to the restroom, then circled around to the service part of the bar and leaned over so I could see the man. I recognized him: deep-set eyes, very white teeth, and a thin mustache dividing a long face. When we started the gig, the barmaid had offhandedly pointed out some of her regulars. He called himself the "Jazz Poet" and hung around jazz musicians. Very tall, dark-skinned, and striking looking, he affected a wide-brimmed hat and a black raincoat slung over one shoulder, like a movie star.

I didn't think too much about the cat until I was having lunch in the hotel with my dancer cousin, Doris. I looked up from the menu—and there he was! The hair on my neck began to rise. He didn't say anything. He just stared. "Doris," I whispered out of the side of my mouth, "this cat keeps poppin' up. What should I do?"

"Don't look at him and don't act frightened! Boy, I've had many a lunatic hangin' round the stage door. You gotta know how to handle the situation."

I wasn't frightened. I was getting mad. He had invaded my space.

The cats always dropped me off at the hotel after work. One night as I got off the elevator, I saw a tall dark shadow standing between me and my room. "Hey," I yelled at the top of my lungs, and away he went, down the stairs. My hand trembled as I used my key, flew into my room, and slammed the door. I stood there leaning against the door for God knows how long.

The next night I talked to the boss of the club. I knew he was a member of the Greek mafia that ran part of northern Ohio. He listened in silence while I told him my story.

"You want I should have his legs broke?"

"Oh God! Do you have to?"

The boss laughed—not out loud, but his shoulders shook and his lips turned up at the edges. "Don't worry! Don't worry! He won't bother you anymore."

He didn't. But I never again felt the sense of security that had been tied to childhood. The stalker forced me into unwanted action. In restaurants I sat in a corner so I could cover the room with my eyes. I looked around before I entered the club, and I looked around when I came out. I felt furious that he had interrupted my fun. His fixation on me forced me to question the motives of people who came up after a performance to express admiration and thanks. I carried a long steel hat pin at all times.

My days of innocence were fading fast—and so were the good jobs. New cats moved into our territory, walking the bar and blowing one note over and over on their tenor saxophones. While the rhythm section banged away, the tenor player would run out the door into the street, and when he came back, still blowing, he'd bring a whole crowd of people with him. The honkers and shouters had arrived! Curt Parnell said, "Well, it looks like it's time to move on down the line. We had a good run and did a good job. I'm headed back to Toledo."

"Yeah," the bass player and drummer agreed wistfully.

"You have to make up your minds," Curt continued, "whether you are weekend warriors or way-of-lifers!"

We looked at each other. Curt snapped his sax case closed. "Weekend warriors do day jobs and play only on the weekend. Way-of-lifers are dedicated to a life of performing. That means you got to keep movin'. I've done both, and both have their druthers. But it takes a special kind of person to stay out on the road. A special kind of temperament! Roll with the punches, and take care of yourself and your fellow band members. You gotta have stamina. Most of all, you gotta have *heart* and a large dose of confidence. You gotta believe there's always gonna be a next gig! And a tomorrow!"

* * *

Curt drove me back to Akron. I wasn't sure that the stalker wasn't following us. I kept looking out of the windows, checking out the other cars. It began a lifelong habit of memorizing license plates.

I knew Curt Parnell was right on the money about the business of music in northeast Ohio. Boy! I didn't let any grass grow under my feet. I called most of the local cats who were really good players, and almost everyone came to the same conclusion. The honkers-and-shouters style of music was fast becoming the flavor of the month.

That weekend I got a gig at a country club—featuring the usual format of comedian, shake dancer, and vocalist—with some musicians I had known since high school. We talked about the gigs drying up for us beboppers. "The H-and-Ss got all the choice gigs!" the drummer moaned. "Len Hope, that sax player from Cleveland, started the whole mess!"

"You call that music?" the bass player's voice dripped with disdain. "Just a buncha no-playin' cats oof-goofin' around!"

The sax player agreed, "They have an audience. They don't have to be good. They just have to be new!" That was the operative word: new. We had worn out our welcome in our own hometown. The bones of the bebop cats had been picked clean. Night after night they sang the same sorry song: "Woe is me and my music!"

I began to get really impatient with their hopelessness and haplessness. Finally I blurted, "Listen, I still have a pretty good agent, who can get us something in Cleveland, or I can take a chance on Columbus. We need steady house-band gigs so we can make some real dough." I paused for breath. "Are you with me?"

"We with you all the way. You can count on us!"

I promised, "I'll be back with a contract . . . guaranteed!"

"Okay, we'll be ready for Freddy! We don't wanna go into no factory."

I took a cab back to my dingy little room to pack. I couldn't help feeling a little let down because none of the cats had offered to drive me to the Greyhound bus station in the morning.

I perched on the edge of the rickety old bed, leaning forward to keep from rolling backward into the center, and thought about what I was about to do. "New York!" "Go now!" The words of Norris Turney and Tadd Dameron rang in my ears. If I were living at home, I wouldn't have hesitated a New York minute. I would have jumped on the first thing smoking and headed straight for the Big Apple—the very next morning. I took my things out of the chest of drawers and placed them on the bed. I reached for my suitcase on the closet shelf and stopped, hand in midair. All at once I was horrified at the thought of disappearing into the great maw of New York City and M'Ma's never knowing what happened to me.

Stop! Perish the thought! Maybe, I mused, if I could go to Columbus first and get a gig, I could save a little more money and get up a little more courage. Then I could cut out for New York City. I pulled down one of the suitcases of my matched set of Samsonite and packed enough clothes to last at least two days. Besides, I thought, I wouldn't wanna disappoint the cats! I gazed at the brown roses on the wallpaper. The cats were the closest thing to a family that I had right then. But Sadik Hakim's words flashed warning lights in my mind: "Don't carry no dead weight."

I stood up and began to walk up and down the narrow aisle between the bed and the old mahogany dresser. *Jeez!* I missed my brothers. I missed my sisters. I missed the room that I shared with my sisters! Most of all I missed M'Ma—I guess I always was a "mama's girl." I longed to hear M'Ma's voice again and to tell her how mixed up, how very frightened I felt.

The fiery anger started up again, inflaming my heart and my head. The thought that my very own father's jealousy and alcoholism stood between me and my family enraged me. I sat down on the edge of the bed, crossed my arms tight across my narrow chest, and rocked back and forth, back and forth. The threat of the stalker also enraged me. Mean and low-down white people added to the mix. Betrayal and fear! Like gasoline and matches—a volatile combination.

After a while I got ready for bed, then got down on my knees and prayed that I would be forgiven for wanting to kill them all—dead! But as I jumped into bed and hunkered under the covers, I knew that when the sun came up in the morning, I'd still feel the very same way.

Kill them all dead!

Amen!

Just Get On the Greyhound, Girl

. . . .

I don't wanna be no playgirl—
Don't need no diamond ring!
Just gimme plenty room—
To try my brand-new everything!

The Greyhound bus rumbled into Columbus three hours and some odd minutes later. I had mistakenly chosen the "local" instead of the express bus. That meant stops at every mail drop and milk run along two-lane Highway 41 as it snaked through cities called Mansfield, Ashland, Wooster, and towns that didn't even have a name, only a sign: "Population 56." But thank God! The long ride helped me sort out some of the snarls and tangles that had become such a troublesome part of my life.

I brushed past the spraddle-legged blonde who was still sleeping, her hair falling like a curtain over one black-ringed, mascaraed eye. She had slept all the way on that long ride, her head falling again and again onto my shoulder. I'd kept pushing her away so the drool trickling from her slack lips wouldn't damage my designer suit.

The driver helped each passenger off the bus. I walked stiffly into the station and looked around for the ladies' room. *Jeez!* There was the usual long line of women with small children hopping on first one leg and then the other. Never enough toilets! It was maddening. I was in a big rush to get out of the restroom and get to a telephone.

The station was swarming with civilians, and the military presence was also everywhere—uniforms of all kinds and lots of military police and shore patrol standing at the ready. Women had on little hats like the one Claudette Colbert had worn in her recent movie, and some had their hair in little snoods in the back, with pompadours in the front. Some tottered on great-looking platform shoes, waving hands encased in little white gloves. Most older men wore suits, ties, and hats or caps; some were getting their shoes shined at a stand manned by Negro men and boys. Above the din, the loudspeaker called out the arrivals and departures of the buses.

I spied the telephones in a long row along one wall; phone books for almost every major city were swinging underneath. Rushing over, I stood in line again and finally grabbed a phone. I thumbed my way through the yellow pages, found the theatrical section, and ran my fingers down the list until I came to an ad that said: "If you tried the rest—now, try the best! Lou Posey, Theatrical Agent."

Yay! I thought, this cat has a real sense of humor. I'll call him first. I dialed the number and a female voice said, "Mr. Posey's office." I told her who I was and why I had come to Columbus. "I'd like to see Mr. Posey today, if possible, as I have other appointments tomorrow." I gilded the lily a little.

In a few minutes, a deep, resonant voice said, "I'm Lou Posey, Miss Evans. Could you come over to the office right away? I'll be leaving for the day in two hours." He gave me the address.

I hurried through the crowded station and out a door marked "Cabs, Taxis, and Ground Transportation." "Right this way, miss." The cab driver opened the door and gestured for me to get in. He helped me with my bag. I checked out his name, Otto Braverman, gave him the address, and off we went—or flew! Otto took off so fast I was thrown against the back of the seat and had to cling to the strap with all my might!

"Boy, this town is really full of strangers these days! Well, it is the capital of Ohio and the university is here! Forty thousand students, and factories all around building tanks and secret military materials." The cabby spoke as fast as he drove. He glanced at me through his rearview mirror. "I know, I know!" He grinned. "Loose lips sink ships!"

He drove on nonstop, wheeling around a corner so fast that I planted both feet against the back of his seat. "Near here is First Street. It's what they call German Village, but nobody seems worried. I guess they been here long enough to feel that this is their country too." He took another turn and threw me to the other side of the backseat. "There's the First Lutheran Church," he pointed out. "We're pretty good churchgoers here—even the capital politicians show up once in a while! Hee, hee, hee!"

"What's that tall tower we just passed?" I asked.

He wheeled hand over hand around another corner. "Why, that's the tallest structure in Ohio, the Lincoln Leveque Tower, 'bout forty-six stories high!" Otto looked at me again through the mirror and wheeled the cab to the curb, stopping so abruptly that I almost joined him in the front seat. "Here we are! All in the same day!"

He jumped out, ran around the cab, and opened the door with a flourish. I crawled out. As he handed me my bag, I said solemnly, "Now, Otto, I really appreciate you getting me here safe and sound, but I must ask you a question."

"Ask away." Otto's blue eyes sparkled.

"Do you-all have *four* tall towers in this fine city?" I watched his face turn pink, then red.

"Ah, not that I know of."

"Well then, Otto, somehow we must have passed the tallest building in Ohio four times!"

"Er, ah, hee, hee, hee!" He looked at the ground, then squinted at the sky.

"I'm gonna pay you exactly one-fourth of what's on the meter, and I must really thank you, and tell you how much I appreciated the lovely tour of downtown Columbus."

"Okay," he smiled. "Do you want me to wait for you?"

"Thanks, but no thanks, Otto. I don't know how long I'll be."

He tipped his cap, ran around his cab, jumped in, and took off like he was running in the soapbox derby.

I walked up the five steps to Mr. Posey's office with my heart in my hands. Fifty-five minutes later I strutted down those same five steps with a lucrative contract in those same hands. Two weeks in one of the better clubs in Columbus!

Mr. Posey had ushered me into his office, looked at the lobbies and the club owners' letters of recommendation, then made three telephone calls: to the union in Canton, Ohio, to see if my dues were paid up; to the club owners in Cleveland, where I had played for Billy Farrell, Savannah Churchill, and Johnny Ray; and to a nightclub owner in Columbus to discuss the band taking Rusty Bryant's place while he was away promoting a hit record.

"The club owner pays me, I pay you, you pay me ten percent."

"I understand." The secretary typed up the contract, and it was done.

"Ever thought about organizing an all-girl band?"

"Wha-a-t?"

"Never mind. It was just a thought." He laughed.

Well-mannered, he wore a loud, checked sports jacket and a white shirt with a matching polka-dot tie and a pocket handkerchief. His eyes, set deep in his pale face, could read your soul. A no-nonsense gentleman! "Well, Miss Evans, see you and your band next week."

Lawd-ee! Was I elated! Jump for joy!

The cab ride back to the Greyhound station was swift and sure. I caught the five p.m. express back to Akron. Less than two hours later, I called the cats from the bus station.

"Meet me at the Sugar Bowl. I've got good news!"

"Uh . . . okay . . .! Okey-dokey!"

Less than an hour later the table in the back corner of the Sugar Bowl began to fill up with musicians—my ace boon coons! I pulled the contract out of my bag and laid it on the table. The cats peered suspiciously at the document. "What is this?"

"Read it!" I grinned from ear to ear.

The sax player read it out loud to everybody. There was silence, then he cleared his throat. "Uh . . . I can't go . . ."

"Me neither!" piped up the bass player. "Our girlfriends and wives had a meeting. They said we couldn't go *nowhere.*"

"What! What do you mean your girlfriends said you couldn't go? Didn't you-all sit right here at this very table and tell me this was what you-all wanted?" I was getting heartless mad. I couldn't believe my own ears.

"We didn't think you could do it," the drummer ventured timidly. "In fact, we *knew* you couldn't."

"Well, I did! And it's more money than any of you *ever* made!"

"No woman 'sposed to get that kind of money," the bass player said, looking everywhere but at me. "Well . . . I promised my wife I'd be home early." They all stood and bumped into each other hurrying out of the Sugar Bowl.

I sat there in my chair—stunned—as my hot chocolate cooled, untasted, a slimy skin growing slowly on top. Lord! Lord! Lord!

Night shades began to gather, the street lights began to flash on, and street people began to amble down the sidewalks. I pulled myself together, folded up the precious contract, placed it back in my bag, and went out into the street. I hailed a cab and went back to the west side, back to my dingy little room.

Dusk was still turning into darkness as I readied myself for bed. I was truly exhausted. To the bone! I lay in the deepening gloom, thinking about knowing when to fight and when to run away. Gramma Hattie had said when I was born that I would know the difference. "I'll decide in the morning," I whispered to myself, and went on musing. What is this thing about men and women's money?

The Evans Exodus

. . . .

You don't has to run with the hounds—
If the hounds won't hunt—an'
You wants to keep runnin'
Then you has to run with the foxes!

I woke up in a cold sweat around three a.m. with these words ring-ing in my ears. I had rolled over into the chasm in the middle of the lumpy old mattress, and the pillow had fallen over my face. I lay there gasping for air, and I realized that I must have been dreaming.

"Yo' soul flies away and visits with the ancestors when you sleep." Great-Gramma Lizzie's words came from a long way off. I lay very still. The mes-sages came crystal clear.

"Time to fight!" My heart started to pound.

"Find someplace to put yo' rage! It makes a hole in yo' soul—and it makes a body constipated!"

Gradually, I came to myself and rolled over to the more level part of the mattress, muttering to myself, "Hey, Lawdy Lawd!" My ears picked up the sound of rain pittering and pattering on my window. "I sure hope it doesn't rain all night an' all day," I spoke into my empty room. "I got a lotta work to do. I gotta get *all the foxes* ready to run!" I went back to sleep, and this time it was dreamless and sweet.

I woke up with the morning sun shining straight into my eyes through the holes in the old dark green window shade. Rolling over, I sat up, rubbed my eyes, and suddenly recalled my late-night visit with the ancestors.

I jumped up and hit the ground running! My mind was made up and my heart was set. I'd get a new group together, honor the contract, and keep on playing good music! A list of cats who could fill the bill soon filled almost three pages of music paper. I also talked to Ethel and her mama (my landladies) to get their input. I called Connie, the pro. "Who always the biggest part of a music audience?" she asked slyly.

"Women," I answered.

"That's exactly right! And who always follow the women?"

"Men!" I laughed. "It's always been that way, even in St. Paul's Baptist Church. The flock is always women. The deacon and preachers is always men!" We both laughed.

"Baptists or barnyards, it's all the same! Chickens, hens, and *one* rooster!" Connie was philosophical. "Get some cats that have *IT!*"

"It?"

"Sex appeal. Charisma. Of course they should play good music. A man can blow 'snakes,' but if he don't have *IT,* he won't draw flies!"

So I narrowed the field down to four cats.

The drummer was known for great, interesting drum solos, and he could sing and harmonize. The sax player played a C melody sax (an instrument more suited to an early learner), but had the styles of Lester Young and Stan Getz down cold! He had one of the most beautiful tones in the Great Lakes area. He had "big ears," which meant that although he wasn't a great reader, he could play anything he heard. Both men were pleasing to the eye and smiled a lot.

I chose a handsome devil of a vocalist instead of a second horn. Copper-colored, he had dazzling white teeth and a slightly crooked smile. His hair was like Cab Calloway's: straight and black as a raven's wing. He wore it long enough to fall into his eyes when he sang love songs with his rich baritone voice. He knew all of Al Hibbler's hit songs and Billy Eckstine's ballads.

And last but not least I chose my old friend from high school—a tall, light-skinned young man with a long solemn face and heavy eyebrows over deep-set, soulful dark eyes. He played a blonde bass fiddle and was our comic relief. He performed all of Louis Jordan's songs, including "Saturday Night Fish Fry," and a traditional bawdy narration called "Last Saturday Night." It went, in part, like this:

> *Last Saturday night when I came home*
> *Drunk as I could be*
> *I saw a head layin' in my bed*
> *Where my head s'posed to be!*

I woke up my wife, my darlin' wife,
I said, "Wake up! Talk to me!
Whose head is that, lyin' in my bed,
Where no head s'posed to be!"
She said, "Fool, you damn fool!
Can't you plainly see?
That's just an old cabbage head
That yo' mama sent to me."
People, I traveled this world
For miles around an' I
Hope to travel more,
But I ain't never seen a cabbage head
With hair on it before!

He was funny and he was sensual. His name was Shakespeare, and he could read people's palms and tell their fortunes. He even read his own palms.

But he was really mad at God! Both his parents had died at once, and his oldest brother and oldest sister each bought a house with the insurance money. The brother raised the younger brothers; the sister raised the younger sisters. Then the oldest brother contracted stomach cancer.

We would hang out with Shakespeare at his house, and his poor brother would sit on his couch, holding his arm across his middle and try to laugh at our antics. He tried his best to hide his pain, but a shadow would cross his face and wipe out his sweet smile, and he would excuse himself and slowly climb the stairs to his bedroom.

Shakespeare came to our house when his brother died, and M'Ma and all of us tried to comfort him. After the funeral, M'Ma made his favorite food, "pork chops that taste like chicken." He did not cry, and he would not be comforted. He really hated God.

We rehearsed the band every day at the YWCA and melded all our special talents into a great revue. The minishow was a fast-paced heartwarming event tied together with my own offerings—a theme song to get us on and off the stage and a couple of piano features: Avery Parrish's "After Hours" and Lionel Hampton's "Hamp's Boogie Woogie." All of us harmonized on "Goin' to Chicago" and "Wee Baby Blues."

We went to Columbus and took no prisoners. The cats were handsome, dressed in dark suits, white shirts, and red ties. Shoes polished to the nines. And my cocktail dresses were ahead of the herd in style. It was tradition for entertainers to dress for where they wanted to go, not where they'd been.

The joint was packed every night with women come to listen to the music, watch the vocalist's shiny, long black hair fall over his handsome face, laugh at Shakespeare's antics, and close their eyes and sway to "After Hours."

The men would stomp and cheer for the drummer's solos—the sticks flying, the sounds of shimmering cymbals, the flams and paradiddles and tom-toms taking everybody back to Africa or back to Blackfoot country. It was glorious! And the review that appeared in the *Black Dispatch* was glorious too. I bought six copies, cut out the review, and mailed one to every one of my ex–ace boon coons. Oh, but the foxes ran a fabulous race.

* * *

Mr. Posey was overjoyed. "I have plenty jobs if you want them!" He was really impressed with us and came to see us again and again.

When the job was finished, our sax player wanted to go back home to settle some business. So did the vocalist. Well, it was fun while it lasted. "We could get another sax player and be a darn good quartet!" declared Shakespeare. "I like what we put together. I like to travel, and I'll be with you as long as you need me." He smiled his shy smile and smoothed his hair. He was always so very neat. His friendship was genuine. And he had a car, so we wouldn't have to make Greyhound any richer!

* * *

Back in Akron, as we planned our next moves, the time came to say good-bye to my sister Charlotte and my brother Jerry. They had both joined the air force. M'Da signed for Jerry because he was underage. It seemed like the exodus of the Evanses! We met for one last time at the Sugar Bowl. I knew M'Ma must have had a hole in her heart, but nothing could be done about it.

"Listen!" Charlotte told me, "M'Da is drinking more and stayin' drunker longer!"

"Well," Jerry's deep bass voice was matter-of-fact, "the three little ones are there to keep her company."

"They won't be there long if things keep goin' the way they goin'!" Charlotte stood up. "Take care of yourself." She smiled her pretty smile. We three made a small circle, and then they turned and walked away, tall and proud.

My eyes filled with tears as I went to the door of the Sugar Bowl and watched until they disappeared up the hill by the drugstore, its windows full of St. John the Conqueror roots, candles, and potions guaranteed to keep yo' man tied to yo' side.

* * *

My blue-eyed leprechaun of a union man in Canton came through like a champ! He contacted the president of the union in Dayton, Ohio, and we hit pay dirt!

"C'mon down!" he told me on the phone, "plenty good musicians down here! Snooky Young, trumpet player with Jimmy Lunceford *and* Count Basie, lives here. And there's Booty Wood, trombone with Tiny Bradshaw *and* Erskine Hawkins, gotta know somebody you can use."

He paused, "Lemme see, and Jay McShann is playing at the country club this week!"

"Jay McShann!" I gasped. "He's my idol! I grew up listening to his music! I know all his songs and piano solos . . ." My heart was beating so fast I could hardly breathe. "Man, oh, man! I'll finally get to see the man alive and in person!"

Shakespeare picked me up the very next morning in his Ford and off we went, armed with minced-ham sandwiches and two jars of Alabama lemonade.

It was a long drive. Dayton was farther than Columbus, but it was a fun drive. We laughed about the television shows *Beulah* and *Kay Kaiser's Kollege of Musical Knowledge;* discussed with great pride Jackie Robinson's breaking into the major leagues—and with great anger the threats against his life just cause he was a different color; and noted how scarce the bathrooms were becoming as we continued our trip. In fact, we noticed that bigger and bolder black lawn jockeys were beginning to appear in more and more front yards. "Down south—up north!" Shakespeare remarked dryly.

By the time we arrived in Dayton and found the union president's home, close to the center of town, we could hardly say "Howdy!" before asking for use of his restroom. "I don't know about 'rest' and I don't know about a 'room,' but the outhouse is right through the kitchen and out in the backyard under that big tree." We made a beeline for the facility, all the time marveling that the president's house was so close to the center of town and still had no indoor plumbing!

Whoa! What kinda town was Dayton?

He was happy to have company, and talked on and on about the great musicians born in Dayton. "Uh, we better get on our way, don'cha think?" Shakespeare was polite, but all business.

"Now, listen," the president was still holding on, "you go down to the Hotel Dayton. That's where all or most of the musicians hang out! Surely you'll find someone to fill the bill!" We thanked him for his kindness and hospitality, jumped in the car, and drove away. The day had come to a close, and evening shadows were falling fast.

The Hotel Dayton was a ramshackle building on a rundown street. We looked around, a little nervous because the streetlights were far and few between. But upon entering the hotel, a friendly Negro girl at the desk in the shabby lobby answered all our questions. "Look," she waved her hand toward the stairs, "go downstairs to the basement, rooms ten and eleven. They all hang out down there."

"Thanks."

The stairs were dark; only a dim bare lightbulb swung from a cord at the bottom. We felt our way down, made a turn into a narrow hall, and then heard music playing softly on someone's record player: Coleman Hawkins's "Body and Soul." And murmuring voices, punctuated by occasional bursts of laughter.

Shakespeare knocked at the door, and the room became completely silent. Someone cut off the music.

Then a voice said, "Who . . . who is it?"

"The president of the union sent us. We from Akron, and we looking for a sax player to join our group."

Silence.

Then, at last, the door was opened a crack, and part of a face appeared, looking at us with one eye. "Well, come on in . . ."

We entered, and the darkened room greeted us with red bulbs in the lamps casting people's moving shadows on the walls. Our eyes became accustomed to the dim light, and finally we could see at least eight people lounging around on twin beds and three hotel chairs. We coughed and choked on thick marijuana smoke and the perfume being sprayed on the red lightbulbs. Over in the corner, some cats at a hotel desk waved at us, but then went back to hovering around a collection of syringes, spoons, and ties.

"What's yo' pleasure?" They were very friendly. "We got plenty of whatever Cookie just copped!" They all laughed, and someone started playing the record player again.

"No thanks," we hurriedly replied, "we just passing through. We come to find a sax player for our group. We got plenty work and a good agent." We repeated. We had to. Ev'ry livin' A was so blind from getting blasted that we knew nothing we said was sinking in.

"Hey! Now that's progress! Somebody come here to *give* us work!" More laughter.

They finally gave us names, some with phone numbers. "Listen," one of the men said, "go down to the Glass Bar. Lots of cats are there to listen to Miss Cornshucks. After she finish singin', they usually jam, an' you can take your pick." He seemed to be the leader—quiet spoken and nice looking.

"Well, thanks a lot. We'll be going on, then. We don't wanna miss the show." As soon as we got up and started to thread our way through the prone bodies and the legs stretched out in the aisles, a great crash came from the windows that were near the ceiling of the basement room.

CRASH! Axes bit into the wooden frames, and the door was battered open. At least ten police and plainclothes detectives rushed in. "POLICE! THIS IS A RAID! YOU'RE UNDER ARREST. LAY DOWN ON THE FLOOR!"

We were scared out of our wits, but we obeyed. Everybody hit the floor at the same time. Let me tell you how humiliated and frightened Shakespeare and I were as we were led out through the shabby lobby, people staring and whispering.

We went to jail in Dayton, Ohio, handcuffed to a band called Cookie and His Cupcakes.

Gramma Hattie was right.

OMYGOD!

Jailhouse Blues

. . . .

The jailhouse doors clanged shut behind me, and I was left standing in a cell, bereft of my belongings and my dignity.

I wasn't strip-searched, thank God!

"You couldn't be hiding nothin' in your narrow bee-hind," the police-woman announced. She was built like the wrestler Man Mountain Dean: large, tall, broad shouldered, and no neck! She and her fellow officer snickered as they walked away.

I stood with my back to the door, looked around the cell, and shuddered.

"Well, what are *you* in for?" There were three women in the small cell, lolling, lying, or leaning on three bunk beds. All three were white. One—heavyset, with permed, curly dark hair, wearing a black dress with a plunging neckline, no stockings, and stiletto-heeled patent-leather pumps stared up at me with bleary, world-weary eyes.

The second woman was raw-boned, tall and gangly, with hair dyed many colors, though the predominant color was red. She wore a royal blue dress cut on the bias so it hugged her frame, as tight as her skin. Her eyes were pale blue, and her thin lips curled around a cigarette. The smoke collected in the middle of the cell because there was no ventilation.

The third woman appeared younger—very petite, with long, loose blonde hair and friendly brown eyes. She was all decked out in an apple green satin cocktail dress, one thin strap fallen from one pale shoulder. Her shoes were magnificent gold platforms! I guessed she was trying to look taller.

I didn't answer.

"I said, what are you *in* for!" the raw-boned woman repeated. She took the cigarette from her mouth and flicked the ashes onto the cement floor. "You look like you robbed some church collection plate!" They were all looking me up and down and coming to God only knows what conclusion! "You can take the bunk over there by the john," she went on.

I guessed she was the leader of the pack. Nobody else seemed to be allowed to speak. I carefully hooded my eyes and thoughts. I didn't want them to know that I knew that they were prostitutes. I've seen all kinds in the clubs and standing under the streetlights outside the clubs. I didn't want to challenge her position as boss of the cell, so I went over to the bunk and sat down. I put my elbows on my knees and covered my face with my hands. It was past dinnertime, and I was hungry and thirsty. My stomach growled.

The petite woman came over and stood in front of me. "C'mon! It's not that bad! Cheer up! It could be worse!" She smiled. I looked around the cell and shook my head. "Fess up! What did you do to get thrown in the clink?" She preened herself with quick little movements, as friendly as a puppy.

Disarmed, I told them my whole story. The raw-boned leader's eyes softened. "What a shame! I knew you didn't really belong in here."

The black-haired woman chimed in, "Look, you have to get ready for court in the mornin'. You have to sleep in your underwear. Put your clothes —no, fold 'em first—this way!" She showed me. "That way they won't get too wrinkled."

Ms. Raw-bone nodded. "You just a kid! You dressed real fine and all, but you don't know *nothin'!*" I agreed. "Now listen good," she barked. "You wash your face clean—no makeup! And when you go upstairs, look 'em in the eyes and be real dumb and humble. Course, you already them things, anyway, so you won't have to pretend."

They all laughed. So did I. I was beginning to relax. I knew they weren't gonna jump my bones, so I did as they advised. "Lay on your back so you won't muss your hair. They won't let us have combs or toothbrushes."

The petite woman rolled her eyes. "I guess they think we'll use them as weapons!"

"No mirrors either!"

"Lights out! On and off!" came a shout from some place outside the cell, and we were plunged into darkness.

"What's she mean—on and off?" I asked, keeping my voice just above a whisper.

"On your ass and off your feet!" All three replied in unison. We all giggled.

I lay on my bunk, my arms across my chest, sleepless, body rigid with fear and anxiety. What's gonna happen in court, I worried.

I thought about my folks, wondering what they were doing while I struggled through the most frightening day of my life. Probably looking at the new TV—Charlotte had told me about the new exciting addition. I shuddered to think what they would say about my being thrown in jail on a drug charge. M'Da would sing his same old song: "See, Lizzie! See how you raised these kids?" M'Ma would be mortified, but would probably get Mr. Rulak, the family lawyer, to get me out. She always was a woman of action.

They just couldn't find out. No way! No how! I prayed, "Dear Father in heaven, please get me out of this mess. Amen!"

Wide awake and listening to the alien noises of that awful place, I worried about Shakespeare, taken away with all those doped-up cats. The fact that he couldn't pray—not even a little—twisted my guts. Ill-fated Shakespeare just didn't trust God. I thought, oh well, I'll say a little prayer for him, and maybe it'll help both of us.

I don't know when I drifted off to sleep, but I woke up with a start. The cell door clanged open, and Ms. Man Mountain Dean came in and yelled, "Off and on!" (Off your ass and on your feet!) "Git up and git ready!"

Her helper shuffled in and handed us a cup of coffee, bitter and black, and an enormous, squishy-soft sweet roll with white cement icing all over the top and sides. Ugh!

"You better eat it! That's all you gonna get till court," Ms. Raw-bone declared. "What did you expect—ham 'n' eggs an' your mom's oatmeal?"

I ate it, went to the john (community nose-holding and laughter), washed my hands and face, then brushed my teeth with my fingers.

"Thanks." I was sincere. "Thank all of you for helping me. I'll never forget you-all!"

They smiled shyly. Ms. Petite reached out and touched my hand. "Good luck! You don't belong here—don't come back!"

I put on my designer suit and waited for Ms. Man Mountain to come for me. It didn't take too long. I could hear her footsteps clump, clump, clumping down the hall and the keys ching, ching, chinging as she came to our cell. She unlocked the door and yelled, "All right! Off and on!" She looked at me and barked, "Follow me!"

I waved good-bye to my three cellmates. "Kill 'em!" Ms. Raw-bone called out. I winced.

I hunched my shoulders and walked quickly in front of Ms. Man Mountain. We got to an elevator and, zip, up and up to the top floor of the building. "Where we goin'?" I asked.

"No questions!" Ms. Man Mountain declared, scowling.

We marched out of the elevator and down the wide carpeted hall. Whoa, where are we? I was thinking fast. This is no courtroom. Ms. Man-Mountain knocked on the huge old oak door. A gruff voice said, "Yes, come in!"

We entered the room, and Ms. Man Mountain said, in a completely different tone of voice, "Sir, er, uh, this is Miss Evans."

"All right, officer, you may go now."

And there I stood in a huge, airy room with large windows displaying a panoramic view of Dayton. The carpet was the color of doves, and very thick. I faced a huge ornate desk behind which stood a tall white man dressed in a dark suit, white shirt, and black tie. Standing on my right were three other white men, all dressed in dark suits, white shirts, and dark ties. Dressed for success—or to intimidate. They got my attention.

"Well," the man behind the desk made a cathedral out of his fingers. "So tell me what you and your friend were doing in the basement of the Hotel Dayton with a bunch of junkies and dope fiends!"

I remembered what the women in the cell had told me. I looked straight into the man's pale blue eyes and answered softly, "My friend and I went to the hotel on the advice of the president of the musicians union to find a new sax player for our band."

"Really?" I didn't volunteer another word until he asked more questions. "Did you know any of the men in the room?"

"Not me! Not my friend!"

"Did you bring any contraband with you to the room?"

"No, we did not!"

They went into a huddle, and my heart was beating like a tom-tom. Then the man behind the desk said, "Well, Miss Evans, my name is Agent Thomas. We've been observing the hotel for six months, and we've been taking photos of everyone entering and exiting that facility." He paused. "Frankly, we were surprised when you and the gentleman arrived. But, as I said, you are very fortunate. The leader of the group in the room verified your statements. *And* the president of the Dayton union." He looked out the window.

"You may go now, and I hope you and your friend never have to come to this office again. This is a federal offense. We will rid our state of the proliferation of drugs *in my time!*"

His face turned red and his lips thinned. "By the way, you don't look like the show-business type. Perhaps you should rethink your objectives, go home and get married, or teach school!" (So much for no make-up.)

I wanted to run out of that office, but one of the other gentlemen escorted me to the elevator and downstairs to retrieve my belongings, and to meet Shakespeare. We were taken to a place where they had impounded the car—they had searched every last inch of it! But, at last, we were in the car, in the sunshine, with the windows down all around, breathing sweet, fresh, free air!

And as we drove away from the jailhouse, I knew that I would never, ever forget the helpful hookers in my cell. And I would always remember the honesty of Cookie and his Cupcakes. They were each sentenced to seven years in the federal penitentiary.

From Hell to Heaven Blues

· · · · · · · · · · · · · · · · · · · ·

Shakespeare's face was grim. "Let's get the heck outta this funky-butt, bad-luck town!" I nodded.

As we drove along, I noticed that October's bright blue weather would soon be ending. The leaves were beginning to turn, and the leftover cornstalks in the fields beside the turnpike were stacked together in rows, like old ladies in long skirts.

Shakespeare suddenly pulled the car to the side of the road, his expression as desolate as the harvested fields. "Why are we stopping?" I stared at him. "What happened to you in the jailhouse?"

"Don't ask!" he growled, brows lowering over his eyes. "I kept my back to the wall and didn't close my eyes all night long!" His words cracked my control. I started to tremble and couldn't stop. "Hey! Hey!" Shakespeare said soothingly. "It's all right! We made it outta there in one piece."

"Yeah," I whispered. "But we almost got seven years! All on a *humble!* All for nothin'!"

Shakespeare hunched his shoulders, looked out the window and spat. "Well, we didn't—so onward and upward!"

He started the car. "Wait!" I yelled. "We can't let those fools run us outta town! We came down here to get a sax player and to see Jay McShann, and I'm not goin' back to Akron without doin' both of them!"

"But, what'll we do till night? We can't go back to that hellhole of a hotel!" He eased the gear into park.

"Well, we can go to the hotel called 'movie' or 'picture show,' if you will!"

He laughed. "Okay, it's cheaper than any ol' hotel, anyway."

We drove downtown, parked the car in the theater parking lot, went into a double feature with newsreels and cartoons and previews, ate hot dogs and popcorn and malted-milk balls, drank Dad's Old Fashioned Root Beer, took a long nap, woke up, went to the bathrooms, and cleaned up. I put on fresh make-up and stepped out into the cool of the evening as fresh as a daisy.

"Let's take care of business first," Shakespeare's mood had lightened considerably. "Let's go find us a sax player!"

"Okay, let's go!" I felt more like myself also, so he stepped on the gas and we sped off to the Glass Bar.

They were just finishing up their version of happy hour when we arrived. The clink of glasses and buzz of conversation bounced off a backdrop of walls and walls of mirrors. We could see ourselves reflected over and over and over again.

The bandstand, up near the ceiling, would be graced by the presence of Little Miss Cornshucks later on in the evening, singing songs in the style of the time—drenched with emotion and dramatized to the nth degree. The patrons said she could make your heart jump out of your chest! There were at least a half dozen musicians sitting around chewing the fat.

We quickly connected with a saxophone player who wanted to get out of town because of a broken romance. We checked each other out and found that we were on the same wavelength: same repertoire, same sense of fun. He was thin, and his handsome brown face was accented with movie-star sideburns and a thin, Clark Gable moustache. And he came highly recommended by the owner of the club.

The owner came highly recommended by the bartender. "He's a sharp cookie," said the bartender, speaking of the owner with affection. "He just has one weakness. He gets drunk on pay night, puts all the cash in neat bundles in front of himself on his desk, then puts his revolver on top of the money. If you go into his office Saturday night to get paid, he pulls the pistol on you. He just has a hard time giving up any of that money when he's drunk!" The bartender shrugged. "You come back on Sunday morning, he just fine! Smiles and pays ev'rybody off. No pain, no strain!"

He poured us another drink—beer for Shakespeare, ginger ale with a cherry for me. (I had vowed not to drink alcohol or smoke until I reached twenty-one, and I was not there yet.) The bartender took a drink of his own whiskey and grinned, his teeth pearly white against his dark face.

I went to the ladies' room. Yep! Glass mirrors galore! I used the potty, flushed it with my foot, washed my hands, and pushed open the door to the main room. Every soul in the club was looking at me and laughing, and all eyes followed me back to the bar. "What's goin' on?" I asked Shakespeare. He was laughing too.

The bartender tried to stop laughing while he explained. "The owner is weird, and the bathrooms are weird, too. When you flush the toilet, all hell breaks loose out here. Bells ring and whistles blow."

"What!"

"Yeah, ev'rybody knows your bizness!" Tears ran down his face. "It's a real crowd-pleaser!"

I smiled weakly. "Well, we gotta get goin'."

We exchanged contracts with the sax player and said, "See you in two weeks in Springfield, Ohio, at the Springfield Hotel."

"You bet!" Firm handshakes all around.

* * *

We drove way out on the outskirts of town to the colored country club, and had an early dinner of black bass fried whole, collard greens, corn bread, and peach cobbler. And then it was showtime. The musicians assembled onstage and tuned up, and the joint began to fill up with patrons who were dressed to kill and ready to be entertained.

Suddenly, there he was, his body large and round, his face like a happy Buddha's, his smile lit up by a gold tooth right in the middle of it. He was dressed in a dark suit with a white shirt and dark tie.

"Baby, here I stand . . ." He started singing and playing the piano using that unmistakable long fourth beat—romping along—Kansas City style. Feet started tapping and heads started shaking, and the fears and tensions of the last forty-eight hours dropped from our shoulders and melted like snow.

Jay McShann's inner clock was rhythmically reflected by his head nodding in a curious manner as he played. Tick-tick-tick-TOCK! Tick-tick-tick-TOCK! The whole crowd was in perfect rhythmic agreement with McShann and his music—tick-tick-tick-TOCK! One gigantic groove!

At intermission I went up to the bandstand and greeted him. "Hi, Mr. McShann!"

"Baby *Doll!*" He stood up and took my hand. "Where you come from, Baby Doll?" He was feeling real good. He was carrying a lot of liquor.

"Akron. Uh . . . Mr. McShann . . . I know all your songs *and* your piano solos. My uncle played your records on my gramma's Victrola for me when I was a little girl. I'd really like to play for you and with your band." The words rushed out of my mouth like a waterfall, and the cats—bass player, sax player, and drummer—all laughed.

Jay was feeling no pain. In fact, he almost fell off the bandstand. "Whoa!" "Hold it, Hootie!" They shouted and helped him back to the chair.

"Help yo' self, Baby Doll. You can play *what* you want, for *long* as you want!"

Jay was magnanimous, especially after Shakespeare and I bought a round of drinks for the band. The cats were in a really good mood, laughing, drinking, and telling road jokes.

When it was time to start the next set, I sat down at the piano and started playing a style called "lock hand" piano, which had been perfected by a pianist named Bill Gitney and an organist named Milt Buckner. Both had played around Cleveland and Youngstown. I knew it would get their attention.

They fell right in, and we had a great time. I played Jay's solos note for note, and they laughed: "She got you, Jay! She on you like white on rice!"

All of a sudden, Jay came up to the piano, grinning from ear to ear. "Baby Doll! You sure didn't lie! You really know your way around the black 'n' whites!" He applauded with the crowd, which whistled and stomped at this unexpected addition to the show, but his eyes were suddenly sober and his smile was stiff and strained. "That'll do, Baby Doll! Ol' Jay will take it from here!"

The applause followed me all the way back to my seat. My head was spinning and my heart was singing. I had fulfilled a longtime dream.

The long drive back to Akron was like a blur. "You really played good with those cats." Shakespeare mused, "That sax player was really good, really dif'rent. But we wouldn't want him for our group—he leans up against the wall a lot."

"Thanks! What was his name?"

"He said it was Charlie Parker."

"What! Whoa! *Charlie Parker?*" I was stunned. I had played the man's music many a night, but had not recognized him. He looked much older than his photos and much older than his years. But what joy!

I felt like a kid way up high on a ladder putting the star on top of a Christmas tree. From hell to heaven in forty-eight hours! Halleloo!

Snowbound

· · · · · · · · · · · · · · · · · · · ·

*T*he Springfield gig was good, but not great, because the sax player was distracted and deeply depressed. His girlfriend in Dayton had put him out, and since he had no gigs in sight after ours was finished, he had to go back to his wife.

His wife had a good job as a nurse. She laid down the law and told him in no uncertain terms that he had to get a day job and become a "weekend warrior"! It broke his heart, but he didn't have the wherewithal to front his own group or even to hang with us. He just didn't have "IT."

The Springfield audience was really a down-home bunch, more down-home than we had encountered in a long time. In fact, the whole town was down-home. And it had a dirty little secret.

One day Shakespeare and I put on our coats and scarves, and ventured out into clear cold air, and went downtown to explore. We decided to stop in Isaly's Ice Cream Parlor.

Now, Isaly's was known all over Ohio, and specialized in ice cream, rich and many-flavored and shaped like a pyramid. We went into the parlor, and the place was really crowded. When people saw us, a hush fell over the whole store. We waited our turn, finally got our orders of rainbow-colored ice cream, and pushed our way out to the sidewalk, licking the outrageous, wonderful, creamy cold confection.

As we stood in front of the store, an old Negro woman carrying the shopping bag of a day worker sidled up to us. "Y'all just come outta that sto'?" she asked. Her dark face was a road map of hard work and hard times.

"Yes, ma'am," we replied.

"An' they served you dat ice cream?"

"Yes, ma'am!" We were surprised.

She looked over her shoulder nervously. "I been livin' here in Springfield all my life an' I nevah knew Negroes could go in there."

We stared, ice cream forgotten. "Well," Shakespeare said, "Today is your lucky day! We gonna treat you to ice cream in Isaly's on Main Street in Springfield!" She looked frightened, but we each took one of her arms and marched back into the parlor and ordered her choice: vanilla ice cream shaped like a pyramid.

As we marched out the door and onto the sidewalk, she stopped, licked the ice cream, and said, " Lawd ha' mercy! Thank you, Jesus, an' you young-ens. I cain't wait till I git home an' tell *ever*-body what the Lawd had done for me to-day!" With that, she walked down the street, shoulders squared and head held high, her pink tongue lick-lick-licking that cone! She waved, turned the corner, and disappeared.

I felt like laughing and crying at the same time.

Shakespeare remarked dryly, "They fought a war for the United States all over the world, but somebody forgot to tell the Negroes in Springfield that they could buy ice cream at Isaly's on Main Street!"

We returned to Isaly's during the afternoon of the last day of our gig. No Negroes were to be seen. "Say, did my gramma ever come back in here again?" I asked the little pink-cheeked girl who had waited on us before.

Her pink cheeks turned beet red. "No, no one came in here but you two."

We took our ice cream and left the store. "Well," Shakespeare shook his head sadly, "old habits die hard!"

I agreed. "I bet her Negro neighbors thought that old lady was halluci-natin' when she told them they could feel free to go in Isaly's."

That night we had to work really hard to keep up our spirits. But the show must go on.

The new band that was booked to follow us came in from Cleveland that night. They checked out our last show, and after the crowd started thin-ning out, they came up to the bandstand and introduced themselves. Our drummer, Jay, who was usually off on his own pursuits, started showing the new drummer his sticks. The piano player was a shy, very young white boy. He just stood around and smiled. The leader was a wiry dark-skinned man, about forty-something. Since we were still in our teens, except Jay, who was in his thirties, he seemed old.

"My name is Jimmy Colvin." He had a classy air about him, a friendly gap in his teeth, three deep creases between his eyes, and deep lines run-ning down on either side of his nose to his mouth. He also had a dimple in his chin. He wore a long, very expensive topcoat, a well-tailored dark suit, and a white shirt with a Billy Eckstine collar and a striped silk tie—a real gentleman from Alabama.

He said, "Look, I hear y'all are looking for a sax player." We nodded wearily. "Well, I like what y'all do. You looking for a front man—I'm looking for a group. Why don't we get together?"

We were wary. We didn't know beans about this cat or, more importantly, how he played. "Well, we leavin' tomorrow, so . . ."

"Hang over one more day! You can check me out and then make a decision." We had a week between gigs, so we agreed. "That's good!" He smiled, his whole face a friendly crinkle. "Everything will be copacetic!"

We said good night. I went to the office and picked up our wages, paid the cats, then went to my room to pack. It was strange and wonderful, after all the sax searching we had done, to have a sax player searching for us for a change.

* * *

Snow is beautiful!

It's beautiful when you look out the window and see the sun reflecting a million points of light. Pure and artful are the shapes of the drifts completely covering everyday things. It's wonderful when you venture outside and tilt your face up to the sky to accept the cold perfect many-sided gifts on your eyelids and lips. It's magic how sound is brought down to a level as still and hushed as the quiet in a cathedral.

But it ain't magic, wonderful, or beautiful when it turns into a blizzard that shuts down the whole state of Ohio!

Every musician knows that dreaded clause in his contract that contains the words "ACT OF GOD," words that mean "if it ain't sunny, you git no money"!

Thank God, we had finished our stint and had our money in hand, but since we couldn't get out of the hotel, the meter was running on the rooms. The Colvin Band was just out of luck—period. They had not even begun to play, so their contract was invalid, and the meter was running on their rooms also.

The owner of the hotel was a battle-scarred octoroon (a person having one-eighth Negro heritage) woman who had seen better days. She immediately assessed the situation, called both bands together, and said, "Well, Colvin, an act of God has presented itself." Jimmy Colvin put both hands over his eyes. "Both your groups have to have rooms. Well, you don't have to pay for them." We all looked at her warily.

She looked out the window. Her blue eyes stared at the unrelenting snow. She was the last of her family line. She had never married because—

what could she do?—everybody in town knew her background. She was at least seventy years of age, but time had treated her fairly well. She was small-boned, and her hair was styled in a beautiful white rope of braids going twice around her small patrician head. She had creamy skin and thin lips. She couldn't marry white, she had told me, and she wouldn't marry black, so here she was, left with the last bit of her dowry, a ramshackle old hotel.

"Until the snow emergency is over, both your groups can play for your rooms. You each will play a set, and I'll give you both a small stipend for your trouble." We all bristled at the words "small stipend." "Now, hold on. The alternative is to move out of your rooms, and I'll rent them to other people. The National Guard has been called out. People are sleeping in bus stations, libraries, the armory, and wherever else they can lay their heads. The hotel is full up. They need entertainment at night." She was being logical. Then she turned up the pressure. "The mayor has decreed that anyone that will help shovel snow will get a ton of coal and a bag of groceries. So if you prefer to take that route . . ." She waved her elegant hands in the air.

"Er, well, all right, but we need extra money to get back to Cleveland when the snow lifts." I spoke up quickly 'cause we were in the better position to make a deal. I felt pretty good. This was like manna from heaven, since we had a week in Cleveland before we were to start on our new gig. It was found money!

Colvin was proud, and he was a gentleman. "Done!" He slapped the table. The old lady said, "Done deal!" And so it was.

Playing alternate sets gave us ample chances to observe Colvin's musicianship—his stage presence and his ability to entertain the stranded audience. Oh, he was good! But he was of a different generation and played a style that was primarily swing, not bebop. But not to worry: my experience playing all those old, stock arrangements for all those old cats in Akron really paid off. We started rehearsing with Colvin every day and melded quite well with his style.

He taught us all his showstoppers, and we taught him ours. "Is You Is or Is You Ain't My Baby?" he sang, and also a nice rendition of "Hey, Good Lookin'." He couldn't cut the mustard on "Cherokee," but did a great job on a very fast "Flying Home."

So we agreed to join Colvin. We set up the bylaws for the new band: We would be a co-op band, meaning everyone would kick in travel expenses for Colvin's big old Cadillac, which would be our new mode of transportation. We would be called the Colvinaires. I was only too happy to unload some of the burden of band business!

"So, Shakespeare," I said in a quiet moment, "look in your palm and tell Jay and me what you see for our future with this cat."

Shakespeare shook his long fingers and started checking the lines criss-crossing his palms. Jay, impatient with what he called hocus-pocus, walked away, ever alert for some heavy chick. "Well," Shakespeare drawled after a long pause, "it'll be okay for a while—a good while. He has two roads to travel." He stopped and closed his eyes. "This band was born in a blizzard!" His voice deepened. "And it will die in a blizzard!"

The Song of the Colvinaires

· · · · · · · · · · · · · · · · · · · ·

C'mon, Babe! Come along with me!
I'd like to take you for a ride in my 'auto-be-mine'
But belong to the finance company!

The Colvinaires, our brand-new band, started moving down that long and winding road, through snow, sleet, ice storms, and sudden dense fog, to fulfill the contracts given to us by Jimmy Colvin's agent, Mr. Moe Gale.

Many a mile was charted for us by the big-rig drivers who allowed us to follow close behind them during terrible weather. They waggled the tails of the rigs when it was unsafe to pass and flashed their lights when it was safe. They were our guardian angels.

We were packed like sardines in that old Cadillac. The bass fiddle nearly filled up the car, its neck across the front seat and its behind spreading out into the backseat. Jay and Shakespeare sat in back on either side of the fiddle; Colvin and I sat in front, mostly because I was a great talker and kept whoever was driving awake while hurtling through the dark of night on some of those long 500-mile jumps.

The trunk of the caddy was as large as some of our hotel rooms and held the drums, saxophone, clothing, and repertoire.

We did no one-nighters, thank God! Mr. Moe Gale's contracts were all for two weeks with a two-week option. We prided ourselves on getting the options picked up. And in most cases we refused to go beyond the four weeks because they would then immediately sign us up to come back in six months—when we'd be as fresh as a daisy!

We worked a circuit in Pennsylvania from Pittsburgh to Hershey, where everything in town smelled like chocolate—even the soap looked and smelled like a Hershey bar!

Then it was up to Minneapolis, down to Green Bay, Wisconsin, over and down to Naptown (Indianapolis), where they make the best chili in the entire world! There we ate breakfasts of ham steaks, hash browns, hot biscuits, and eggs over easy while listening to a jukebox play Little Jimmy Scott's "Everybody's Somebody's Fool" with the Lionel Hampton Orchestra. At night we played in a club that was across the street from a tiny joint called Henri's (on-rays), where three brothers held court. Monk and Wes and Buddy Montgomery played to a packed house, all the time inventing a brand-new sound.

Then on to Harrisburg, the capital of Pennsylvania. We checked into a rickety old hotel, strictly for Negroes, and made contact with the hotel bartender. Bartenders always know what's happening in a town—where to find cleaners, Laundromats, Negro barbershops and beauty shops. "The best Laundromat is downtown," he said. "Most people 'round here use Ma Brown's Laundry, but you can't be in no hurry."

"We *are* in a hurry," we said. "Thanks anyway."

We drove to downtown Harrisburg. We should have suspected something was wrong at the Laundromat from the scowls on the faces of the two white women folding sheets. After putting our clothes in the machines, we went next door to a little bar for a drink.

It was early, and no one was in the place except the bartender, a large white man with red hair and a moustache, wearing a white shirt and apron. He served us—beer for Jay and Shakespeare, ginger ale for Colvin and me—and when the drinks were finished, we ordered another round.

CRASH! CRASH! We turned toward the bartender, who was busy breaking the bottles and the glasses we had drunk out of! "What the . . . ?" We looked at each other, finished the second round, and ordered again. CRASH! The bartender broke all the glasses and bottles again!

"Sir," said Shakespeare, "we gonna leave yo' joint. You gonna put yo'self outta business if we stay any longer!" The bartender glowered, brought a knife down, and obliterated a lemon.

"Good-bye, my friend!" Colvin said, as we exited. "See you when the last trumpet sounds!" He broke more glasses, and we hadn't even drunk outta those!

"Let's get something to eat before we pick up the laundry and go back to the hotel." We walked down the street a ways and checked the menu outside a small restaurant. We went inside. There were quite a few people filling the tables, and we noticed they were all white. But we slid into a booth and started talking . . . and talking . . . and talking . . . Pretty soon we noticed no one had come to take our orders.

"Whoa! What's goin' on?" I felt a knot in the pit of my stomach.

Colvin raised his hand and summoned the waitress, who was standing by the door of the kitchen, whispering to the chef, who was whispering to a man in a business suit, who was obviously the owner. She finally came over slowly and said, "I can't serve you!"

"What! You all outta food?"

"No!" Her pudgy face was red as fire. "Listen. You're in downtown Harrisburg, and we don't serve Negroes downtown."

"But, this is the capital!"

"It don't make no dif'rence! Go someplace else!" She hung her head down. "Please, I don't wanna lose my job."

We looked at each other. "This is down South—up North again!"

Colvin was really upset. I had never been South, and neither had Jay or Shakespeare, but Colvin was from Birmingham, Alabama, so I guess it was a very unpleasant reminder of where he'd come from. We got up and tried a dignified exit. We didn't want to push it because those people were known to spit in your food back in the kitchen or put ground glass in it as a warning to others! We went across the street and ate Chinese food. "They don't serve me there either!" the Chinese owner told us cheerfully.

When we got to the club that night, our spirits lifted. It was located on the edge of town, but was really fine-looking: walls draped in red velvet and gold braid, and statues of dead cats from the Roman Empire everywhere. A lot of the men sitting around the bar and at the tables had five-o'clock shadows at twelve o'clock on their faces. They were all dressed in dark suits and black shirts with silk ties. Pinky rings on all of their little fingers. Their women were dressed fine, with flashy jewelry and gold and silver evening purses and shoes. All their women were brassy blondes. All their wives were at home.

There were two bandstands, and another band was already playing on one of them. Jimmy Colvin took in the situation with one glance. "Don't set up all your drums," he spoke behind his hand to Jay. "This is trouble!"

Sure enough, the cats in the black coats wanted the two bands to challenge each other near the end of an evening of playing alternate sets. The owner wanted both bands to play "Flying Home" until we dropped! "The band that plays the longest gets paid extra," he said, taking the fat cigar out of his mouth, just as though we were boxers in Madison Square Garden or gladiators in the Colosseum!

Jimmy started putting his horn in his case and said, "We quit!" But the men surrounded the bandstand and told us to keep playing. The other band rolled their eyes and began to blow their fool heads off. "I think we're going to have to fight our way out of here! They been drinking all night, and I don't think they're going to cool down. When I give the signal, ev'rybody grab his stuff and leave!"

Colvin pulled a gun outta his sax case, and we ran out of there, threw the instruments willy-nilly into the Caddy, and stepped on the gas! And we *never* went back to Harrisburg.

* * *

Playing Mr. Flint's club in Columbus was a real pleasure after Harrisburg.

Constant bad treatment diminishes anybody! It eats at your sense of self, even when you know better. When it's happening to you, at first you're so amazed—you feel like an actor in a bad movie. But afterward you grow cold, and even though you fall into a murderous rage, you feel helpless. The only good thing is that we could move on down the line. The shame of it all was the people who were stuck in those dark places and had to suck on that bitter tit until they died. Hey, Lawdy Lawd!

We were entertaining Negro audiences again, and again became the house band. I think we felt that we really needed a rest from strife, so we let our option get picked up over and over again. We backed up Jimmy Witherspoon, who drove an automobile with leopard-skin upholstery! He was handsome and the women adored him. When we sat around after the show, listening to and telling lies, he always interrupted everybody else, saying, "Lemme tell you this! Lemme tell you that!"

Wynonie Harris was a different type. He was classy and good-looking, with light brown skin and gray-green-hazel eyes. Jo Jones (the drummer with Count Basie) was his cousin. Harris possessed psychic powers, and sometimes he put on a turban, sat at a table, and told fortunes—but only for the most beautiful women! He and Shakespeare walked a wide swath around each other. Very weird! He called me "Miss Box" (slang for "Miss Piano") and had a hit song called "Don't Roll Those Bloodshot Eyes at Me!"

Larry Darnell was a pretty young man—black and beautiful, with a gorgeous pompadour hairdo (done up by his boyfriend) and a voice that made a body shiver. He had a hit called "For You, My Love (I'd Do Most Anything)" and a tearjerker of a song—half spoken, half sung—called "I'll Get Along Somehow." His momma came to every show, and when the women cried and fell on the floor, she screamed, "That's my boy! There he! That's my baby!"

Early one Saturday morning during this time, Shakespeare knocked on my door at the rooming house that we all called home and said, "Jeannie, I want you and Jay and Colvin to come to the courthouse with me!"

"What's the matter, Shake, you stick up a bank?" Colvin was always witty.

"No," Shakespeare rubbed his hands over his eyes, then his hair, "I'm gettin' married."

The silence was ghostly. "You what!" I finally found my voice.

Jay said, "I can't come. I gotta date." And he disappeared.

We knew Shakespeare had been hanging out with this girl for about two weeks. She was a high-yellow girl with jet-black hair, very pretty, and as quiet as a mouse. She sidled into the club one night, met Shakespeare, came to the club every night after that, and never left his side. We never heard her speak; she just smiled.

Shakespeare looked as if he were in a trance—I wondered if he had read her palm.

So Colvin and I went to the courthouse as best man and best friend and watched in disbelief as Shakespeare and the silent lady got married.

We had the next night off, so they did have a little honeymoon in the rooming house. Sunday and Monday went by—down time at the club. Tuesday morning, Shakespeare knocked at my door and called, "Jeannie! Hey! Open up!"

I opened the door and there he was, alone.

"What's happening?" I queried, one eye barely open.

"Come on down to the courthouse with me!"

"Why? You gonna marry again?" I was joking. His face fell, and he looked at the floor.

Colvin came out of his room, dressed for town. "Okay, you woke me up, so let's get going."

"What's going on?" I began to feel alarmed. Certainly, I was mystified.

Shake said, "I've arranged for a judge at ten a.m. I'm gettin' an annulment!"

I cried, "You what?"

Colvin looked at me and put his finger on his lips. "Let's go!"

I got dressed as quick as I could and joined them in the lobby. In complete silence, we drove to the courthouse and finally stood before the judge. He had bulging, pale blue eyes and wore his glasses on top of his head. His hair was like a halo around his bald head. He looked just like Benjamin Franklin. "Well, what's this all about? You were married last Saturday and now seek an annulment?" He looked down at the document. "I see this is uncontested. Where is the . . . er, er, um . . . bride?"

"I took her back home to her mama," Shakespeare mumbled.

"Well, pray tell, what happened? You two witnesses?" He looked at Colvin and me.

"Yes, sir." "Yes, sir."

Shakespeare cleared his throat.

"Speak up, young man!"

"Er . . . Judge, I married the woman, and we were happy at first. But I live in a rooming house, and the bathroom is down the hall, and we had our food delivered to our room." Colvin and I looked at each other. We had noticed the trays piling up outside his room.

"Get on with it, young man!"

"Well, Judge, the woman never took a bath!"

The judge stared. "You mean she never left the room after days . . . ?"

"No, sir. I have a john in my room, that's all."

The judge raised his gavel and brought it down with a bang! "Annulment granted!" he bellowed.

Shakespeare was a free man. Nobody ever mentioned it again.

*　*　*

South Bend, Indiana, was the headquarters of the Studebaker auto factory. Everybody in town drove one. Everybody in town had money to burn.

The club we were booked in after Columbus was an all-white club with all-Negro entertainment. The Colvinaires were again the house band, only this time we played mostly for shake dancers and apache dancers rather than vocalists. (The apache dance was a French import—French street criminals were called "apaches"—portraying a fight between a pimp and a prostitute for her money, usually played to the tune "My Man.") After the show, we played dance music.

Colvin's friends came to hang out with us. Conte Candoli, a great trumpet player, took us on a tour of the Selmer musical-instrument factory in Elkhart, Indiana. The artisans there put all the scrollwork on Selmer saxes by hand! They told us that they were afraid there would be no one to do this kind of artistry when they died.

Earl Hines, a friend of Colvin, also visited us. He was a well-known pianist who invented the trumpet-style solo for the piano. He performed with many a great musician: Jimmy Noone, Charlie Parker, Dizzy Gillespie, Wardell Gray, and Louis Armstrong. He wrote the hit song "Rosetta." He was as deep as a river, born at the turn of the century, a legend in his own time.

"You play great piano," he told me. I was staring at his hair, it looked a little askew. I felt really nervous about his checking us out. "Really great fingering," he added.

"Thanks." I glowed.

"But," he continued, "you don't know your progressions!"

"What's a progression?" I was curious.

He looked a little surprised, then he leaned back in his chair. "I know how you missed learning them. You on the road all the time, making things up as you go along. In the old days you could hang out ev'ry night and listen to other piano players." I nodded. "But progressions are basic, and you must learn them!"

So Mr. Earl Hines met me at the club the next afternoon and showed me what I needed to know. Another guardian angel!

The very next week while playing the Saturday afternoon matinee, Shakespeare leaned over and, without missing a beat, whispered, "Jeannie, look like somebody we both know just came into the club."

"Who?" My back was to the audience because the piano was an old high-back upright that had to be placed against the red-velvet-draped back wall of the stage.

People were having a high old time dancing to "One O'clock Jump." As soon as that was done and they had gone back to their tables, Colvin announced the show's headliner. "Ladies and gentlemen, the performer of the hour is ready to perform her fascinating and wondrous dance. Straight from the crowned heads of Europe to the bald heads of South Bend . . . *Miss Chicken Lockhart!*

We played a fast and furious chart on "Cottontail," and out of the curtains burst a woman dressed in an outfit made entirely of chicken feathers. Her head was encased in a huge chicken head, its beak open so you could see her attractive brown face. Her legs and feet had been made to look like yellow chicken legs, and her yellow shoes had chicken toes on the ends. She flapped her wings and danced wildly around the stage. Then everyone, except Jay, stopped playing. He kept the rhythm going and accented Chicken Lockhart's moves as she pretended to look for food, pecking around the floor and squawking and flapping her wings.

"Look over there in the second booth on the right-hand side!" Shakespeare whispered.

I looked, and almost fell off the piano stool. There, sipping a drink in a tall glass with lots of fruit and an umbrella stuck in it, was—M'Ma! She was wearing a little blue hat on her perfectly waved black hair and a blue silk suit with white collar and cuffs. Her little white gloves lay across a blue purse sitting on the table.

I couldn't believe my eyes. My heart raced, and a lump came up in my throat.

Just then Chicken Lockhart hopped up on a chair, croaked loudly, furiously flapped her wings, gave a loud squawk, jumped off the chair, and, miracle of miracles, left a giant golden egg on the chair! We joined the drummer and played a really fast "C Jam Blues" while she danced around. The crowd was hysterical, applauding and whistling. I turned and sneaked a peek at M'Ma. She had her hands over both eyes!

Then Chicken unzipped that chicken costume, hopped out of it, and stood there in only pasties and a G-string. M'Ma pulled one hand away from her eyes, but when she saw Chicken shaking everything on her body and taking her bow in next to nothing, she covered her eyes again.

Lordy have mercy!

The lights went up and the show was ended. I left the stage and walked slowly over to the booth. So did Shakespeare. "M'Ma! Whatever are you doin' here?" I sat down beside her and gave her a big hug.

"Mrs. Evans!" Shakespeare shook M'Ma's hand and grinned all over.

"How did you get here?" I asked. I didn't know whether to laugh or cry.

"I took the Greyhound bus this morning from Akron. It's over three hundred miles, you know." She was staring at me.

"Well, you look none the worse for wear." She smiled. "How long you gonna stay? You can stay with me at the hotel . . ." My words rushed out and tumbled over one another.

"No," M'Ma said quietly. "I'm not gonna stay. In fact, my bus leaves in one hour. I just came to see if you were all right. You too, Shakespeare."

Shakespeare was pleased. He wriggled like a petted puppy. "I take good care of Jeannie," he said grandly. "She is more than a sister to me. She is my one true friend!" He stood up as Colvin and Jay came over to pay their respects. M'Ma knew Jay's momma in Akron, and brought regards from her to him.

"Well, I know you both have a lot to talk about." The three men went into the kitchen for a late lunch.

M'Ma told me that Charlotte was loving the air force and was taking up nursing so she could have a trade when she got out.

"How 'bout Jerry?"

A shadow came over her face and her lips disappeared. "Well, he got in some trouble 'cause he wanted to play in the Air Force Band, but they wouldn't let him. He resisted. So now he's driving big ammunition trucks around narrow mountain ledges in the dark, in Korea!"

I tried to comfort her. "He'll be okay. He's got a guardian angel." I let the thought hang there for a little while. Then I asked, "How're the little ones?"

"Well, Jo-Anne inherited Mr. Riley, and the little boys are wonderful!"

"M'Da?"

She sighed, "He's not doin' any better. In fact, he's worse."

"Well, I sure won't be back anytime soon. We're really booked up solid!"

"That's good." She smiled. "The band sounds very nice . . ." She was silent for a moment. "You know, Great-Gramma Lizzie made quilts."

"Yes, she made us thread her needles when we were really little."

"She was asked to exhibit them in the same department store where you exhibited your paintings."

"Really?"

"Yes, and she won first prize, also, and they put her picture in the *Akron Beacon-Journal*. When she went to pick up her quilts and her prize, they were gone!"

"Gone? Where?"

"No one knows. No one ever found out who took those quilts out the window of the department store and spirited them away."

"Whoa . . ."

"She was heartless mad all over again at white people—for making her a slave when she was little and now for stealing her life work . . . So I really understand your deep disappointment in life, but I truly hope you don't let it fester inside."

"I won't. Don't worry! I truly believe all that stuff got me ready for my real, true love—music."

"Well, as long as you're okay." She looked at her tiny watch. "Time for me to go. I ordered a taxi to pick me up in a couple minutes to take me to the Greyhound station."

"Hey, let us drive you. The matinee's over, and we don't have to play again till eight o'clock."

"No, you stay here. I got what I came for. Y'all are doin' all right." She hugged me, and we walked outside to her waiting taxi. After she climbed in, she leaned out and said, "There are four thousand two hundred and fifty days of childhood."

"What's that mean?" I was astonished.

"It means what it means. Bye-bye!"

She had come three hundred long miles, and would travel three hundred more miles to get back home—all in one day—just to see if I was okay. How on earth did she find me? My heart was full. The lump kept growing in my throat, and I just stood there, waving long after the taxi had disappeared.

* * *

Jay, the drummer, and I fell in "like." We fell out of "like" just as fast as we fell in, experienced unexpected consequences, but remained civil, and continued to make music together.

New Baby Blues

. . . .

You need a permanent solution
For these temporary love affairs!
This live-in, light housekeepin'
Ain't gonna git you any where!

Some women say that having a baby is like pulling your lips over your head and tying them into a bowknot! It was not that way at all with me, not after playing three shows and a three-hour jam session on a sultry Saturday night in July 1951, in Erie, Pennsylvania.

It was the last night of our engagement at the Pope Hotel. I felt a few cramps, so after the job I checked into a prearranged hospital, got undressed, put on a white gown backwards, lay down on a bed in a room full of women screaming and groaning and cursing their husbands—and promptly fell into a deep sleep. I woke up with the woman in the bed next to mine screaming, "Nurse, nurse! Come quick! This girl has had her baby!"

I was wheeled at a record-breaking clip down the hall and into a delivery room. The cord was cut, and a beautiful, brown baby girl was snuggled into my arms. She smiled, and I fell in love.

* * *

Charlotte Evans, USAF
Lowry Air Force Base
Denver, Colorado

Dear Charlotte:

Hi, Sis! How you doing? I'm glad you like Denver! So you think you'll settle down there when you get out the Air Force? In the mile high city? Seems like World War II and the Korean War kinda ran into each other, doesn't it?

Sister mine, I truly wish I could empty my heart out to you. I'm just babblin' on, making small talk, because I'm so full of confusion that a lump stays in my throat like the stopper in a bottle full of the unspeakable.

Well, I'm back in Columbus, Ohio and I'll be here for a little while. I won't beat around the bush—I've got news.
Remember when I wrote you about Doctor W. H. O'Reilly who examined me and told me he thought I had a tumor? He called it a fibroid tumor and said that most Negro women had them 'cause they had too many female hormones. He said I had to have a hysterectomy!

Oh, Sis, my heart dropped and almost stopped beating! Hysterectomy meant early midlife problems and no children! They say you're only half a woman with one!

As I wrote you when you were stationed in Texas, my period was still regular but sparse and I had no pain except goin' to the john a lot, so I kept on steppin'! I gained a little weight, thinking the tumor was growing, so I put two big safety pins together to fasten my skirt, and I wore loose jackets on stage, mostly 'cause that's the style now. I saved money for the operation.

Sister, I called M'Ma and told her about the hysterectomy, and even long distance I could hear her catch her breath. She asked me to come back to Akron for the operation so she could be there with me. She said no girl should go through that awfulness alone. I did go to Akron.

We went and checked out hospital costs, and she insisted that I come back to the house instead of staying with my old roomie, Ethel, for a few days. M'Da just nodded his head when I came in, and kept sitting in his chair reading. I sat on the couch, and M'Ma went to the kitchen to make tea. In an instant, he went on the attack. "You were really bad when you were little!" he said without looking at me.

Sister, the rage started moving up my body to my head like an erupting volcano! "No, *you* were bad when I was little!" I spat out the words in a low voice. I didn't want M'Ma to hear.

"I want you to leave here," he looked at me with such meanness my heart almost stopped. "Everything has been peaceful since you been gone! I want all of you to leave!" His finger started pointing at the air for emphasis.

All of a sudden, all panic, all anger left with a whoosh. I stood up. "Listen, you mad at the wrong somebody! You know, I know your secret—in Cleveland—I suggest you cool your row and try to be decent. I didn't come back here to stay. I didn't come back here to fight. You ought to be ashamed of yourself!"

M'Da stood up, almost knocking over his chair, and I saw something on his face I had never seen before. Sheer fear. "I . . . I . . . I never get to be with your mama alone. I want to be with my wife without one of you needing something!—What about Cleveland?"

"Let's just keep it the way it is—you know I know—but it all depends on you!"

He glared at me, then went out the door, slamming it behind him.

I said good-bye to Jo-Anne and M'Ma and the little ones and hit the road. I long to tell you of this, my dear, but it goes deep down into that place that I cannot reveal.

Well, Sis, hold on to your hat! I went back to Doctor O'Reilly six months later as he suggested and lo!—my tumor had changed into—you won't believe this—a BABY!

Yeah, me! The girl who never wanted to get married to nobody and never wanted to settle down into the land of "Ho-hum," has the cutest, sweetest little girl baby you'd ever wanna see!

Charlotte, she so pretty and she never cries. She smiles all the time.

The doctor was so mortified 'cause he misdiagnosed my condition that he pulled some strings. (I really hollered and yelled and threatened to stand on main street with a megaphone if he didn't help me!)

Dear Sis, I'm so very alone. I try to be brave and positive and matter-of-fact, but I cannot tell M'Ma about the baby because I cannot bear the thought of M'Da pointing his finger and standing over her saying hurtful things, "See, see Liz? See how you raised her? What you gonna say now?" I so long to share the baby with her and have her advice on how best to continue our lives.

Doctor O'Reilly hurried up, Charlotte, and made some contacts with his priest and now I'm living in a nice place with the Little Sisters of Mercy with Shirley. That's what I named her. The nuns are wonderful and very curious about Negroes.

The band is on hiatus. We've worked steady without a break even for holidays. So they don't mind. Colvin went back to Cleveland and Jay went back to South

Bend chasing the elusive 250 lb. "Sireen" who seemed to fascinate him so. Jay doesn't seem to want to do the "father" thing. You can lead a mule to water but . . . Oh, well!

I have my own room, and the other girls are very nice—they are all white because this place is for white women and white girls "in trouble." We take care of our babies, but some babies are here alone 'cause their young mothers never came back for them.

Shakespeare comes ev'ry day. (It's better to have a faithful friend than a lousy lover!!) He stayed here in Columbus with a hair-dresser friend of both of ours. Shakespeare and I play with Shirley and we also play with all the babies who don't have anybody. He picks them up and, boy!, do they laugh and gurgle when his big brown hands cradle them and rock them and hold them high in the air. Their little pink cheeks turn rosy red! He goes down the rows of cribs and picks up each and ev'ry one!

Sister, dear sister. One night, after everybody was quieted down, I slipped into the chapel, made my way up to the little platform that held the organ, and sat down. I ran my fingers over the keys, and by the light of the flickering candles lit by the prayerful little sisters, I started playing a Bach toccata—it came from a faraway place, wending it's way down the years till it rested some place in the logjam in my heart. I played until my desert-dry eyes filled with much-needed tears. They welled up and out and down my face and made little patterns on my shirt. When I finished playing, I put my head down on my arms and rested there. Tears to sobs—sobs to hiccups. And, finally, it was done. I dried my eyes on the sleeve of my shirt, stood up, and turned to leave the little stage. The Mother Superior was standing there, smiling at me.

"Well, miss, perhaps you have found your true calling. You are born to music. You must not neglect it. I can tell it has chosen you."

She turned and, without a sound, disappeared through one of the side doors.

Charlotte, I'll have to leave here soon 'cause I have to go back to work—the band still has contracts, you know. At first, I thought I'd go crazy wondering what I was gonna do. I felt like I had stepped on the gas of a Ford V-8 and run myself into Summit Lake—just like Aunt Catherine!

If I go back to Akron, since I haven't been able to finish college or get a teaching credential, I won't be able to get work that pays well—only day's work, or take a job living "on the place" with white folks, taking care of their kids and having Thursday afternoons off. Or, perish the thought!, marry some man so I can have help paying the rent. There sure isn't much choice for Negro women right now.

Sometimes, my sister, I feel like I'm standing outside myself watching a scene in a play—my soul coolly watching events unfold, just measuring, waiting for something I cannot even name.

We're going to Sherbrooke, Quebec, next month and since we will play in a nice French hotel, I can take the baby with me and the French-Canadian maids will babysit the three hours we're playing. Shirley will be asleep the whole time.

The group will drive up to Quebec, but Shirley and I will fly up. It's better for her. I bought her a beautiful white sweater outfit and a snugglie with feet, and a white blanket for her first airplane ride.

Well, I guess I better wind this letter up. Jay's mama said I could bring the baby to Akron after the Sherbrooke job and that she would love to look after her, and Jay and I could pay for Shirley's keep and send clothes and things.

I'm really thankful for her offer. She's alone and they'll be company for each other. But more than that, no matter what I do for a living, in Akron or anywhere else, I will have to leave Shirley with someone most of the time. And being on the road with a band is no way to grow up. Shirley deserves a stable environment, not a succession of hotel maids. I'll be able to stay there on breaks between gigs and whenever I possibly can. It's not great, but it's the best I can do.

Well, Charlotte, Great-Gramma Lizzie, Gramma Hattie and Aunt Catherine all took care of us and we turned out okay!

I'm still in a daze 'cause I only had two months to get used to going from a tumor to a baby!

Take care of yourself and when you hear from Jerry, tell him he's an uncle!

You know, Charlotte, I just thought about something—neither one of us really ever talked about weddings and long white dresses and all that fairy tale stuff as little girls. I never played for any weddings at St. Paul's Baptist Church—only funerals! I guess we're a whole new generation!

> *Take care*
> *Your Sis*
> *Jeannie*

P.S. I'll get some photos made and send you one soon.

P.P.S. It really breaks my heart at the thought of leaving the baby—even for one minute! I guess my 4,250 days of childhood are over forever. They belong to Shirley, now!

See you on the late watch,

Jeannie

A Blizzard of Birdshit

. . . .

"Where is ev'rybody?"

We were driving slowly down the main drag in Clinton, Iowa. It was early afternoon and we were trying to find the nightclub we were booked to perform in that week. The street was completely deserted. The car suddenly veered, fish-tailing over to the side of the street.

"What the heck was that?" "I dunno! It's not ice and it's not snow." "Well, it sure is slick!"

Colvin righted the wheel. "Hey, there's the club!" He turned the car into a circular driveway and slip-slid up to the club entrance. It was protected by a striped green awning that was completely covered with a glistening white substance.

"Okay, let's get the equipment out and set up so we can get back to the hotel and take a nap before dinner."

We got out of the car and almost fell on our behinds. "What the . . . ?" Whatever it was, it was slippery and white and covered the entire sidewalk. We hurriedly hauled the equipment out of the car as the white stuff rained down on us.

"Geez!" We looked up and almost passed out. There, covering all the telephone wires, the roofs, the awning, all the buildings as far as we could see were hundreds—thousands—of dark, hunched, ominous bird shapes.

"Hey!" Shakespeare shouted and clapped his hands. A cacophonous sound went up from the multitude as they flapped their wings and took off like black fireworks filling the sky, wheeling around and around, spiraling up, covering the sun! We dashed into the club and wiped our feet on a tremendous drop cloth that covered the entrance.

"What was that?" we asked the waiter who was peering at us, mouth open.

"Starlings," he said, his bright blue eyes filled with laughter. "They've taken over the whole city! The mayor and ev'rybody are trying to figure out what to do about them." He added, "Shoot 'em, I say! Have a contest — whoever bags the most birds gets a prize."

The chef came out wiping his hands on his apron. "They're messing up ev'ry car and taking the paint off our houses!" He shuddered. "They've got germs! The police was shooting in the air yesterday, but them birds just flew around and around till the shooting stopped, then landed right back where they started."

"They've broken down telephone wires," the waiter interrupted, "and people have to walk around in the daytime with umbrellas and galoshes."

"Whew!" Shakespeare exclaimed. "This is a bad-luck town!"

My mind raced ahead. Perhaps I would have to come back to perform that night with brown-paper bags over my good grey high-heeled Andrew Gellar shoes!

"Bad-luck town!" Shakespeare muttered one more time.

That night, the club was packed. Every table and booth was filled with people drinking their fool heads off. From frustration, I knew.

It was safe to come out at night because the birds would hightail it to a big grove of trees way out on the outskirts of town. Nobody knew why they chose that spot, but then again, nobody knew why they chose Clinton, Iowa, in the first place.

The people were boisterous and applauded every single thing we did, and at intermission, when we retreated to the kitchen to catch our breaths, some of them came back to chat and get autographs. (The club management didn't want us to sit out front with the customers.)

Colvin was over at a corner table talking to two well-dressed men with pinky rings and cigars. Jay, Shakespeare, and I were sitting in the opposite corner when, all at once, a man came up to our table and said, "All right, friends, my name is Al and I'm your union man and I came to collect your dues."

His black hair was hanging down in his face, his brown suit was rumpled, and his shirt collar and tie were wrinkled. He was about two sheets to the wind, just like everybody else. "You guys really play good music." He sat down, put a briefcase on the table, and opened it. "Look, I know you-all know a good deal when you see one." We looked at each other. What the heck was this all about? "I'm selling fake books — the best in the country — and I know you-all need one."

Now, fake books contained copies of all the best-known Broadway and pop songs. They were illegal because they were copied without the permission of the copyright owners. And to have a drunken union man selling them on the side was really bizarre. He piled the books on the table, dove back into his briefcase, and brought out an unlabeled brown bottle. "This is the best white lightnin' in the country," he chortled as he screwed the top off the bottle, wiped it off under his armpit, and offered us a drink.

"Uh . . . we don't drink . . ."

"Okay, all the more for me," he said. "Listen, you guys really come through here with one of the best contracts I ever saw for this club." He took a big drink out of his bottle.

"What?" Jay queried.

"Yeah." He named the sum on the contract. "That's good bucks!" We looked at each other again, barely breathing, his words sinking slowly into our brains. It was not the amount of money Colvin had quoted to us! It was many, many greenbacks more! "Well," the union man took our silence for a yes, "you-all buying a fake book—that's good. I'll come back the end of the week and bring your books and collect your dues and collect your money for the fake books. Nice meeting you-all!" He lurched to his feet and went back into the main club room.

He really took the wind out of our sails!

We played the rest of the week, and when pay time came around, we all jumped on Colvin. It was a bitter confrontation! We were furious and hurt because we had been going great guns. And we were supposed to be a co-op band, sharing equally in the expenses and the money. Colvin was nimble and he was quick: "I was going to tell you-all, er, uh, it was going to be a surprise . . ." Oh, Colvin was smooth all right, but we knew a lie when we heard one.

We shed Colvin like the skin of the snake. And just as Shakespeare had foretold, the band that had been born in a blizzard in a town called Springfield broke up in a town called Clinton, barraged by a blizzard of birdshit!

The Colors of Many Changes

. . . .

Shakespeare found God!

He had hated God with a passion for a long time for all the trauma and tragedy that he thought had been visited upon his family from on high.

We don't know when or where he found God, but he did tell us what he had to do about it. "He called me to preach his word," Shakespeare continued. His long face shown like the rising sun, and he looked at his palms, fingers splayed out like a gospel fan. We stared at him, speechless.

"I'm going back to Erie. You-all needn't worry; I'll stay till you find a new bass player. I won't leave you-all in the lurch." He mused, "It won't be long now!"

After the breakup of the band and the episode of the birds in Clinton, we came back to Akron to regroup. Boy, we were in luck! We found Lee, an old high school friend, who played wonderful Lester Young–type saxophone, then called the agent, who was only too happy to continue booking us, and started rehearsals.

The band had begun to recover from Shakespeare's blockbuster declaration. But the thought of losing Shakespeare left me numb. He had been a true friend, through thick and through thin. What would I do without him? O Lordy!

I was staying with Jay's mama. She was helping me take care of Shirley by day, and at night when we rehearsed at the Y. Shakespeare stayed with one of his sisters. And nobody knew where Jay was staying; he was always so mysterious.

Shakespeare's prediction was coming true even as we spoke.

Cruising nonstop cross-country, doing a "gangsta lean," driving his "green machine," fresh from the Korean conflict came my brother Jerry.

Keeping him company in his fine seafoam green Cadillac were two cartons of Camel cigarettes, a jug of Hennessy cognac, a dog-eared copy of a book by the philosopher Schopenhauer, and a brand-new blonde Kay bass fiddle. He was coming home from hell, back to a world where fickle fortune had us all "hot-sock dancin'" to a whole new set of tunes.

When we first left Akron, Euclid Avenue was mostly Caucasian, except for our family, the very Reverend Mr. Yancy and his family (who were mixed mulatto and Blackfoot Indian), and one other Negro family, the Millers, who lived next door to the Evanses. Mrs. Miller looked after the two little boys while M'Ma and M'Da worked.

When we returned, all the white people had moved way out on the outskirts of town to someplace newly named "the suburbs."

Some cat in Levittown, Long Island, had built a lot of identical new houses on huge tracts of former farmland, and white people had snapped them right up—sold their old houses and left their old lives behind. Inside the brand-new houses, and inside the old houses they left behind (purchased with pride by the Negroes), there were great changes also. Muntz TVs, some with radios and record changers attached, took the place of discarded pianos, which were soon followed by the dining room tables. TV dinners served on newly invented TV tables broke up family conversations and family songfests. Nightclubs grew dark. Howard Street was becoming a ghost street, and show folks and older musicians hung it up forever.

It also seemed as if Shakespeare wasn't the only one who found someone bigger than himself 'cause President Eisenhower took a pause from playing golf and ordered troops to Topeka, Kansas, to help a little Negro girl named Linda Brown attend an all-white school. At the same time, we jazz musicians were cheering because Louis Armstrong had sent a nasty comment to Eisenhower, declining the president's invitation to help spread democracy on foreign soil. That tune seemed to run along the lines of "Ain't nobody goin' nowhere to no foreign country to preach no freedom while there ain't no freedom at home!"

The powers that be, led by Joe McCarthy, a senator from Wisconsin, were really getting the blues over the reds (Communists). All kinds of investigations were breaking out over colors. Pinkos. Blacklists. Whites rabid over "separate but equal" and "forced acceptance" issues. The yellow peril and the domino theory were causing kneejerks throughout the military community, the musical community, and the whole country at large.

We decided that since, on top of all this frenzy, the Ku Klux Klan was beginning to stir again (it seems they had only been taking a nap) that we would never go below the Mason-Dixon Line to perform. Ever!

We were also trying to stay abreast of the flood of new sounds that were becoming popular and pushing the old music aside. "Rags to Riches," sung by a newcomer named Tony Bennett in an incredibly high tenor voice, and "Love Is a Many Splendored Thing," sung by the Four Aces, were added to our group, and Jay sang them with great feeling to the ladies in our audiences. We turned "Secret Love," performed by Doris Day, into a multi-keyed jazz instrumental. "Oh, My Papa" by Eddie Fisher, "Vaya con Dios" by Les Paul and Mary Ford, "Tennessee Waltz" by Miss Patti Page, and a ditty called "Sh-Boom" by the Crew-Cuts—a little preview of the future—were nice, but not for us.

Louis Armstrong's "Mack the Knife" suited us fine, and at the same time, a little Latin music was creeping in around the edges, with the likes of "Cherry Pink and Apple Blossom White" by Perez Prado. Lee, our new sax player, with his beauty of sound, really sold this tune to our audience. We also drew from a goldmine of other hits: "Chances Are," sung by a very original vocal stylist named Johnny Mathis; a beautiful love song called "Blue Velvet," sung by Bobby Vinton; and "Unchained Melody," a spectacular comeback offering by my old pal, Al Hibbler, from the sound track to *Unchained.* "Canadian Sunset," a hit piano solo by Eddie Heywood, became one of my features, and last but not least, a catchy tune by that rotund music maker from down in the Big Easy, Fats Domino's "Blueberry Hill," topped off our choices.

We never performed these songs as pop tunes. Perish the thought! We always played jazz solos on them all, fast or slow, using the coat of many colors of jazz and altering the changes and progressions at will, making a whole new music even out of the new music.

* * *

In the middle of all this shufflin' and scufflin' and pickin' and choosin', M'Ma took a cab and rode in the pouring rain up the hill to Jay's mama's house.

I opened the door when she knocked, and there she stood, shaking her dripping umbrella. I was stunned to see her. She pushed past me, and Jay's mama greeted her with delight. She made some tea, chattering away with M'Ma. I just sat there at Jay's mama's dining table, mute and miserable.

Finally, M'Ma could be polite no longer. She shoved back her chair, leaped to her feet, and yelled, "WHERE IS YO' BABY?" Jay's mama smiled slyly, picked up the cups and saucers, then went into the kitchen. I didn't know who had told M'Ma about the baby; all I knew was that it hadn't been me!

I stood up, knees knocking, and led M'Ma into the bedroom where Shirley was sleeping peacefully, smiles playing around her little mouth. M'Ma leaned over the crib and "ooohed" and "aahed" and clucked and finally sat down on the bed beside me. Her copper-colored face was full of pain. "Why didn't you tell me?"

I swallowed hard. "You remember when I came home to have the operation for the tumor? She nodded, her hands clasping and unclasping. "Well, the tumor turned out to be Shirley!" Then, like a dam bursting, the whole story spilled out—the doctors' (three of them!) misdiagnoses, little time to prepare, M'Da's ordering me to leave while she was in the kitchen, and his hopes that *all* of us kids would get out as soon as possible.

M'Ma sprang to her feet, clenched her fists, and finally hissed through lips that had disappeared altogether, "THAT . . . THAT . . . NIGGER!" I was shocked past my socks, clear down to the basement. That word was not *ever* to be used in our family. M'Ma sat down and seemed to be gathering her composure.

Finally, clearing her throat, she murmured softly, "Well, what's done is done. But I must tell you about your brother Jerry. He's home, and he's a nervous wreck. He stares out into space, and then, out of the blue, he'll say 'They just kept on comin', and they died, an' they kept pilin' them up like cordwood.' "

She paused. My mouth was open with complete wonder; I couldn't muster even a gasp of disbelief. "You said Shakespeare is leaving yo' band? I want you to consider taking Jerry with you." She smiled, held up one hand to stave off any comments on my part. "Oh, he's a good player, he told me he played at the officers' clubs—showed me pictures—"

A light came on in my brain. "Oh man, oh man, oh man! That's a great idea! He was good before we left, he can't be anything but better now."

"I'll make a deal with you," M'Ma continued. "Jay's mama is getting too old to care for a lively child. I'll share Shirley's care with her, and when the time comes, I'll come up and get her, and she can grow up with the little boys. Jo-Anne is going away to study music at a Methodist college, so there'll be plenty room." She looked at me intently. "You take care of mine, and I'll take care of yours."

"Well," I smiled, relief flooding over my whole body, "I took care of the bottom of him when he was little, so I guess I can take care of the top of him now that he's big!" We laughed together, sitting close together on a bed, two women smiling at each other, understanding each other, as equals.

Then her expression changed, the look in her eyes grew hard. "I will take care of yo' father!" And so it was.

* * *

Jerry fit in the band like a hand in a glove. He was a marvelous player, much more modern than Shakespeare (Jerry's idol was Percy Heath). He possessed a real basso voice, and could play and sing songs like "Ol' Man River" at a really fast tempo and not drop a stitch. He was also featured on a cute Nellie Lutcher tune called "Fine Brown Frame." He had really long, strong fingers with corns on them that he had cultivated and maintained, so he had a very good solid sound. And he was left-handed, which really intrigued the musicians who came in to check us out.

M'Ma helped us get new uniforms, and we were all set. And not a moment too soon! My stash of money was getting mighty low. We said our good-byes to Shakespeare, and then he and the old days were gone. The new days, with all our hopes, dreams, and wishes, were waiting just around the corner.

Way up in God's country!

Triumph, Tragedy, Turmoil, and Tenor Players

. . . .

*G*od's country was Canada—north, south, east, and west. And the operating words were "acknowledgement" and "acceptance." Canadians looked at me, not around, over, or through me! It was marvelous how much this simple human contact filled up my soul. The schoolchildren would spot me on the street, their faces wreathed in smiles, and say, "Hello, brown lady!" It's hard to describe how it felt to be somebody on *and* off the stage. None of us ever took it for granted.

We always performed at hotels where we each had a nice room with maid service. Breakfast and dinner were thrown in—free.

The weather meant nothing to these big-hearted people. When it was forty-one degrees below zero, they had to keep their car batteries in their homes. But it never stopped them from coming to see us perform. The joint stayed packed every night and during the Saturday afternoon matinee, which was mainly for women shoppers. They would pile into the room, put their shopping bags beside their chairs, and order up! Women weren't allowed to sit at most bars. They drank mostly ale, Guinness stout, and gin and tonics. Black Cat cigarette smoke filled the air.

These women seemed to absorb straight-ahead jazz and improvisation more easily than the men—I don't know why—applauding and stomping their feet after solos and unabashedly singing along on "Blueberry Hill."

Jerry began to relax more and more. Even so, many a night after the gig, he would sit in the big ol' brown armchair in my room and read until morning, long legs stretched out and crossed at the ankles. I would lie in bed and listen to my shortwave radio. Symphony Sid and Morry Bloom, famous jazz disc jockeys, pumped out all the latest, and the earliest, jazz music. Occasionally, I'd tease Jerry about "Too-Loose"-Lautrec and all the other depressing heroes residing in his favorite books.

Sometimes Jerry and I would take in a flick, although you had to stand up every time the queen showed up on a newsreel or somebody in the movie played "God Save the Queen." Jay and Lee made it a habit to lose themselves until just before showtime.

Our work permits allowed us to stay in Canada only about nine months a year; then we had to leave the country for three months, after which we could return. Our agent made sure we had gigs in the United States— usually in Buffalo, New York—for the three months we were away from Canada.

The next four years were spent gigging in Toronto, Ontario; London, Ontario; Niagara Falls, Ontario; Montreal, Quebec; Sherbrooke, Quebec; and Quebec City, where we once appeared at the Latour Arena on the same bill with a vibraphonist duo, a Hungarian father and his nine-year-old son, who played the instrument backwards; a troupe of monkeys that pedaled tricycles and jumped rope; and nine violinists who only spoke French and had been hired to play Illinois Jacquet's "Flying Home" with a tenor sax player named "Big" Bill Moore, who was in tears because he had requested nine musicians (a rhythm section and six horns). We taught the violinists the riffs—they were delighted—and played with Big Bill on the tune. In return, he played on ours and did battle with Lee, our tenor player. The crowd went wild. He was really grateful, and became our ace boon coon!

We really lived the good life in Canada. Big time!

Buffalo, New York, was like night to Toronto's day. It was ninety miles from Toronto. We tore down the Queens Highway in ninety minutes straight into an amazing scene.

First of all, Bethlehem Steel was king! We arrived around two a.m. on Sunday morning, but the streets were full of cars and people. Folks stopped their cars in the middle of the street to start a conversation. We were amazed to see barbeque bones flying out of car windows. Music blared from everywhere, ribs were turning on spits in the windows of restaurants, and afterhours clubs were packed with show folks and civilians. It was like Howard Street in Akron, only bigger and bolder. Lights were flashing, and people looked spit-shiny and sported all the latest threads. And people talked loud; no murmuring in this town.

This was our first impression of that big ol' brawling, rusty-butt steel town embracing the banks of the Niagara River, just across the Peace Bridge from Canada.

In Buffalo, we played at a club deep in the Negro section. We were the house band, backing such performers as Mabel "Big Maybelle" Smith, a sweet-faced, huge chocolate mountain of a woman, who wore long black gloves to cover up the heroin tracks on her huge arms. She had a major hit with "Baby, Please Don't Go" and a torch tune called "Candy." We also backed Dakota Staton, a really fine-looking brown-skinned woman with a lilting vocal style. She had a hit with "Broadway," and nobody could out-sing her on "Funny Valentine." She always tried to jive us by saying, "I'm sorry, could you just try to pick it up if I hum it? I left my music on the plane." (Every time?)

We played for T-Bone Walker, a real gentleman, always polite, dressed in a white shirt, black suit, and tie. He played jazz and blues on his guitar, cracking up the audience, declaring in song, "Woman, you must be crazy . . . !" His composition "Stormy Monday Blues" was his signature song, and artists all over the world were singing it. T-Bone was great fun, but he had one troubling problem. He dearly loved his "nephew." He taught him to play guitar just like himself and insisted that the young man appear with him. But the kid couldn't keep time. He jumped meter and leaped across musical bar lines like a frog. We had a hard time keeping him sounding coherent. But we tried because we had the greatest respect for T-Bone. But we felt sad for him because we knew the kid would never be able to carry his torch.

Jimmy Rushing played the club. Dubbed "Mr. Five by Five" (because he was so short and stout!), he was known all over the world as the vocalist with the Count Basie Orchestra. He also played excellent piano. We also backed Little Jimmy Scott, a small-boned light-skinned man with an uncanny voice and style; he hung far back on the beat and made a hymn out of "When Did You Leave Heaven?"

Many of the famous and not so famous played the club: Bo Diddley, a born hit maker with "Bo Diddley," his signature song, and "I'm a Man" a close second, sung in his strong, rough-hewn voice that soared over driving, hypnotic back-country rhythms; the Drifters; the Turbans, who had a runaway hit that caught them so much by surprise that they were still trying to learn to tie their turbans on their heads so they wouldn't unravel and fall off while they were performing; the Swallows and the Robins, shy, young, one-hit wonders.

"It's ring-around-the-rosey for them!" Jerry was hard but fair, oh Lord.

"Yeah, the promoters gonna get all their money; they all gonna go home broke!" Jay mused.

Then came Willie Mabon with "I Don't Know." Willie didn't know any other song, so we had to fill out his show by featuring ourselves. Paralleling the jazz and pop singers, the "bird" groups were beginning to become popular, along with soul singers like Ray Charles, drowning in his own tears.

* * *

"What is it about sax players?" I complained to Jay and Jerry. "They're just like lightning rods attracting trouble. Lee always seems to fall in lust with women with black eyes. And I don't mean the color!"

"Yeah," Jerry mused, "How 'bout that lady wrestler from Calgary who mopped up his hotel room with his body in Toronto?"

I grinned. "When the Mounties came and broke that one up, I thought we were gonna be deported."

"She looked just like Man Mountain Dean!" Jay needn't have been quite so critical; he seemed to love big fat women himself.

Jerry laughed, then in a high, feminine voice he mimicked the excuse the lady wrestler had given the Mounties: "He said he didn't love me anymore."

"Talkin' 'bout a man," I sang, "kept his hat on all night long. / 'Twas a signal to the women that he'd *soon* be movin' on!"

We all snickered. But our laughter soon turned to dismay.

Lee got in trouble again—this time with a big yellow girl who wore baby blue baby doll shoes. She came into the club where we were backing Sonny Til and the Orioles, and, yes, she had one black eye. Someone had closed it with a fist. Lee left the club with her that night, and they became an item. But love faded much too soon. And when Miss Baby Blue Shoes hung Lee out a third-story window by his feet, the cops had to talk her into pulling him back into the room to safety. For an encore, we had to rush him to the emergency room after another woman bloodied up his face with a "diamond" ring—a gift from Lee—that turned out to be glass!

He decided to go back home to Akron. The bright lights of show business seemed to blind the poor boy to anything close to real, true love.

Our next sax player was from Buffalo. We took him to Toronto to play in a hotel with a restaurant that featured prime-rib dinners. We were given free dinner privileges, but the sax player would eat two or three prime ribs! The owner had to cut him off—to our great embarrassment—so he ate salmon while we ate prime rib. He fell in love with a beauty queen with long blonde hair and innocent eyes. She fell for his soulful tenor playing, so she gave him the gift that keeps on giving—the clap. Three times! After the third time, the doctor said, "Lads, this is moral turpitude. You can get deported, you know. I won't report this, but don't ever come back to this office again!" After we got back to Buffalo, we gave the cat notice and sent him on his way.

The next sax player was from Baltimore, just passing through Buffalo. He had a wife who stole things. She stole a frozen turkey from the market, stashed it between her legs under her long skirt, bought some chewing gum, and walked out.

She invited us to Thanksgiving dinner.

Her husband, an outstanding tenor player, had recorded with some famous New York cats, but after we went back to Toronto (without his wife, thank God!), we found that at every full moon he would go into a trance. He'd sit in his hotel room for two or three days and not move.

Becoming a trio every month was worse than having your period!

Our time away from Toronto came around again, so we were booked into Newport, Rhode Island, to play a joint that catered to nothing but sailors. A little Greek man about five feet tall ran the club. It was a hard job. Every week, the boss booked a blonde, country-and-western lady vocalist and a shake dancer. They came from Boston, though they were billed as "straight from Texas and New York City." The singers couldn't sing and the dancers couldn't shake. The owner went berserk at rehearsal and ordered us, "Show her how to bump and grind! Bump an' grind, I say!"

The sax player declined by going into a trance, so it was left up to Jay. And he did a remarkable job in a short period of time. He told the dancer to pretend to have three long strings hanging from her mouth, a carrot tied to one, a string bean tied to the second, and a coffee bean tied to the third.

"Pretend to hit the carrot with your, er, your pelvis," he instructed. "Then pretend to hit the string bean." We watched in wonder. "Hit the carrot! Hit the string bean!" The girl's hips were swinging like an unlatched gate in a high wind.

"What about the coffee bean?" I asked.

Jay was determined to transform the girl into a shake dancer; our job (picking up the option for an extra two weeks) depended on it. "You'll see," he said.

He faced the girl, who stood waiting and eager, her red hair wet with perspiration. "Okay! You ready now? Hit the carrot! Hit the string bean! Now," Jay yelled, "GRIND THAT COFFEE!"

It worked. The girl tore up the place, and the sailors threw their white caps up in the air! Jay had saved the day.

The admiral came to the club, fell in love with our group, and invited us aboard his aircraft carrier for lunch. Doris Duke, the millionairess, invited the admiral to lunch at her big ol' estate, and he brought us along, just for fun.

But playing seven nights a week became a real downer. We needed one day to recharge. I could tell that the cats were getting too wound up, but we had two weeks to go before we could take a much-needed break.

One night after work, walking the empty streets of Newport and trying to reduce the tension so we could have a good night's sleep, Jerry, the sax player, and I stopped in front of a music store to check out the instruments displayed in the window. Jerry and the sax man had been drinking cognac all night. (The sailors bought the band plenty of drinks.) Suddenly, Jerry whispered, "They're all around us!"

"Who?" The sax player turned and scanned the street.

"They're comin' over the ridge!" Jerry dropped to one knee and threw a punch right through the plate-glass window!

Blood was everywhere. I yanked off my scarf and wrapped it tightly around Jerry's hand. Then the sax player and I took him under his arms and, somehow, got onto the main drag, where we were lucky to get a cab. We rushed him to the emergency room at the nearby hospital.

The whole scene at the hospital felt surrealistic. Everything seemed to be moving in slow motion, and the voices sounded far, far away. Nurses and doctors swirled around, barking orders. When I told them I thought Jerry had had a flashback to the Korean War, the doctors were kind and gentle. Having to deal with sailors every day, they knew exactly what to do.

I felt faint and my eyes began to blur. To steady myself, I held onto the sax player's arm and stared at the long hair growing out of the head nurse's chin—it was only one hair, why didn't she tweeze it out? I closed my eyes and shook my head. Nothing to do but wait, and pray.

They stitched up Jerry's hand—thirteen stitches—but were really concerned about one of his tendons. We all feared that he might not ever play again. Lawd! Lawd! Lawd! We watched Jerry come back from the hell in his head to the emergency room in Newport. He smiled his slow, beautiful smile and said, "Hey, how long this train been gone?"

"Long enough, little brother, long enough."

We took him back to the hotel and put him to bed. Then I made arrangements through our boss to pay for the window.

That night during our show, I called on the spirit of every piano player who taught me everything I know. I walked the bass line and played boogie-woogie and stride piano to make up for the missing bass. Jay steadied the rhythm by using four beats to a measure on his bass drum, just as musicians played long ago, before there was a bass fiddle.

The sax man called one of his Baltimore bass-playing buddies in to finish the gig, and Jerry took time off to walk down by the water and sit on the dock and watch the big ships sail on by. O Lawdy! I trembled many a night after that to think how close I had come to breaking the promise I had made to M'Ma to take good care of her baby while she took good care of mine!

We were really happy with our next sax player! Tommy Turrentine, a fine jazz trumpet player, composed and arranged a song called "T's Tune" for our group, then asked if we would please take his younger brother, Stanley, a gifted sax player, with us to Milford, Maine, so he wouldn't get sucked into the drug scene in Pittsburgh.

Milford was a village so small that the mailman, postman, and the policeman were the same man. He changed his hat for each job, but drove the same long black automobile. The village was a resort for bear hunters. Right after the swarms of black flies disappeared in September, hunting season began, and swarms of hunters appeared.

After we settled in, the waitress, a middle-aged bottle blonde, tall and rangy, always quick with a quip, asked us, "Do you guys swing?"

"Well, I hope so!" I replied.

"I mean *swing!*"

"Ev'ry time we perform." I assured her.

She looked at us sharply. It was after hours in the club, and we were waiting for "Charlie," the chef, to fix us some broiled chicken to take to our rooms. She tossed her hair, sighed, and impatiently tapped her long red nails on the table. "Swinging here in Milford is our village pastime." Her tone belonged to a teacher of three-year-olds, overly patient and long-suffering. "We have a party and throw our house keys in a hat. Then we go home with whoever pulls out our key.

"Naw, we don't play that."

"Well, you don't know what you're missin'!" She giggled. "We had to stop for a while five years ago 'cause a young red-haired man came to town an' we had a high old time—till red-haired babies started showing up." Our mouths dropped open in amazement. "Yeah, two, three, of the little buggers! So that kinda put a damper on things."

Whoa! "Thanks, but no thanks!"

We took our chicken and hurried to the safety of our rooms. Red-haired babies are one thing; Negro babies are another!

We resumed our swingin' *on* the bandstand, but the sax curse struck again!

Uncle Sam found Stanley Turrentine way up north in bear-hunting country, where Stanley's draft notice finally caught up with him, and marched him and his sax straight into the U.S. Army!

Back in Toronto, we set up shop again with a tenor player named Bill Forte, from Memphis, Tennessee. His habits shook up the bartender. Every morning he would go to the bar and order a shot of everything white or clear: gin, peppermint schnapps, white vermouth, vodka, and white rum. Then he'd down them one by one, wipe his mouth with the back of his hand, and leave. That was his breakfast!

"He makes me bloody nervous!" the bartender would complain to us every single night. "He plays music most beautiful, but he doesn't seem to know what he's all *aboot!*"

A ray of sunshine through all this was that Jerry's hand healed like brand-new. Thank God!

But things were changing fast. The queen came to Canada, did a square dance, and changed the whole music scene in all the provinces except Quebec, of course. Cowboys and hillbillies came out of the United States in droves and took over. In fact, we had to appear on the same bill with many of them. Most were from New Jersey, but that didn't seem to matter.

"Look, cats, things ain't what they used to be. We gonna have to find a new track to run on." I really felt a sense of finality. The scene was over.

That last Saturday night we drove ninety miles in ninety minutes down the Queens Highway, down to Buffalo, to a smart new supper club where they were holding jam sessions all night and serving ham and eggs, sausages and biscuits, fried chicken and waffles, and Bloody Marys. Jerry, Jay, and I sat in as a group and did our stuff, and the people went wild. The two bosses put their heads together and hired us on the spot.

It had been a great ride, the last four years: all-white audiences in Toronto, all-black audiences in Buffalo, but we played the same music for both. Weird and wonderful!

But it had been a little lonely for both Jerry and me. In fact, I had not even thought about needing or wanting a man-friend. We were just too busy. But on a fluke, completely out of the blue, when I wasn't even looking, I found my own true love!

A Little Love Song

· · · · · · · · · · · · · · · · · · · ·

The moment I met my man
I loved him from the start—
That's when a little bitty blue bird
Flew—into—my heart.

The supper club was dimly lit; the smell of stale cigarettes and beer hung heavy in the air. The jukebox was turned way down low, playing "Do not disturb the hangovers" music: "Sweet Sixteen Bars," gospel-tinged blues in 6/8 time by Ray Charles.

The bartender was getting the place ready for the night, washing glasses, chopping ice, and polishing mirrors that reflected a blue neon sign that said "Schlitz Beer" behind the long, curved wooden bar. His eyes hung at half-mast as he went about his familiar tasks, humming and whistling through his teeth. It was the afternoon after the night before, and Jerry, Jay, and I were in the showroom on stage, waiting to rehearse the new show person.

We were always on time. That way when the show person would show up late, apologizing all over the place, we already had the upper hand. That was how we maintained the balance of power, and, believe me, there was always that struggle.

Then suddenly HE appeared in the doorway of the darkened showroom, and we watched as he walked quickly and gracefully between the tables and chairs already in place for the evening's performance. Trailing behind him with slow, measured steps, pelvis thrust slightly forward, came a tall shapely woman. Her skin was the color of cocoa topped with melted marshmallows. She had Orphan Annie eyes, her lips were covered with Max Factor Cherry Red lipstick, and her black brows were heavily penciled into a shape of permanent dismay.

The man, wiry and well-proportioned, carried some weight in his wide, wide shoulders. Large fierce black eyes fringed by long lashes dominated the face they shared with a small nose and a neat black mustache. Stern lips hid a friendly gap in his top front teeth. A dark beret covered his coal black hair. The impressive shoulders were draped in a striking, elephant-eared hand-tailored tan jacket.

He placed his brown valise on the front table, snapped it open, and quickly began passing out arrangements to each of us while the woman intoned in a deep contralto voice, "This is my music director, Jimmy Cheatham, and I . . . I am Miss D!" Then, "Sorry we're late."

We introduced ourselves, but the woman's music director hardly acknowledged the introductions. Impatient, he snapped his fingers and said, "Take it from the left hand corner!"

Now, what he had handed us wasn't lead sheets (simple guides with words, lead lines, and chord symbols). Mister Cheatham had prepared piano-conductor scores, which are written in an orchestral style, filling both hands with the exact sound of a big band. The bass part was complex, to be played pizzicato and bowed, and the drum parts were meticulous.

Well, we cut through the music like a hot knife through butter. We really showed off, both because we were good musicians and because we were delighted to have music that challenged our prowess. And the arranging was brilliant. This man had found the soul of the song and had married it to the soul of the singer.

The music director's eyes opened in disbelief, then narrowed as he snapped his fingers and stomped off the next song. "He's all business during business hours, I see," I murmured to myself. Glancing up from the keyboard, my eyes met his, and, I swear, I felt a sharp electric current sizzle through my whole body. I shook myself, dragged my eyes back to the music. What the heck was that?

We romped through the whole show, and when it was done, I turned to compliment the vocalist, who really had a remarkable voice and presentation. She opened her show in the back of the room (just like Big Maybelle Smith), singing without a mike until she came up onstage to finish the song (the same song sung by Big Maybelle Smith), "Why Was I Born?"

Miss D most often spoke of herself in the third person. "Well, she thanks you for the compliment. She is very pleased!" Very weird.

I turned to compliment the music director, but he had taken his brown valise and disappeared out the door and into the street. I was surprised at how disappointed I felt. I looked for him that night, but he didn't show up for Miss D's opening.

After the last show, Jerry and I took a cab back to the flat we had rented together in Cold Springs. As the cab passed the Colored Musician's Club on Broadway, I saw him! There on the sidewalk, lit up by the lights of Gerald's Restaurant, the after-gig hangout for show folks, he was standing with a bunch of cats all dressed in identical dark suits. Oh, he had a gig tonight—that's why he was a no-show.

I watched him as our cab idled at the red light. He stood a little apart from the other musicians, smiling slightly, one foot planted slightly in front of the other. He wore beautiful navy loafers with tassels on the toes. My heart leaped into my throat, then started pounding. As the cab pulled away, my head swiveled to keep him in sight.

What in the world is wrong with me?

Jerry's eyes were closed, his head resting on the back of the seat. He didn't notice anything.

At our pad, I pushed past Jerry and into my room. "Night, Sis," he called. "Night, Bro!"

Sleep hovered out of reach. I tossed and turned. Finally, exhausted in mind and body, I fell asleep, deep and hard, and dreamed. In the dream, the one-armed man played heart music, just as he had played so long ago, back home on Bina Avenue.

> *He wrapped his little bluebird wings*
> *Around my beating heart*
> *He nestled way down inside me*
> *Just happy as a lark!*

The next morning I awoke, and the musical perfectionist in the tasseled loafers was still there—on my mind! I jumped out of bed and raged at the woman reflected in my mirror. "I don't want any more complications in my life! I don't want nobody! I don't need nobody! I'm not lookin' for nobody!"

A still small voice deep down inside replied, "I knew him before I was, and I'll remember him after I am not!"

Shaken, I called my friend Rose. She and I had become friends when our group first arrived at the supper club from Toronto. She was as dark as a blue-black evening sky, with almond-shaped eyes and a heart-shaped face. I think King Solomon was thinking of a woman just like Rose when he wrote (in the voice of a woman), "I am black, but comely, O ye daughters of Jerusalem!" Her great figure and her sensuous walk turned heads wherever she went. She didn't have many women friends; because she was so striking, she made a whole lot of women feel dull and dowdy. But Rose and I hit it off right from the start. She had a son around eight years old and a little girl near Shirley's age. Whenever Shirley came to stay with me, Rose acted as babysitter.

"Rose!" I took a jitney cab over to her house and burst in, breathless and excited. "I saw this cat," I blurted out. "He's really somethin' else—and I don't know what to do about it!"

"Hold on!" Rose laughed. "Sit down an' let's have some tea." We did what women do the world over when a new man comes along. I mean, we chewed the fat about him until all the grease was gone! Finally, Rose asked, "So, what are you gonna do about him?"

I shook my head in despair. "I don't wanna do anything; I don't wanna feel this way, neither!"

"You already do. So I'll ask around and find out what I can about him, then we'll take the next step."

"Okay," I answered, not sure I wanted her to investigate, not sure I didn't.

A couple of days later, on a Sunday evening, Rose called me. "It's your night off, and we're goin' out on the town."

"Oh, noooooo!" I wailed. I was comfortable in my jammies and curlers.

"Oh, yessssssss!" she laughed.

We decided to wear flame red: Rose in a tight-waisted satin coatdress, and I flaunting a Lili Ann two-piece suit with a petal peplum.

We arrived at the Colored Musicians Club, climbed the steep wooden stairs, rang the bell, and waited for someone to look through the peephole and let us in. We knew we were as sharp as Gillette razor blades: two brazen, dark babes in flamin' red. We stopped just inside the door to see and be seen.

The joint was packed with jazz lovers. The stage was full of cats from all over—Cleveland and Erie and Pittsburgh—jamming away on "All The Things You Are." As we seated ourselves at the end of the bar, I saw him standing by the piano, gleaming trombone silent in his hands, head down, eyes closed, listening intently to a sax player who was telling a story about a place where we had all hung out. I was distracted momentarily. The music was really romping, and my every instinct was to focus completely on the happenings on the stage, where the cats were really takin' care of business. Reluctantly, I dragged my attention back to the business at hand.

Thick smoke from Pall Malls, Chesterfields, Camels, and stogies floated halfway between the tables and the ceiling, weaving ever-changing patterns in the air. Faces turned in our direction. Speculating eyes watched Rose and me as we settled ourselves onto the barstools, crossed our legs, and pointed our toes. We ordered drinks—gin and tonics—sat back, lit cigarettes, sipped, and studied HIM. Boy, was he into the music!

"Humm," Rose exclaimed, "I see what you mean!" She teased, "If you don't want him, I might take a chance."

The waitress—a sturdy, attractive woman—came over and introduced herself as Evelyn. "You-all new in town?"

Rose answered, "No, just new in this club."

"Me, too," I said. "Ah, can you do me a favor?"

She smiled at me and bristled at Rose. "What is it?"

"See that cat over by the piano, the guy with the trombone, wearing the dark beret?"

Evelyn peered through the smoke. "Oh, you mean Jimmy Cheatham?"

"Yes!" I paused.

Then Evelyn revealed some information that Rose hadn't gathered. "He's been in California, in school, and just got back."

"Take him whatever he drinks," I said, suddenly bold.

"That would be gin and tonic or sometimes a new drink called a screwdriver—vodka and orange juice—from California. Sometimes he drinks cognac." Evelyn seemed enthusiastic about the topic of conversation.

"Well, send him some gin!"

We watched as she wended her way through the tables and broke into his reverie. We watched as he looked up at us while she spoke and shook his head no.

Evelyn made her way back to us, the gin and tonic untouched on her tray. "He said he didn't care for anything." She grinned.

"Take it right back!" I was imperious. Not many men had said no to me for lo, these many years. "Tell him to drink it, or wear it!"

Evelyn's eyes gleamed, "All right. Here I go!"

Back through the crowded tables she trudged as the music became more intense and the people more excited. Two tenor players were challenging each other, playing four measures apiece—a real musical duel. The bass player laid a solid carpet underneath the sax players; the piano darted in and out, chords adding spice to the mix; the drummer's sticks sounded like a machine gun before a phrase, then added exclamation points after the phrase was done. People started yelling, "Go 'head! Go 'head!" It was a lively backdrop for the light-hearted duel between the music director and me.

Rose and I watched intently as Evelyn sidled back over to the music director and spoke to him. He looked startled, then threw his head back and laughed. He accepted the gin and tonic, raised it in a salute to me, made a courtly bow, and took a sip. Evelyn trotted back over to us, grinning from ear to ear, and exclaimed, "Now, that's the way to meet a man!"

Rose said, "Let's go!"

"What?"

"Leave him curious! C'mon! He teaches downstairs in the Union Hall during the day. You can connect with him there, in private, in a couple days." I obeyed her. Rose was a "nat'chell born" courtesan, wise in the ways of the world, and wise in the ways of men and women.

I went to bed thinking of him. I woke up Monday morning still thinking of him. At noon I dressed up in a copper-colored cotton dress with a short, waist-length jacket. The skirt belled out like a flower, and a crinoline petticoat peeked out from under the skirt, modest but enticing. I slid my feet into high-heeled pumps fastened with thin straps that drew attention to my slim ankles. The shoes were the exact shade of the dress. For the pièce de résistance, I carried a little umbrella that also matched the copper shade.

I took a jitney cab down to the Colored Musicians Club and Union and walked right in. I greeted the president, who was a friend of mine, and marched into the rehearsal hall. He was sitting at the old upright piano, writing music. The front of the piano was mirrored, so he spied me the moment I entered the room. "Yes?" His voice was crisp and business-like.

"Do you teach trombone?" I queried, my voice a little breathy.

"Hm-mm-yes, why do you ask?"

"I thought I'd like to take a few lessons." The moment the words left my mouth, I could have kicked myself. I should have just said "like," not "thought."

He laughed, his eyes crinkling at the corners. O Lawdy! He had dimples in both cheeks.

"You? As small as you are, you'd go right through the slide!"

I bristled. "Wanna bet?"

"Yeah!" His horn rested on a stand in the corner of the room. He strolled over and picked it up. "C'mon!" he challenged, his tone derisive, "hit me a B-flat."

I took the trombone from him, wiped the lipstick off my mouth with my hanky, put the mouthpiece up to my lips, and blew a perfect B-flat.

His eyes narrowed, then opened wide as I hit another one, and another. I knew he wanted to ask where I had learned to push clear sounds out of the awkward instrument. It was one of the residuals left from my brief sojourn at the University of Akron: I had had to learn brass, strings, and piano, plus ear training, to qualify as a music teacher. God knows how I remembered the technique after so many years, but I just could not let that man beat me!

He eased the trombone out of my hands. "Come to the piano." I sat down and arranged my wide skirt demurely over the piano stool. "Play this!" He opened a book of Czerny compositions.

"No problem," I murmured, then marched my fingers nimbly through the piece.

His dark eyes twinkled. "Play this." A book opened to Bach's Two- and Three-part Inventions.

"No problem," I trilled. And it wasn't.

"Well," he stood back, one hand on his hip.

I remembered what Rose had taught me. "Well, I must be going now!" I slid off the piano stool, patted my skirt into place, and picked up the precisely matched, copper-colored pièce de résistance.

I was halfway across the room before he had gathered his wits enough to call after me. "Wait! What about the trombone lessons?" I waved good-bye, and I and my umbrella waltzed out of the rehearsal hall—my heart beating fast, but singing a happy song.

* * *

Ordinary days turned into magic, and the nights, ordinarily filled with daring feats of music and entertainment, no longer became the end of the evening, but the beginning of my time spent with Jimmy. We began to meet casually after our gigs and hang out at Gerald's Restaurant.

There we sat in a booth, plates of eggs growing cold, listening intently to the jukebox while a new artist named Benny Golson played his behind off on a new tune called "Along Came Betty." Eyes closed, heads bobbing, we laughed out loud at some delicious phrase spinning out of the soul of Benny Golson. This was better than sipping blackberry wine. Sharing the music was heady and heart filling.

The one consistent complaint civilians make about artists is that in the midst of everyday conversation about everyday matters, the artist is always listening and responding to color and sound—a church bell, a bird's song, a buttermilk sky. Away they fly (the artists), leaving the exasperated civilians to exclaim, "Are you listening to me?" and, bitterly, "There's no there, there!"

Wives of musicians complain to the men they married (because they yearned to touch the magic they saw onstage), "There you go again, ga-loompin' off in your head to only God knows where!" The musicians reply to themselves wearily, "Even a *broken* clock is right twice a day. You're right! Only God *does* know!"

Lawd, it's so hard to explain that you are born hearing color and seeing sound. "It's just like breathin' out and breathin' in," Shakespeare used to explain to the blank faces on his lady friends.

A German scientist in Toronto, for whom we played the opening music, gave a lecture about primal relationships: "The iris of the eye contains elements that either attract or repel when meeting another iris." He declared, "The iris that repels cannot look straight into the iris of the other person. Therefore, there will be no lasting relationship! The iris that attracts another iris can look deep and long into the other person's eyes. In this case, there will be a long-lasting relationship."

On my nights off, Jimmy and I gazed into each other's eyes hour after hour over late steak dinners at a historical little hideaway restaurant by the railroad tracks called Ann Montgomery's. We ate clams oreganato on the west side at Frank and Theresa's Italian restaurant. We finished each other's sentences and laughed until the tears came when we said the same words at the same time. I felt as if the sky was bluer, the grass looked greener, and the air smelled sweeter. I felt that all my senses were heightened, lengthened, and deepened.

"Gimme your hand!" He would say as we crossed the busy streets, and he would admonish, "You make me feel like you gonna step right out into the traffic!" Of course, I wasn't going to do any such thing. But, Lawd, didn't it feel wonderful not to have to be in charge!

Great-Gramma Lizzie told us long, long ago, that some African tribes and slaves would have the females run up and sniff the armpits of their intended. If she could survive this test, she could survive anything! Well, Jimmy Cheatham was always as clean as a chitlin, so I guess things were copacetic.

I began to go down to the rehearsal hall and accompany some of the vocalists he coached and built acts for. He was mercurial: fierce and gentle, stern and soft, but never, ever boring! Both of us understood, and never resented, our need for alone time to replenish and rewire the ever-probing antennae fueling our creative juices. Glory!

Summer was almost gone, but the fire between us never wavered. It burned brighter than bright, and things were beginning to really feel all right!

* * *

"I'm gonna take you to a place," he declared one afternoon after his clients had departed. "I'm gonna take you to my secret place."

I held my breath, and it slowly dawned on me: I was being courted. A good old-fashioned courtship. I was thrilled, but torn; I knew we would soon have to move on down the line. Our contract had been renewed over and over, but now it was almost time to go.

His secret place was in a park, in a small hidden glen: beautiful old trees spread their limbs over green grass bordered by flowers, and a little pond sparkled nearby. Birds sang and butterflies fluttered around, their wings a sudden burst of color against the old trees. It felt as peaceful as a cathedral there, looking up, up past the sheltering branches to the sky.

And there we sat and talked and talked about our hopes, dreams, and wishes. I told him about my little girl and the never-ending pain of being away from her so much of the time. He told me of having to leave Hollywood for Buffalo, and interrupting his steady climb toward success, because of his mother's illness.

I took a deep breath and turned toward him. "Jerry and I are thinking of leaving soon. Jay seems to be caught up with a woman, and, we aren't advancing as a group at all. We were thinking of going to California. Our agent thinks we'll do just fine as a duo, says we ought to try some of the high-class joints in Beverly Hills or even Palm Springs."

"Well," he turned his head and looked up at the sky, "if that's the way it is, that's the way it is."

I pulled my knees up to my chin. It was quiet except for the birds' occasional burst of song and something splashing in the pond. "So . . ." I said in a little voice, "maybe we'll meet again in Hollywood."

"Um-m." He looked at the ground.

I stood up. "Well, I guess I better get back to my crib. I'm expecting a long-distance call from the agent."

All of a sudden, I felt pain! As if all the air went whoosh! right out of my body. I closed my eyes and got lost. The sheltering grove had disappeared. I was rushing through a long dark tunnel. I felt alone, and terribly frightened. I started walking ahead of him out of the grove, faster and faster. Then I turned and came back. I gazed up at him. "I dunno! I just dunno!" My voice broke. "Since I met you I haven't been able to sing my blues the same way and make people cry!" I tried to laugh, but the laughter caught in my throat.

"Well, take your pick," he said softly, his black eyes luminous.

"I just can't—I just cannot leave you—I really, truly *cannot*."

We stood close together, holding hands, and everything felt all right. Then all right headed straight into wonderful. "I never wanna lose you again," he said.

Mercy!

Little Mattie, Big Mama, and the Beautiful Miss M

· · · · · · · · · · · · · · · · · ·

I been a long time comin'
From the place where I have been
Can't tell nobody why, Lawd
Can't tell nobody — when!

"Bells!"

"Lester Young," announced my new love, Jimmy, the music director, "the president of the tenor saxophone, always used this phrase."

Jimmy had enlisted in the army at age eighteen and found himself at Fort McClellan in Alabama, with the 173rd AGF (Army Ground Forces) band, in the same company as Papa Jo Jones, Chico Hamilton, and Lester Young. In fact, Chico slept on the bottom bunk and Jimmy slept on the top. They were all older than he, but they became his lifelong friends and mentors.

"Lester didn't like ugly," Jimmy continued, "he liked ev'ry thing smooth running — that's why he also used the phrase, 'Stay pretty.' " That was the way our affair tripped along, smooth and pretty. But up jumped the devil.

I knew that Miss D had big, bulging, Orphan Annie eyes for the music director, but I really was taken aback by Jay's reaction to our new romance. He woke up like Rip van Winkle after a seven-year snooze, rubbed his eyes, looked around, and realized that lo! his meal ticket had been all punched out.

We put up a good front for the audience, but the bandstand became a war zone. Jerry, who usually liked everybody, detested Miss D from the very beginning. "She should apply for a gig with a rent-a-fool company!" he declared.

Jay and Miss D formed an unholy alliance hell-bent on breaking up the music director and me. Miss D ranged far and wide with her venom, and even tried to enlist the aid of the music director's mama. But Jimmy's mama, a lovely, highly spiritual little lady, saw right through Miss D and found out that the woman had six children and a husband in another town.

Buffalo was a strange town, known to break up *all* the bands. The town was like a giant strip of flypaper: you zoomed in, got stuck, and had a hard time getting out. Everybody had an unlisted phone number.

We called Buffalo "down South, up North." It had two musician's unions, one for Negroes, one for whites. The west side was mostly Italian. The east side was mostly Polish. In between — everybody else — mostly Negroes. Part of the Underground Railroad was still evident in this section.

The Polish and Italians had one thing in common: they were all dyed-in-the-wool Catholics. That meant that any woman who wanted to be outfitted with birth control had to get past an army of Catholic doctors who had orders from headquarters not to give out any kind of artificial contraceptives. Considering what was imminently possible, I started asking around about what, when, and where to get what I needed.

One afternoon, I strolled into Adam, Meldrum, and Anderson, the best department store in town, to try on one of the new sack dresses by Balenciaga. Considered all the rage, they sold like hotcakes because they fit like a chemise and covered a multitude of sins! The saleswoman who always waited on me was also a good friend. She snickered when I told her, "The men love this new sack dress. When they see women in it, they call it goodies in a sack." Later, while trying to make up my mind between a red wool or a beige sweater-type sack dress, I confided in her about my problem with the doctors.

She said somewhat mysteriously, "I'm going to make a phone call. Wait here." Less than fifteen minutes later, back she came into the dressing room, looked around, and said loudly, "Well, have you decided which sack you want?" Then she whispered, "I'm going to give you the phone number of a doctor who can help you." I nodded, my heart beating fast. "You mustn't give this number to anyone else. Promise?" I promised. And I bought both dresses — one for day, one for night — then rushed home and called the secret number.

The doctor was a white woman who lived way out on the outskirts of town. She agreed to see me.

My friend Rose borrowed her boyfriend's car, and in the driving rain near the midnight hour, out we went to a big white house in the suburbs. There was no light shining on the porch. We rang the doorbell. After a few minutes the door opened, and we were greeted warmly by a tall elegant woman with braided white hair wrapped twice round her small head. She announced in a crisp alto voice, "Leave your umbrellas in the stand. I'm Doctor G. Which one of you needs assistance?"

Rose pointed to me. The doctor told Rose, "Have a sit-down. We won't be long. There are magazines on the table." Then the doctor motioned me through a doorway next to a table on which a single white candle burned, its flickering flame casting changing patterns on the wall.

Once inside the room I looked around, and my mouth dropped open in amazement. It was a complete operating room. The walls were painted off-white and were filled with diplomas and certificates from some of the most prestigious universities and hospitals in the East.

Her assistant was a heavyset dark-haired woman with heavy dark eyebrows. She wore a nurse's white uniform and cap. She nodded at me and intoned, "How do you do?" Her black eyes bore into mine. "We do not need to tell you that the Catholic doctors in this area will not issue birth control. We, the women of the future, believe it is every woman's right to have access to whatever she needs for her own body." She spoke with passion, though her face never changed expression. "Go behind that screen, undress, and put on this white coat, backwards."

I did as I was told, and when I emerged from behind the screen, the nurse patted the examining table and said, "Hop up here!" She covered me with a white sheet.

I was fitted with a diaphragm and instructed in its use. Then I was cautioned again not to reveal its source. The doctor placed the diaphragm in a pretty little ivory-colored container shaped like a seashell. The lid closed with a snap. I realized I'd been holding my breath, and let it out in a sigh.

I dressed as fast as I could. The doctor accepted the envelope filled with cash by turning her back, placing her hand behind her body, and wiggling her long white fingers until I placed the money firmly into her hand.

There were hugs all around. Once more, with a finger to her lips, she opened the door, and Rose and I went out into the rainy night.

We were silent as we hurtled through the darkness, listening to the rhythm of the wipers sweeping across the wet windshield. I felt elated and triumphant. I thought about Great-Gramma Lizzie admonishing us about ladylike behavior, " 'cause nobody wanted to see possible," but I felt empowered, preparing for the possibility of "possible" and contemplating the delights of nights, playin' the changes of the Kamasutra.

* * *

Little Mattie Fields, Big Mama Thornton, and the beautiful Miss M entered our lives almost simultaneously.

Miss M was a vocalist on a revolving stage in a large Main Street nightclub called the Town Casino. It was run by men with five-o'clock shadows on their faces at noon. The revolving stage held six other blondes of varying talents. They sang songs like "Two Little Girls From Little Rock," among many other pop songs.

Miss M was a tall slim Nordic woman with wide-spaced blue eyes that drooped slightly at the corners and lips that were always smiling. She wanted to get off the wheel, as it was called, in the worst way and become a headliner. She came down to the Colored Musicians Union so Jimmy could coach her vocally and create a nightclub act for her. Primarily a dancer, she possessed a pretty good June Christy–style voice. She was honest and had a great sense of humor. The three of us became good friends. She was embroiled in an intense battle with her ex-husband for custody of her little girl.

Little Mattie came down to the union one afternoon, a sweet, shiny-faced brown woman with a sturdy square body dressed in a light coat over a uniform. In her hand, she clutched a piece of paper torn from a three-ring binder; the story of her life was painfully printed on it.

"I got your name from Miss D," she said, in a shy, light, breathy voice. "She stays at the Little Harlem, where I work."

My eyes hooded when she mentioned Miss D. I realized Miss D had tried, in her own convoluted way, to get Jimmy's approval by sending him a client. Bitch!

"I wrote this poem, and I need somebody to put music to it," Little Mattie continued. Her voice grew stronger and more confident.

"Has it got a name?" I gently removed the paper from her hand and placed it on the piano. "Everybody's Happy but Me," we read. "That's a great title!"

Little Mattie smiled and took a deep breath. "It's the truth." I started playing the piano, fashioning a melody for the little song. While my fingers moved over the keys, Mattie began telling us about her life. "I'm a maid at the Little Harlem Hotel," she explained. "Big Mama Thornton stays there too."

"Big Mama Thornton?" I turned on the piano stool and stared at her in amazement. "I didn't know she was in town!"

"Nobody does. She been sick. She came here with her band to play at a blues club, but the gig got canceled and they all got stranded."

"Whoa!" Jimmy and I both exclaimed at the same time.

"Yes, I been helping them out with food and buying medicine for Big Mama." We stared at Little Mattie. It was hard to believe that this modest, shy little woman was taking care of Big Mama Thornton and her whole band.

I finished the simple melody, and Jimmy made a nice lead sheet. Little Mattie's eyes got bigger and bigger at the sight of her heart's desire coming alive on the manuscript paper. Jimmy gave her a copyright blank, which we helped her fill out, and we told her to send it to Washington, D.C.

"I want to thank you. Would you like to come over to my house tomorrow night? You could meet Big Mama and her musicians."

"Would we!" We all laughed.

She took the precious song of her life in her brown hands and walked toward the door, then turned and said, "I'll make you-all my famous leg of lamb."

"We'll be there with bells on!" I replied.

My music director agreed. He called to her as the door closed—"Bells!"

The next evening we arrived at Little Mattie's modest home and found ourselves bombarded by bruising blues music and surrounded by a crowd of happy folks: a gang of musicians; five children; Mattie's shy, earnest-looking, very slim husband; and sitting at the head of the long dining table like a queen on her throne, Big Mama Thornton.

Little Mattie introduced us to the family, the band, and finally to Big Mama, who looked at me, smiled, and said, "Hullo." Her black eyes snapped as she turned to Jimmy, and she pulled herself up taller in her ladder-back chair and said, "Well, hello there, you handsome devil, you!" Jimmy gallantly took her hand in his and kissed it. Big Mama glowed like a lantern, smiled her most beautiful smile, and said sweetly and seductively, "Sit down a little while and let's visit."

I felt shocked to see her condition. No longer the rounded, well-padded woman of her early photos, she began to show the angular, raw-boned figure that forecast the shadow of things to come.

I went to the kitchen and helped Little Mattie bring out the eats—mashed potatoes, corn on the cob, hot biscuits, green beans with bacon, and, finally, the biggest and best leg of lamb I had ever tasted.

Big Mama ate very little. She picked at her food, but drank a lot of milk from a tall blue glass. She laughed at the musicians' road stories and the children's chatter, but soon everybody could see that she was tiring. "I think I'll take a little snooze," she said and stood up, her tall, rangy figure swaying a bit. She walked regally to the doorway and paused dramatically. "Good night—one and all!" Then she turned and disappeared.

"Good night," we called after her. "Don't let the bedbugs bite!" and "Sleep tight, Big Mama!" She poked her head around the door and smiled one last time, waved, and was gone.

Mattie said to me in a low voice, "She really is not well. She won't eat—only drinks gin and milk."

"So that's what was in the blue glass?"

"Yep. The doctor said if she didn't stop drinking she wouldn't last much longer."

I felt terribly sad, "I'm so sorry to hear this."

"Don't be. She's a tough old bird, and she'll go when she gets good and ready—and not a moment sooner!" Little Mattie smiled.

Jeez, I said to myself, this little woman is really strong!

She and I went into the kitchen and dished up peach cobbler with ice cream and carried it into the dining room. Everybody was laughing and drinking and eating and listening to the blues. It felt wonderful to sit around a dining table with a family and have fun. For a moment I missed Akron and my own family, but I also remembered the unhappy parts, and put all of it out of my mind.

When the last bite of cobbler had been scooped from the last dish, Little Mattie and I cleared the table and cleaned up. She washed; I dried. Little Mattie talked about Big Mama and herself. "We were both born in Montgomery, Alabama. We went to a one-room schoolhouse. Big Mama was always very tall. The kids teased and tormented her and pulled her long black hair. She hunched over, trying to be small as the other kids."

"That's a cryin' shame!" I exclaimed.

"Yeah. I used to fight for her. She just would not fight for herself."

"But you were much younger than she was!"

"Yep, I know. Big Mama's folks were church folks, so naturally she sang in the choir. But her mama died when Big Mama was in the third grade. So she left school and never learned how to read and write."

"No kiddin'?"

"That's right. She got a job washing and cleaning spittoons in the local tavern, and she learned to play harmonica from watching and listening to her older brother, Calliope. He wouldn't teach her, and she had to use the old harmonicas he threw in the trash."

"Jesus!"

We finished cleaning up and sat at the kitchen table. Little Mattie put her elbow on the table and her chin in her hand. "Well, one night the regular vocalist got drunk and didn't show up, so Big Mama convinced the tavern owner that she could do the job. She never looked back after that, and hit the road with her own band."

"Good for her!"

"You sure you don't want some more peach cobbler or lamb? I'm gonna make care packages for the band to take back to the hotel."

"No, thanks, I'm stuffed. Girl, you sure can burn!" I meant that she could cook like a professional chef. Little Mattie beamed. I asked, "So what did you do, follow her?"

"No," she began putting sliced lamb and biscuits in bags for the band. "I finished school and fell in love, got married and moved to Buffalo, New York. Me and Big Mama always stayed in touch, though. I had five kids and Big Mama had a son . . ."

"What? Where is he?"

"She kept him with her on the road and tried to be a good mother, but the authorities took her boy away from her." Little Mattie looked away and fell silent. After a while she said, "Big Mama never talks about him, but she kept him with her a long time, so it must have broken her heart. She never knew what happened to him. And she never had another child." We were both silent.

After saying good night to the musicians and Little Mattie and her husband, Jimmy and I went to Gerald's Restaurant and ordered hot chocolate. I told him what I had learned about the two women.

That night, in my own bed, alone in my apartment, I thought about Big Mama Thornton and cried. I wondered if even the fame she had begun to rack up and the acclaim from her hit "Hound Dog" would ever make up for this dark place in the fabric of her life.

But the love and care of Little Mattie seemed so beautiful—another indication, like defiant Dr. G and her passionate nurse, of the web of women who were slowly but surely becoming a part of my life, taking the place of the "hard-ankles"—the men—I had hung around with for years.

The Blues and the Buffalo Scuffle

. . . .

I played in Kansas City
With the finest in the land
But Lawd, the babes in Buffalo
Always break up all the bands!

McKinney's Cotton Pickers' chief tenor man and arranger, Eddie Inge was born in Kansas City at the turn of the century, made musical history alongside players like Don Redmond, Jimmie Lunceford, and Louis Armstrong, and now stood at the bar of the Colored Musicians Club, a double Black Label scotch held daintily between his thumb and first two fingers. His brown felt hat perched rakishly on the back of his head. He stared suspiciously at the latest influx of new cats who had suddenly invaded Buffalo.

Inge, called "Father" by most of his friends, was a light-colored man with large eyes, and carried himself with the bearing of a big-time champion. In fact, one could still see in his eyes the eager young man who had conquered the stages of the world, inventing and polishing a new music, refining it to perfection, then, all too soon, looking out at an audience that had turned away.

He was in the history books as the famous arranger of a song called "You're Driving Me Crazy," and now ran the house band at the Club Moonglo, part of the Chitlin Circuit for Negro entertainers. He backed a dynamic, young new vocalist named Della Reese, among others.

The new cats were a huge threat! Their music was strange and atonal. They blew long, winding cascades of notes for solos. They broke tradition and didn't seem to care whether their shoes were brown, even when they wore black tuxedos.

Never you mind that their idol, Dizzy Gillespie, had accepted an offer from the U.S. State Department to do a goodwill tour and spread bebop all over the world. Louis Armstrong had turned down that gig years before.

Never you mind that Negro people were beginning to boycott buses in Alabama, and that a new cat named Martin Luther King was beginning to shake up old "Reverend Uncle" preachers, just as the new jazz cats were shaking up old Eddie Inge.

"I've seen better days on the farm!" declared Shorty Baker, Duke Ellington's trumpet man. He was the exception to the rule. He was almost as old as Inge, but had recently come to Buffalo to live with his sister after a bitter fight with Duke over longevity and a long-overdue pay raise. He stood at the bar with Inge, surveyed the new cats, and chewed the fat about the old ways versus new days on the road.

"Ol' Duke is smooth! I give him that," Shorty continued. He hitched up his pants over his rounded stomach with his elbows. Jimmy and I were eavesdropping shamelessly. We wanted to learn everything we could from the old cats *and* the new cats. We saw ourselves as a bridge between the two factions.

"Duke wrote 'Satin Doll' cause he and Lawrence Brown had a big fight over a fine chick," Shorty told us, "and Duke won the woman. Then he rammed a stick up Larry's ass and 'heisted' it!"

Inge explained, "Duke wrote the song, and Larry had to play it—over and over again!" Inge and Shorty snickered and we smiled, delighted to be in the presence of such grand fellows.

Jimmy and I became real friends with Shorty, hanging out at his sister's house, where he regaled us with stories of the Ellington Orchestra and his marriage to his ex-wife, Mary Lou Williams. Now, Mary Lou Williams could play piano and arrange with the best of them. She led her own groups, played with Andy Kirk, kept up with the times with bebop, and played excellent boogie-woogie piano.

"Are you a prima donna?" Shorty asked me playfully. "Can't have two prima donnas in one family!" We laughed, but I could tell that he was a little autocratic, so I could see why Mary Lou wouldn't take any crap from him, or anybody else. I hooded my eyes and kept my thoughts to myself. I knew in my heart of hearts that he would go back to Duke Ellington sooner or later.

Three young men from Memphis blew into Buffalo: Herman Green, tenor sax; Jimmy Brown, a superb drummer who had a voice like an angel;

and Bill Forte. Yes, he had returned—he of the white-liquor breakfasts in Toronto.

These cats had three things in common: they could play like the wind; except for Herman, who wanted to teach college-level music, they all had insomnia, nervous tics, and clinical depression; and they had all grown up playing with Phineas Newborn, Jr., the finest, fastest pianist in the Midwest—outside of Art Tatum. Phineas also suffered from emotional quirks and assorted symptoms. Maybe it was something in the water in Memphis?

A long, tall, somber young man rode in from Texas. He carried his trumpet under one arm and, like my brother Jerry, Schopenhauer and William Blake under the other. Richard Williams, or "Notes," as he was known, had notched his belt playing with names like Charlie Mingus and Lionel Hampton.

It was a gathering of eagles.

Jimmy and I wasted no time. We held a meeting and presented an idea to these eager young men. We suggested that they come together, write and arrange their favorite styles and songs, and play them at monthly jazz showcases that Jimmy and I produced. Jimmy would also arrange songs for the talented vocalists who came to town, and for their participation in the showcase, give them the arrangement—free! It was like manna from heaven for them.

Let the good times roll!

The showcases were a great success, and because admission was free, people came early to get a seat. The club made lots of money from just the drinks and Evelyn's fried-chicken dinners.

"Three hundred dollars an hour!" crowed Percy, the head cat at the club. But when he hired Doristine Blackwell, a tiny, gorgeous, light-brown-skinned woman with wavy, coal black hair, to help at the bar, all the wives in the musicians' wives' club mutinied.

"It's gonna be a hanky-panky club!" they declared. But Percy gave not an inch, and Doristine became a permanent member and vocalist for many of the big bands.

Donald Byrd, that great musician, was celebrated in a composition called "Amen" that Jimmy arranged, with Jimmy Legge playing the melody with his tuba. Notes provided a change of pace with his arrangement of "Whisper Not" by Benny Golson. The other cats in the band were well seasoned: George Holt (trumpet) of Cozy Cole's band, Elvin Shepherd (tenor sax) of Lucky Millender's orchestra, C. Q. Price (alto sax) of Count Basie's band,

Eggie Riding (trombone) of Roy Eldridge's group, brother Jerry on bass, and, naturally, myself on piano along with Notes and Shorty Baker brilliantly leading the trumpets. Jimmy acted as conductor-in-chief. It was a great ensemble—ready and eager to show off their many talents.

Bells!

* * *

The man from Alabama, Gene Lee, tall and elegant, immaculately dressed, his brown face shining beneath a tall, wavy, coal black pompadour, walked into the union hall. Jimmy and I were working on a lead sheet for a big-boned red-haired young man who stuttered so badly he could not be understood when he spoke. By some mysterious fortune, he could sing without a trace or whisper of a stutter. He was blessed with a beautiful baritone voice. Jimmy picked out "This Is My Beloved" for him to sing. His session finished, flushed with the success of his own personal miracle, the baritone strutted out the door.

Then Gene Lee told us his story.

"My whole group got busted and sent up the river to the big house," he announced. "Caught with a stash of heroin and a gun." He sneered, "Fools, fools, fools!" We shook our heads in agreement. "It really left me in a hole," he added. "I've got contracts to fill and no band. I need some lead sheets of most of my show so I can hire cats to read the music on sight." He sighed. "I'm really gonna miss my band, but they got twenty years . . ." He sighed again. "I guess it ain't no dice."

Gene composed most of his own music, some in the style of Johnny Ace—blues ballads dripping with emotion. He also did a jam-up rendition of Little Willie John's "Fever."

"I found some cats that can play the style," Gene declared, "mostly young cats. They can read some, and they got 'big ears.' The piano player is an old cat, but he's the best reader." He turned a chair around backwards, straddled it, and rested his hands on the back. "Maybe you-all heard of him. Name of Pete Johnson."

I stared at Gene. "*The* Pete Johnson? Roll 'em Pete? That Pete Johnson?" I cried.

"Yeah. We're playin' tonight at this little old joint around the corner. It ain't much, but it buys me grits and pays my hotel bill." He smiled. "Why don't you-all fly by tonight?"

"Will we!" I was ecstatic. I could hardly believe my ears.

After Gene left the union, I jumped from the piano and turned to Jimmy.

"You know, I studied and memorized every Pete Johnson, Albert Ammons, and Mead Lux Lewis piano book I could get my hands on when I was just a kid!" I hugged myself. "Just like I studied Jay McShann's music."

"Really?" Jimmy looked a little skeptical.

"Yes, really! I'm gonna be at that joint tonight!"

That night we went to this little hole-in-the-wall joint, walked through the dark narrow bar, entered the back room, and after our eyes became used to the dark, found a table near the stage. We both ordered gin and tonic.

There he was, on a high stage, sitting at the old upright piano with a drummer, a bass player, and Gene Lee, who had his hands resting on his tenor sax, singing a song called "Why Wasn't I Made of Stone?" Pete Johnson had a square head on a short neck, and his body was square also. His brown face blended into his brown suit, brown shirt, and tie. His fingers played flowery runs that curled around Gene's voice like morning-glory vines. The mournful song came to an end, the audience applauded and whistled, and suddenly Gene spied us at our table. Gene pointed to Pete Johnson, who waved his short arms and smiled.

At first, I was mesmerized. Then it seemed as if somebody or something pulled me out of my seat and propelled my legs up on that stage. Gene looked surprised. Then he grinned and did a little dance like a chicken, flapping his arms wildly around in the air.

Entranced, I walked up to the piano, put my hand on it to steady myself, and said, "Pete Johnson, I know *all* your music. Every note! Please, let me play a duet with you."

"All right. Set yo'self right down! Bottom or top?" he inquired.

"Top!" I grinned. That was courtesy and protocol: it gave Pete the lead position to play the bass patterns on the bottom. I was his guest, so I took the auxiliary position at the top of the piano.

Two hands for both of us, of course. Our twenty fingers dancing on those eighty-eight keys turned that piano into a train driving down the tracks—eight to the bar, on the L&N Railroad. Everybody in the bar joined us on the journey.

As we played, Pete Johnson whispered, "Are you from Kansas City?"

"Nope. Akron, Ohio."

We played on. "Girl, you *sure* you're not from Kansas City?"

I started to execute a trill between G and B-flat, so it took me a little while to answer. "In my heart, I guess I am."

He smiled and relentlessly dug into the left side of that piano keyboard, and the rhythm permeated the room, penetrating bodies to get at the souls hidden inside. We played a half hour without stopping, the audience standing, out of their chairs, applauding, the energy rising higher and higher. A person could have floated across the room on it.

We drove that train into the station, wheel in a wheel, pistons turning. Pete made a Count Basie ending, and we rolled the final chord to a crescendo—it was over. We threw our arms around each other. Pete, tears in his brown eyes and on his brown cheeks, said, "Girl, you took me back to Carnegie Hall with Mead Lux Lewis and Albert Ammons! You play yo' bee-hind off!"

"I'm honored." I spoke softly. I felt as if I had just shaken hands with the Grand Canyon.

Jimmy and I hung around with Pete and his wife quite often after that. She told us of the illness that took him off the road. I told Pete about my lifelong admiration for Jay McShann, and he smiled. "Ol' Jay's a hoot," he said. "He got his own style, and he keeps a good band. Lord, he's a hard player!"

Pete Johnson's own piano playing was almost feminine at times, with gentle eight-bar blues and undulating boogies. His liquid piano runs brought to the mind's eye sepia-toned pictures of lazy lakes filled with drifting lily pads, or maybe Tiffany lamps and lovely filigreed lace doilies spun-sugared into perfection.

Pete's wife, a tiny Caucasian woman with short salt-and-pepper hair, a clean-scrubbed face, and guileless eyes, was completely devoted to Pete and his music. She informed us that they had received no royalties from his compositions in years. "Give me the name of the music publishers," Jimmy declared. "Those people don't *wanna* find you! We'll find them, I promise!"

Pete and I continued to play duets on his little studio piano in the couple's tiny apartment on the second floor of the old redbrick building not far from the union. Though the stroke he had suffered sometimes weakened his arm, and sometimes instead of four hands at the piano there were only three, he never complained and he never stopped smiling. And the spirit of the music remained strong and powerful.

Once in a while, when he was feeling whole, we would sit back and listen as he transported us back to another time, when the center of the earth was Kansas City at the corner of 12th Street and Vine.

* * *

"Day-O!"

Harry Belafonte had the whole country singing "Day-O!" and our workplace was no exception. Almost overnight, the supper club was turned into a tropical-island retreat—phony palm trees in every corner, waitresses in long ruffled skirts, and drinks with little umbrellas sticking out of them. The boss hired two West Indian guitarists (one black, one white, both authentic), and we talked fast and convinced the boss that we could play calypso music.

"First thing we do," I convinced Jay and Jerry, "is go to the costume shop down on lower Main Street and get some 'Day-O' duds." We bought ruffled shirts and tight black pants for the cats, and I invested in a couple of off-the-shoulder peasant blouses and ruffled skirts, one bright red, one multicolored. I topped the whole look off with myriad arm bracelets and huge golden hoop earrings.

Overnight we put together our portion of the show—"Song of the Jumbies" and "Calypso Blues," originally sung with bongos by Nat "King" Cole—and we listened to records, records, records. The West Indians were delighted with our correct interpretation of their music, and gave me a gift of a shak-shak, a handmade metal can filled with stones, for extra rhythm sounds.

There was no place for Miss D and her Broadway show tunes in this new set-up, so she was let go. But back she came for opening night. She and Jay would often disappear into the dressing room after our sets, so Jerry and I and the West Indians would hang out at the bar.

"The place is packed," the bartender was pleased. "More people, more moolah!" He crowed, "You guys are amazing. You play jazz and Tin Pan Alley and—pow!—you switch to calypso, and the people go for it! Maybe you-all should print your own money!" We all laughed, and he poured us drinks on the house.

Another person who came to see us do "Day-O" was a woman Jerry had met. She was a high-yellow woman with straight jet-black hair, and she wore really crimson dime-store lipstick. She just appeared out of nowhere, and suddenly she and Jerry were an item. She came to the club, sat at a front table, drank a Tom Collins or two, and started yelling, "That's *mah* man! He playin' that *big* ol' bass! *Beat* that thang, baby! *Beat* that thang!"

We were so embarrassed we wanted to go through the floor of the stage! Instead, we tried to be cool and tactful. "Jerry, uh, we don't wanna get in your business, but your lady is makin' it kinda hard for us. We can't maintain our status and dignity." I was really mad. "Can't you get her a table in the back? *Way* back!"

Jerry just smiled his pretty smile and shrugged his shoulders. Jay stared at him. Jerry walked away. He seemed to be under some kind of spell. Jay ventured, "Maybe he's having another flashback . . ."

"*I* think maybe he just didn't get enough of the Korean War!" I told Jimmy, who looked a little shocked.

"Dif'rent strokes for dif'rent folks." Jimmy replied.

And thus began the reign of "Red the Terrible." She declared, "*Ever* body calls me 'Red' 'cause I'm so evil." She smiled with those blood-red lips when she said it. Little did we know how much truth she spoke—or how much she would cause our lives to change forever.

* * *

If I were superstitious, I would blame the winter snows, the blustery winds, and the icicles like stalactites, so large and pointy they could lodge in your skull like a sword plunged into a stone if they fell on you. So people walked in the middle of the street. The blizzard bombarded Buffalo and the whole snowbelt in the middle of the night. The area should have been renamed "Antarctica North."

Since I'm not superstitious, I argued with myself, what else explained the dread that knotted my stomach, the awful feeling of panic that came over me at unexpected moments? I tried to shake the feelings off, but they persisted. I phoned my agent. He answered, "Hallo! Hallo! Who *is* this?" I hung up without replying.

That was last week. Red the Terrible's entrance spurred my newly awakened resolve to make an exit, to take my loved ones and get out of town, maybe next week. I'll think about it, I promised myself.

The snowplows came out early and made bad matters worse. People couldn't move the cars that were parked in the streets, since they were completely buried in snow. So the plows went along the middle of the streets and threw all that snow onto the already submerged cars.

We brought out long winter coats, heavy sweaters, brightly colored wool scarves, and galoshes. We had to carry our calypso clothes and shoes in garment bags and change on the job. The Buffalo jitney drivers were used to horrible weather; we climbed aboard and slipped and slid down the middle of the street to the gig. The boss hired some winos to clear the walkway so people could get into the club. And still they came! Nothing seemed to stop Buffalonians from coming out in any kind of weather to party.

The blizzard brought frantic phone calls from the president of the union. "Hey, Cheatham. The big concert scheduled for tonight at Kleinhans Music Hall is in big trouble. Joe Williams (of the Count Basie Band) is here, but his group is stuck in New York City and can't get through the snow. Nancy Wilson's supposed to be here. She can't get through either. Can you get a group together and play some music as well as play behind Williams?"

Jimmy said, "Bells!" Then called together Eddie Inge (tenor sax), C. Q. Price (alto sax), George Holt (trumpet), Cubby Copeland (drums), and Jimmy Legge (bass). Jimmy assigned himself to trombone, me to the piano. It was rush, rush, rush! In fact, we received Joe's music only minutes before the curtain opened. And surprise, surprise! Miles Davis and his group went the long way around and arrived, stomping their feet and blowing on their fingers, ready to do the concert.

The piano part of Joe Williams's arrangement called for an opening piano solo. Though my heart was coming out of my chest, I called on all my tricks and started with really soft, Basie-like tinkling at the very top of the piano. The audience started applauding, and Joe Williams turned from his mike and said, "Go 'head!" And then, "Go 'head, again!" I played half a dozen choruses with his gentle prodding, then he called out to the crowd in his bass voice, "Give that little girl a *big* hand!" The thunderous applause sounded sweeter than music to my ears.

Jimmy led the band with such class that Miles Davis stuck his head out the side curtains and called, "Leave some for me!"

When we came off, Joe Williams leading the way, Miles Davis, pretending to be nervous, said in his growly, cracked voice, "Y'all made it mighty hot for us to follow all that!"

A Buffalo bright spot!

* * *

"Where's our next gig?" Jay inquired on our next play night. I looked at him, a little surprised. Jay didn't usually ask about our itinerary. Hm-m, I thought to myself, he's feeling left out because of the exciting extra gigs we been playin'.

Before I could answer, Jerry stopped tuning his bass and said, "No gigs outta town!"

"What?" Jay and I exclaimed at once. I stared at my brother.

He leaned his bass on the stand, picked up his bow, and started rubbing rosin on it. "I'm not goin' 'cause I'm gonna get married."

I felt like somebody kicked me in the middle of my stomach. "Married?" I whispered.

Jay stopped tuning his drums, put his drumsticks under one arm, and swiveled around on his drum stool. His eyes opened wide. "To who—to whom?"

"Red," Jerry spoke defiantly.

"Jesus H. Christ!"

"And I want you and Cheatham to be our best folks." Jay appeared visibly relieved at this announcement.

"Help!" I cried weakly.

"Listen, Sis, we gonna get married with or without you, so what's it gonna be?"

In families, sometimes it BE that way!

The very next week, on a miserable Monday morning at the courthouse in Buffalo, New York, Red the Terrible became Mrs. Gerald Allen Evans. I loaned her my grey, ankle-length, Mouton fur coat and matching hat. So she looked nice and sounded demure, except for the "Hot damn!" when the clerk told Jerry to kiss the bride.

Jimmy looked grim, but managed a hug and "Congratulations" to Jerry, who was grinning like a fool. I gazed at his happy face and the scar tissue all around his battle-scarred eyes, and I knew this was one war he would not win.

The apartment Jerry and I rented became the honeymoon hangout. That evening, the four of us went to a restaurant, had a nice meal (no Tom Collins, thank God!), then took a jitney back to our crib—slipping and sliding in the snow.

They disappeared into Jerry's room, and Jimmy and I sat in the dark on the couch in the living room, talking over the events of the day. We didn't have a television—who had time to look at it? But we did have a radio always tuned to the music stations. Oh, we heard about Uncle Miltie, *I Love Lucy*, and all the other popular TV shows, but coaching vocalists, rehearsing bands, doing arrangements, and playing the club at night kept us plenty busy.

We were listening to Johnny Mathis singing "Chances Are" in his typical vibrato-filled fashion when there came a tap-tap-tapping at the door. "Wonder who that is?" I hated to get up from the comfort of the couch, my stocking feet sliding over Jimmy's, but the tapping became a knock. Jimmy and I went to the door and opened it a crack. A mass of people huddled there, standing in the dark.

"Yes?" I asked. I knew they had the wrong address.

"Does Red live here?" A young man stepped out in front of the others.

"Who wants to know?" Jimmy replied with a question of his own.

The young man seemed weary. His shoulders drooped and his head hung down. "I'm Red's brother. I drove all day an' mosta the night, all the way from West Virginia."

"Well, Red *is* here but . . ."

"Well, good!" Delighted, he turned to the others. "Here we are, kids . . . this is it!" With that, he pushed the troop forward past us into the apartment, along with their many shopping bags and heavy boxes tied with twine. The intruders—that was how I viewed these strangers invading my home—wandered around the living room, touching things. I turned on the lights so I could see what the heck was happening.

The young man informed us, "These are Red's children. All five of them. The oldest, she has a six-month-old baby—that makes six." I gaped at him, mouth working like a fish out of water. "Red's mama, she tol' me to bring them up here 'cause she tired of takin' care of them. Got the address from Red." I nodded, as if all of this made complete sense to me. My mind whirled. I grabbed Jimmy's arm for support. "I'm goin' back to West Virginia right now—tonight." He smiled. "Have a good night!" He wished us well, turned, and bolted down the stairs. Moments later we heard his jalopy roar off moving at high speed, even on the ice-covered street.

I left the door open, hoping they would all go away. "What's goin' on?" I asked the oldest girl, who had a lumpy bundle hanging on her.

"These are my half-brothers and half-sisters." She pointed to two little boys and two little girls who stared at Jimmy and me through soulful eyes, as only a homeless urchin who has been coached can manage. "And this is *my* baby." She lifted the bundle to show us the child inside.

"JERRY!" I ran back to the honeymoon hideaway and banged on the door with both fists.

"Wha . . . what . . . What's the matter?" I heard Jerry's feet hit the floor. He opened his door an inch. "What's the matter out here! Is it a fire?"

"Worse!" I snarled. "Tell yo' new wife to bring her buns OUT HERE NOW!" Red poked her head around Jerry and blinked her eyes, her black hair hanging limply onto her yellow shoulders.

"AARGH!" I couldn't speak. I pointed toward the living room and pulled hard on Jerry's arm. Red hung on to him, but fury gave me strength. I dragged them both into the middle of the living room. Dead silence.

Then Red shrieked, "What are you-all doin' here? How did you get here?" She put both hands over her eyes.

"Gramma sent us." They found their voices. You can always tell if children have been raised by old people—they usually don't speak unless spoken to. "We come here to live with you and our new daddy." They looked around, bright eyes curious, then burst into excited chatter: "I like it here!" "Can we stay?" "I'm hungry!" "I wanna go potty!"

The oldest girl remained silent, wary, taking in Jimmy, Jerry, myself, and the apartment. "I guess you-all didn't know about us," she observed, her voice just above a whisper. "I'm fifteen. Gramma and I been takin' care of these kids since I was little. She go away," the girl pointed at Red, "and bring back a new one, then go away again."

I heard the radio playing "Smoke Gets In Your Eyes" by the Platters.

Jerry stood in the middle of the room, surrounded by those children like Gulliver among the Lilliputians—struck dumb. Red crumpled in a heap in a chair, her forehead pressed against her knees, her tangled hair scraping the floor, her yellow arms hanging listlessly on either side of her legs. She had fainted dead away!

* * *

The snow fell softly from the dark blue skies as we headed for work the next evening. The new snow made the pavement extra slippery, even in the middle of the street. Along both curbs dirty snow piled up like the walls of Jericho under the fresh dusting of white. Our jitney driver was a pro, and we moved along at a reasonable speed.

"I hope we don't get too much more of this stuff," I tried to make simple conversation. Jerry sat slumped way over on his side of the jitney and didn't answer. After all, from the time he had gotten married in the morning until his honeymoon was unexpectedly interrupted, he had become a husband, a father of five children, and the granddaddy of one.

"Er, maybe, ah . . ." I stumbled past the start of a suggestion, "I think maybe we better draw all the money we can from the gig tonight, so we can buy food for all those crumb-crushers." They cleaned out a week's supply of food in one day. He grunted, or was it a whimper? I shut my mouth. I didn't want him putting his fist through any more windows.

We arrived at the supper club a little later than usual because of the condition of the streets, so we went immediately up on the stage.

Jerry tuned his bass while I went into the dressing room behind the piano and placed my overnight bag on the make-up counter. I had packed the bag for a stay at my friend Rose's crib because I had to give my room to Red's three girls and the baby. The two boys slept on a pallet on the floor of Jerry's room.

I looked in the mirrors and shook my head. The gold hoop earrings swung back and forth catching the light. I pulled the peasant blouse down a little off one shoulder, drew a deep breath, and tried to shake off the emotions and chaos of the day so I could slip into the role of the Caribbean charmer—a creature of the night.

"Day-O!"

The show that night went by without a hitch. I looked out at the smiling crowd and spied Miss D, who had come down to the club to see if she could get some unsuspecting white man to buy her a steak dinner. At intermission, I went to the boss and drew out all the money Jerry and I had coming for the week. I hated doing this; I preferred to receive all the money at once, not in little dribbles.

Jerry sat by himself, looking so forlorn that my heart squeezed and lost several beats. I observed the room from a rear table—the crowd milling around, getting ready for the next set; the waitresses working the tables, flashing their neon smiles, picking up glasses, bringing back drinks, pocketing their tips—then I saw Miss D and Jay go into the dressing room. There go Miss Sodom and Mr. Gomorrah, I said to myself, up to no good!.

Jerry gave up his seat to a waiting customer and came over to stand with me against the phony palm trees until it was time to play the last set. Finally, the night was over, and I said, "See you tomorrow" to Jay and the two West Indians. I trudged into the dressing room and grabbed my overnight bag. "Let's go, Jerry, the jitney's here. I'll drop you off."

He got wearily to his feet, sighed heavily, and said, "I'm taking my bass home to reset the sound post." That seemed odd to me, but I figured he needed something familiar to do the next day. He zipped up the heavy canvas case and picked up the bass. "Okay, Sis, let's go."

* * *

Later at Rose's comfortable flat, after her kids were tucked in their beds, we sat around in our jammies to discuss the invasion of the West Virginians.

"We have to move," I told her.

"No!"

"Yep! Our landlady heard all the feet in our flat and came upstairs to see what was going on. She took one look at Red and all those children and told us she only rented to Jerry and me, that we were great tenants, but she couldn't stand to have all those kids upstairs over her. Too many people, she said." I groaned. "Oh, God!"

"You can always stay here," Rose offered.

My eyes misted. "Thanks, good buddy! But I'm really worried about Jerry. What can he do?"

"He needs to get an annulment," she said grimly, "or a pistol!"

"The woman never told him she had *any*body, let alone all those kids—and a grandchild!"

Rose pursed her lips. "Wait!" I said. "You haven't heard the worst part!"

"Can it get any worse?"

"Yeah, and it is! She is forty-five years old!"

"What? Why . . . why, Jerry's only twenty-two!"

"Yeah, and it's a cryin' shame!"

Rose sounded stunned. "Girl, I'm gonna go to bed! We gotta figure out what to do—tomorrow! So, good night."

I finished my tea, rinsed the cups and saucers, and went wearily into the little guest bedroom. I started unpacking my overnight bag. "Wait! What is this?" My hands trembled as I dumped everything out of the bag onto the bed. "What the? . . . Rose!" I called. "Come in here! You won't believe this!"

Rose came running into the room, her finger on her lips. "Shhh, you gonna wake the kids!" She took one look at the jumbled objects on the bed and whispered, "What's the matter?"

"Somebody stole my birth control!" Outrage vibrated from every word.

"What, are you crazy?"

"Somebody went into my personal belongings and stole my birth control!" I plowed my hands through my things, searching once again. "It's just not here." I sat down heavily on the bed. "Nobody went into the dressing room but me and Jay and Miss D . . ." my voice trailed off. The heat of my anger started from my feet and shot up my body to the top of my head. "I'm gonna kill 'em. I'm gonna kill 'em both—dead!"

The very pettiness of the act overwhelmed me. I pulled my feet up, put my arms around my knees, and rocked back and forth, the contents of the overnight bag strewn all around me. Rose threw her arms around my shoulders and let out a stream of profanities. "That bottom-feedin' broad! That scum-suckin' scutter! That puffy-gut hound dog!"

"I'm gonna have to get it back."

"It's long gone, Jeannie . . ."

I grew silent and cold. I thought about the good doctor's warning: "Don't come back!" I'd have to find another source. Oh, Lawd! How low can you go? Buffalo seemed to bring out the worst in people. The last question on my mind as I slipped off into a fitful sleep: WHO STOLE THE BIRTH CONTROL?

* * *

Rose decided to go to the club with me the next evening, and she invited a friend of ours named Big T, a humongous woman, known to best many a man. I don't know how Rose got Big T to wear a dress, but she showed up in a huge, long black sack dress. Her hair, cut short like a man's, showed off Rose's gold earrings. She disdained all make-up. Big T announced, "This is my funeral dress. Somebody might die tonight!" I shivered.

We picked up Jerry, who was standing out on the porch, waiting for us with his bass. He was surprised to see Rose and Big T, but he didn't ask any questions. We all squeezed into the jitney with the bass. He looked older than his twenty-two years. In less than two days his eyes had lost their live-liness. He sure didn't look like a bridegroom.

We pulled up to the club. As we got out of the jitney we were surrounded by a milling crowd.

"What's going on?"

We pushed our way up to the entrance to the club. Nailed to the door was a large sign that said: CLOSED. A padlock hung from the door handles on a thick chain.

"What's going on?" I demanded again.

The bartender came up behind us and said through gritted teeth, "Those bastids! They closed the club and disappeared. None of us got paid!" The waitresses were wringing their gloved hands and blinking back tears.

Somebody up there watched over us because I had drawn out all our money, and Jerry's bass was with him, not locked up in the club. Thank God, and somebody say "Amen!"

I turned to Rose and Jerry and Big T, who looked real disappointed be-cause she had worn her funeral clothes and had come ready to kick ass. Miss D and Jay were nowhere to be seen. "Jay came earlier," said the bar-tender. "To eat dinner." Miss D had not shown up at all.

"Really?" I said bitterly. "That's odd, she usually comes to mooch steak dinners off the customers." I asked the bartender, "Where do the club owners live? They can't get away with this." I knew we had to strike while the iron was hot.

"They own a grocery store out in Cold Springs. That's where they got their first money; the rest came from banking the numbers game."

I pried the location of the grocery store from the bartender, who wrote it down while we all stood around stamping, trying to keep our feet warm. We took the jitney back to our cribs: Big T to hers, then Jerry and his bass to his, and finally Rose and I went back to her house.

The premonitions that had brought cold-blooded dread to the pit of my stomach were now realized. I had ignored the urge to get outta town before it was too late, and Buffalo's siren song had drowned out the intuition I had always listened to and acted upon. And now there I stood: No gig! No apartment! No birth control!

But that was not the end of this bitter tit! Monday morning the steel mills went out on strike. It was to be the longest steel strike in U.S. history. The Chevrolet plant closed also. The barbeque joints were all boarded over. People lost their mortgages, their homes were foreclosed on, and they had to move in with relatives. Houses were packed to overflowing with people; others were boarded up—row after row—whole neighborhoods stood blighted, their deserted homes dark against the snow.

People became afraid to go out at night because of the young folks' robbing, stealing, and selling the drugs that always entered poverty-stricken neighborhoods, as if by some evil magic.

"There was a study done in Montreal," said Notes, the scholarly trumpet player. "When you pile rats all together in a small space, they start eating their young!" He was dead right. Except that with people, it seemed just the opposite: the young started killing their elders and anyone else they considered helpless.

Jimmy's coaching and arranging business skittered to a halt, and he started doing part-time bartending at the Colored Musicians Club. People drank more than ever!

Miss M and I found work as a duo—just piano, and both of us doing vocals. She drove us to the gigs in Niagara Falls, Canada, in her lavender Lincoln convertible with chrome everywhere. She wore black evening gowns and I wore white, so we made a great pair: her Nordic, June Christy persona and my urban, "Black blues" spirit.

All at once, a lightbulb came on in my head. Still hot on the trail of the club owners who had stiffed us, I decided to go down to the unemployment office and make a claim. Jerry went with me. He was so thin and haggard it nearly broke my heart.

"You must have proof that you and your brother worked for those two characters," the woman behind the desk advised us.

I hightailed it down to the union, talked to the president, and got a copy of our contract, which I took back down to the unemployment office. Thank God, I was always a stickler for detail. Jerry and I had both signed the back of the contract. Jay had refused to sign. "Somebody can always get you," he said haughtily, always afraid of being tricked.

"You have proof, young lady," the woman said. "We'll find those two rascals. But you two must come down every Monday and sign up." She was thin, birdlike, her hair cut into a short bob. She always wore crisp white blouses and thick glasses that kept slipping down her small nose.

"Thank you, thank you, thank you! We'll be here. But where do we sign up? There's no provision for jazz musicians on the forms."

She looked a little puzzled. Then she smiled. "You two make this dull job exciting. You've set some kind of record—we never had jazz musicians sign up here before. Um, let's see, just come to me at this office and sign up. Every Monday." We all laughed. No standing in long lines for these kids!

So every Monday, Jerry would pick me up and we would go down to her office, sign up, chew the fat—she enjoyed tales of our road adventures, especially the raunchy parts—and be on our merry way. Jerry had started driving a jitney to make ends meet. In fact, Jimmy's mama convinced Jerry to put Red the Terrible's big old family on welfare so he wouldn't be responsible for them. He, gallantly, had decided to raise the whole brood. The welfare people got them a big house, drafty and creaky, but nonetheless a house of their own, along with food and clothing. He gave an occasional bass lesson, also.

Miss D finally left town. She could no longer mooch steak dinners at the club or, for that matter, mooch everything else off Little Mattie. Big Mama got her health back, such as it was, thanks to Little Mattie, and went back to California. And Jay finally turned his big fat Polish woman loose—sent her back to Erie—and came by to announce that he was moving to Boston to go to school. He certainly had the smarts to do just that.

The snow seemed endless. The ice and sleet never seemed to stop preying on the besieged city. Finally, spring came and the snow melted, fading away drop by drop into the earth and along the gutters, as mysteriously as it had come. Buds appeared on the trees, birds began to sing, and nature started doing its job, getting the earth ready for renewal. But there was no renewal at Bethlehem Steel; the strike wore on and on. People really suffered, especially those with children. College students, without money for tuition, had to drop out and come home. Everyone's future was put on hold.

The only real joy for me in Buffalo was the fact that Jimmy and I were together all the time. Our love grew deeper in spite of all the strife around us. "We just live in Buffalo, baby!" Jimmy always said. "We don't let Buffalo live in us!" The rehearsals with the cats at the club were lifesavers, and the gorgeous jazz showcases were still bringing more people than ever once a month.

But everyday life got leaner and meaner. I was almost down to my reserve stash—the get-outta-town bus or train fare and hotel-for-one-week money that would let me ditch Buffalo if I ever decided to leave this hectic life behind.

One day Rose said, "Jeannie, there's a job for *all* of us if you want it."

"Bring it on!" I cried. "Where is it? You know, I always wanna pay my rent on time!" Rose had a boyfriend who helped her out, but she was pretty independent and refused to become a "kept woman" with two kids. "What kinda job?" I inquired, then exclaimed before she could answer, "Take me to it!"

She laughed. "Well, I talked to this ofay cat, and he said he was hiring women to plant seedlings for a canning factory."

"What?"

Rose looked grim. "Look! Things are scarce here in Buffalo. We don't have much choice!" She was right. Some low money was better than no money.

So, early in the morning, around four a.m., before the sun had risen, we walked down to the designated corner and waited. There were a lot of silent women—Polish and Irish, Italian and Negro, old and young—standing, and shivering, and avoiding one another's eyes.

I had no work clothes and neither did Rose, so we borrowed some from Big T and put belts around the huge pants to hold them up. We added big, heavy sweaters over plaid flannel shirts and two pair of socks under galoshes—we couldn't find any work boots that fit. We tied bandanas over our hair, looked at each other, and laughed to keep from crying. We made our lunch of kosher baloney sandwiches, an apple, and a bottle of Coca-Cola, packed with an opener, in brown paper bags.

At six o'clock, two big, open trucks lumbered up, and we all piled in. One woman struck up a song, and pretty soon we all joined in: "Row, row, row your boat . . ." then "I Shall Not Be Moved." The trucks meandered through the traffic to a farm way out on the outskirts of town. We spilled out of the trucks and looked for a bathroom. There was none, only two outhouses.

"What y'all expect," Big T whispered, "the Waldorf?"

"No, but we didn't expect this!"

A mud-spattered car drove up, and a short stocky white man jumped out. He wore his sweat-soiled brown hat pushed back on his round head, his wrinkled suit coat too tight on his body, and his black tie loose at the neck of his worn shirt.

"Well, ladies, welcome to real work!" His face shown as red as fire, a scruffy stubble on his cheeks and chin. He laughed, blew his red nose on a patterned blue bandana, stuffed it into his back pocket, and continued, "Stand in a row. My assistant will pass out boxes of seedlings and show you how to plant them. You have to finish five boxes to get paid." He cleared his throat and spit. "Do you understand?"

I looked at the boxes. My Gramma Hattie had taught us how to set seedlings in the earth when we were little, but I didn't say a mumbling word.

We all went to work, leaning over the loamy black rows, and planted and planted and planted. At first there was some light conversation in Polish, Italian, or English, but as the sun rose in the sky, words dried up like a desert. All you could hear was "Jesus" and "Oh, Lawd!" from some of the women. My back caught on fire, so I said, "Shit! The only way to do this is down on my black knees!"

Pretty soon everyone was down, knees hugging the damp, bitter black earth.

We called a halt at high noon. Or rather, the red-faced little booger drove up in his dirty car, yelled, "Lunch!" and drove off, leaving a cloud of choking black smoke behind. Everybody hit the outhouses and lined up. Nowhere to wash our hands, but Lawd have mercy, those kosher baloney sandwiches tasted like pheasant under glass! The Coke tasted like fine wine!

We went back to work and labored until sundown, when the assistant, who was also the tallyman, cried out, "Work done! Line up at the pay shack for your money!" Every woman there drew a deep breath at the same time and then slowly began to rise from her knees, Polish and Irish and Italian and Negro.

I remained on my knees a little longer, trying to get myself together. Suddenly, I began to pray. I couldn't help myself; the words just poured out. "God" I said, looking out at the setting sun, "if I get outta this field alive, I'm never, ever gonna do this again. I'm getting outta this town. I don't know how, but I'm goin' to, and when I do, I'm never gonna live here again!" I had come full circle from Gramma Hattie's farm to the bright lights and hundreds and hundreds of people applauding me. "Now, I'm back on my knees on a farm again! Mother of Jesus, help me!"

I got up and walked slowly over to the pay shack, got my money, climbed on the truck with Rose, Big T, and all those other exhausted women trying to put bread on their tables, and closed my eyes. A song ran through my head:

> *Lawd, there's fifty weepin' women on their knees—*
> *Fifty weepin' women on their knees!*
> *And they all rose together*
> *And faced the settin' sun*
> *Cryin', "Lawd, have mercy, if You please!"*

Earl Hines in South Bend, Indiana. He taught me about progressions.

Me with the Colvinaires in South Bend, Indiana, 1950.

My brother Jerry and his beloved bass, 1949.

My brand-new love, Jimmy Cheatham, in Buffalo, New York, 1957.

Willie Mae "Big Mama" Thornton, about 1979. She had a #1 hit with "Hound Dog" in 1953, three years before Elvis Presley covered it. Photo courtesy CTS Images.

Little Mattie Fields. I met her and Big Mama in Buffalo in 1959. Photo courtesy Mattie Fields.

Band rehearsal at
Local 533, Colored
Musicians Club,
Buffalo.

'CHEATHAMS' JAZZ SHOWCASE
MUSICIANS CLUB - BUFFALO, NEW YORK

LEFT TO RIGHT: GENE LEE/VOCALIST, ELVIN SHEPARD/TENOR SAX, BOB CRUMP/ALTO SAX, MUSEYF
SHAREEF/TROMBONE, EGGIE RIDING/TROMBONE, JIMMY CHEATHAM/CONDUCTOR-ARRANGER,
JEAN CHEATHAM/PIANO, JERRY EVANS/BASS VIOLIN, CUBBY COPELAND/DRUMS, JIMMY
LEGGE/TUBA

Pete Johnson, composer
and pianist ("Roll 'Em,
Pete" and "Cherry
Red") with whom I
played many duets.
Buffalo.

PETE JOHNSON
GTS IMAGES

Escape from Buffalo

· · · · · · · · · · · · · · · · · · ·

I'd rather drink muddy water
An' sleep in a hollow log
Than stay here in this city
An' be treated like a dirty dog!

"My ship has just come in!" I danced around Rose's parlor, waving my arms over my head, a long white envelope clutched in my right hand. "My ship has boogied into the harbor," I sang, "an' I'm gonna get myself together, an' me an' my man gonna blow this mean ol' town!"

Rose came into the room, one eye made up with a thin, powder blue line drawn above her long black lashes, exotic and mysterious looking. "You mean your rowboat with two oars, don't you?" she teased.

"Don't bring me down! This missive is from the New York State Unemployment Office, giving Jerry and me all our back money and granting us twenty-six weeks of checks. Paying the maximum!"

Rose started dancing her dance of the seven veils. "You got it! You got it!"

"I knew if I prayed hard enough it would happen." I murmured, mostly to myself.

"Yeah. You always thought God lives in your closet!"

"What?"

"Never mind. Whatcha gonna do now?"

"Well, I know I gotta plan this getaway real careful. I'm gonna take Jimmy with me. He didn't graduate from two music schools just to get stuck here and wither on the vine!"

"What about Jerry?" she inquired. "You gonna leave your brother?"

I blew out a gusty sigh. It was all too sad. I didn't even want to talk about him and the horrible situation he'd gotten himself tangled up in. I changed the subject. "Maynard Ferguson called Jimmy to go on a short tour with his band. It was Jimmy's music-school pal, Willie Maiden, who recommended him." Rose appeared properly impressed, her mouth made a little "o" shape beneath rounded eyes. "He didn't have to tell me how happy he was to hang out with those cats. It's been really slim pickin's here."

"You think he'll come back, or keep on steppin'?"

My heart squeezed and then restarted itself. Perish the thought!

* * *

"You and Jimmy are always together, so why don't you both consider movin' in here with me an' helping me with the rent?" Jimmy's mother smiled until her eyes disappeared. Her face got really rosy, flushing up under her thin light-colored skin. "Then you can get that good love anytime you want!"

We both laughed so hard that tears came to our eyes. We understood each other perfectly. There was something unspoken between us—respect. She had raised Jimmy and his sister without their father. She had left her husband in Alabama and come to Buffalo when her children were small. She worked hard and, with the help of Jimmy's gramma and trusted women friends, kept her family together, even though she had to leave them whole summers sometimes.

We were on the same side: our mutual love for Jimmy. Thank God!

* * *

1959—the last year of the fifth decade of the twentieth century. The world and the music were changing fast. Elvis Presley and the Colonel dominated the pop world with songs and movies. Little Richard, dressed in astounding stage outfits and sculptured, wavy black hair, wrote "Tutti-Frutti"; Chuck Berry, with his gravity defying duck walk, performed a tune called "Maybelline." We did this, but parodied one line with, "Why cain't you be clean?" A quiet young man, Clarence Becton, who had played drums with Gene Lee and me on many a gig, left Buffalo to join the gospel group, the Swan Silvertones. Their sound was the same sound that Sam Cooke brought to the world with "You Send Me."

The jazz world was changing also. There was Horace Silver, whose songs we copied and spread all over western New York: "Doodlin'," "Nica's Dream," "The Preacher." Horace was a pianist I admired greatly, and I played his "Song for My Father," even though I was not very close to my own dad. Even at Polish weddings where we played authentic polkas, the guests nodded their heads and patted their feet to Horace's music.

Miles Davis's "Kinda Blue" was replaced on the jukebox of the Colored

Musicians Club more than any other disc. I mean, we wore it out. That recording transcended all eras, all styles. It seemed to be the calm before the storm of world events.

Jimmy and I had our own little production during that awesome, creative period.

JIMMY AND JEANNIE CHEATHAM
WISH TO ANNOUNCE
THE BIRTH OF THEIR SON
JONATHAN
BORN ON VALENTINE'S DAY, 1959

No, my lips were not pulled up over my head—only up to my ears.
WHO STOLE THE BIRTH CONTROL?

* * *

For the next four years, Buffalo was like a junkyard dog tied to a stake driven into the ground at the entrance of a plantation named "Steel Mill." Nobody could go in and nobody could get out! You could almost taste the fear. The big bosses had shut down the "company store," and all the field hands and house folks alike had to "root, hog, or die poor."

Jimmy and I were luckier than a lot of folks. Miss M and I played quite a few gigs. Jimmy played with a series of musicians, including Little Willie John of "Fever" fame.

I secretly planned and prepared to get out of town. The State of New York gave Jerry and me an unprecedented series of extensions on our unemployment checks, and I squirreled away every greenback dollar that I could. Rose, an incredible seamstress, began to help me alter my gig clothes to bring them up to date.

"You bring little Jonathan over anytime!" Pete Johnson was an amiable and gentle babysitter. He and his wife bought a special white blanket for Jonathan to play on and nap on.

Doristine laughed and said, "Boy! When you-all bring Jonathan to rehearsals, all the cats turn into 'Big Mamas'! The whole group is a band of uncles."

Jonathan was never sick and never cried. He walked around the horns and touched them all gently while the cats smiled with approval.

Our main babysitter—for both Miss M's blonde and blue-eyed baby girl and Jonathan, our little chocolate child—was Little Mattie. She became caregiver to us all. But one day Little Mattie came to the union rehearsal hall, poked her head in the door, and said in a wee voice, "Can I talk to you-all a minute?"

Jonathan was taking a walk with Mr. Plummer, the ninety-year-old secretary of the union, who looked exactly like Eisenhower—even his color. He often ambled down a few blocks toward Main Street to buy fresh-roasted peanuts, and loved to take Jonathan with him because Jonathan was the only person who walked as slow as he did.

"Come on in, girl! What's happenin'?"

Little Mattie didn't smile her usual sweet smile. She sat down heavily on the old red leather couch, pockmarked with countless cigarette and cigar burns. Jimmy and I left the piano, walked over, and sat beside her.

"What's wrong? Kids all right?"

"Um-humm."

We sat quietly and waited until she chose to speak.

"You know my husman works on a giant forklift for this company for years. A long time. It's a good job and pays good. The steel strike never stopped them." She covered her face with her hands.

"He wasn't hurt, was he?" Jimmy stood up.

"No, nothin' like that." She coughed. "Well, his boss, a nice enough white man . . . he even been to our house . . . he ate my cookin' . . ." She stared at her two hands twisted in her lap, not able to meet our anxious eyes. "Well, I'm tellin' you . . . I can hardly voice it . . . he and my husman fell in love!"

"He what?"

"Yeah, my husman left me and the kids for his boss. Even told me he and my husman would pay for me and the kids . . . that I shouldn't make a fuss . . ."

"Whoa!" My chin dropped. "What will you do? What can we do?"

"Nothin'!" She stood up and shook her head. "I guess I'll wait a couple years till the older kids get through school, then go out west an' live with Big Mama. She always callin' me to come out an' manage her an' her affairs."

"Oh, Mattie, we so sorry . . ."

"Nothin' to be sorry about!" She squared her shoulders. "He don't want us. We don't want him!" She walked to the door, then turned. "I'm gettin' a divorce. It should be real easy to get alimony and child support. The judge—any judge—will gimme that and more when he finds out my man fell in love with another man."

With that she lifted her chin and walked out, brave and proud, dismissing her betrayal with one wave of her hand.

* * *

Jimmy and I floated easily between all strata of the Buffalo community, university professors to winos. It was one of the terrific gifts we brought to each other. We were both easily adaptable and took great pleasure in meeting people of all kinds on their own level. And, boy! The gap between haves and have-nots became wider and wider.

In the area where we lived, once tree-lined, marvelous German-built two-story homes began to deteriorate. Trees were cut down for firewood or died from neglect. No one had money for a mortgage as well as repairs and paint. The bank moved away, the drugstore, the grocery stores. Even the German butcher, who was rumored to have included his two missing fingers in some sausage rather than throw out the whole batch, moved away, taking his wonderful supply of fresh meats.

We had to go farther and farther away for food and supplies. The buses stopped running earlier and earlier. But I was getting closer and closer to my goal of cutting Buffalo loose.

Still, all was not lost. We—the whole jazz showcase band—played a job in Jamestown, New York, for the Four Lads. The president of the black union in Jamestown called the president of our local, looking for a big band to play the show.

The manager of the show people thought he had called the white union. You should have seen the looks on the faces of management when we piled out of the automobiles, black musicians in dark suits, white shirts, and red ties. They didn't say much as we took our places, tuned up, and took a look at the opening number.

"Hu-mmm! This is a great arrangement," Shorty Baker said to Richard "Notes" Williams. The arrangement opened with a trumpet cadenza, a long series of 'leventy-'leven notes cascading and tumbling over each other.

One of the Four Lads said, "Er, ah! Listen! Uh. Maybe your trumpet player should leave out the cadenza. It's *very* difficult . . ." We looked at each other, and nobody said a mumblin' word.

Later, in front of a packed house, the MC ran out, grabbed the mike, and announced, "Ladies and gentlemen . . . the Four Lads!" Shorty Baker stood up and hit that cadenza and played those 'leventy-'leven notes off the paper! And when he finished, he took a deep bow. The Four Lads were so astonished, they couldn't sing! Then they laughed and laughed while the audience gave Shorty Boo a standing O.

"I dare you to do that again!" the lead vocalist challenged. Shorty stood up, repeated the astounding performance, and took another bow. The crowd went insane. The vocalists started singing in a hurry before the event turned into the Jimmy Cheatham Jazz Showcase Band featuring Shorty Baker.

We felt terrific—and vindicated. At that time, most white studio musicians thought that most black jazz musicians could not read music. What a night!

* * *

These years were marked by struggle, not only in strike-ridden Buffalo but also in the Deep South—in Birmingham, Alabama, the birthplace of M'Ma and M'Da and Jimmy and Jimmy's momma and dad. There were sit-ins and demonstrations and protests. Straddling the late fifties and early sixties, as we went from colored to Negro to black, we became aware of a different voice in the music, sounding louder and louder in the land, forecasting things to come.

To be honest, I felt deeply moved by the voices and the struggles. John Coltrane—his sound strained, yet insistent, like being born over and over but never quite getting free of the birth canal—was a weird kind of revolving or retrograde reincarnation. So different from Charlie Parker's beautiful, orderly quicksilver and Gene Ammons's deep, throbbing probing of my solar plexus.

I felt. But I was so busy trying to morph me into we and into three, and trying to realize the ever-present dream of making a home for Shirley, that the rising conflict was forced to the background of everyday life.

At the Colored Musicians Club (I guess we'll always call it "colored"), we sat around after rehearsals and discussed Martin Luther King's latest speech and people marching and going to jail. Jerry became excited about a bass player named Charles Mingus, and for a few brief moments I saw the old fire in his battle-scarred eyes. But it was short-lived.

The jukebox played soft and low, and Jimmy and I sat in our favorite corner of the club, talkin' trash with Doristine. The club was empty because of the early hour. Jonathan was with Jimmy's mama, and we were lost in a little world of just listening to music—Ahmad Jamal's "Poinciana."

Suddenly the old wooden stairs rumbled under running feet that stopped at the top, and then came a frantic knocking at the door. Jimmy got off his bar stool and looked through the peephole. "It's Jerry." He buzzed the door open, and my brother fell into the room. Jerry's face looked ashy, his brows were knitted together in pain. He stumbled over to me, threw his long legs over a stool, and slumped onto the bar's polished surface.

"What's wrong, Jerry?" I moved onto the stool next to his. He wore his jitney driving clothes, the cap pulled way down low onto his face. "The kids alright?" He didn't answer.

Doristine grabbed a bottle of Hennessy. "He needs a drink." She poured a good shot and gave him a "water back." He didn't touch the drink, just stared at it. We knew that if he ignored his favorite Hennessy, something had to be really wrong.

"She did it!" The words finally came out his mouth. "She really did it."

"You mean Red?" My heart sank. "Did she kill somebody?" He put his head down on his folded arms on the bar. I moved his drink so he wouldn't spill it.

"She broke my bass!" We all froze.

"She what?" Doristine gasped.

"She said she was sweepin' the floor and somehow my bass fell down the basement steps."

We couldn't grasp what he said. "Wait a minute! Can it be repaired?"

"It's in splinters." Tears coursed down his lean dark cheeks and mingled with the beard he had grown this past year. "I'm done. I'm finished." He stood, stumbled to the door, and pushed the buzzer, letting himself out. We listened to his slow heavy footsteps descend the narrow stairs.

"Jimmy, go after him!" I felt suddenly cold with fear. I didn't want to think what Jerry might do.

Jimmy rushed over to the door and called over his shoulder, "Can you get home alright?"

"Yeah."

I never knew what he said to Jerry—what was there to say? It was the war I had foreseen, the war that my brother would not win. There was no way in heaven or hell, without tremendous energy and willpower, that Jerry would be able to purchase another blonde Kay bass in these hard times. It was the year that Red the Terrible ripped the heart out of a wonderful young man and a marvelous master musician.

* * *

The president of the union called. "Jeannie, where's Jimmy?"

"He went to buy manuscript for some arrangements. He got a nibble to do an act for a vocalist."

"I hope she pays him!" Prez snorted.

He referred to one girl who took the arrangements and cut out without paying. She was blonde and beautiful, but she was bad, bad, bad! Her sugar daddy was a big-shot lawyer from Detroit. He gave her the cash to pay us, but she bought dozens of pairs of white gloves with the money.

"White gloves! For what?"

"I dunno," I said. "We found out that she was turning tricks in her hotel room in spite of the fact the lawyer sent plenty of money to keep her. She told Miss M that wearing white gloves made her feel clean."

Prez snickered. "No accounting for taste. Well, I'm callin' 'cause Bull Moose Jackson needs a tenor player for his organ group. He's in St. Catherine's, Ontario."

"Bull Moose Jackson?"

"Yeah, you know, the lady-killer. I don't know what he got, but it drives all the women crazy. He is one homely cat! But he opens his mouth, out comes this knock-out baritone voice." Prez sang "I love you—yes, I do!" Horrible, wobbly, loud. Hilarious.

"Never mind, Prez," I laughed, and moved the phone over to my other ear. I thought a moment. "Almost all the cats have left town." There had been a big fight over what to do with the money brought in by the jazz showcases.

Prez snorted, "I don't blame you guys for quittin'. They weren't payin' you, an' they acted like you an' Jimmy was s'posed to produce those shows."

"Well, no more, no more. Shorty Baker went back to Duke Ellington. Ev'ry body else scattered to the four winds." A light bulb went on in my head—a real fluorescent flood of light! "Hey, how about a trombone player? Jimmy played with the Hank Roberts organ trio a whole lot of times." My suggestion met with silence. I waited, not breathing.

"You know, you're right. I'll call Moose in Toronto and call you right back."

The breath I'd held rushed forth. "Okay!"

My mind raced. I ran to the walk-in closet, pulled out Jimmy's suitcases, and opened his dresser drawers. I gathered six white shirts, seven sets of underwear, black socks, white socks to wear under the black socks to protect his feet, three ties, a bow tie, and black shoes with extra laces. I brushed off two dark suits and his topcoat, packed the suitcases, and laid the folded topcoat across them.

Jimmy hardly ever complained about anything, but he did say, "You know, you always stay ready to pack—like you gonna leave anytime."

"Babe, you gotta realize I been packin' to perform since I was five years old, in M'Ma's children's choir. I don't know any other way—clothes dry-cleaned or washed and folded, toiletries replaced as soon as they're almost used up." I smiled to myself, happy that he worried I might leave. He needn't worry. He could count on me. For the long haul. For life.

The phone rang. "Jeannie," Prez sounded excited, "Moose said he would love to use the trombone!" Jimmy was to meet Jackson in St. Catherine's that evening. He wanted Jimmy to finish the tour with the group.

"He'll be there." I hung up and called Miss M. "It's beginning! Can you drive us up to St. Catherine's today so Jimmy can take this gig?"

"Yep, sure can. It'll be a nice change." She paused, sounded pensive, "Maybe you and I can hook up something. We'll drive back tonight. Be over soon as I can."

I turned into a whirling dervish. I got Jonathan ready for Little Mattie and dressed myself in one of my revamped designer suits. When Jimmy came up the stairs whistling, I met him at the top with his suitcase and his trombone. In St. Catherine's, right off the bat, Jimmy fit the Bull Moose Jackson group like a hand in a glove, so down the road they went, making beautiful music together. Hall-le-loo!

The very next day, Miss M called her agent. He booked us into Albany, New York, to perform with a comedian and a dancer in a roadhouse run by the Mafia. The owners were very courteous, almost old school. They paid us a lot of money. We performed weekends and drove back to Buffalo every week. Each time I picked up more of my clothes.

The kids, Jonathan and Miss M's daughter, were very happy with Mattie's big family, but Miss M and I had no intention of ever going back full-time to Buffalo.

"We know Bull Moose Jackson's itinerary," Miss M pursed her lips. "We can meet them at the end of the tour, in New Bedford, Massachusetts. Jimmy and you and I can drive on into New York City."

I knew her ex-husband was breathing down her neck. He had remarried. Dead set on getting revenge for Miss M having left him, he planned to take her child away. Little Mattie's home served as a great temporary hideout.

We all met in New Bedford as planned. Jimmy said his good-byes to Moose, his band, and the vocalist, Phyllis Branch. Phenomenal, with a four-octave range, she sang in several languages, including Yiddish. Everywhere she performed, she left her audiences laughing at her wit and weeping with her heart-rending songs. Under the lights, her skin shown deep blue-black, something she felt really sensitive about. Not exactly light-skinned myself, we hit it off. She was headed to New York City also, and promised to keep in touch with us. She wanted Jimmy to do some arrangements and lead sheets for her.

Jimmy declared, "Here we go. Here's to 'la grande' adventure!" We packed his things into Miss M's lavender Lincoln convertible along with our stuff.

My heart beat like a trip-hammer. What waited ahead for us? We gave ourselves one month to get settled into the New York scene. Jimmy had contacted one of his fraternity brothers, who lived out on Long Island in a huge house. He agreed to rent us rooms—one for Miss M, one for Jimmy and me. Sight unseen.

I had a few doubts. Would we like these people? Would Jimmy be able to get work? Miss M and I already had a gig booked for an indefinite period, starting in two weeks. "Hooray for Salvatore!" I joked. "I think I love the mob!" We owed this booking to Miss M's "friendly" friend, whom she met while singing on the wheel at the town casino in Buffalo. He called his connections at a joint called The Golden Bar and Dance Palace, and we were in like Flynn.

Jimmy and I and Miss M hugged one another, juiced up that lovely lavender Lincoln, and headed out of New Bedford and into the canyons of New York City. We escaped from Buffalo, city of bondage, city of broken dreams, city of unborn hopes and wishes. I knew our future wouldn't be easy, but Gramma Hattie told it to the world when I was born: "She really knows when to fight and when to run!" Lawd have mercy!

New York City, Ditty-Wah-Ditty

. . . .

New York, New York
Now don't that sound nice!
But the City so tough—
They named it twice!

The lovely lavender Lincoln convertible carried the three of us into a veritable wall of noise. Sheets of sound assaulted our ears: yellow cabs darting in and out of traffic, pounding on their horns; sirens screaming from rescue wagons and police cars; delivery cyclists whipping in and out of traffic like roadrunners; clouds of smoke gushing from buses and trucks; jackhammers, with men at their mercy, ripping up streets and sidewalks. Folks in automobiles gave one another the arm and the finger and yelled curses in every language under the summer sun. Every kind of smell swooped up and assailed our nostrils, and our eyes began to water from the debris-filled air.

The vibration of the city was so high and energy-filled that it made my body tremble. Our heads whipped around like ping-pong balls from trying to take in all the sights, but when we cruised down the Boulevard of Broken Dreams, past the belly button of Tin Pan Alley—the Brill Building, 1619 Broadway—we was cool.

With the top down on the lavender Lincoln, Miss M and I, heads held high, sat in the front seat while Jimmy lolled in the backseat like some powerful potentate. All the would-be songwriters, wannabe hit makers, and "no way in hell" hangers-on stared at us as we tooled by. Oh, we was cool!

We drove around the block and came right back around to 1619 Broadway again, giving them all another good look. O Lawd, we was *cool!*

We parked the convertible around the corner in a space hard come by and walked back toward the entrance of the Brill Building. A scruffy, elfin, middle-aged man, the silver hairs on his face glinting in the sunlight, his piercing blue eyes scanning the crowd, leaned against the mailbox. He saluted us as we passed by. We smiled and waved back, then threaded our way through the crowd milling around the entrance of the building.

The three of us took the elevator up, knocked at the door of Pete Johnson's music publisher, and entered. "Yes?" A skinny, sandy-haired, fidgety woman looked up from her desk and stared at us through the cat's-eye glasses perched on her nose. "Yes?" She asked again in a sharp nasal voice.

"We're here representing Pete Johnson, the boogie-woogie king," Jimmy declared.

She tapped her pencil impatiently on the walnut desktop. "Do you have an appointment?" The rhythm of her New York City voice rat-a-tat-tatted in our ears.

Jimmy's tone matched hers. "We don't need one. This meeting is long overdue."

A short swarthy man dressed in a tailor-made grey pinstriped suit emerged from an adjacent office. He patted his black toupee and adjusted his black-striped silk tie. "What's going on out here? You gotta song for sale?"

"No." Jimmy's eyes glinted. "I'll get right to the point. We came here to find out why Pete Johnson has received no royalties from you-all for over eight years."

The man stepped back. "Er . . . yes . . . well, he's deceased, is he not?"

"Not last time we looked. He's alive and kickin' in Buffalo." Jimmy's tone turned sarcastic. "He also lives on Broadway." Jimmy produced a letter authorizing him to act on Pete's behalf. The man ushered us into his plush office, offered us seats on his leather sofa, and had the secretary serve us coffee. He ogled Miss M while he produced records of Pete's account. With apparent difficulty, he tore his eyes away from our friend and studied the papers spread over his desk. Finally, he assured us that the money would be winging its way to its rightful owner. Mission accomplished! (Pete informed us later that his first royalty check was in four figures.)

Back in the hall, we pressed the down button and waited for the elevator. The doors opened. Our mouths opened. Standing there, bigger than life, was Big Maybelle Smith. Her eyes lit up her baby face as she recognized us. "Hey, soaks!" she cried out in her contralto voice.

"Hey, Maybelle, whatcha doin' in the Big Apple?"

We piled into the elevator and grabbed her in a group hug, all of us at once with room to spare. We couldn't reach all the way around her huge body, but we did the best we could.

Her black hair was pulled back, slick and shiny, and she wore a black rayon crepe dress. Its long sleeves covered the heroin tracks on her huge arms; the color cut down on cleaning bills.

She laughed, her voice throaty and warm as it worked its way up out of the deep canyon of her huge breasts. "I'm checkin' out my traps. Come to get me some money from the people who published 'Candy.' " She stopped, her face as innocent as a newborn babe's, "Say, lemme have five dollars. If you don't have five, lemme have two dollars." Up to her old tricks—we knew Big Maybelle was still shooting up heroin. She said grandly, "I'm trying to buy my mama a home."

Jimmy silently reached in his pocket and pulled out two one-dollar bills.

The elevator reached the ground floor with a thump and we walked out to the street. Somebody was raising a ruckus on the sidewalk. The scruffy cat from the mailbox spit at one of the songwriters, one who carried an expensive alligator briefcase. We moved aside to watch. Big Maybelle whispered, "The puny cat's name is Spitty. If he don't like you, he spits at you!"

Spitty spat again at the songwriter and this time gave him the arm *and* the finger.

"Hey! You stupid moron! Somebody ought to put you away." The songwriter leaped out of the line of fire and stomped into the building.

"The cats are scared of Spitty," Maybelle declared. "They think he can hoodoo them and put a hex on their songs, so nobody complains to the cops. If he likes you, he smiles and waves. Some folks say he's psychic and can tell whether you got the right stuff, or not."

He had smiled at us. Amused, relieved, and wondering if the opinion of a crazy man might be a good omen, I nodded, my face serious.

"Well, good to see you soaks. I gotta go make my rounds."

"Okay, Maybelle, take care of yourself!" We hugged her once more and watched her waddle away, stopping here and there to hit on the cats for a dollar or two. We never saw Big Maybelle again.

As we ambled around the corner to the lavender Lincoln, we heard the cats say, "Who are they? Where they from?" First impressions—there ain't never but one.

On the long ride out to St. Albans to Jimmy's frat brother's home, tired but happy, we summed up the whole day's experience. In spite of all the noise, grime, smells, and frenzy, New York seemed to be a place of magic, full of the promise of a grand adventure.

"Boy," Jimmy exclaimed, "we sure got Pete's business straight."

"Yes, indeed!" Miss M carefully positioned the convertible so she could join the insane traffic. "And we got hustled big-time by Big Maybelle Smith."

I felt high, my mind full of possibilities. "We got the go-ahead from the uncrowned King of Broadway, Spitty, ruler of the sidewalks of New York City!"

* * *

"Ain't these some of the same cats that manacled Billie Holiday to her bed and took away her cabaret card while she was dyin'?" a thin, dark-skinned musician sporting a beard and a beret complained bitterly to his friend, his voice soft but intense.

We stood in line in a Manhattan police station, waiting our turn to have our mugs shot and our fingers printed. Musicians had to suffer this ordeal in order to get a cabaret card, which would allow them to play in the clubs of New York. "Yeah," his friend agreed, "these New York cops think musicians live in a constant state of pre-criminality."

Other denizens of the line joined the muttered discussion. "Cops don't take no prisoners—just take away your card if you mess up." "How you gonna make a livin' with no card?" "Who started this crap, anyhow?"

"Well," said one who knew, "during World War II they tried to keep tabs on foreigners, you know, waiters and casual workers. The cops and FBI figured they were spies, so they made 'em carry ID cards."

"Man, I ain't no damn spy!"

"I know that, you know that, but they don't know that!"

Laughter all around.

I began to feel faint. I recalled the jail in Dayton, and shuddered to think that they might pull up old records of my brief incarceration, then deny me a coveted cabaret card. In my agitation, I put my hands over my eyes.

"You okay?" Jimmy asked.

"I'm fine . . . just fine!" But I had an awful time standing there, waiting until they called our names. My knees trembled, and I wiped the glistening sweat off my nose. It wouldn't take much to make me leap out of line and run for the door. Don't panic, I steadied myself. Be cool, a voice in my head repeated over and over.

The night before, we had been made most welcome by Jimmy's frat brother and his family—wife, two sons, and mother-in-law. The house in St. Albans, Long Island, turned out to be one of the many large, stately homes acquired by upwardly mobile black professionals. In fact, lots of very successful musicians, including Duke Ellington's son, Mercer, lived nearby.

The mother-in-law, a sunny, smiling woman, her hair dyed jet-black, owned the house, bought with her earnings as a high school principal. Jimmy's frat brother worked in the post office, and his wife was a travel agent. Everybody was professional.

"My Aunt Helen, M'Ma's baby sister, attended your alma mater," I informed the mother-in-law as we sat around the kitchen table. We had unpacked our gear in our large, airy rooms and come back to the kitchen to be sociable (and to find out if we could use the kitchen, or not!).

"Wilberforce?" The mother-in-law was delighted. "Did she belong to AKA?"

"Yes, and she teaches math in a Cleveland high school."

The woman really loosened up then, and poured us cups of the inky black coffee to which her daughter seemed to be completely addicted.

"I'm going to throw the cards for you-all." My mouth dropped open in surprise. A psychic school principal? I glanced at Jimmy out of the corner of my eye. Beyond him, Miss M shot me silent signals. *Whoa!*

Our hostess shuffled the well-worn playing cards and placed them on the table for each of us. Diamonds and hearts kept coming up, time and time again. "My gracious!" She peered at the cards. "You young people are really fortunate!"

She read Miss M's cards. "You, miss, are very beautiful inside and out, but . . ." She pointed to the ace of spades, as conspicuous against the sea of red cards as a black widow spider. "You must be careful not to give your heart to a short dark handsome young man!"

Miss M giggled and tossed her silvery-blonde hair. "My man friend is an older man with grey hair." She was speaking of her sugar daddy.

"Mark my words!" The mother-in-law tilted her head back, closed her eyes, and sighed.

"You," she said to Jimmy, "have more energy than most people. You have to slow down so you won't run out of this precious gift." Jimmy nodded.

"And you, miss," she turned to me, "you are the bravest woman I ever met in my life!" This stunning accolade left me unsatisfied. I really wanted to hear about Shirley and Jonathan and fabulous jobs and lots of money. Topics one might expect from a fortuneteller. "You and Jimmy," she continued, as if she understood my unspoken need, "will find your success in the West. The farther west you go, the more successful you both will become." This was specific. We were impressed.

"Thank you." We drank one more cup of the midnight brew and went to our rooms to rest up for the challenge of the next day.

Standing in line, I thought about the mother-in-law's psychic card reading. Lord, I prayed, please help me! Here I stand and I don't feel brave at all!

"Next!" The cop in charge barked.

I wobbled up to the table's edge. He grabbed my wrist, rolled my fingers across the blue ink pad, and pushed one finger at a time onto one of the pages that littered the tabletop. There I was: branded and exposed before the world.

"Smile!" He growled and thrust a camera toward my face. I mustered up a weak, halfhearted smile as he snapped my photo.

"Here's a temporary permit to work. We'll check your background, and in a few days you will be informed of your status." His voice rat-a-tat-tatted in my ear. Wait . . . wait . . . The words echoed in my brain. I turned away and rammed my hands in my pockets, feeling like a felon waiting for the jury to bring in the verdict. I swallowed a moan.

While Jimmy took his turn at the table, and then Miss M, the frightful thoughts mounted, one over the other, until I shoved them to the back of my mind. In a rush of sheer relief, we pushed our way through the line, out the police station door, and into the deafening din of the city.

"I'm gonna tell you both how to stay alive in this city," Jimmy said. From the police station, we had trekked over to the union hall and transferred from Buffalo #533 to New York #802. "Let's go to Chock Full o' Nuts and eat. That's the first rule: always eat, little-bitty meals, all the time, and lots of Orange Julius."

The menu offered good solid food, hearty but cheap: grilled-cheese sandwiches, hot split-pea soup, and coffee or hot chocolate. As we plowed through our lunch, Jimmy continued his lessons in survival. "Look around you at all times—360 degrees. Keep your purse hanging in front of you at all times. Separate your keys and money. Don't keep everything in your purse. Keep some money in your shoe or the belt around your waist. Make sure you buy purses with a zipper closing at the top. Buy a newspaper—small, like the *Daily News*—so you won't have to catch anyone's eye on the subway."

He paused, looked at our amazed faces, and laughed. "When I was living here going to school at the New York Conservatory of Modern Music in Brooklyn, I rode every subway in the city to the end of the line and back."

"That's neat." "Jeez!"

Jimmy continued. "If you see a crime goin' down in the subway, get up and move to another car." This advice left us speechless.

"You'll get used to it," he reassured us. "Miss M, you gonna have to get a garage for the Lincoln. You don't wanna be hung up in an interview and not be able to feed the meter or move the car. And these cops will tow your 'short' in a New York minute!"

Miss M made a face. "I heard. In fact, I'm gonna take care of that little thing today. I'm gonna check out a couple of old girlfriends from the wheel in Buffalo. They may have some leads on future gigs."

We split up after agreeing to meet at the Russian Tea Room that night. Jimmy and I went to meet Papa Jo Jones at Jim and Andy's on West 48th Street, one of the more popular hangouts for musicians. We walked into the dark, smoke-filled bar. The place was buzzing, with cats hanging at the bar, lounging in the booths, and crowding the aisles. We spotted Jo Jones, known all over the world as "the man who plays like the wind." He came to fame playing with Count Basie. He was holding court at the bar, surrounded by cats I knew only from their famous recordings. I recognized some from TV shows and concert posters: J. J. Johnson, Ernie Royal, Thad Jones, Sarah Vaughan (one of the few women who hung out there), Stan Getz, Al Cohn, Zoot Sims, Clark Terry, and Jackie Williams. A&R Studios was upstairs, so lots of the cats waited at Jim and Andy's between recording dates.

Jo spotted us and jumped off his bar stool to greet us. "Well, here's my kiddies!"

He looked at me curiously. We had never met before, so we measured each other carefully. Oh, he was dapper! A slight figure of a man with straight, coal black hair fringing his balding head. A wide smile lit up his copper-colored face and illumined black eyes that never rested on anything for very long. He wore a dark suit made on Savile Row in London, a light blue shirt especially made for TV appearances, and a dark knitted tie.

"My kiddies!" he exclaimed again. "Let's go over to a booth and get away from all these *yan-a-gans.*" And thus began a friendship that lasted over twenty-five years.

He ordered Hennessy cognac for us and himself. I sat back and sipped.

"Always eat before you come in here," Papa Jo advised us. "These cats would rather buy you a drink than buy you a sandwich. Their hearts are not as big as a mustard seed!"

I looked around the room, checking out the scene. Then I felt a pull, as if some subtle force was drawing my attention toward the bar. At the very end stood a heavyset man dressed in a rumpled dark suit, his hat pushed to the back of his head, a cigar clenched in his teeth. He'd been there since we entered the place, in the background, unnoticed until I felt his eyes on me. Vivid blue eyes stared into mine. He smiled. Then he ambled over to our booth. Jo Jones stopped talking. He seemed annoyed, but said with a wave of his hand, "This is Sunny."

We said, "How do you do?" not inquiring about his last name.

"I been checkin' youse out," he informed us in a gruff voice. "Youse are alright!" He turned and ambled through the milling crowd and out of the bar.

Jo watched him leave, then informed us, "Sunny used to be a member of the Dutch Shultz gang." He stopped for effect. "I mean an *active* member."

"Really?"

Jo leaned forward and spoke in a hushed, conspiratorial voice. "If he likes you, you'll never have to worry about *any*body bothering you in New York City." He grinned and added, "He plays the horses, and he doesn't rub people out anymore."

I was fascinated, feeling like I had been swept into the midst of a George Raft gangster movie. But Jimmy nodded, his face set and serious.

We went back to discussing possible career moves with Papa Jo. The bar reeked of blue-gray cigarette smoke, and Jo contributed a lot of it. A *stone* chain-smoker, he lit a new cigarette from the glowing ash of the last. Jimmy and I smoked too, but this was the first time I felt like I was doing it in self-defense.

Suddenly, Sunny stood beside us. He had arrived so quietly, he startled me. He handed Jimmy a large shopping bag. "Here's something for youse." He stepped behind me and said to Jimmy, "May I?" In his hand he held a fine gold chain dangling a beautiful gold cross. Jimmy nodded, his eyes full of wonder. Sunny placed the chain around my neck so the gold cross settled at the base of my throat.

I touched the little cross with my fingertips. "Why, Sunny, thank you."

"It's nothin'." Sunny smiled and returned to his favorite spot at the end of the bar.

Jo Jones made a sideways motion with his hands. "Don't open that bag here." Jimmy obeyed.

Hours passed before we could satisfy our curiosity. We said good night to Jo, picked up Miss M at the Russian Tea Room, made the long trip back to St. Albans, and tiptoed up to our rooms before Jimmy finally opened the shopping bag. He pulled out an expensive suit from Saks Fifth Avenue—brand-new, with the tags still swinging on it. It fit perfectly and stumped us with a mystery. How did Sunny know Jimmy's size?

* * *

It seemed a whole lifetime ago when the country was galvanized by initials: FDR, WPA, CCC, NRA, and KKK.

Now, in the early '60s, the whole country was again galvanized by the initials: JFK, RFK, MLK, and KKK. The business of the nation took place against an agonizing background of marches on Washington, the murders of civil-rights martyrs, and disorder at the border as young men slipped over into Canada to live rather than die in Vietnam.

Against this backdrop of change and confusion and violence, Jimmy, Miss M, and I kept on pushing to make a life in New York City.

Frank Como, one of Jimmy's schoolmates from the conservatory in Brooklyn, greeted us warmly at his office. "Hey, Jimmy, want some work?" Tall and handsome, Frank had large eyes, and his ready smile reflected pleasure. He immediately gave Jimmy a gig copying music parts for the symphony. When he found out that I was a jazz pianist, he seemed overjoyed. "My wife, Roberta, is also a jazz pianist!"

"That's a groove!" I replied. "I'd like to meet her."

Roberta Como and I were introduced to each other at Steinway Hall. Jimmy and Frank arranged the surprise, and were beside themselves with glee as we warily looked each other over, surrounded by dozens of Steinway pianos. Roberta, a tall, willowy woman with a decidedly New England accent, said "Pleased to meecha!"

"Don't just stand there," Frank pointed to the two baby grands that occupied the stage at one end of the hall, "go up there and play!"

The two men were insistent. I felt like knocking their heads together. I was more than a little annoyed at being blindsided like this—so was "Bert." But we took our places at the lovely Steinways and began to mess around on the keys, feeling each other out. Then, glory! Bert and I romped through the jazz repertoire. She and I fit together like soda and Black Label scotch!

Jimmy and Frank decided then and there that the two pianos *must* be recorded. Frank said, "I'm gonna call a friend of mine. He's from England and has his own label."

"All right!" Jimmy caught fire. "I'll get Jo Jones on drums and George Duvivier on bass."

No quicker said than done.

Bert did the arrangements, including a lovely and, for its time, far-out treatment of "Over the Rainbow." She had each of us playing in a different key. In fact, George said, "This is one of the most interesting and longest bowing recording I ever made. I enter playing arco in one key, and you ladies are in different keys—it's like walking on eggs!" He grinned at Jo Jones. "This is pretty far out!" Bert and I glowed.

The record, called *Academy Awards in Jazz*, on the Grenadier label, received great reviews from Dan Morgenstern. The decision to record the two pianos turned out to be a momentous move. Today, it is in the archives of Rutgers University in the George Duvivier ocollection.

We made another momentous move when we visited Jimmy's father and stepmother up in the Bronx. "It's only a duty call," Jimmy growled. "He never raised me. But I guess we should go up and see them and get it over with."

Andrew Cheatham looked like a brown Edward G. Robinson. He had retired from the L&N Railroad in Birmingham, Alabama, and now owned his own cleaning shop in the Bronx. His second wife, Marge, was a fine-looking woman—taller than Andrew, with beautiful high-brown skin, naturally wavy black hair, and the voice of a five-year-old, childish and sweet.

Jimmy's father, known as A. C., was delighted to see us. We had a great time, and when our host and hostess went to the kitchen for refreshments, I whispered to Jimmy, "Hey, the old guy really loves you." Jimmy didn't say a word.

When the couple returned bearing lemonade and cake, A. C. blurted out, "We'd like it if you two would move in here. Whatever you can afford is all right with us." Marge nodded, smiling.

Jimmy stared. Then I saw storm clouds gathering on his face. So did his dad, who quickly said, "Er . . . just think about it and let us know. You're welcome anytime."

Swaying back and forth on a seat on the D train heading back to Manhattan, Jimmy was very quiet. "Well," I prodded, "you know, we're gonna need a sitter for Jonathan. I want him with us sooner rather than later."

I glanced across the aisle where a weird-looking man with long, grey hair and an unkempt beard, dressed in three coats and gloves with no fingers, glared at me. "What the hell *you* lookin' at?" he howled.

"Read your paper!" Jimmy hissed, reminding me that I'd forgotten New York etiquette.

I buried my head in the newspaper. "What about Jonathan?" I persisted.

"A. C. didn't raise me," Jimmy repeated from behind *his* newspaper.

"So what? At least he's asking for a second chance. He's not putting you out like my dad did, he's taking you in!"

Silence. The D train hurtled around a sharp curve. Clackety-clack! Clackety-clack!

"Okay. But if I don't like it, I'm gone!"

Mission accomplished.

We moved in that weekend. Mapes Avenue, a beautiful tree-lined street, was right around the corner from the Bronx Zoo. The house used to be a synagogue. The apartment buildings lining the street were full of Italians. The candy store on the corner sold egg creams. Heaven!

Miss M moved into a one-room walk-up apartment in the Village. The bathtub, right in the middle of the living room, was covered and used as a table when nobody needed a bath. She installed a telephone so she could call me when she was on her way to pick me up in a long black limo, on the way to a Mafia gig.

* * *

"We can't accept your check." The voice of the grey-haired blue-eyed bank teller dripped as cold as ice water. He peered at my paycheck again. His eyes opened wider. His pink face flushed redder.

"I'm not taking money out. I'm trying to put money in," I explained. Miss M and I got paid $800 apiece for the two-week gig for her Mafia friends. I went to a bank on Southern Boulevard to open a checking account.

"You have to bring your husband to sign for you in order to have *any* kind of account. And he has to show proof of a steady job."

"What?"

The teller curled his lip, "That's all. Bring him with you and we can do business. Next in line, please!" I couldn't believe my ears. We were living in the 1960s, but I felt as if I had plunged back into the 1860s. Down South, up North, again!

I returned to the house and told Marge about the bank's policy. "Oh, everybody knows that! Never you mind. I'll take you down to my friend Lena's store. She'll cash it for you."

Lena greeted us in her thick Italian accent, took the check to the back room of the store, and came back with crisp greenbacks. "Mama Mia!" her throaty voice rose in awe. "What do you do to make so much money?"

Marge peered at the bills in Lena's hand. "How much money is that?"

I felt disaster coming on.

"Eight hundred dollars." Lena sounded impressed.

"Eight hundred dollars?" Marge gasped. The two women stared at me. Marge declared, "I didn't know a woman could make that kind of money!" Oh boy! The old, hateful war with M'Da flashed through my mind.

Lena said something in Italian and handed over the money. "Madre di Dio!" Madre my bee-hind! I fumed to myself. I guess I could have explained that I didn't make that kind of dough all the time. Mostly, money in our business came in like little droplets, not a waterfall. And where the hell are people like these two women when we have to "drink muddy water and sleep in a hollow log"? From that moment on, Marge's fun-loving relationship with me changed, and I realized Jimmy and I would have to move again.

Funny. An old white man at the bank, an old black woman, and an old Italian woman—all of them heartless mad because of my hard-earned money. Even *women* wanted women to stay barefoot and pregnant.

* * *

Beginner's luck and a daily dose of determination, inspiration, and perspiration—a surefire antidote to failure—carried us through barriers and past obstacles like a dose of croton oil.

We got lucky fast. I played at Town Hall with a trio and a vocalist named Rita Abbey. Eubie Blake and Noble Sissle headed up the program. What an honor it was to appear on the same show with these time-tested giants. Jimmy arranged all the music, and Larry Gales (bass) and Eddie Cornelius (drums) made for a wonderful evening.

"Boy!" I marveled to Jimmy. "Every time it seems that we've run out of steam, something good happens."

"Seems that way," he agreed.

We "checked all the traps" constantly, going from the Turf on 49th Street, known worldwide for its cheesecake, to Jake Koven's studio, where Jimmy and most of the cats practiced to keep their chops ready for whatever, to the Metropole, where Cozy Cole, legendary drummer known for the hit tunes "Topsy Part I" and "Topsy Part II," held sway. George Holt, our friend and trumpet player from the old Buffalo days, played with Cozy.

On George's recommendation, Jimmy did a killer arrangement of "Slaughter on Tenth Avenue" for the five-piece group.

Attitude was everything. Feast or famine, that's the game—getting over, that's our aim! Sometime we up, sometime we down! And the hustle was a never-ending constant.

"Babe," Jimmy announced one evening when we had a no-show by one of the "no singing" vocalists we coached at the little studio we rented by the hour, "I don't know how we gonna get back to the Bronx. I spent all the money I brought with me to rent the studio."

A dismal picture of us pickin' 'em up and layin' 'em down across the George Washington Bridge flashed through my head—and we were booked for a vocalist at ten a.m. the next day! If we had a few bucks, we could have stayed in one of the all-night movies in Times Square.

I felt too weary to get angry. We made our way along the crowded sidewalks of Broadway, the myriad neon signs beginning to light up the night, flashing on and off, on and off. At the bottom of one of our lowest periods, they seemed dimmer, somehow.

Just then, Julius Watkins came swingin' down the street. A premier French horn player, we hadn't seen him in a long time. Not since Buffalo, in fact. "Hey, you guys! I didn't know you-all were in town." He informed us he'd just gotten back from Europe. "How you guys doin'?"

"Fine, fine." We smiled. "Never let 'em see you cry" was the motto of most musicians. You had to look successful and act successful to be successful.

"Okay! Glad to hear it. Good to see you again." He gave me a hug, shook Jimmy's hand, and went on swingin' down the street.

Jimmy slowly unfurled his fingers. Julius had placed a tightly folded bit of green paper in Jimmy's hand. A hundred-dollar bill.

Speechless, we stood rooted as the crowd split and flowed around us. Julius Watkins's heart was bigger than a mustard seed. We weren't lucky—we were blessed.

* * *

Three letters arrived on the same day, forwarded from St. Albans to Mapes Avenue. The first two granted Jimmy and me our permanent cabaret cards. Thank God! The feds had not spread my Dayton arrest data across the country. Now, much relieved, I was free to work the nightclubs of New York City.

The third letter read as follows:

Dear Sis:

I'm really glad you and Jimmy are in New York getting relocated. There certainly was nothing for you-all in Buffalo. I wish Jerry would get out—alone!

I'm glad to be settled back in Akron again. I sure wanted to live in Denver where I was stationed so long ago, but I guess that's the way the cookie crumbles. I sure bounced around a lot—different cities, different boy friends (smile) and different jobs.

Now, I've been studying nursing in Cleveland and am now content to be in Akron working at Akron General Hospital. Shirley and I are great friends. I know you enjoy her letters and talking to her on the phone.

Dad is still clowning!!! Maybe even worse this year than last year, so, it's no sense in you planning to come back here. You'll have no peace.

Now, I have something serious to ask you. Shirley's father has remarried—to a wonderful lady. They've been here to visit Shirley. Now, don't have a fit! You know Shirley's really smart and should go to a good private school.

Jay and his wife (by the way, she is a black woman) want to take Shirley to Boston and let her go to Girl's Latin School there. Mom and I checked it out. It's a first class school and Jay and his wife have a house. (I think it belongs to her.*)*

Jeannie, Jay is really sincere about paying Shirley's school expenses and sending her to a fine college.

You have to give her the chance.

I know he can't do it without your permission and I also know you will do the right thing. Everybody deserves a second chance.

Let me know as soon as you possibly can so Shirley can sign up this fall. Trust me, I trained people in the Air Force. I know who is real and who is not. This woman will do the right thing.

> *Your sis,*
> *Charlotte*
> *XXX*

P.S. I've been going out with a man named Carl Mans. He used to be a gamblin' man but now he's working at Goodyear. He is quite the gentleman but he don't put up with no stuff! More about him later.

P.P.S. But I have hopes!?!

Enraged is not the word for how I felt! Tears ran down my face as I sat in the room alone and reread the letter. *Jesus H. Christ!* Jay had a lotta damn nerve coming into the picture after all this time. He never seemed interested in the slightest, from the day Shirley was born. He wouldn't even sign her birth certificate.

I wanted to commit murder. If thoughts could kill, Jay would be stone cold dead in his grave. I paced up and down the room with my hands over my mouth. I didn't want Marge or A. C. to hear me. I tore the letter in two and threw the pieces across the room.

After a while the rage burned itself out, and I collapsed onto the bed, hardly able to breathe. My longtime dream of providing a stable home for Shirley was shattered. It all boiled down to money—and I had none. Schools like the one Charlotte named were completely out of my reach.

It was devastating to think that Jay could waltz into Shirley's life and give her all the things that I dreamed of providing her but could not afford. I found it even harder to believe that he really intended to take on the responsibility. How could the world's worst womanizer change that much? But Charlotte sounded positive that he had.

I picked up the wrinkled pieces of the letter and smoothed them out on my pillow. I reread Charlotte's words. That "second chance" comment caught my eye. I had told Jimmy the very same thing about his dad. Oh, God!

Suddenly I felt very lonely. Jimmy was in Manhattan, copying music for *The Jimmy Dean Show*. With a deadline looming, he planned to work two or three days straight, getting the show ready. This was my battle.

I decided to sleep on the whole mess. Tomorrow I would get up and go down to 180th and Southern Boulevard to the magazine store owned by a friend, an elderly Jewish lady; I could use the phone there. I didn't want Marge or A. C. to overhear when I spoke to Charlotte. I wanted to talk to my sister privately and see what was what.

Next morning, I dressed and quietly let myself out. During an anguished night I had decided not to stand in Shirley's way—to let her go. "I despise the whole thing!" I cried to Charlotte. "I hate, hate, hate it! But the way the world is, the way women are treated by men and banks and other women, she's gonna need all the education she can get—like being armed for battle. She needs the biggest guns she can handle so she can be her own boss and live her life at the top of the heap—not buried at the bottom!"

"Good Lord!" Charlotte said, "you really sound upset. Don't worry, you doin' the right thing. Shirley loves you. She won't forget you're her mother. But if she doesn't get this chance, everybody goin' to regret it as long as they live."

I knew my sister spoke the God-awful truth, and truth is supposed to be the light. I will be brave. Have mercy!

* * *

"Please come right away!" The wee voice on the phone jarred me awake. I sat up in bed and swung my feet to the floor. The old lamp with its tasseled silk shade threw weird shadows on the flocked wallpaper, Marge's idea of genteel decorating. Huge velvet wine-colored flowers marched in rows from the ceiling to the floor. She had no idea that the same flocked paper adorned the walls of a house of ill repute we used to jam in after hours in Columbus, Ohio.

It was five a.m. when I woke Jimmy. Without hesitation we got dressed and took the train down to Miss M's walk-up. We found the door ajar and pushed it open. Cautious, we entered the darkened room. Jimmy called out, "Hey, are you here?"

A wee sound, almost that of a mewling kitten, came from the bed in the corner. I found the switch, and light flooded the room. She was lying half on, half off the bed, white as a sheet and wrapped in nothing but a blanket.

"What happened?" I sat on the bed beside her and took her hand in mine. Her fingers were cold and clammy. Her silvery blonde hair, damp and lifeless, clung like pond fronds to her face. "How long you been like this?"

"Two days," she quavered. She whispered a tale of love and rejection and violence. She had fallen in love with a young Mafia character she met while dancing at the Copa. She wanted him to marry her, but he had a wife. Miss M stubbornly proceeded to get pregnant, hoping to force his hand. Instead, he sent a couple of goons to her apartment, drove her out to Brooklyn in a limo, and had some back-alley abortionist do a job on her. Afterward, the goons drove her back to the Village, shoved her bleeding body through her front door, and split.

Jimmy and I exchanged worried glances. We didn't want any part of the Mafia. Helping Miss M might be dangerous if the ex-boyfriend found out and took offense. In unspoken agreement, we dressed Miss M and caught a cab to the nearest hospital.

At the hospital, confronted by suspicions and pelted with questions, we deliberately became a pair of dimwits. "I don't know what happened!" "We have no idea how she got this way!"

Eyes were everywhere, probing, cross-examining. There we stood, two black people propping up a bleeding white woman. In my mind, I pictured us doing a "hot sock" dance to get down the corridor and out the front door.

That's a dance without shoes and with hot coals underfoot. But friendship overcame fear, and we stood by Miss M until she was safely settled.

Miss M stayed in the hospital for a week, she had lost so much blood. Then they transferred her to the psychiatric ward, where she confided her thoughts to a shrink. Her doctor told us that even after suffering such terrible abuse, she refused to believe that the cat would never, ever return her love. The psychic school principal's warning to Miss M had been in vain.

New York, New York—a city so tough, they named it twice!

Fatback

· · · · · · · · · · · · · · · · · · · ·

"*Y*ou hasn't begun to live till you fishes the fatback from out yo' bowl of black-eye peas!" Old Uncle Sid, the sage of Bina Avenue, would utter, his head tilted to one side, a sly smile on his lips.

Our "fatback" turned out to be a fat little old man from Denmark who lived in a nice building with a striped awning stretching out to the street, one block down from the home of Jimmy's dad. "You two! Stop!" he called out to us from across the street one early morning. We were "quick stepping" along the sidewalk, trying to catch the crosstown bus to the Grand Concourse. We didn't want to miss the D train to Manhattan.

"Come! Come!" He gestured as if he meant to scoop us off our sidewalk onto his. "I want to talk to you both." We were in a hurry, but curiosity got the better of us, so we scurried across the street and joined him under the awning.

"Listen," he said, his sky blue eyes twinkling like old St. Nick's on Christmas Eve, "I've watched you two lovebirds for a long time. I like what I see." His rosy cheeks blushed even rosier. "Are you looking for an apartment? Rent controlled?" His accented words danced to the lilting sound of Scandinavia.

"*Are* we? Yes, we *are!*" Jimmy and I exclaimed at the same time.

"Well, me and my wife have been in this country for over forty years. I was merchant seaman. We never have children . . ." His blue eyes clouded, just for a moment. "Now, I take Else back to our home in Denmark." He swept his hand toward the lobby of the building, "Come! Upstairs. We talk."

Jimmy and I exchanged glances. It was Wednesday, "fishing day" at the union, the day when musicians picked up gigs and small checks. Every musician in town would be there—big fish and little fish—but we followed the old man up four double flights of stairs to apartment 4E.

He unlocked the door and called out, "It is me, Else, and I have the young ones with me!" A short stout woman came into the hallway to meet us. Round and rosy-cheeked, her face was wreathed with smiles. Her eyes were china blue. Her snow-white braids wrapped around her head in a double row like a crown. Her feet were encased in black "space shoes," and we could tell she had trouble walking.

"Come in, come in!" She invited us to sit on the sofa. She served me tea while her husband poured whiskey for Jimmy. Then they sat opposite us in two high-backed chairs. The old guy told stories of his adventures as a merchant seaman, and the laughter grew louder and louder. The time flew by as he kept Jimmy's shot glass, and his own, full of scotch.

"Skoal!" he shouted and threw the whiskey down his throat.

"Skoal!" Jimmy answered, really getting into the swing of things.

Else and I drank tea and ate homemade cookies and smiled at the men.

When the whiskey bottle was almost empty, our host wiped his mouth with the back of his hand and intoned, "Well, young people, this apartment is yours if you want it. You can really hold your liquor, young man! I'll go with you to the office of the apartment owners on 163rd Street and turn everything over to you."

"Er . . . what will be the cost?" My voice quavered as I voiced the fear that Jimmy and I might not have enough ready money to take advantage of this gift from heaven.

"Not a thing! You two help us pack our belongings, take us down to the ship, and help us depart."

Else added wistfully, "You must take care of my geraniums in the window."

"I will," I promised as I watched her sky blue eyes mist over. Mine did, too.

Up and down, up and down four double flights we traipsed with the trophies of their lives in America, properly packed and labeled for the long voyage home. And down we all went to the sea, to the bustling docks.

Jimmy bought one dozen red roses for Else and expensive cigars for her husband. As we helped them to their stateroom, the old man said in his thick accent, "Else and I come to this country in steerage. We go back to Denmark in first class!" We hugged and kissed the two old people, then at the call "All ashore that's going ashore," we left the stateroom and made our way down the gangplank to the dock.

As the two little figures stood at the rail peering through a rainbow of colored paper streamers thrown from ship to shore and everybody cried "Bon voyage!" my breath caught in my throat. I realized that the couple had neither chick nor child to help them face old age and record their visit on this planet.

We were their children—two black children of Africa in a sea of blonde and white-haired children of Norway, Denmark, and Sweden, standing on the shore and waving farewell as the ship disappeared beyond the horizon.

* * *

We rushed back to apartment 4E, 2141 Mapes Avenue, put the key in the lock of our first, very own home, entered, hugged each other, and danced and boogied from room to room! We found the original royal blue Little Orphan Annie mug on the sill of the frosted bathroom window, and the geraniums in three delft blue flowerpots were freshly watered. Else left behind a pair of six-sided candelabra with ivory inserts hand-painted with scenes of windmills; they had been made for her great-grandmother in Norway in the 1800s. Everything had a place and everything remained in its place: silverware, dinnerware, pots and pans, handmade potholders with little Nordic scenes sewn into them like miniature quilts. The hardwood floor shown like a newly minted penny.

The darling couple left a plate of cheeses and crackers and a bottle of Black Label scotch in the refrigerator. In the bedroom, the lovely old mahogany bed was freshly made with clean white sheets, and on the pillows with cases edged in handmade lace we discovered a book full of the raunchiest pornography we had ever seen.

* * *

Lawd have mercy!

It was a "great gettin' up morning" the day we brought our little son, Jonathan, from Buffalo to our brand-new home in the Bronx! He bounded into the hallway the minute we unlocked the front door, then ran through each room, his little travel bag swinging from his shoulder. We watched as he finally skidded to a halt in the living room and smiled as he announced, "There's an old lady in the bathroom with white hair like a crown and big black shoes on her feet!"

Jimmy and I looked at each other in amazement. Jesus! It was my first inkling that my son had inherited the family gift of "sight." I needn't have worried; Jonathan seemed unconcerned. He threw his bag on the floor, climbed up on the couch, and began to jump up and down. "Mom and Dad! I like our new house!"

My heart righted itself.

"I'll make us some hot chocolate—with marshmallows."

* * *

Our new home was a little corner in paradise. In fact, I named it "Outer Eden." Spending spring and summer Sundays in the Bronx Zoo right around the corner was like being in the Garden of Eden: the beautifully tended grassy knolls bordered with lovely multicolored flowers nodding in the breeze beside winding paths; unexpected glimpses of secluded ponds reflecting azure skies; people from all over the world strolling along in their colorful native dress, speaking in a hundred tongues; the universal sounds of "ooo!" and "ahhh!" as people viewed all the animals and birds on display in their man-made homes.

We chose a nice shady spot where our son and a couple of his friends could run and play freely while Jimmy and I broke out the Sunday *New York Times*, fried chicken, biscuits, fresh fruit, lemonade, and cupcakes home-made from the old 1-2-3-4 cake recipe from Bina Avenue.

We, the women of the fourth floor of "Outer Eden," had a *thing* goin' on.

"The smells that come out of your apartment!" the Italian lady across the hall exclaimed after she rang my doorbell. I laughed as she rolled her eyes and rubbed her stomach.

"Braised lamb shanks marinated in red wine with garlic and rosemary," I said, pleased with the compliment. "Would you like a taste?"

Without hesitation she countered my offer. "I'll trade you spaghetti and meatballs for some of your lamb." She paused and pursed her lips, as if considering international banking rates of exchange. "And a plate of anise cookies—homemade!"

"Done!"

My Jewish neighbor, in the third apartment, bartered her cabbage rolls for my London broil. And so the ritual began. Our fourth-floor walk-up became the nucleus for the extended neighborhood, reminding me so much of the old days on Bina Avenue.

The voices of children rang out, "Roly-oly-oly-oh!" and the sounds of the stickball games at dusk, just before the streetlights came on, were loud and lusty.

"Anthony! Anthony!" the call came from the building full of Italians in the middle of the block.

Next door to Jimmy's dad, a thin, nervous little black man with "duty" stamped on his high forehead was raising his six children alone in a house with a neatly kept yard fenced all around with black metal stakes. His wife had decided that she could not endure domesticity another minute and split, jumping back into the life of a party girl with a vengeance.

The family in the next house came from Puerto Rico—a kind, happy group. The papa headed the neighborhood Boy Scout troop and taught karate and jujitsu, even though one of his legs was much shorter than the other.

Li'l Jimmy O'Brien lived across the street from Anthony's family. His mother and father were "fallin' down" drunks. Li'l Jimmy was eight, small and thin for his age. "It's a darn shame," A. C. drawled. "That kid has to cook, clean, buy groceries, wash clothes, and get himself to school— all by his lonesome." A. C.'s eyes were steely. Li'l Jimmy often scampered across the street to sit on A. C.'s front steps or on the porch swing. The child always seemed exhausted, could hardly speak. He'd just pant and bob his head.

"Did you eat today, Jimmy?"

A shrug, a sag of his head. "No."

A. C. and Marge and Marge's sister fed him and let him be a little boy for just a little while. Then his pale pinched face relaxed, and his big blue eyes, ringed with dark circles, began to sparkle, and his thin shoulders would straighten a little. "I better go," he would sigh, "Mama and Papa will be wakin' up."

Marge would hand him a bag of food. "In case you wanna snack later." He nodded, his face returning to the tense, worried look of a child forced to be too old, too soon. Paradise lost.

* * *

We went out from Eden to forage far and wide, following up on gigs and promises of gigs.

Thank God for A. C.! He and Jonathan had a grand old time together. I tried very hard to set my schedule around my son's school times. Sometimes, on holidays and weekends, he came with us to Jim and Andy's, where Sunny, the ex-mafioso, and Al Cohn's father kept him happy. Al Cohn was a world-renowned tenor player.

"I looked around and our son was sitting in Sarah Vaughan's lap," Jimmy reported to me after a record session.

I laughed. "He knows whose lap to sit on. Only the greatest!"

Jimmy went everywhere and knew everybody. He played Broadway shows, ice shows, jazz bands; arranged and copied music for artists to appear on Merv Griffin's show; and, along with me, coached vocalists. I began extracting more music from recordings for Wes Montgomery, a great jazz guitarist, and became a sought-after rehearsal pianist.

I did a stint with Ed Ames, of the Ames Brothers vocal group, while he got ready to go solo. "That was a bitch! That was a *real* bitch!" Ed's manager repeated as we finished "Bridge over Troubled Water." Ed's beautiful baritone voice soared up to the high ceiling of the brownstone apartment. I really played the mess out of the very difficult piano-conductor part, the Steinway baby grand talking back to my fingers, answering everything I asked of it. They taped the session, but to my regret I never received a copy. Still, their validation of my ability that day carried me through many challenging episodes in my career.

Papa Jo Jones was a constant in our lives. He took us to the Embers, where he was playing with Joe Bushkin, that venerable pianist, who swore to anyone who would listen, "I take a pill to go to sleep, and I take a pill to wake up." Joe carried all his pills around in a small metal case.

"I'm going to take you to meet a pianist, not a piano player!" Papa Jo said one evening. The pianist turned out to be Dorothy Donegan, a slim woman dressed in "showtime-show folks" fashion, draped and glittering, golden slippers on her feet. The woman astounded everyone with her prowess, all the time telling jokes and pulling her wig askew and kicking up her heels. I never heard such great piano playing. She was all over the keyboard, just as unbelievable as Art Tatum—both true virtuosos.

We hung out at the Copper Rail on Seventh Avenue, across from the Metropole, and ate soul food and kept company with Lockjaw Davis, straw boss and tenor player with Count Basie's orchestra.

"Those yanagans are great musicians, but it's like herding cats tryin' to keep them on time, on the bandstand, on the bus." He clutched his stomach. "They givin' me ulcers!" We nodded sympathetically and tried to calm him down so he could eat.

The Brill Building became a major waystation for us, also. Joli Gonsalves and Joe "Tinker" Lewis's publishing company, Suite #405, was firmly entrenched at the Brill. The two men were alumni of Harry Belafonte, Leonard de Paur, and other famous vocalists. You never knew what was going to happen in that office.

One day, one of their clients came bursting through the door and shouted, "Hey, you gotta help me out! We're doing a limbo album 'round at Harlequin Studios, and we need one more tune. Tell me whatcha got!"

Limbo music was the flavor of the month. Joli and Joe began flipping rapidly through their catalogue. I started just as quickly going through my head, my mind turning like a subway turnstile. "I have a song," I spoke up.

The client turned to me and snapped his fingers. "How soon can you get it to me?" He spoke with a decidedly West Indian accent.

"One hour."

"Okay." He glanced at his watch. "I'll be back!" He darted out the door, then ran back. "One hour sharp, mon!" And, zoom, he was gone again.

While I sang the song I had just made up to Jimmy and Joli, they wrote it down, then quickly made a lead sheet.

"How Low Does Lulu Limbo When Lulu Limbos Low?" was recorded that afternoon. It was placed in Joli Tinker's catalogue. In turn, they signed for Jimmy and me to join ASCAP as artists and publishers. Jim-Jean Publishing Company was born.

Lawdy!

* * *

Joe Lewis introduced us to Mrs. Big D, a lady who opened her heart and home to struggling musicians and vocalists. The first person we met there was my old friend Tadd Dameron.

"Hey," he beamed, "what you doin' so far from home? What's goin' on in Ohio?" We hugged. He looked so frail that my breath caught in my throat. He seemed quite resigned to the fact that he was getting ready to leave this earthly plane. I resolved to visit often.

"Hey," he said to Jimmy and me one afternoon, "I'd like you two to have my latest tune."

"We'd be honored."

"It's hot off the presses!" Tadd handed us a brand-new sheet-music copy of "I'm Not Very Happy Anymore." It was hard to keep from crying.

On Joli and Joe's recommendation, we were coaching a slim, handsome young man, very much a bird of another feather compared to Tadd. Pale of face with a shock of thick dark hair that he tossed from his eyes with a jerk of his head, he sat hunched over, hands pressed between his knees. He sang like an angel and was being groomed to open for Phyllis Diller, the tart-tongued comedian.

Jimmy asked, "What are your plans for your career?"

He tossed his black hair, "All I want," he declared, "is an apartment on Sutton Place!"

Jimmy directed the full force of what some of our students called "Cheatham's Ray" at the kid.

"Is that all you think of your talent?"

The young man hung his head. Oh, not because he felt contrite. He was very ambitious, and we found out that he would do anything to further his aims.

"I'm gettin' married this weekend," he announced at one rehearsal not long after.

"What? Oh, er, to whom?"

We hadn't realized he even knew any young ladies. It turned out he had met a girl fresh out of the insane asylum. She was very pretty, but very fragile, nearly transparent, as if she were a veil between us and the pale winter sunlight. She smiled, then in an instant, the smile would disappear, a shadow would darken her pale blue eyes, and she would hold her head with both hands.

With a few questions to people who knew the kid, we found out why he wanted to get hitched so fast. The young woman had a bank account with about $900 in it—and the cat was broke. Jimmy declared, "We are not going to that wedding. It's an affront to all that's decent!"

But Mrs. Big D prevailed upon us to at least come to the reception at her home, which we did. The girl's mother was the only family that the bride had at the reception—a pale, anxious twin of her daughter.

The next week we heard the story of the fallout from the wedding. Tadd Dameron told us, "After she gave him the $900 in cold hard cash, the cat told that girl on her wedding night that he had no intention of ever consummatin' the marriage, 'cause he was gay."

As he related the sad tale, Tadd accompanied himself on the piano. Knowing Tad, Jimmy and I were not in the least surprised and asked, "What did she do?"

Tadd played minor chords. "She climbed out on the hotel's window ledge and threatened to jump off. In her white wedding gown!" Tadd's fingers made the music cascade down the keyboard.

"Jeez!"

"All's well that ends well . . ." He continued to play very soft and sad. "The cops came an' talked her back into the room. She wouldn't come in till the cat left. Now she's back in the insane asylum."

How low did that cat limbo to get his greedy hands on that poor girl's dough?

I gave you all my money, babe
What mo' could I do?
My stocks, bonds, securities
An' all my lovin' too!'

Tadd Dameron, composer of many lovely songs, including "Our Delight," "Casbah," and "If You Could See Me Now" (my favorite) went to
the great jam session in the sky in 1965.

Bronx Gulag and Agoraphobia

....

*T*wo hulking goons walked into the office of the two brothers Cohen, who owned most of the apartment buildings on Mapes Avenue, including our own, and shot them dead.

"The sky is falling!" intoned Papa Jo Jones. "The whole world is having a nervous breakdown." He took a sip of his Courvoisier and, with a wide gesture of his hand, declared, "Look around you! Cats don't cut their hair anymore . . . and not a please or thank you in a carload!"

He was right about the hair. Afros or "naturals" were all over Jim and Andy's. For the white musicians, it was long hair with long sideburns. Out on the sidewalks of New York, long hair, ironed straight on an ironing board, was swinging on the heads of women wearing short skirts and hot pants. In fact, every day at high noon, a blonde-wigged woman stopped traffic and caused all the maintenance men to catcall and whistle on Seventh Avenue and Forty-seventh Street by parading up and down in pink hot pants. She weighed 300 *pounds.*

Thank God for Yves St. Laurent! He designed the pantsuit, which covered all those women's knobby knees and less than lithe limbs that shamed the nation.

A chaotic half decade was bracketed by assassinations, starting with those of JFK in '63 and Medgar Evers in '64. History-making events tumbled one upon the other: the "I Have a Dream" speech by Martin Luther King Jr. at the March on Washington, the riots in most major cities (Cleveland, Chi-town, Detroit), city streets and college campuses filled with protesters, the Black Panthers' quest for equal access, disco music sounding a death knell for clubs with live music, the live-televised shooting of Lee Harvey Oswald by Jack Ruby, the assassination of Malcolm X in the Audubon Ballroom (where Jimmy's father and Marge had danced to big bands in the early years). The sixties closed, unofficially, with the assassinations of Martin Luther King and Robert Kennedy in '68.

"The whole country is hangin' on to a blade of grass, tryin' not to fall off the earth." Sonny, the old soldier for Dutch Shultz, was grim. "Ain't no respect, no more!"

The killing of the brothers Cohen changed our lives, also. The city took over the buildings, and the effect was dramatic and immediate. All of a sudden, our building was overrun by women who had no husbands, but at least a half dozen kids each. All the original tenants moved out, or were moved out by their grown children, who had watched this influx of dubious females with growing alarm.

"We hate to leave you here." My neighbors came to say good-bye. They brought me little gifts of anise cookies and Chianti wine. "We really hate to leave our little homes. We thought we'd live here till we died," my Jewish neighbor said in a melancholy voice, "well, until we died . . . or *whatever.*"

Dope dealers and addicts took over the neighborhood. Across the street, in the vacant lot where Boy Scouts used to play games, a new industry sprang up. "They are out there in broad daylight, teachin' kids how to strip cars in record time!" Jimmy complained.

"No!"

"Yeah." He shook his head as if the movement might dislodge his dismay. "I don't want you to go down to the mailbox anymore without me."

He was right. The three of us, Jonathan, Jimmy, and I, came from Manhattan one Saturday night, and starting from the first floor, all the way up the double walk-up to the fourth floor, we discovered a dark, shuffling line of people moving up to the apartment next to ours. A young woman—very thin, with bumpy light brown skin and bad teeth, and always sporting a greasy bandana on her head—had moved into that apartment with her little son. The super told us she had no furniture, only a mattress on the floor. Now, all the traffic was going into her apartment—one by one.

"That's it!" Jimmy was furious. The crowd moved aside while he put the key in the lock and shepherded us into our apartment. "I don't care *what* she's doin' in there, it *can't* be legal!" My heart froze. What had happened to our Eden? What did it all mean? We got the answer sooner than soon.

The kosher market closed, the Italian greengrocer closed, the shoe shop closed, and the cleaners closed because the new people didn't seem to wear clothes that ever got cleaned. The drugstore stayed, but installed double bars on its doors and windows. Break-ins and robberies became rampant.

The garbage that used to be picked up twice a week, with fines enforced for uncovered or dented cans, now wasn't picked up at all.

"You'd think, since Mayor Lindsay sent all these people here and the city is payin' their rent, that he could figure out that more people means more garbage!" The thin black man was outraged. "Can't the city count? More people, more garbage . . . more pick-ups!" He shouted at the top of his lungs. We were all sitting on A. C.'s porch, trying to figure out what to do. We took turns calling city hall—to no avail.

Jimmy went on the road with Duke Ellington's orchestra, and I assured him that Jonathan and I would be okay. A. C. said, "I'll look out after them—don't you worry."

But then came the time when I decided to go down to the magazine store to chat with the owner, one of the last of my female friends still living in our changing neighborhood. It was high noon. "Oy, vey!" Startled, she threw up her hands. We had been talking quietly across the counter when three men barged into the little store. Swiftly, they hit the old lady over the head, shoved me onto the cramped floor of the phone booth, yanked the money out of the cash register, and split. To my terrorized mind everything seemed to move in slow motion.

Then, in comparison with the robbers' frantic activity, it became suddenly very still. I slowly uncurled myself from the floor of the phone booth and pushed open the door. I stumbled across the store and behind the counter, where I fell to my knees beside the old lady, who lay moaning on the worn linoleum. The wound on her head looked ugly, and I felt grateful that she was still alive. I scurried back to the phone booth to call the police. It never crossed my mind to run out onto the sidewalk. What the hell good would that do? Everybody on the street was either an addict or a crook. While I waited for the cops to arrive, I cradled my friend's head in my lap.

When the cops came, *they* would call for an ambulance. In New York, nobody calls an ambulance except the police. If you try, rival ambulance companies sometimes stop to fight over territory, and you're likely to be lying there a long time. New Yorkers always call the cops first!

After the police officers took my statement for their report, I went home —walked up the four double flights to my door, unlocked it, went in, and sat in Jimmy's big ol' chair. Then I began to shake. I thought about sinking into a bathtub of warm water to heat up my ice-cold body, but was afraid I wouldn't be able to climb out again. So I just sat there—and shook. I didn't move from that chair, trembling and exhausted, dozing fitfully until it was time for Jonathan to come home from school, and then the door-bell rang. "Lord," I prayed, "please help me get myself together before that child comes in this door!" I got to my feet—and became Jonathan's mom.

For the next eighteen months I wore sunglasses because the sun seemed too bright. I found that I could not stand in line anywhere, for any reason. The subway terrified me. At unexpected moments my heart took off at a mile a minute, racing even while I was sleeping. Several times I went to the emergency room and after sitting there for hours, they would tell me, "We can't find anything wrong with you or your heart."

I started thinking, Hey, maybe I'm insane. Then I'd tell myself, You can't be insane; insane people don't know they're insane. Small comfort that, particularly since my fear prevented me from taking any jobs at the re-hearsal studios. I stayed in our apartment and extracted music for other musicians and listened to Joe Zawinul and Cannonball Adderley playing "Mercy, Mercy, Mercy!" on my record player.

Jimmy installed an alarm system in the apartment. For comfort, he put in an air conditioner. And bars across the windows near the fire escape. I became aware that I was truly in prison all over again. Not in a steel-barred cell as in Dayton—worse! Freedom marches and student demonstrations at colleges and universities were all over the television. A woman named Bernice Reagon appeared on the flickering screen and sang "Before I'd Be a Slave, I'd Be Buried in My Grave," and I cried and cried. I was locked behind *invisible* bars.

* * *

I was not alone in the (visibly and invisibly) barred apartment. Besides Jonathan and Jimmy, an army of roaches had taken up residence in the once varmint-free building. The city wouldn't pay the excellent super who cared for our building, and though he tried, he just couldn't buy the necessary repellents and cleaning materials with his pension.

The super's son, a likable young man, really loved Jimmy. "You can go to college. You can be anything you want!" Jimmy would encourage him. The advice meant even more, with the neighborhood under assault.

"This is Armageddon!" the old man moaned. "For twenty years I've prided myself on being a good super!" He stood only five feet tall and had a small hump in his back. His wide mouth usually smiled at everyone, but now he shook his head, his walnut-colored face dejected. "I don't know where these new jokers come from." Not long after, the super suffered a stroke. It seemed he just couldn't face a building with feces smeared under the stairs, children pissing in the halls, and grown people throwing their garbage out the windows into the inner courtyard. With a snicker, they called it "the airmail special."

The son tried valiantly to take his dad's place. We mopped our hall floor with hot water and bleach to help out, but nobody could win the war of the roaches. The new tenants brought them with them, nesting in their furniture and hidden inside boxes of belongings. The roaches seemed almost tame, used to humans. When we turned on the kitchen light, they didn't scurry away; they just stood there with one leg up and checked us out.

The gang that hung out in the vacant lot across the street stole a bike from the son of A. C.'s friend, the same man who had been outraged when the city stopped picking up the garbage. He told A. C., "I'm going to get that bike back! I paid good money for it and nobody messes with my kids!" Off he went around the corner to start his search. When he spotted his son's bike, the gang resisted his furious shouts and herculean efforts to wrest the bike away from them. One of them pulled out a stolen pistol. A. C.'s friend found the bike, and found a bullet right between the eyes.

The murder shocked the whole neighborhood. "It's a cryin' shame!" they mourned. More militant voices declared, "This is a war zone!" We found ourselves in the midst of what we thought of as "the *Un*civil War." The protester's body was taken south by his old mama and daddy, along with his six children.

*　*　*

The winter winds howled, and the blowing snow fell on the South Bronx, covering the mounds of garbage and junk and refuse with a pristine blanket. It looked like a fairyland for a little while, but inside our building the temperature was frigid, and we had to wear sweaters, scarves, and coats to keep from freezing to death. There was a shortage of heating oil, and Mayor Lindsay and his cronies would not allocate oil for the furnaces of the South Bronx. We called city hall in vain. Babies got pneumonia, and everybody coughed and sneezed and shivered.

The last straw came when the city allocated a couple million bucks for oil to heat the cages of the animals in the Bronx Zoo and millions more to build a new aviary for the zoo's display of caged birds. But none for the human beings hunched together for warmth in their freezing apartments.

A numbing despair settled over the whole neighborhood. Even the junkies and the roaches moved in slow motion. "Maybe we should move to the zoo!" A. C.'s house was just as cold and clammy as our building.

"Maybe we should all move to Gracie Mansion!" The Puerto Rican's jesting threat didn't elicit a single smile. Between chattering teeth he added, "In fact, maybe we should all move back to Puerto Rico!"

I called M'Ma. "We've tried to call city hall, but their phone stays off the hook." M'Ma remained silent for a long moment or two.

"The birds and the foxes have a place to lay their heads, but the sons of men have none," she whispered. "I do believe that Earth is the Alcatraz of the universe!"

The Light Shineth in the Darkness

· · · · · · · · · · · · · · · · · ·

Ev'ry body—sometime—
Lives a life they did not choose—
Lives of quiet desperation
Down in this basket full of blues!

I lay on the couch in my living room looking at *The Joe Franklin Show*. I had just returned from the emergency room at Bronx Hospital. The racing heart, shortness of breath, and other scary bodily betrayals had returned with a vengeance, just because I had gone downstairs to get the mail. I really thought I was dying—all alone.

Jimmy was on the road with Paul Mauriat, a French bandleader touring America with a hit song, "Love Is Blue." Jimmy was the only black musician in the group and the only one who could speak English. Under normal circumstances, I just missed him when work separated us, but now I felt very lonely. Making my isolation worse, I hadn't confided the depth of my mysterious malady to Jimmy, because I knew he had to work to pay the rent and buy food. Jonathan was enjoying an overnight with his grandparents.

Lying there in the empty apartment, I felt tired, bone weary. My heart ran a hundred miles an hour while I remained motionless. I fought down my fear, trying to ground myself. Joe Franklin's voice droned on and on from the television, but I focused inward on pictures from my past: the Reverend Uncle Frank, Uncle Sid and Aunt Catherine, Aunt Bessie, M'Ma in her red velvet dress, the Reverend Mary. Ahhh!

The dark place inside me began to lighten up . . . The China-Man and—oh!—the lake, cool, blue, serene . . . "Wash my sins. Wash my sins away!" Weeping willow trees trailing long green fingers in the cool blue waters . . . Grampa. "No tears now! Not now!"

The sound of the television faded away. *What?*

Someone coming through the window. Floating in the middle of the air! No. Not floating . . . Feet paddling in the air. Right over the chair opposite the couch where I lay. Face smiling, eyes so full of love they blinded me. I rubbed my eyes. "Gramma Lizzie?" Hands stretched—beckoning fingers—love filling the whole room—blotting out the furniture, the rug, the ceiling. Coming closer, closer. Her head tilted a little to one side. Such pure love! Tears streamed down my cheeks. I could not wipe them away. I could not move a muscle. Then . . . My mind couldn't grasp what was happening to me. I felt my body lifting, lifting. Gramma put one finger across her smiling lips and slowly shook her head from side to side.

"Not yet."

I heard the words, not from her lips, but from somewhere deep down inside my soul. *My soul?* The love deepened in her eyes and she gradually withdrew backwards out the window.

I lay motionless, unable to make my body answer my commands. Gradually, I became aware that the television still filled the room with trivial sound. I knew, at that moment, I had not dreamed.

I closed my eyes and fell into a deep sleep. When I awoke, I looked at the clock on the table beside me. Only twenty minutes has passed. I shook myself, made my way to the bathroom, and splashed cold water on my face. I stared at the haunted eyes reflected in the mirror and knew we had to get out of New York.

Back in the living room, I collapsed on the couch, deep in thought, reliving the extraordinary events of the last half hour. An idea took possession of my mind. The telephone book. Yes! Feverishly turning the yellow pages, I found the number for a Christian Science church. I figured it had brought Grandma Hattie through and out of the South, so it should be able to bring me through and out of the South Bronx.

A woman answered the phone. After listening to my story about the assault and the hellhole conditions of our neighborhood, her dry, quiet voice replied, "Start by being grateful."

"What?!"

"Start by being grateful," she repeated, then hung up the phone.

Stunned disbelief was followed by a flash of anger. "I *am* grateful!" I sputtered. Then, anger turned to confusion. Grateful for what?

To cover my disappointment, I turned the television's volume up. Joe Franklin introduced a middle-aged woman. She wore no makeup, her grey hair stood up around her face like a halo. From Australia, she spoke like a missionary, saying she had come with a message for the women of America. She described an illness, mysterious and misunderstood, that doctors failed to diagnose: the racing heart, the crippling free-floating fear, the inability to stand in line anywhere, the closed-in "gotta get outta here" feeling that came with riding on a bus or subway train.

"She's describing me!" I whispered.

The woman went on, waving her arms in excitement. "At the bottom of it all," she said, "is unaddressed anger. The body is in a fight-or-flight mode—constantly."

I huddled on my knees in front of the television screen so I wouldn't miss a thing. She continued, "You must change your MO. Say continuously: 'I am whole, perfect, strong, powerful, loving, harmonious, and happy.' Take deep breaths," she advised, "move through it."

I mouthed the words, then grabbed a pencil from the little electric piano nearby and wrote them out on some music paper. I am whole, perfect, strong, powerful, loving, harmonious, and happy! I fell on my knees again, listening intently. When I got up, night had fallen, the apartment dark except for the flickering light from the television screen.

I heard the shuffling feet of the dope addicts lining up and down the stairs, waiting for the dealer in the next apartment to open shop. I turned on the lights and took slow, deep breaths. "I'm grateful for the lights." I grinned. "Well, it's a beginning!"

From Hell to Academia

·····················

I ain't gonna let nobody
Give me the blues all day—
I work so hard
An' they don't ever wanna pay!

They say every dog has his day, but I say: Some dogs have *two* days! Determined to overcome my illness, I found myself stumbling one step backward for every two steps forward. Still, I repeated that mantra over and over. I am whole, perfect, strong, powerful, loving, harmonious, and happy. In time, the words became a permanent tape playing deep in the far reaches of my mind.

I bought a new pair of dark glasses to help diffuse the light outside, and learned they also helped me keep myself *to* myself in crowded areas. I sat and meditated and wrote a list of the things that I needed to change. I discovered to my surprise that I was filled with fury.

I hated the hoodlums who had attacked me and my elderly friend in her little magazine store. I felt angry at myself for thinking that I could fix it alone, and heartless mad at the fact that I had stopped performing in the way that I knew I had been born to do.

I despised the bubble-eyed bottle-blonde no-talent women we coached and tried to teach how to sing, despised the way they took me for granted and didn't want to pay for their lessons, despised the same lame excuses we heard time and again. The capper came from a boorish little twit from the East Side. She said, "You'll have to wait for the money this week, Jimmy. I had to go down to the dock and pay the automobile import fees for my new Triumph."

I followed her into the bathroom and closed the door, leaned against it, and folded my arms. I am whole, perfect . . . The tape played in my head. "What do you think of my new suede suit?" she asked. "I got it at Bloomingdale's."

"Never mind the suit." I pitched my voice low so it wouldn't carry past the closed door. "Give me the loot!"

"What?" Shock stopped her hand halfway to her lips, the lipstick she held as red as the color creeping into her cheeks.

"Give me the money you owe for the two lessons last week and for the lesson you had today!" I stared at her. . . . strong, powerful . . . The tape played on.

"But," she sputtered, "I already told Jimmy . . ."

"Jimmy not *in* here!" I broke in, "You gonna pay *me* today!" . . . loving, harmonious . . . "You gonna pay me in this bathroom, today, or I'm gonna kick yo' narrow white behind!"

Without another word, her ringed fingers trembled as they searched her purse and pulled out a wad of greenbacks. "Take what you want!" she whispered.

"No," I said, "Just give me what you owe, no more, no less." She did. "And," I continued, putting the money in my pocket, "you better not tell Jimmy anything about this!" Her head bobbed up and down in agreement, her face beet red. "We have the arrangements for your opening night, and you will not get them till you pay for them," I hissed at her. . . . loving, harmonious and happy! The mantra came to an end. So did our conversation. I stepped aside and she hurried out. "See you next week!" I called after her. She didn't reply.

Jimmy looked a little puzzled as she rushed out, but he was preparing for the next vocalist and paid no attention.

She came back the next week. And the week after.

* * *

I wanted out. I think I might have felt a little better if we could have afforded to move from the Bronx to Manhattan, but no matter how hard we worked we couldn't save enough. The rents were just too high. Still, we struggled to get ahead.

Jimmy worked deadlining (staying awake two and three nights and days at a stretch), copying music for industrial shows. He substituted for Melba Liston, a great woman arranger and trombonist, on Broadway and wrote arrangements for vocalists appearing on television and at ice shows. He was a regular typhoon. He confessed to me one night that he had made a mad dash for the subway when suddenly his heart stopped. Jimmy's voice shook as he told me what happened. "I dropped to my knees, I just stayed down, until it started again."

"Oh, my God! That's what that psychic schoolteacher warned you about!"

"Yep. I got a big flash of her face while I was struggling to breathe."

"You all right?"

"Yeah, ev'rything's copacetic."

And it was. Jimmy continued to work just as hard as before. He was writer, arranger, orchestrater, and contractor for and with Chico Hamilton. He loved Chico like a brother. After all, they had served in the army together—one on the top bunk, the other on the bottom.

As contractor, Jimmy hired lots of great musicians to record commercials for Chico—musicians such as Thad Jones, Snooky Young, Art Farmer, Ernie Royal, Jimmy Hamilton, Danny Bank, Toots Thielman, Clark Terry, Richard Davis, George Duvivier, Britt Woodman, Jimmy Cleveland, Benny Green, Joe Beck, Russ Andrews, Slide Hampton, Jim Hall, Steve Potts, Tom McIntosh, and Ron Carter. Jimmy and Chico did several wonderful scores for *Wide World of Sports*, "Ski Ski," and the "Willie Mays Story," which were shown on ABC-TV. The group traveled all over, even as far as Mexico City.

If we had lived in Manhattan, I would have been able to contribute more to the family finances. I could have performed in clubs—there were so many kinds, types to fit every taste for entertainment, scattered along the streets of Manhattan—and been paid a lot of money.

And, most importantly, I could get a cab home. No cabby ever wanted to come to the South Bronx and no woman was going to feel safe coming home alone at four a.m. on the subway. Trapped in the South Bronx, I got madder and madder, but at least now I recognized it.

* * *

Dear Jean:

I take my pen in hand to write you that I think I'm going to have to dee-vorce your daddy. Things are really bad here. His drinking and taking the door off its hinges is really terrible. It makes me so sad.

Love, Your Mom

Dear Jean:

I take my pen in hand to write you that your daddy finally told me what was eating him all these years. He took the regular physical at Firestone when he was forty years old. They told him he had only three months to live! He did not tell nobody. He started drinking that very day!

Twenty years later he read in the obituary in the paper that the doctor who examined him years before was dead as a door-nail. It struck your daddy that he himself was still alive. *He never (so far) has taken another drink!*

Things are good here. I'm glad I do not have to dee-vorce your daddy.

Love, Mom

* * *

"Bennington College?" Jimmy's awed tone echoed his disbelief. "In Vermont?"

"Yes. I would like for you to take my place at Bennington. I've been asked to take Cecil Taylor's place in Madison, Wisconsin, at the university there. I already recommended you. Of all the people I know, you're the one who can do this."

These were the words of Bill Dixon, a fine musician with whom Jimmy had rehearsed many times and had recorded a record called *Metamorphosis*. Bill had come all the way to the South Bronx to our apartment, so we knew he meant business. The protests, marches, and the riots on college campuses had brought about the birth of black studies programs all over the country. All of a sudden life made a U-turn, and we became part of a whirlwind of change.

My prayers were being answered and more. I thought about Gramma Hattie. She always said, "The Lawd may not come when you want him, but He *always* come on time!"

Commuting to Vermont, Jimmy taught Black Music History for one semester. Then, in no time, the game of musical chairs among Bill Dixon, Cecil Taylor, and Jimmy began again. Bill Dixon asked Jimmy, "Hey, man, would you like to go to UW at Madison to finish Cecil's contract?"

"Take it!" I said. My heart beat like a trip-hammer.

Jimmy hesitated, a frown creasing his forehead. "Madison is a long way from New York and all . . ." I understood his reluctance. He was into a lot of things—exciting events and intoxicating drama. But that stuff never, ever lasts. In New York, when you hot, you hot—and when you not, you not! "I'll do it," he said. "*We'll* do it!" Bill smiled and nodded.

I flew into action. I sublet our apartment, and Jimmy's father volunteered to collect the rent and mail it to us. I called UW–Madison for data on housing, which they sent in record time. I phoned U-Haul for rates and availability and rented a station wagon and a trailer. "Big Jim" Neely, the driver for Chico's band, offered to help. "I've never seen that part of the country," he smiled. "You-all just send me back on the plane, and I'll be your driver." A sweet, sweet man, Big Jim had a wife, Winnie, who was just the same—just plain, good folks.

The University of Wisconsin referred us to an apartment building in Madison owned by a Mr. Divine. I contacted him, but he was not sure about us as tenants. When I told him Jimmy had played with Duke Ellington, it was like magic. It seemed that Mr. Divine had owned a ballroom in Milwaukee in the thirties and forties and had booked Duke Ellington's orchestra many times.

Duke Ellington had written Jimmy a letter of recommendation, and so had Lena Horne, and this information so impressed Mr. Divine that he rented us the furnished apartment sight unseen. We sent the money order for first and last, and the deed was done. Halleloo!

The super's son helped us pack our clothes, books, music, electric piano, trombones, the old lady's plants, which I had dutifully tended even in the depths of my illness, the Orphan Annie glass, the old candelabra, and our freshly laundered sheets and towels. We planned to leave the furniture, since the new apartment in Madison was completely furnished and we didn't want to bring any extra baggage—creepy crawlies or cockroaches, if you will.

The station wagon and trailer pulled up to the curb in front, and we piled things inside. "It's just too small," sighed the super's son. "You gonna need the next size bigger!"

We all laughed wearily, then unloaded everything out on the sidewalk. *Nobody* was gonna haul all that stuff back up the four double flights of stairs. The Puerto Rican man and Sam, the Italian candy-store owner, A. C., Jonathan, and I guarded our things while Jimmy and Big Jim exchanged the trailer. When we had packed everything away a second time, even the junkies standing across the street waved, "Good-bye! Good luck! An' don't come back!" They needn't have worried about that. I had drunk enough muddy water to last me for a lifetime.

As Big Jim Neely maneuvered the station wagon through the crowded streets of the South Bronx, trying to adjust to the weight of the trailer attached to the rear, I closed my eyes. I didn't want to look back. I had a fleeting image of Lot's wife heading out into the great unknown and turning for one final glimpse of the only home she had ever known—and never escaping. I'm grateful! I am grateful! I repeated silently as the car carrying me from my prison crawled along, too slow.

Then Big Jim hit the accelerator and we were off. I swear that I'll never come back to the South Bronx! I promised myself. Never, ever! When I come back this way, it will be to Manhattan and the Great White Way. I will come back as a conqueror! My thumbs were folded into my fingers, and my hands were jammed into the pockets of my camel-colored pantsuit jacket.

Seven long years had passed since I had graced a stage—in a red satin outfit, doing what I was born to do. Now, as the car sped along the highway, my heart leapt in my chest, and I felt so full that I didn't know whether to laugh or cry. I was hungry for applause, nay, *starving*, for cheers, stomps, and whistles. I had no idea what might be in store for us, but I knew one thing for sure: I would never let life force me to stop performing ever again.

As we tooled along the interstate from New York to Chicago, I leaned my head back on the seat and started to ask myself questions. Will we like the new apartment? This commonplace worry compared to the worries we had just left behind brought a smile to my lips. Any apartment away from the South Bronx, I'm gonna like!

But what about Jonathan? Children don't like to be uprooted, and he was sure to miss his grandfather. What about his new school? Will Jonathan like it? So many kids had overdosed on drugs in his South Bronx school that now I closed my eyes for a moment and prayed that Madison would prove to be a safe haven for my son.

Jimmy sat in the front beside Jim Neely, not watching the highway ahead, his head turned to the side, looking out at the passing landscape. I stared at his profile and thought: Will Jimmy like this university? He loved Bennington and its open and accepting attitudes, but this university was a different breed of cat. The civil-rights uprisings across the campuses of the nation had forced university administrations to accept black studies as a viable part of the curriculum.

Cecil Taylor had left the University of Wisconsin–Madison in an uproar. Cecil had come to Madison to teach black studies, and he had come with his mind made up and his heart set to teach the truth. He warned the huge class that gathered to view this jazz giant that he would be giving them lessons, lectures, and examples, just as in any other subject. He also warned them that they would have to take an exam.

Somehow, despite Cecil's warnings, the students thought, and bought into the myth, that the presence of a jazz musician meant that they could come to class in droves, party, get stoned, and say "Right on!" Well, "Right on!" became "Right off!" when at least two-thirds of the class flunked Cecil's extensive exam. The shocked university muckety-mucks tried to force Cecil to reverse the failing grades. Of course, being a man of integrity, he refused and resigned.

Bill Dixon had come in and, with the same attitude about the seriousness of the subject matter, maintained the validity of black studies. The university wanted to keep the funds supplied by the federal government, so an uneasy truce existed on the Madison campus.

Jimmy was walking right into this buzz saw of a situation. Anyone who knew him would have been able to predict which side of the controversy he would advocate. I knew that the minute we arrived in Madison he would get to work establishing his own tough criteria, picking right up where Cecil Taylor and Bill Dixon had left off: no screwing around, good attendance, and compulsory participation in class. No more, no less. I was confident that after Bill's firm and righteous stance was reinforced by Jimmy's stern, no-nonsense, "invite you outside" approach to teaching, there would be pain, but there would be gain. Cecil Taylor, Bill Dixon, and Jimmy Cheatham all had two things in common: integrity and the fact that jazz was a way of life to us all.

I watched Jimmy watching the countryside slide by and I smiled. I guess I answered my own question.

We were supposed to be in Madison only one year. After that one year, then what? The future loomed uncertainly before me. Always, I had relied on music to fill that void. Can I still play good piano after all this time? Have I lost my touch with an audience? I shuddered. Then I reminded myself that we were heading west, away from the South Bronx with all its dangers and disasters. Out of the blue, our luck had changed. Our guardian angels probably have run-over heels and holes in their golden slippers from running interference for us!

Jim Neely steered the station wagon with its cumbersome trailer onto the Madison belt line, then off at John Nolan Drive toward Capitol Square. He drove around the square while we all gawked at the beautiful capitol rising over the city. Then we wended our way onto State Street, continued up the hill past the Madison Inn, turned into Mendota Court, and we were home.

As we climbed stiffly out of the station wagon, a short stout leprechaun of a man hurried out of the adjacent building. "Well, you've arrived, have you? I'm Mr. Jimmy Divine. Which one of you is Jimmy?" His pudding face was crimson with pleasure. His wire-rimmed glasses sat on the tip of his round nose.

"We both are!" grinned my Jimmy and Jim Neely.

"Well, that's fine," Divine chortled. "Which one of you played with the Duke?"

"That'll be me."

With that, Mr. Divine rushed Jimmy and pumped his hand up and down so hard that Jimmy looked around at us with a mock expression of "help." "It's an honor to have the great Duke Ellington's right-hand man here in my building." Raised eyebrows all around. No one said a word.

Our ecstatic landlord spun around, pulled at the great bunch of keys at his waist and led us into the building. He ushered us into the elevator and away we went—up, up all the way to the twelfth floor. No more walk-ups for us.

A grinning Mr. Divine unlocked a door at the end of the carpeted hall and gave what looked very like a little bow as he gestured for us to enter. The apartment had two bedrooms flanking a nice-sized living room with cream walls and thick beige carpet. The furniture was upholstered in beige and tan and the bookcases and hutches were rich walnut. The modern kitchen had an island for casual dining, an ultramodern dark brown refrigerator that matched the cupboards, and an electric stove, just like the one on Bina Avenue; there would be no gas fumes as in the Bronx. To our delight, we discovered two full bathrooms. And, wonder of wonders, sliding doors in the living room opened out to a balcony with white wrought-iron furniture and a view overlooking the blue waters of Lake Mendota.

Our building was surrounded by frat houses, dark bricked, with dark green ivy growing up the walls, like a movie version of academic life. My eyes swept back to the lake again. It was so like Summit Lake way back in Akron, Ohio, that it took my breath away. Cutting across the still water, a line of boats full of young men dressed all in white practiced rowing for a race. The voices of the coxswains calling cadence rose to our balcony, music to my ears.

I turned back into the living room. "Mr. Divine, this is perfect! Just marvelous!"

His Irish face folded into lines of pleasure, and his blue eyes sparkled. "I own all three of these buildings," he said with pride. "I'll have some of my work crew help you bring up your belongings."

The men huffed and puffed and unloaded our stuff. Then I stepped out on the balcony, closed my eyes, and said, "Thank you God, we made it safe and sound!" I opened my eyes just in time to see the boats swinging round the bend, oars sweeping the waters in perfect precision, the voices of the coxswains swallowed up by distance. Then they were all gone, hidden by trees along the lakeshore, their branches trailing down into the lovely blue lake. I am whole, perfect, strong, powerful, loving, harmonious, and happy. And above all, I am grateful. I grinned. And, Lawd, I'm livin' in a penthouse! "Thank you, Jesus."

We sent Big Jim Neely back to New York on a plane, and as we waved goodbye, I knew that we would never, ever go back to the Big Apple to live.

Gonna appetize my life
Tomorrow's gotta bring good news!
I ain't gonna spend my life
Down in no basket full of blues!

TOWN HALL
Affiliated with New York University
123 WEST 43rd STREET • NEW YORK 36, N. Y.

Town Hall, Sunday Evening, October 14th 1962 at 8:15 p. m.

Ray Crabtree Presents

CAVALCADE OF MUSIC

MUSIC AMERICANA...Sissle & Blake
TRIBUTES TO: Jerome Kern, Mr. And Mrs. Vernon Castle, W. C. Handy,
J. Lubrie Hill and J. Rosamond Johnson

MUSIC AMERICANA.....................a. The birth of the Spirituals
...............................b. The birth of the Blues
Noble Sissle & Eubie Blake

Rita Abbey

Bewitched	Hart & Rodgers
My Man	Yvain & Solabert
Ain't Misbehavin'	Waller & Razaf
Let Me Come Home	Jean Cheatham
Homeward Bound	Jean Cheatham
Come Running	Roc Hillman

TRIBUTE TO: Miss Lena Horne

Jean Cheatham, Piano....Eddie Cornelius, Drums...George Tucker, Bass
Arrangements by Jimmy Cheatham

Town Hall Concert,
October 14, 1962,
with Noble Sissle
and Eubie Blake.

Academy Awards in Jazz
(about 1964). Jean
Cheatham and Roberta
Como, piano; Papa Jo
Jones, drums; and
George Duvivier, bass.
A copy of the album is
included in the
George Duvivier col-
lection, Institute of
Jazz Studies, Rutgers
University, Newark,
New Jersey.

Big Mama Thornton, Edmund Hall, and Papa Jo Jones. New York City, 1967. "From Spirituals to Swing." David Berger photo, © Milt Hinton.

George Duvivier, bass. Courtesy of Ed Berger and Roger Field.

Welcome to Wisconsin

· · · · · · · · · · · · · · · · · · ·

My first gig in Wisconsin was for the Ku Klux Klan. It happened in Monroe, at a place called the Monroe Gun Club.

One morning, after the two Cheathams, father and son, charged off to their prospective new lives at their new schools, I carried a second cup of coffee and the yellow pages of the telephone book out to the balcony. The clear autumn air made my lungs snap, crackle, and pop. Overhead in the pale blue sky, a whole convoy of birds was winging its way south, the lead bird unerringly obedient to orders from headquarters. "Maybe it's a good sign," I murmured. "If they can find their direction, I can find mine."

I began feverishly thumbing through the yellow pages as if they were an oracle. "Hey," I called out to the departing flock, "here's an agent right on State Street!" The agent's office was one block down the hill from our apartment.

Now, I was delighted that we had had the good sense to withstand the urgings of the university person in charge of relocation. He recommended that we live where most of the professors and other high muckety-mucks hung out—way out on the outskirts of town. "No more isolation for this kid!" I had vowed at the time. Our polite but stubborn refusal to be swallowed up by the suburbs proved to be a blessing.

I blew a kiss to the lake, now shimmery with little whitecaps sparkling in the morning sun, went inside, and called the agent. I made an appointment to bring in my bio and photos in an hour. No New York pretensions of a "too-full calendar," just "Come on down!"

Down the hill to State Street I ambled, leaning back a little to balance myself in my high platform shoes. Their wooden soles echoed clackety-clack, clackety-clack. In my camel-colored pantsuit, with my woven leather briefcase under my arm, I felt my heart beat fast, trip-tripping at the prospect of meeting and dealing with an agent after seven long years.

I reached State Street and stood still while I decided whether to turn right or left. The street burst upon the senses in a blaze of color and sound. At high noon it was teeming with activity. Young people paraded up and down wearing platform shoes, long flowing hair, sideburns, big bushy Afros. They bustled in and out of places like The Brat House, a New York-style deli, and Rennebohm's drugstore, with its fabulous lunch counter featuring beer-battered cod—all you could eat. Burger joints perfumed the crowded sidewalk with the smell of grilled onions. An array of little shops lined the street, including the university ice cream shop, whose rich, creamy confection was made from cream that came directly from cows grazing on university pastures right on campus. Thirty-two thousand students considered State Street part of the campus. Heaven!

I wended my way through the jostling crowd and finally stood in front of the address given me. It belonged to a psychic shop. Its windows were filled with psychic paraphernalia, turquoise jewelry, and candles large and small. Whoa! Shades of Akron, Ohio, with its St. John the Conqueror roots, incense, and candles in the drugstores down on Howard Street.

I stepped across the threshold and looked around. Yep, this was a root town, all right.

"May I help you?" A mild voice drifted from the back room through a doorway draped in dark curtains.

"Jeannie Cheatham here!" I called, and that was the beginning of a most interesting saga.

Bob was a very well-mannered well-dressed man in his middle years, with coal black hair, manicured nails, and an air of "nothing surprises me." We chatted while he looked through my bio, then he said, "I really like Duke Ellington and his alto player. I practice my saxophones every day and listen to Rabbit" (the nickname of Johnny Hodges). Then, "Your bio is impressive, wonderful!"

"What about booking me?" I demanded.

"There's a job in Monroe, not that far from here. I've already booked the bass player, named Dennis Oliver, and a drummer named Stefan and a clarinet player named Smitty." He looked at me sharply. "You want the job?"

"Sure, but someone will have to pick me up an' bring me back." I left the shop walking on air. I'm back on track! I'm back! I'm back! I floated up the hill to Mendota Court. Clackety-clack, clackety-clack.

That weekend we arrived at the job and found out it was a gun club. We carried in the instruments, mikes, and music stands and found men and women, at least one hundred strong, sitting in rows of chairs facing a tall tanned man, his long flowing white hair the exact color of his suit and shoes, standing on a small podium.

"We need money!" he bellowed and pounded his right fist into his left palm. "We want our own land in north Wisconsin—a land of plenty, a land where we can raise our precious children, the fruit of our loins, far away from spics, Jews, queers, 'n' niggers."

I looked at the clarinet player, Smitty. He was eighty years old, but he was still a cat. "Jeannie," he murmured, "this looks like a downer. You wanna leave?"

Dennis was cool. Over six feet tall with long, mixed grey hair, and way on the sunny side of forty, Dennis had beautiful, calm blue Irish eyes and a ready smile. He began putting up the mikes and music stands on the stage opposite the speaker. Swiftly and quietly, he uncoiled the long black wires and plugged them into the "head."

I replied to Smitty in a low voice. "Look, none of us are here to stop this man's speech. We're here to play music while they eat. We gotta play if we want our pay!"

Smitty grinned. "Okay. We're with you!" So we moved over to help Dennis.

When the man in white spotted me, he stopped talking. His face turned as red as fire and he shook his head in disbelief. The audience began to mutter and shift their feet. I guess they were waiting for a sign from on high, and since none came, they just sat there. "Let's play," I whispered. Smitty and I started "Take the 'A' Train" while Dennis and the drummer finished the set-up. We knew they would have to pay if we started, and I didn't want nobody messin' around with my money!

"Friends," the man in the white suit said with a grand gesture, "let's eat!" The enticing buffet—catered by Rennebohm's—was spread across several paper-covered tables and heaped on huge platters: baked beans, potato salad, coleslaw, sliced Virginia ham, and beer-battered cod fillets.

Nobody in the audience seemed very hungry. They kept sneaking looks at me or glaring at all of us. After we played "When the Saints Go Marching In," Mr. White Suit gave me a really dirty look, crossed his arms, climbed back up on his podium, and told his people, "Folks, this meeting is over, but don't ever forget what I said. We must separate ourselves from"—he gave me another baleful look—"those people!" Then he shouted, "The Ku Klux Klan lights up the cross!" We took the money and ran.

The gig lasted only thirty-five minutes, but it was long enough to tell me that I could still play—and play well. Glory!

When I took Bob's commission down to the psychic shop and told him about the gig, he didn't look outraged, he didn't even look upset—he seemed mildly amused. "Well," he murmured, "welcome to Wisconsin!"

* * *

"Guess who's coming to dinner?" I blurted.

The third evening after my encounter with the Klan, I met Jimmy at the door. Usually, like most guys, he and Jonathan needed a breather after a long day. We would exchange greetings, then they both would drift away to opposite sides of the apartment, seeking a little solitude. This time I was so excited that I couldn't contain the news.

"Who?" Jimmy put down his loaded bag, his eyes glazed over. He had more than a hundred students in his lecture class, and no teaching assistant to help him, and he was bone weary.

"My sister Charlotte, her new husband—the gamblin' man—and M'Ma!" The words flew out of my mouth. "They are drivin' all the way from Akron to see if we're okay."

Jimmy sat on a stool at the kitchen counter and smiled. He loved company. "Hey! That's heavy!"

"Guess who else is comin'?"

"Hm-m-m—who?"

"M'Da!"

Jimmy stood up. "You're kidding!"

"No! He's comin' after all this time. He is comin'! M'Ma says he's been sober for a long while and is lookin' forward to seein' us and Wisconsin."

We rushed around spot-cleaning, dusting, and putting out guest towels. I decided to serve broiled lamb chops, curried rice, fresh asparagus—and cookies, since I didn't have time to bake a 1-2-3-4 cake. I felt so nervous that my mind flip-flopped, going over different scenarios. Should I shake hands with M'Da or just nod?

The doorbell rang and I ran to open it. There they were! In the flesh! We all hugged and exchanged introductions with Carl, Charlotte's new husband. Jimmy whirled M'Ma around in a bear hug. Then there it was—the moment. M'Da and I stood face to face. Either I had grown taller, or he had shrunk. We were looking at each other eye to eye. Who was this little old guy? Last time I saw him, he seemed like a giant, forbidding and dark and powerful. Now, he was grey and short and smiling. *Smiling?*

"Hi, Doll," he said quietly. The tenor voice that had quoted Longfellow—"Half a league onward!"—and brought tears to our child-eyes with his rendition of "My Bonnie Lies over the Ocean" was just the same.

"Hi, Dad, come sit and be comfortable."

The tension fell away from me like a heavy black cape shrugged from my shoulders, and suddenly we were a family again. Almost.

We talked and ate and laughed until our sides hurt. Carl was funny, and knew lots of tall tales from gambling on Howard Street in the bad ol' days. He was tall, dark, and elegant and at least twenty years older than Charlotte. No longer a full-time gambler, he had taken a job running the elevator at Goodyear. No overalls for him! Only neatly pressed uniforms.

Charlotte told me in a private moment that on their wedding night, Carl put his pistol on the nightstand in the honeymoon hotel and said, "This is my last marriage! My other two wives were unfaithful. I'll never marry again!" Charlotte and I snickered as only two sisters do when sharing such moments.

Jimmy and I showed them the whole city. They were especially interested in Lake Monona, sister lake to Mendota. On our tour along the lake, Jonathan piped up and said, "Mendota means 'morning'!" Named by the Indians, Monona, which means "evening," became the watery grave of Otis Redding, composer of "Sittin' on the Dock of the Bay." One bit of local lore in Madison claims that a vintage World War II plane called the *Grey Goose* hit Otis's more fragile Beechcraft, and then it was curtains—the *Grey Goose* wasn't even dented. But the truth was that Otis's plane had crashed into Lake Monona in a storm ten years before we arrived.

The second impressive place, especially for Carl, was the dairy on the campus. He had never seen cows milked by machines before. He was so astonished he told us, "Come back later and pick me up! I'm going to sit right here all afternoon and watch this." And he did.

The third unusual sight was licorice ice cream at the shop on State Street. "Black as the ace of spades!" M'Da's and Carl's red tongues licked the dark confection with great relish.

Yet, all the good times aside, it was a bittersweet reunion for me with M'Da. He was an old man now, kind of sweet, but awkward. I circled around him because I really didn't know how to act or what to think. When it was time to say good-bye, there were hugs all around, and, wonder of wonders, M'Da gave *me* a hug.

"You an' Jimmy are good together with Jonathan," he said. "Good-bye for now. And don't forget to get a pap smear every year!" With that, the elevator took them down to the waiting car and the long drive back to Euclid Avenue in Akron. I stood there in the doorway, stunned. Pap smear?

On the Move in Madison

. . . .

*B*ob the booking agent knew where all the bodies were buried in Madison. We struck pure Klondike gold when we hooked up with him. By the time the autumn winds blew all the brilliantly colored leaves from the trees, and the lakes froze over and became an icy playground for hockey, curling, and skating, we began to feel that chilly breeze come blowing through our BVDs. A brand-new band—Bob on reeds, Jimmy on bass trombone, Dennis Oliver (big and Irish) on bass, Stefan Sylvander (small, neat, and Swedish) on drums, and myself on piano—began gigging all over the area. We played the *Godfather* theme, "You Are the Sunshine of My Life" (Stevie Wonder), polkas, and Duke Ellington.

What would have taken years elsewhere, gaining entrée into the higher reaches of society, took only a few months in Madison because of Bob's position and influence.

"The west side is progressive, ya' know, way out," Bob informed us as we drove to the country club there to perform. "Lots of homes and buildings by Frank Lloyd Wright, particularly up on Maple Bluff."

"The famous architect?"

"Yes."

"And the east side is mostly 'way back when' folks and features the Oscar Meyer meat-packing plant," quipped Dennis. "I worked many a shift there before I decided to get my degree in French lit." The east side also sported its own country club. The lawmakers and the lunatic fringe coexisted uneasily in the center of the city, and Bob guided our group into every venue. We played only on weekends, as in most small towns. The schedule suited me. It left all week to be a mama and a mate.

Every morning I woke with a smile and looked forward to the demands of the day. Jonathan, Jimmy, and I took turns doing breakfast—we all loved to cook. The kid made great omelettes. "Maybe I'll be a chef," he declared.

"Well, Applehead,"—when Jonathan was a baby, his head had been perfectly round, and Jimmy used the nickname when he felt particularly fond of his son—"whatever you want to do, we'll help."

"You'll be ahead of the game," I teased Jonathan. "When you get a wife and she has to go to the hospital, or anything like that, you can take care of your family."

"Yeah," he would smile shyly.

M'Ma had taught my brothers how to wash clothes, cook, clean, and iron. "So you won't ever need the services of the woman next door," she declared. It was a different time, but it still made good sense.

Every evening I cooked from scratch, great meals, because Madison had some of the most fantastic markets I had ever seen. Tender, milk-fed veal, corn-fed beef, and succulent young pork. The cheeses were superb. The three of us loved shopping together, and entertaining new friends added to the food and the fun.

Jonathan's friend, the daughter of one of the professors at UW–Madison, came over fairly often. A brilliant girl, tiny and brown-skinned, with a ready smile and big glasses that slipped down her nose, you could tell she was going to be somebody. Another friend, a long, lanky boy with pale skin and liquid eyes, brown hair always falling in his face, became a familiar figure, lounging on the couch or poking around in the kitchen while I prepared dinner. Jonathan sometimes left them with me in the apartment to pursue his own interests.

Very bright, Jonathan read at the twelfth-grade level while still in the third grade. The taller he grew (to almost six feet), the more he exhibited traits I have seen in lots of predominately intellectual musicians: inflexibility, a tendency to be self-seeking and self-serving, and lots of "won't" power. A lot of kids enter their teens and suddenly become self-involved strangers preoccupied with their own growing pains. Jonathan's behavior was nothing to become alarmed over.

Jimmy's friends included Cecil Lytle, a fine figure of a man striding across campus, his wide-brimmed leather hat keeping time with his every step. A world-class pianist, both classical and jazz, Cecil and his wife, Becky, were both going for their degrees. Robert Rhymes, well built with classic features, taught school, played in Jimmy's black music ensemble, and was always ready for some serious discourse.

Four women, new friends, offered sustenance for my soul. A hectic search for a hairdresser introduced me to Ruth Harris. She had been Mahalia Jackson's accompanist, and played both organ and piano. Five feet tall, feisty, fiery, and full of the spirit of the true Gospel, Ruth didn't bite her tongue about anything. We clicked like a well-oiled machine, not needing to talk when we played together. And she turned out to be a great hairdresser.

Jere Hilton, who knew all things "Ellington," was wise in the ways of the world and became a good pal of mine, easy to converse with about our world of music, because of her close association with Duke Ellington's star soloist. She kept a ready smile on her lips, and her lilting voice concealed her own secret pain.

Bob the booking agent's friend, Tamara, who lived with one foot in the world of the spirit and one foot in this world of the material, with all its troubles, became my confidante and champion.

Hazel Symonette, truly attractive, with honey-colored skin and soft eyes, wore no make-up and sometimes wound colorful scarves around her head. She lived nearby in another of Mr. Divine's buildings. She had been through the early uprisings and had come out unscathed, but cautious. When Hazel walked, her feet never lost contact with the ground. When she talked, she never raised her voice. A lovely magnet for the African men on campus, she became a lifeline of support that made it possible for us to work weekends. She and Jonathan hit it off right away, and she volunteered to keep an eye on him in our apartment while she studied for her degree.

In New York, we would play from ten at night to three in the morning. Madison wasn't New York; most gigs ended early. "We ain't never gonna turn into pumpkins in this town," I told Hazel. "We'll be home before midnight."

Ruth Harris, Jere Hilton, Tamara, and Hazel Symonette: all steel butterflies and sister-mama-friends!

* * *

"Expubidence!"

Babs Gonzales had come to call. He stomped around our apartment and out through the sliding doors onto the balcony. "This whole town's expubident!" His voice rang out into the crisp air as he repeated the words. Then he turned and bounced back into the apartment.

Jonathan, Jimmy, and I grinned from ear to ear as we watched the antics of the wiry figure known as the prince of the bebop scat singers.

"Papa Jo Jones told me where to find you-all." He took a bow and clicked his huge, yellow wooden clogs together and saluted us. Babs had purchased the shoes in Holland during one of his many European jaunts. He made a startling sight clackety-clacking up and down the streets of New York. It was no less startling in Madison. He had invented the word "expubidence," and found it fit for all occasions.

"I really miss you cats in New York—not many cats talk to me . . ." He stopped to run his slim fingers over his straightened, coal black hair cut Dutch-boy style. "Or, at least, let me talk to *them!*" He threw his head back and roared with laughter, his teeth plentiful and perfect.

The men sat in the kitchen and told lies while I made Alabama chicken smothered in milk gravy, a big bowl of salad, and pineapple upside-down cake topped with real whipped cream. After dinner, Babs pulled out a slim book with a red, yellow, and blue cover. "This is my autobiography—hot off the press. I'm travelin' around promoting it. This one's for you." He opened the cover and scrawled "With love to Jeannie and Jimmy Cheatham from Babs." "I wrote it all by my lonesome," he said with pride. "It's called *I Paid My Dues.*"

A great performer, musician, and composer, he was a fabulous promoter of his and other people's talents. A friend of my friend Tadd Dameron, Babs wrote many songs, including "Oop-Pop-A-Da" made famous by Dizzy Gillespie. Considered uneducated by Madison's ivory-tower academic standards, Babs held a PhD in bebop.

When it was time to say goodbye, Babs leaned out of the taxi window and called, "I be done seed ya! A-reba-dutch!" (his version of the Italian farewell).

Though he was gone, the air was still charged with his energy. That, too, was his trademark—always the giver.

* * *

The spring of '73 came in with the sounds of the ice cracking on the lake. All the little fishing huts that had dotted the ice like West Virginia lean-tos began to disappear. Not that it made much difference to the fish, since the fishermen and women partied in the little hideaways, leaving the fish pretty much to catch themselves. That winter our dentist had confided, "A huge percentage of the brandy drunk in the United States goes down the gullets of the people of Wisconsin."

"Really?"

"Yes. Did you know that blue gums are only found in people of African descent and Scandinavians?" He paused for effect.

"Really?" That was the only word either Jimmy or I could manage, since the dentist was working on us both, tilted back in side-by-side chairs, and had his hands along with all his paraphernalia in our mouths.

"Yes." His ice blue eyes sparkled behind his wire rim glasses. "King Olaf of yore sent to Africa for some fierce fighting mercenaries to help him with a war he was losing. The Africans came, fought the war, and won, then decided to stay. They married beautiful blonde maidens, and the rest is history."

Jimmy and I had seen coats of arms displayed in bars in small towns that pictured—surprise, surprise!—black, curly bearded, broad-nosed men with generous lips, brandishing swords and wearing iron helmets complete with Scandinavian-style horns. The tale told by our dentist cast new light on the subject.

Shortly after our arrival in Madison, we decided to take advantage of the opportunity provided by the university to get dental work done and to have physicals. Through Bob, we acquired an excellent CPA to put our far-flung finances in order, just in case Jimmy's contract was not picked up in June.

"Babe, it's white-knuckle time." Jimmy was worried. This year-by-year thing was becoming more and more nerve-wracking. So our primary emotion was relief when the contract was renewed for the '73–'74 period. But our relief was short-lived; 1973–1974 began well, then day by day turned into star-crossed years for us.

"Let's take a trip this summer and get away a bit." Jimmy had another reason for the trip. We did not like Jonathan's choice of friends. He was floundering.

So we boarded a train and had a terrific time rolling across the country to see Jimmy's folks, especially his mama, and my brother Jerry. We did not see Red the Terrible. She had broken her false teeth for the umpteenth time, taken a whole bottle of aspirin, and been consigned to the Buffalo mental ward for observation—all because Jerry was divorcing her. Thank God!

M'Ma started driving at the age of sixty-five. "I just decided one day that I wasn't gonna take another bus. So I told your dad to get me a car."

"You! Drivin'?" I felt almost as excited as she was.

"Your dad called Firestone, and I started takin' lessons. Two weeks later, I came home and found a brand-new four-door Ford LTD parked on the driveway. I still can't get over it!"

"Me either."

M'Ma ignored my remark and, in a tone of supreme confidence, cooly continued, "I drive ev'rywhere I want! But I have trouble turnin' into our driveway around that big ol' tree, past the house, and into the garage. I told your dad he gonna have to move the house over so I can drive that big car into the garage."

"What did he say?"

"Said he'd take a nap and think about it."

* * *

Shirley graduated from Mount Holyoke that summer, and we went to the graduation. The shah of Iran's daughter and the daughter of Telly Savalas, who played Kojak on TV, graduated also. It was a grand affair, and our pride knew no bounds.

* * *

Back in Madison, I began to plan for our eventual move. I put living-room furniture and lamps on layaway and began collecting African artifacts from a dealer's shop on the square. And miracle! The dealer imported real African kente cloth in the same colors as a magnificent, framed batik wall hanging that I had purchased. We found two hand-woven rocking chairs and an African chair carved from a tree trunk—all in one piece, no nails. The furniture I put in storage, but the runaway wife of an old German tailor made pillows of the kente cloth.

As soon as she finished ten small pillows for our couch, she left her little blonde baby, birthed on her last runaway trip, and disappeared for a week. No one knew who the baby's father was. "Why do you run away? I asked her on her return. The old tailor had taken the baby for a walk.

"I don't know. I just have to go . . ." She looked a little sad, her brassy, dyed-blonde hair falling in her brown-hazel eyes, eyes with gold glints in them, like a forest animal's. "I know I break Gustav's heart every time I leave, but this time when I came back with the baby, he told me if I leave again I can't take him with me. Gustav accepts him as his own little son." She paused and lit a cigarette. "I'm lucky, I guess."

"You're not going to fly the coop before you finish the pillows are you?" She hadn't finished the two huge floor pillows I had ordered.

"No, I promise," she took a deep drag on her cigarette, "but it's gettin' near time . . ." She looked faraway, almost as if someone or something was calling her.

"My son keeps doing the same thing." I felt a sudden need to confide in her, knowing she would understand. "He started last year, but now, it's beginning to get worse. He disappears for days at a time. We don't want to call in the authorities, 'cause we don't want him to have a record."

Her hazel eyes turned hard. She tossed her head. "Is he unhappy at home?"

"He jokes, brings me flowers, sits in his room writing out reams of sports statistics. He goes to school, then disappears. He says he must see what's out there . . ." I shook my head, trying to contain my despair. "We've tried physical exams, brain-wave tests, psychiatrists, psychologists, behavioral scientists, church counselors, prayer, and more prayer." Her expression didn't change as I rushed on, pouring out my fear and frustration. "He makes up stories to manipulate people. He went to a white woman's house way out on the west side and told her we had gone to France and left him behind. The woman kept him, fed him, gave him money so he could get by. Finally, Robert Rhymes tracked him down and brought him home. It's almost like he enjoys fooling people."

My intuition that she would understand was correct. She understood all too well. But it was Jonathan she understood, not the hurt that he caused the people who loved him. "Well," she said, "that's what I do best, fool people. It's like I got a big maggot in my gut and I have to keep movin'. My folks were okay, I guess—but boring. I just can't stand routine." She put her cigarette out in her cold cup of coffee.

Gustav came into the little shop carrying the baby, whose cheeks were red-rosy from the crisp air. "Hello, Mrs. Cheatham. Here is my son! I haf named him Josef, like in the Bible."

I smiled at the baby. "Well, hello there, Josef!" The baby buried his face in Gustav's coat. I glanced at the child's mother, wary of her impassive expression. "I'll come back for the two big pillows tomorrow."

She nodded, and kept her word. I went back to the shop with the money and found Gustav there feeding the baby. His face was relaxed, but resigned. "There are your pillows in that bag," he said. He looked beyond me, then whispered, "She has gone away."

I rushed home in a panic as a dreadful premonition wrapped itself around me like a heavy black cape. The apartment was empty, silent. Then the phone rang. I picked it up. My voice shook. "Hello?" The police had Jonathan.

Our guardian angels had helped all of us all along the way. But a twenty-year-old high-yellow bitch bearing a gift of a calico kitten, which Jonathan brought home and promptly ignored, and another gift of angel dust, which he did not ignore, changed his destiny and twisted his life path. He was sent away to a youth camp.

He will write his own story one of these days.

There were young folks in our town
They thought they were so wise—
They fell into a bramble bush
An' scratched out all their eyes!

An' when they saw their eyes were out—
With all their might an' main
Jumped back into the bramble bush
To try to scratch them in—again!

"Here come da judge!" became a familiar refrain to the entire country, including the White House, during 1973-1974. Haldeman, Ehrlichman, Agnew, and others, even Nixon himself, meant nothing to us. The only thing on our minds and hearts was love and fear for our son. After Jonathan was taken away, we plunged ourselves into our work. In fact, we had to play that night—that very night.

"You two are the bravest people I've ever seen," Bob remarked. His friend and mine, Tamara, a beautiful, petite blonde girl, helped us through the terrible ordeal. She had special healing powers and gave of them generously to us. The music washed over us like a balm, and all our friends came to express concern. But we didn't think we were the ones who needed assistance. We thought of Jonathan, and prayed that someone would be able to reach him, to help him heal.

Through Bob, we played dates with Tony Orlando and Dawn, Pat O'Brien, Helen Merrill, who wanted Jimmy and me to go on the road with her, and Odetta. Odetta came to our apartment, sat on the floor surrounded by musicians from town, and told road stories while I served pigs-in-a-blanket and beer to them all. It was a blessing to keep busy.

Jimmy and I organized another group that played Sundays at a former church that was dark as a dungeon. There we filled our hearts with funk and soul music while six ladies of the evening, dressed all in red, undulated in front of the stage. Clyde Stubblefield, who used to play for James Brown, the Godfather of Soul, was our drummer. Dennis Oliver on bass, Bob McCurdy on trumpet, Jimmy and me and a really good soul saxophone player named "Fat" Richard Drake made up the group.

"How come they call him 'Fat' Richard?" I asked Dennis. "He's skinny as a fiddle string."

"He used to be real fat, till some customer put something in his drink one night to see if Richard would play even wilder than usual. He freaked out and had to be hospitalized."

"Oh, my God!" Horror replaced my curiosity.

"Yeah, an' he kept havin' heart attacks an' lost a lotta weight."

Jimmy and I looked at each other. That look said everything. Thank God for the advice given us so long ago! *Never leave your drink unattended.*

One didn't dare go to the restroom at the Church Key, because all the addicts went in there to shoot up or gulp pills. But, Lawd! the music was grand —and helped to heal the broken-hearted. We featured tunes by Herbie Hancock, and the joint stayed packed. When we got home each night, completely wrung out, we fell into bed and into a dreamless sleep.

* * *

Jimmy worked incredibly hard with his lecture classes and his invention: the Experimental Improvisational Black Music Ensemble. It was wonderful to attend his concerts: a row of young hopefuls spread out across the stage in various styles of clothing and in every color of the human rainbow; young men from the African continent, from India, Germany, and America; young women expressing themselves on flutes, trumpets, trombones, keyboards, and percussion.

"I teach each one of my students up to their own highest potential," Jimmy explained to the curious and the bewildered.

"I come to your concerts just to see if you gonna fall on your ass!" one professor needled Jimmy. "But you always pull it off. And I don't know how you do it!"

Our apartment at 661 Mendota Court, number 1204, became a mecca for musicians, friends, students, and for Mr. Divine. We always kept a big pot of chili or gumbo simmering on the back of the stove. Musicians dropped by from all over on their way to and from Chicago, Milwaukee, Minneapolis, and points in between. We hosted the whole Basie band, Freddie Waits, Sonny Brown, and Papa Jo Jones, who came to stay with us for weeks at a time.

Along with the Sunday gig at the Church Key, Jimmy and I started another gig at the Park Motor Inn on the square. "When we leave here, we better be up on our axes," Jimmy declared. "So wherever we decide to go, we can hit the ground runnin'!"

We featured "free music," or avant-garde music, an expression of the times, brought on by various social movements: civil rights, black history, freedom of all kinds. We played tunes like "Forest Flower" by Charles

Lloyd and "Footprints." Our Afros got bigger and wider, and Jimmy's beard became a fearsome wonder.

"Hey, hold the phone!" Curtis Fuller pulled his golden trombone from its case and was rapidly assembling the slide and stuffing the mouthpiece in place. "Don't stop now!"

He leaped up on the stage of the Park Motor Inn and started spitting out notes, the trombone's golden slide gleaming in the spotlight, flicking in and out like the tongue of a cobra. We were jamming on a piece called "So What" by Miles Davis. It was usually played at a rather sedate tempo, but we remade the tune and played it at a breakneck speed, like the old tempo on "Cherokee."

"I want some of that," Curtis exclaimed. "I never played it at that tempo." And away he went.

Boy, the cat could burn, and the crowd knew it. Some of the more staid musicians of Madison came in to see what we were up to. A few confronted us during intermission. "What the hell are you-all playing? We don't understand any of it!"

"The joint is loaded, and they all seem to understand it," Jimmy pointed out, his voice bland. The bewildered musicians didn't leave, but they got very, very drunk.

That night we all went over to Fat Richard's crib—none of us, Dennis, Freddie Waits, Stefan, and a few others were feeling any pain. "I have a artistic masterpiece I must show all of you," Fat Richard declared. He ushered us into his living room, waved us to the couch, and pointed to the wall. "It's cosmic," he said in an awed voice.

"What is it?" Dennis finally blurted out.

"It was a pizza. Last night I put it in the oven, fell asleep, and when I woke up—it was art!" Certainly, it was coal black, and all the pepperoni, peppers, and onions were standing out in bas-relief. They were coal black also. Fat Richard had nailed it to his wall, and there it hung in all its weird glory. We all stared at it for a time, sipping our gin and tonics. Then we politely said, "Good night, Richard! You better call Lloyd's of London in the mornin'!"

No fools! No fun!

Movin' an' Moanin', Groovin' an' Groanin' in Madison

....

Jonathan David Samuel Jones and I were hanging out in Ward-Brodt's music store in Madison. Few people in the store were aware that the dapper man with the copper-colored face and the straight black hair growing around a horseshoe-shaped bald spot was the drummer known to the entire world as "Papa" Jo, the "man who played like the wind." Along with Count Basie (piano), Freddie Green (guitar), and Walter Page (walking bass), Papa Jo set the standard for the rhythm sections of the jazz world and the foundation of the Kansas City style. My hero, Jay McShann, also contributed to this style—big time.

At the moment, my friend was rolling drumsticks on the counter to see if they were warped. "Jenny," he rasped, "these sticks are not good for man nor beast. Kids need to play with the best, so's they won't accept anything less." He always called me Jenny; I don't know why.

The cashier aimed a baleful look at my companion as I paid for a copy of "Sunrise, Sunset" to play at the next country club gig with Bob the booking agent. I didn't know a lot of "square" songs, but sheet music and fake books did the trick.

"How's about a real kosher corned-beef sandwich?" I asked Jo as I hastened to keep pace with him along State Street. Papa Jo played tennis on a regular basis and moved his feet with the same speed he applied to his drumsticks. We turned into a little restaurant and found a booth way in the back. He immediately lit a cigarette. "Jo, you smoke too much!"

He countered. "Sit up straight. You're not that old!"

Jimmy and I quit smoking in 1965, when it became a choice between either renting a studio where we could rehearse, or smoking. No contest. We quit cold turkey. And just like all the converted, we tried to get our close friends to quit.

While we waited for our sandwiches I said, "Jo, it's wonderful you came to hang with us. It's nice . . ." I halted and looked away. "It's good to have someone in Jonathan's room." He looked away also, but not before I saw the mist cover his fierce dark eyes. His own son had also fallen into the bramble bush.

"Hey," I tried to lighten the mood, "I'm doing a special class with kids— music and movement. The University of Wisconsin made me a visiting professor. And guess who's helping me? Ruth Harris! She was Mahalia Jackson's accompanist for years."

He sat up at attention. "Mahalia? I knew her ol' man. He was in the service with Jimmy. Big tall handsome cat from Gary, Indiana, I seem to remember . . ."

"What was his name?"

"Never mind that! Suffice it to say, *all* her money didn't go to the Lawd!" He snickered. With that he went into a litany of stories about his life. How he was born in Alabama, played horns and piano, tap-danced and sang. Good thing he did. "There was this peckerwood I worked for as a teen-ager, or a little older. He always kicked me in my behind. One morning I went to work and vowed that he would never raise his foot to me again." Jo paused. The look on his face belonged to someone I did not know. "When he came up to me and yelled 'work faster!' and picked up his foot to plant it in my behind, I grabbed his leg, took my knife and cut, cut, cut around it and pulled down the flesh like you shuck corn."

"No!"

"Yes, I did." He opened his wallet, took out a folded piece of paper, unwrapped it, and took out a fragile square of yellowed newspaper. He smoothed it out on the table. The article's headline announced "Negro youth sought for heinous assault on prominent citizen." "That's me," he acknowledged grimly. "I'm the Negro. I caught the first thing smoking and joined a carnival. Good place to hide out—up north."

I could find nothing to say. We sat in silence, not looking at each other over the remains of our meal. After a time, I said, "We better get to the crib. Jimmy's class will be ending soon, and I wanna fry some chicken for supper."

"I like chicken." Jo folded the article carefully and placed his past back into his worn wallet. He stood. "I'll pay the check," he said.

After supper that evening, Jimmy, Papa Jo, and I sat around and traded stories about Big Sid Catlett, Big Joe Turner, Big Maybelle Smith, Big

Nick Nicholas, Big Mama Thornton, and Little Jimmy Scott. All three of us had worked with or for all these artists. And Dinah Washington, of course.

Jo and I both had played for this woman who carried all the door receipts in a cigar box clutched to her ample bosom. She played good piano herself, and was quite distant but polite with me. She remarked, "Good job," her eyes searching my face. Jo said she had searched for something with him, but it was not his face. She *loved* men.

Papa Jo Jones never had to buy an airline ticket—some millionaire cat from France set up a standing account for him just because he admired Jo's drumming. It was all very mysterious, the way Jo lived, the cryptic messages he would throw out to everyone and no one in particular. "Pretty soon Gramma's drawers gonna fit little Susie!" he would rasp in a voice of doom. Ray Bryant, a brilliant pianist friend of Jo's, wrote and had a hit with a tune called "Little Susie."

Jo came to wherever we lived and hid out from everyone and everything. He would tell people he was going to Europe, then fly out to hang with us. He would eat, sleep, watch the Road Runner—his favorite cartoon character—on TV, sip his Hennessy, and drink room-temperature beer. When he felt ready to face "whatever," he would leave.

This time, he lingered long. "Jenny," he said one day after Jimmy headed out for his lecture class (The History of Black Americans), "I must tell you something." He lit a cigarette. "I been to the Mayo Clinic. They told me they can't fix what's wrong with me."

"Is it your lungs?" Alarm sharpened my voice and made my question sound like an accusation.

"No!" he shouted.

"Well, Jo, what's wrong? Can we help?"

"Never you mind—it's the final diagnosis—and I just have to live with it."

"Okay, Jo."

He left the next morning. He was smiley and witty and joked with Jimmy as he packed his bag. I fixed his favorite traveling food, pork chop sandwiches. He carried them all the way to France, where he did as he always did—played like the wind.

* * *

Another one of the famous Jones boys came to town—Thad Jones, the other half of the Mel Lewis–Thad Jones Orchestra. Barrel-chested, with smiling eyes and a wide crooked grin, Thad played both trumpet and flügel-horn with ease. Mel was a drummer known for his solid, no-nonsense drive.

Jimmy had met Mel Lewis in Buffalo, when Mel was very young. "Mel's daddy used to bring him to the Colored Musicians Club to cut his teeth at the jam sessions," Jimmy explained.

Thad Jones was one of the trumpet players Jimmy had hired to do commercials in New York City for Chico Hamilton. Jimmy had subbed on many a Monday night with the Mel Lewis–Thad Jones outfit at the Village Vanguard. "Thad is a great arranger. He puts them together with pains-taking care," Jimmy declared.

I was fascinated by the odd pairings—the thickness and thinness and rhythmic variance in Thad's music. Even the monolithic passages were like elephants parading trunk-to-tail, tail-to-trunk. You couldn't hear their feet, but you sure knew they were there. Contrapuntal lines ran oppo-site, then chased each other through the music—racing, but always ending up embracing—and most importantly of all, the band *always* swung! The orchestra was appearing at UW on Jimmy's recommendation to enhance the jazz program. Thad and Mel were living proof of black and white jazz musicians closing the gaping wound between the races. Together they made a "joyful noise," a soul celebration.

Standing in front of the celebration was a willowy young trombonist named Janice Robinson. Her hair, a short ebony cap, clung close to her round head. Powerful, yet as feminine as her predecessor, Melba Liston, Janice stood toe-to-toe with Thad, playing a duet—with their plungers. Yes, the business end of real toilet plungers!

"It's an argument between two lovers," I whispered to Jimmy. I felt ec-static watching this great musician at the top of her game. Recognition of the musical argument rippled through the audience as Janice and Thad used their plungers like the voices of real human beings. The mock dis-pute became more and more heated and the crowd became more and more excited.

"Go, girl!" "Have your say!"

"Hang in there, Thad!"

The climax came with the fierce intermingling of both horns, then sud-denly Thad's character began to plead with and soothe Janice. She re-sponded with whoops and little slide sounds of forgiveness. It all ended in a grand finale of lip-smackin' sounds like kisses, and the whole band roared a musical "Ain't love grand!" The applause was thunderous.

Jimmy and I hurried backstage, where he had a great reunion with all the cats. Janice and I shared a moment of recognition. Here is another survivor, came the silent acknowledgement, another holder of a hard-won place in the sun in the rough-and-tough world of a dedicated jazz musician. I looked deep into her eyes to see if the "fire in the soul" was burning there. Only time would tell.

* * *

"Stand up! Make a circle! Hold hands!" Ruth Harris's voice whipped through the room, wrapping itself around the ragtag bunch of squirming children, causing them to cease their wiggling and giggling. They stared at us, as quiet and still as little statues, eyes round and wondering.

As I reported to Papa Jo Jones, as a visiting professor at the University of Wisconsin–Madison, I was to teach eurythmics, a theory from Germany that held that children had to be taught rhythms in a certain way.

Ruth and I played piano and organ and taught the kids (all potty-trained) to move to gospel music and to clap their tiny hands on two and four —in fifteen minutes! Professors crowded the balcony above the teaching area, watching in amazement and taking notes. However, we had nine more weeks to go, so we taught the kids scales on a little keyboard I bought. They learned how to identify the notes from sound and name. They learned a whole hymnal's worth of spirituals and gospel songs. And did they move? Every bone in their busy little bodies!

* * *

Neither burning sun, nor dark of night, nor rain, nor sleet, nor blowing snow with a forty-one-degree-below-zero windchill factor could keep Jimmy and me from our appointed rounds. We worked day and night— teaching days, playing music nights.

We took the long drive up north to see Jonathan regularly. Sometimes we made the trip alone, sometimes Dennis would drive us, and sometimes Hazel would hang with us. Real, true friends.

Jimmy took his Improvisational Experimental Black Music Ensemble and the University of Wisconsin Big Band up to the Big Ten jazz festival in Eau Claire, Wisconsin, where awards were given to the best musical groups every year.

"Babe! We took out most of the awards!" Jimmy's excitement could not be contained. He was particularly proud because most of the music charts he used were professional ones given to him by Count Basie and Duke Ellington. These charts were in stark contrast to the arid stage-band charts used by the other bands. They were rich with the colors of the people who invented jazz—and most of all, they *swung!* Nothing galls some people like success, especially when the success is not their own. The Big Band was accused of playing "black," whatever that means. Unfair advantage?

At the American Legion Hall–Elks Lodge ballroom in Kenosha, Wisconsin, Jimmy briefly rejoined Duke Ellington. The whole band spread out across the stage, preparing to start the concert. Chuck Connors, the bass trombone player, was on stage also, but obviously feeling no pain. In fact, he was asleep, deep in the land of "the day after the night before."

"I always carry my mouthpiece, as you know," Jimmy reported to me, his voice ringing with excitement. "I went up to the stage, pulled Chuck and his chair off into the wings, and went back onstage, with the maestro's (Ellington's) approval. Then I took Chuck's bass trombone and played the whole gig. How sweet it was to be back with the cats again!"

I was sorry to miss the big event, but I was playing a single at the newly built Sheraton Hotel for the dinner hour, five to seven p.m. After that, Bob the booking agent, Dennis, Stefan, and I went upstairs to play for dancing till midnight. The general manager admired my music. "Look, Jeannie, I'm going to write you a letter of recommendation, so wherever you go, you can present it to any Sheraton general manager and get a job." I thanked him and floated upstairs, where we played music until just before the carriage turned into a pumpkin.

* * *

"Stand up! Make a circle! Hold hands!" Once again, Ruth Harris's no-nonsense voice crackled through the room. Only this time the assemblage consisted of thirty hit men.

Dean Savides, a man of the future at the University of Wisconsin–Baraboo (summer home of the Ringling Bros. circus), asked Jimmy and me to head up a degree program at Oxford Federal Correctional Institution, or the "Big House." Professors of English, math, art, and electronics were to follow. Most of the men incarcerated at Oxford, in contrast to the students at the British university of the same name, were inmates whose claim to fame was that they had murdered men for money.

"If we help someone here, maybe someone will help Jonathan." That sad and desperate thought underpinned our decision to accept the offer. We drove the two hundred miles, round trip, twice a week, in a car provided by the university, through snow and sleet, for three years.

"I never will get used to the constant ID checks and rechecks and the clanging cell doors closing one after another," I whispered to Jimmy as we made our way into the bowels of the Big House.

The students ranged in age from eighteen to sixty, all lifers. In fact, some had been sentenced to three lifetimes for stealing a tank for the Irish resistance. I asked one baby-faced curly-haired blond boy in his early twenties, "Why and how could you kill so many people?"

His clear blue eyes didn't change. No clouds in that sky. "It was easy. I didn't know any of them . . ."

All our visits to Oxford were unnerving. We always rewarded ourselves by stopping halfway home in "The Dells," a beautiful spot in Wisconsin known for its spectacular fall colors. We treated ourselves to a big steak and a "martini salad," gin and vermouth with pickled onions, mushrooms, and olives floating in a chilled glass.

One night we saw a familiar face on a poster behind the bar. It was Miss M in full Western regalia, her blonde hair peeking provocatively from under a white cowboy hat. The print read: "The girl fresh from the Smokey Mountains appearing at the Blue Mountain Bar & Grill, the lovely *Ms. M!*" The date had already come and gone. We smiled and celebrated her "git up and go" with a second martini salad.

As time went by, the inmates began to look forward to the classes. The music was water to dying flowers to these cold-blooded characters. They began to call us the "Dynamic Duo" and cheered us as we walked through the yard to enter and exit the prison.

Some of the inmates had a beef with the officials because they were not allowed to worship in their own faiths. "Only an old ofay who drone on and on about who know what," scowled the black inmates. In fact, there had been a riot and a general lockdown a couple of days before one of our scheduled classes.

When we arrived, we were directed to the warden's office. "Order is restored." His eyes glinted behind his Harry Truman glasses. "Some of the other professors bolted. But the inmates have been asking for you two . . . if you're not afraid . . ."

"We're not!" snapped Jimmy. I didn't say a word.

Later, we went to the warden (who was a huge hero in our eyes) and ran down the reasons for the prisoners' complaints. We asked if Ruth Harris could join us.

"Stand up! Make a circle! Join hands!" The men were so shocked at the nerve of this tiny woman who asked them—O horrors!—to *touch* each other that they stood there paralyzed. "I said stand up! Make a circle and join hands—NOW!" Sister-mama Ruth jumped from the organ, put one hand on her hip, and shook her finger at the hardened group.

Miracle of miracles! They grabbed each others' hands and quickly formed a circle. Ruth jumped back on the organ bench and started singing while I joined her on the piano.

"Oh! Oh! Oh! Oh, what He's done for me!"

"SING!" she shouted. They all joined in, and it was on. You could feel the gospel spirit ricocheting around the room, and tears started streaming from eyes that were spiritually as dry as the Sahara. When the time was up, Ruth Harris led us all in prayer and spoke softly about the many loved ones lost and time that waits for no man. Then we sang "I Shall Not Be Moved" and "Oh, When I Come to the End of My Journey." They filed from the room—quietly and reverently. One turned and said, "We'll be waitin' for yo' return, ma'am."

From that time on, we saw real changes in their attitudes, and also welcomed a black minister and a Muslim spiritual leader for these men. And that was good.

* * *

The cat was a "chicken hawk"! As bad as the chicken hawks that Gramma Hattie had blown out the blue sky with her old blunderbuss. We had witnessed too many of them hovering around the campus of UW–Madison, doing free-floating wheelies in the sky, waiting to pounce on some upwardly mobile, nubile young thing. Spotting a vulnerable victim, they swoop down and capture them in their claws, whisper sweet nothings in their ears, then—bam!—the girls are dumped into a bin labeled "A Dream Deferred."

These cats make a career out of college, never graduate, just grab the fresh young girls, take all their money *and* their honey, then move on when a new group of unwary females arrives the next semester. Most of these men are in their thirties, and pass themselves off as knowledgeable and worldly.

Shirley, my daughter, called, and something in her voice galvanized us into action. "I have found this friend," her soft, sweet voice had an extraordinary ring to it. "He's really something!" That special Morse code, embedded in a mother's mind at the moment of her child's birth, started clicking. Dash, dot, dot. Dot, dash. Dash, dot. Dash, dash, dot. Dot. Dot, dash, dot. DANGER!

"Jimmy," I shouted, "cancel everything. We gotta go to Albany and check out this cat!"

Oh, what a splendid chicken hawk! A would-be Muslim from Buffalo and as handsome as the devil himself, he had dark liquid eyes that flashed as he pounded a fist into his palm and pontificated. He tried to impress Jimmy and me with a waterfall of rhetoric, raving on and on about pyramids and a lost knowledge that he, and only he, possessed. Jimmy remained quiet as the flood of words poured over us. Then he leaned forward and tapped the young man on his dashikied knee. "And where did you acquire all this information?" Something in Jimmy's tone stopped the man cold.

"In my books!" he shouted and jumped to his feet, his fez tipping onto his forehead. "I'm going to go to my apartment and bring 'em back an' prove you don't know what you talkin' 'bout! I'll be right back."

"But I haven't said anything," Jimmy said mildly, not finding it necessary to comment. He had let the man beat himself half to death with his own words, then sat back and watched the hawk try to fly on broken wings. The man scuttled out and slammed the door. He never knew that Jimmy was a thirty-second-degree Mason. "Well, Shirley," Jimmy inquired, "what is he gonna do while you are studying at Harvard Law School?"

"Oh, he'll find something . . ." Her voice trailed off, her eyes lowered. Jimmy and I looked at each other. A stone chicken hawk!

The young man did not return that night or the next morning. Jimmy and I went out to check out "Rocky's Rock Pile" (Rockefeller's famous building project), and when we returned, Shirley was livid. "He came soon as you-all left. He must have been watching an' waiting. He stormed in here an' said 'Woman, fix me some food!' "

"No!" Actually, we were not in the least surprised.

"Yes! An' I told him no man gonna order me around an' make me put on no head rag an' walk behind him—just 'cause he's a *man!*" Her eyes blazed and we knew everything was going to be all right. The scales had fallen from her eyes. We hugged her goodbye and flew back to Chicago.

Then we took the *Grey Goose* (yes, the same plane that the mythmakers claim ran into Otis Redding's plane) back to Madison. Only four people were aboard, along with one stewardess, a bit long in the tooth for her occupation. Over fifty, her waist thick and maternal beneath her grey uniform, she said, "No cocktails!" when we asked. "Only Jack Daniels." She lifted the lone bottle from the snack cart. We accepted the drink in paper cups— water back.

"I'll have one with you. This is the last flight today." She slurred her words.

And that did it. We started laughing and couldn't stop. We felt so relieved that Shirley had decided to keep going on up the ladder of success unencumbered that we laughed until we cried. The timeworn stewardess laughed too and kept pouring the corn as the plane coughed, shook, and, at last, wobbled over the lake and landed.

Snuggled in bed beside my wise and wonderful man that night, my Morse code spelled out: Thank you, God. Thank you for everything.

* * *

Time flies when you're having fun! It was 1976. America had a new president, a peanut farmer named Carter. Madison had one of the youngest mayors ever elected, Paul Soglin.

Alex Haley's book *Roots* was being discussed in our apartment by a motley group of musicians, artists, and hangers-on, who sat on the floor eating gumbo and drinking beer. The music of Miles Davis played in the background.

Dennis said, "You black people believe your own myths!"

"Bridle yo' Irish tongue, or I'll sic the leprechauns on you!" I parried. Startled, Dennis looked around as if a tiny trickster was lurking in a dark corner of the room. We all laughed.

There came a frantic knocking at the door. When I swung it wide, one of our fringy friends fell into the room. His shoulder-length blond hair stood up every which way, and his pale blue eyes were popping out of his head. "What on earth is wrong?" Jimmy stood up.

"Some black men from Milwaukee just robbed my wife's yard sale!"

"What?" "Is she all right?" A deluge of questions burst from all the folks.

"Yeah. They stole twenty-three bucks!" He stood in the middle of the floor and blurted, "Bring back lynchin' an' burnin'!" Silence.

Jimmy said, "Er . . . Maybe you better go home and check out your old lady." The man looked around at the stone faces in the room, then stumbled out the door that I still held open.

"And don't come back! Ever!" Dennis shouted after him.

There was no discussion of the incident. It was as if the Red Sea had closed over the hurtful words just as it had closed over old pharaoh's army. Jimmy sighed, "The more things change, the more they stay the same!"

* * *

How do you meet a legend? Hover around the stage door hoping for a fleeting glimpse of this woman who had made historical inroads on the territory reserved for titans of testosterone? A member of Andy Kirk's Clouds of Joy, arranger for Earl Hines, Tommy Dorsey, Benny Goodman, Louis Armstrong, Duke Ellington, and Dizzy Gillespie, she played excellent stride, boogie-woogie, and bebop. Top it all off with a work commissioned by the Vatican and who do you have? Miss Mary Lou Williams.

I met Mary Lou Williams the hard way—as a last-minute replacement for a stand-up lead singer in a chorus, drafted to sight-read the part of Lazarus, one of the major characters in "Mary Lou's Mass." The other singers had rehearsed for several days. Father Peter O'Brien, her faithful assistant, had worked like a dog to pull the event together. The theatre was jam-packed.

Mary Lou sat at the grand piano like a queen on her throne. She wore a dress that accented her ample bosom, her luxurious hair arranged in the style she had favored through the '30s, '40s, '50s, and '60s. Her eyebrows, pencil thin, were penciled in.

Full of anxiety, I rushed to check out my part, trying to see where the pages turned and if there were any repeats and where it would all end. I wouldn't have been nervous sitting at the piano singing, because I could feed myself the notes. But standing on a riser not far from Ms. Williams's left hand made me so uneasy that I began to sweat. I could feel moisture running down my back and popping out on my nose.

Her large eyes swept over the chorus that was made up of opera singers, little hippie-dippies, Sikhs in turbans, students in platform shoes and a whole slew of men dressed in black robes, the Little Brothers religious group. Truly eclectic.

Ms. Williams began playing the music. The bass player joined in. The chorus began to sing. When it was time for my entrance, I waited for a preparatory nod from the woman. None came. She directed with her head and only gave a quick jerk from side to side, so I wasn't sure she meant for me to begin.

She turned her head and gave me the meanest red-eyed look I have ever seen. In a nanosecond, I thought about Shorty Baker, trumpet player with Duke Ellington's Orchestra, my good friend from the Buffalo days, Mary Lou's ex-husband, and found my voice. I glared back at her and, loud and clear, Lazarus rose up from the dead!

Her eyes opened wide. Still pumping away at the piano, she lowered her head, and the mass moved on up a little higher and became a thing of beauty.

"She gave me the evil eye!" I complained to Jimmy later while sipping on a tall cool one at the Porto Bella Restaurant. "She knew I had never seen that music before, an' she should have acted like a pro an' smiled an' relaxed me."

"You seemed relaxed to me."

"Well, I got that way by thinkin' about all that shit Shorty told us about her."

Jimmy threw back his head and roared. Then he said, "Papa Jo Jones always said the talent is always bigger than the person!"

I sighed, took a sip of my drink, and shrugged. "Give the devil his due. Ms. Mary Lou Williams is a genuine, bona fide, dyed-in-the-wool diva! None better."

* * *

Ms. Mary L. Williams
Box 32
New York, NY 10031

Dear Jimmy:
Hi! What's happening? Am trying to get my new LP started! Got any ideas? Please call or write soon.
Love,
Mary Lou

Humph! Since Miss Mary had ignored me altogether, how on earth did she get our address? And why did she write only to one half of the folks in our house?

Bitch!

* * *

Wisconsin State Journal
October 14, 1976
Mrs. Cheatham is Honored

Madison jazz musician Jean E. Cheatham has been named woman of the year by the Wisconsin Women in the Arts. The conference "Women Together: A Moving Mosaic" is a recognition and celebration of the diversity of women in the arts in Wisconsin.

Mrs. Cheatham, pianist, vocalist, and composer is a visiting professor of Black History at UW–Baraboo. Her appearance, which has been designated as a tribute to her, will be a performance of her band Saturday night at conference headquarters, the Port Plaza Inn.

Conference speakers include feminist artist Judy Chicago, who will be keynoter, and author, Kate Millett.

* * *

Babs Gonzales
870 St. Nicholas Avenue
New York, NY 10032

Hey J & J

How are you and your family? I'm sure you're better than n . . . . rs in N.Y.!
Rigor mortis and depression has really set in here.
The cats are almost all out of work. (Whites included.)
Jim and Andy's closed now since I came back from Europe. Half Note closed.
(Good)
N . . . . rs sick and dying. Ray Nance on kidney machine. Sir Charles got cancer. Joe Newman look like he 90 years old with eye trouble — trying to live too high. (Dig?)
Me, I'm okay. Been in Europe doing my little gigs with Griff, Dexter, Slide Hampton, etc. So I'm selling my book and Billy Holiday 45 that I recorded in 1949 at my birthday party.
New book still not out yet — I need 5,000 but I refuse to ask n . . . . rs or white folks to go down with me, so I wait.
I video-taped my concert last week so I have a hour TV show to sell too.
I go back to Holland Apr. 28 so if I can come out for a lecture and gig before then, good. Me and 3 rhythm $1200. I ain't forgot I.O.U. $25.00.

> *Me an you*
> *La! La!*
> *Babs*

P.S.

If there's a club can use me with local rhythm — that's cool too.

> *La! La! again*
> *Babs Gonzales*

* * *

It was moving day on Mendota court. I sat on the bed in Jonathan's room, hugging his pink polka-dot doggie with the patent-leather ears. He had had it since he was three years old. The other shoe had finally dropped, and the anxiety we felt every year around springtime was over. Jimmy's contract for 1976–1977 was the last contract for him at UW-Madison. "Well," Jimmy said, shrugging his shoulders, "we do have one offer, if we wanna stay in this area."

My heart sank. The one offer we had came from the Oxford Federal Correctional Facility. After we had our first graduates from the degree program, the warden offered us a permanent position, complete with medical benefits, a car, and a house. But the thought of spending the rest of our lives in a home within the looming shadow of the Big House turned my blood ice-cold. We decided that there "ain't no luggage on no hearse" and that more than half the fun in a journey is getting there. We opted for the unknown.

It was heartwarming the way the whole community turned out to say good-bye during the last sessions at the Park Motor Inn. Among the overflow crowd were close friends: Dennis and Stefan; Robert Rhymes, who tried to help our son; Arne Bo, UW guru; Fat Richard; Clyde "Mr. Good Foot" Stubblefield; Jere Hilton, pipeline to Duke Ellington's Band; Ronn Gilbert, guitarist and one of the best blues researchers I've ever known — who, what, when, and where — he had the answers in his head.

Tamara, Bob's friend, gave me a little silver and turquoise ring shaped like a rose from the psychic shop. She and Hazel had sat beside me every day in court through Jonathan's travail. Ruth Harris turned my rough Afro into a lady-like, shiny, curly new hairdo. She was determined. "You don't want to go to Hollywood looking like a heathen!" She touched my cheek. "Goodbye, friend. Don't forget me. Don't forget to pray."

Babs's letter had helped us decide to go west — not east. Jimmy had made a phone call to Buddy Collette, his friend from his school days at Westlake College of Music in Hollywood. Jimmy and Buddy had shared an apartment with John "Streamline" Ewing, trombonist with Earl Hines, Louis Armstrong, and Jay McShann, among others. The phone call bore fruit.

"C'mon out!" Buddy was always generous. "You two can stay with me till you find a place."

Bob the booking agent turned us on to a car-dealer friend of his, who sold us a brand-new Ford LTD station wagon right off the showroom floor for a very low down payment. We packed our immediate needs into the back of the bright red wagon.

I called Bekins Storage in Los Angeles and arranged to store the contents of a large U-Haul truck. Two of Jimmy's students — tall handsome blue-eyed Pat Wick, composer and keyboard player, and Sipho Kunene, diminutive drummer from South Africa — had, with their parents' permission, offered to drive the truck to wherever we wanted to go. We would fly them back to their homes.

In the courtyard below our apartment, my friend Hazel, Pat, and Sipho were loading up the rental truck. The two young men had moved our new furniture straight from storage into the truck. It had taken three days to pack everything.

"Sell me these beds," I cajoled Mr. Divine, when he came up to see if we needed any help.

"Oh, just take what you need." He was smiling, but his Irish eyes were tearful. "You two have been good tenants, and good friends. Jimmy played with the Duke! I hope I get new tenants like you. Not like . . ."—he shuddered—". . . not like that other fellow that was here before you. That Cecil Taylor."

"Who?" Jimmy and I spoke in unison as we both stared at the little man.

"Oh, he was a nice enough fellow, but he left abruptly. Got in a fight with the university."

Jimmy and I exchanged a glance. We knew the story about Cecil justifiably flunking his whole class, but what else? Mr. Divine went on. "He left a cat in my apartment. No one knew the beast was in there at all! At all! One week later, when my housekeeper went to clean the apartment, it was in *shambles!*"

The landlord's face turned beet red from fury as he relived the whole episode. "The beast had torn up the couches, the bedding, the drapes. It pissed all over the carpet, and shit in all the corners. My friends, there is *nothing* like week-old catshit!" We choked back our laughter. "That poor beast had not food, nor water—he drank out of the toilet!" Mr. Divine's outrage grew with each word out of his mouth.

Jimmy became alarmed. "Hold it, Divine, you better calm down before you have a stroke!"

Mr. Divine switched gears abruptly, and his blue eyes lit up. "I see you have a bottle of brandy sitting right here. How about a wee drop?"

"Help yourself."

We went back to packing. Mr. D. wiped the back of his hand across his mouth and poured himself a generous glass of Papa Jo Jones's Hennessy. It was fine with us; we couldn't take an open bottle on the road. He sat there sipping away while the two boys, Hazel, Jimmy, and I marched past his rotund little figure, all of us carting away pieces of the dismantled beds.

The last possessions I packed were Jonathan's: his basketball, his favorite photos, a notebook full of poems, other boy things. Last of all the pink polka-dot doggie with patent-leather ears. All these went into a box marked "Applehead." I knew deep down in my heart of hearts that he would never come back for them.

I took one last tour of the apartment, went out on the balcony, and said a silent goodbye to beautiful blue Lake Mendota. The truck and the red LTD waited in the courtyard with their engines idling. Before I climbed into the car beside Jimmy, I hugged Mr. Divine, who wriggled with delight as he wiped a tear from his eye.

"Goodbye, Hazel! Goodbye, Mr. Divine! Take care."

"May the wind be at your back and may you get to heaven an hour before the Devil knows you're gone!" he called as we pulled out of the driveway and hit the long road west—leaving behind 1,875 days of life lived to the fullest, through heartbreak and laughter in Madison, Wisconsin.

It was August, and the sun made little heat devils dance on the asphalt highway. It was my birthday—I was fifty years old.

Glory!

Performing at the Park Motor Inn, Madison, Wisconsin, 1976. Photo courtesy Tamara Rand.

Jimmy Cheatham and Pat Wick, who was Jimmy's student at UW-Madison and helped us move to Los Angeles. Photo by Leroy.

Sipho Kunene, Jimmy's student, who also helped us move to Los Angeles. He went on to play long-term with Harry Belafonte. Photo by Jim Webb.

Sipho Kunene

Mary Lou Williams. I performed in her jazz mass in Madison. Photo courtesy CTS Images.

Papa Jo Jones. Photo courtesy CTS Images.

Babs Gonzales, hanging out at
our place in Madison.

Me at fifty, Madison,
1977.

The Way West

. . . .

C'mon, Babe! Come along with me!
We gonna take a trip in my auto-be-mine
But belong to the finance company!

We started moving right on down the line. The sun was shining bright in the end-of-summer sky, and I began to feel as if a huge burden had lifted from my life, leaving only memories of the good times. The tensions and trauma of packing and scheduling, the farewells to friends, and, indeed, the whole town had been wearing. The decision to leave Madison without our son broke our hearts. The decision to go on with our lives had taken its toll on both of us.

"Nothin' like the smell of a new 'short'!" Jimmy mused, inhaling the new-car aroma of the red LTD as if it were fine perfume. An excellent driver, he maneuvered the station wagon through light traffic, at ease, but ever mindful of the two young musicians leading the way in the lumbering truck filled with all our worldly goods.

We hadn't gone too many miles into Iowa when all the old rules of the road came rushing back. We rolled through small towns, clusters of small houses with black lawn jockeys as tall as grown men, standing at the ready in their front yards. Some of these cottages had Confederate flags displayed in their windows. We knew from experience never to stop for food or restrooms in these places. And then there were small towns with big black lawn jockeys and the *American* flag hanging in prominent places—we didn't stop there either!

We wanted to avoid putting the boys in harm's way from any racist who hated mixed company. It narrowed our choices down a whole lot, especially in conjunction with the old road caution to never eat in a place called "Mother's" or just "Eat"!

Our next hurdle came when we discovered that neither of the boys knew how to use the gears in the huge truck. We stopped in a full-service gas station to put gas and oil in the truck, and we implored the garage attendant to show them how to shift the gears properly. Alas, the lesson did not sink in. They were musicians, not mechanics, so the truck ate more than the boys—if that was possible.

"Those kids have bellies that keep on eatin' when they full!" I declared, worried because we had only so much money allotted for the way west. In fact, we had traveled less than a hundred miles when it became obvious that the boys needed a good night's sleep.

"At this rate," Jimmy said after we had fed the boys yet again and gone to our rooms to rest up, "we'll probably arrive in LA on New Year's Eve!" He laughed. I didn't. We had to get our things to Bekins Storage at a certain time or we would lose our space.

Next, we found out that long stretches of highway completely taxed the boys' concentration and that they became hypnotized by the lines in the road. They started weaving all over the place. Jimmy kept driving, first in front, then behind, then beside the truck, blowing his horn to keep them awake. Pretty soon, some Good Samaritan truckers, checking out our dilemma, started riding shotgun—a real caravan of honking and shouting.

We outran a tornado in Nebraska and ran into a mining boom in Wyoming—no rooms, in no motels, nowhere! Men were sleeping in eight-hour shifts, leaving barely enough time for the sheets to be changed, if they were changed at all. Everything seemed to be covered in some sort of white powder being mined from the surrounding hills. So much of this dust filled the air that it was hard to breathe.

"I'm gonna stand by the desk and see what's what," I whispered to Jimmy in the lobby in the last motel in town. The motel entrance was full of weary folks, waiting.

I heard the desk clerk calling on the phone to the next town. "Oh, you have rooms!" she exclaimed, then turned to three rough-looking men leaning on the desk and said, "Go forty miles south and there's the Gopher Motel with three rooms."

"Thanks. We'll get our gear, pack it up, and get going!" The men lit cigarettes and began a discussion about what gear to load first.

I scurried over to Jimmy and the boys and told them the news. We didn't *have* to pack. We busted the hell out of that highway and got to the motel first. We took two of the three rooms. The desk clerk there informed us, "You have to check out at six a.m." We didn't care.

"Are those your kids, mister?" the gas-station attendant asked the next morning.

"Yes, both of them," Jimmy replied dryly. The attendant kept staring at six-foot-three Pat Wick, his pale white skin shining in the morning light, and five-foot Sipho, his brown skin reflecting that same light.

The attendant said, "This is a fine red LTD station wagon! I ain't never *seen* such a fine station wagon. Er . . . how did you come by such a fine station wagon?" So intent on his questions, he ran the water with the air conditioner coolant out of the car, onto the ground.

"Hey!" Other attendants looked away with smirks. "What are you doin'?" Jimmy was livid.

"Don't worry, mister. I'll replace the water *and* the coolant." The man hopped around the car like a jackrabbit, wiping windows and performing other random acts, his eyes never quite meeting ours.

Down the road we went, Jimmy still fuming, on into Las Vegas to eat and rest. The next morning, halfway to Barstow through the desert, the sun blazing unmercifully down on man and machines, the air conditioner went dead in the station wagon.

Four-letter words, some five-letter words, some seven- and even ten-letter words flew out of our mouths. Words like "bigot," "racist," "honky," "redneck," and "peckerwood." These all came from Pat Wick! Other words like "asshole" and "sumbitch" came from Jimmy. Sipho just shook his head. I was too damn sick from the heat to say anything except, "Air! Air!"

Thank God, in Barstow, the proper mix of coolant found its way into the LTD. The boys and the truck were filled up. We climbed into our vehicles, and Jimmy and I took the lead to search for the turn-off to Bekins Storage.

We made the turn. But the boys did not. We watched helplessly as the truck kept driving on down the highway. It disappeared from sight, and we pulled into the Bekins parking lot and sat silently. What to do? We had traveled 2,060 miles, and now we had no idea where, in all of Los Angeles County, those boys and our truck could be. We waited and waited, hoping they would retrace their steps, but two hours went by and—nothing!

Jimmy sighed, "Well, let's call Buddy Collette. Maybe, just maybe, they'll go to his house."

The Bekins people laughed and laughed when we told them of our travails, and extended the check-in time.

Buddy was not home. The phone rang and rang. We kept calling, and finally he answered. "Don't worry," his deep voice reassured us, "they'll call, and I'll direct them to Bekins."

Three hours later the evening sun began to set in the West. Palm trees along the driveway, so foreign to my eyes, stood like long, rusty elephant legs, dark against the rose-colored sky. We walked up and down. The men who were to store our stuff walked up and down, also. We were getting more and more dejected when, at last, we heard a horn blowing beep-beep-a-beep-beep. Lurching down the ramp into the parking lot came the wayward truck.

The men all cheered as the boys sheepishly climbed down from the cab.

"I remembered you gave me Buddy's address and phone number for future gigs," Sipho said, as earnest and quiet-spoken as ever. "We called him, but no one answered the telephone. So we drove to his house and waited. When he came back, he gave us directions back here."

The furniture was unloaded and stored in record time—many hands made the task lighter. The truck was delivered to U-Haul, and the boys piled into the LTD. We arrived at Buddy's in time for an invitation.

"You guys want to go to my gig with me?"

"Yeah, we're game!"

"C'mon, let's go play music!" Buddy smiled.

We jammed all night in Laguna Beach with Fred Katz, a cello player with Chico Hamilton, and Henry Franklin, a powerful young bass player who reminded me of my brother Jerry.

We had traveled halfway across America, tested by misfits and mishaps, but had arrived safe and sound, and found ourselves playing bebop and blues within hours of our arrival. We had made our way to the left coast of the country—the land of make-believe—and there we would stay until it was time for us to go.

Pipe Dreamin' in the Valley of Smoke

· · · · · · · · · · · · · · · · · ·

I wanted in!

I could taste it, smell it, feel it. I sat on a rickety folding chair in a corner of one of the dusty rehearsal rooms in the basement of the Musicians Union, Local 47. Standing beside me, leaning on his broom, was the caretaker of the union, "Big" Bill. Yes, the same Big Bill, the tenor player we had rescued in the '50's at the Latour Arena in Quebec City. He had quit the music business, or as he laughingly told me, "The business quit me. The music did *not!*"

Our eyes and ears were focused on the big band grouped in the center of the room—cats with names like Ted Hawke and Duffy Jackson (the son of the Woody Herman alumnus, bassist Chubby Jackson), drums; Mike Price, Al Aarons, and Ray Brown, trumpets; Britt Woodman, Henry Coker, Phil Ranelin, and my Jimmy on trombones; Buddy Collette, Charles Owens, John Stephans, Fred Jackson, and Jackie Kelson, saxophones; and the great Red Callender on bass.

Grover Mitchell, the bandleader, was standing in the middle of this illustrious crew. He was a tall tan handsome man who looked like a sepia Benny Goodman, glasses and all. He was dressed East Coast, in a suit, shirt, and loosened tie. He had played in Count Basie's band for many years and knew better than most how to produce the Kansas City sound.

"He conducts from the middle of his chest like it's a secret," whispered Big Bill.

"Total command," I whispered in return.

The rhythm section was the engine driving the whole band, led by the stalwart Red Callender. The drummer maintained a steady pulse and, at the same time, accented the punctuation marks of the trumpets. The lead alto was leaning and keening, the voice eerily floating above the rest of the reeds.

The trombones were pure velvet, knitting all the instruments together into a well-oiled machine that forced heads to nod, feet to pat, and bodies to rock in total agreement.

My fingers opened and closed in response to the music. I ached to play piano with this band. I had cut my eyeteeth on big bands. But sitting at the old piano was this little blue-eyed cat timidly picking at the changes, fingers limply fanning the keys.

"That is not what I want!" Grover kept riding the little guy while the music roared on.

"But what you want isn't on the paper," the little guy yelled back.

"Well, put it there!" Grover snarled. "You MFs don't listen! It's been played, you know!" Meaning that the man himself, Mr. William "Count" Basie, had put his stamp on Grover's arrangements.

The rehearsal ended much too soon for me. The cats were milling around, cracking and facting and high-fiving, each one secure in the knowledge that he had played his part well and was in complete control of his craft.

I shook my head, squirmed on that rickety old chair, watched the little piano player sneak up the stairs. I want in! I declared to myself. I have to figure out how to make my move. I am gonna get in!

Exactly one month before, we were awakened by the sound of a mockingbird in Buddy Collette's back yard, knocking off tunes from a nightingale. He sang really loud, as if to wipe out the memory of the original melodies.

"Just like the music business," I snickered. Jimmy just nodded. He was exhausted from the long drive cross-country and the jam session the night before. We'd gotten up, dressed quietly, and awakened the boys. We took Pat to LAX to fly back to Wisconsin, then took Sipho to Santa Monica to his cousin's home. We were near tears to see them go, but big hugs all around and we went our separate ways. Then Jimmy and I drove back to the Miracle Mile to breakfast and to set our agenda.

"First things first," Jimmy said between bites of lox, cream cheese, and bagels. "The unemployment office first. That gives us two incomes for thirteen weeks before we have to really hustle."

"That's a good thing," I agreed.

Jimmy was the captain of this West Coast venture. He had lived here back in the '50s while studying at his second professional school, the Westlake College of Music. "I met Britt Woodman at the school and persuaded him to go with Duke Ellington, the *real school.* Britt introduced me to Buddy Collette. I met John "Streamline" Ewing at a bar. He played with Louis Armstrong, Charlie Parker, and Cab Calloway."

"Wow!" I looked around the restaurant. I loved the lox, cream cheese, and bagel, but I was a Midwest breakfast maven—ham, sausage, bacon, a stack of hotcakes, eggs, oatmeal, fresh fruit, and coffee. "I'm still hungry," I complained.

"Okay, okay." Jimmy paid the tab. "We wanna be first in line at the Hollywood unemployment office. You know, Streamline and I rented an apartment at 1406 South St. Andrews, and later we brought in Buddy Collette," Jimmy continued as he maneuvered the station wagon from the Miracle Mile to Hollywood. "It was a great pad! I fried chicken for Charlie Parker there—two for him, one for us. Boy, he could really eat. Just like he blows!"

I looked out the window and checked out the breakfast joints we were passing. "Fried chicken. Sounds great! I'm still hungry."

The unemployment office gave me a chance to size up some of the people —stuntmen, starlets, musicians. They all had a golden overlay on their skins, no matter how light or how dark. The men carried little purses. The women had phenomenal manicures—long nails, some with decorations on them. (Did anyone *ever* do dishes?) And their teeth—white, gleaming, with nary a gap in sight. They held their heads high. No double chins here, and every soul wore shades.

"We gotta get some sunglasses," I whispered to Jimmy as we waited in line, "I feel like the sun out here is so close to the earth that you can get sunburn in your house!"

"I was in line with Lady Barrymore in the '50s," Jimmy declared, "She said the money belongs to whoever put it in the pile—high or low."

Traveling along the wide boulevards of LA and Hollywood, I stared out the window of the LTD at the palm trees lining the streets like tall, rusty-legged sentinels and at the ice-cream–colored stucco structures—vanilla, blue, coral, and green—with manicured lawns, tortured little bonsai trees, and hedges clipped into animal shapes, all of it accented with exotic, brightly colored flowers that stuck their impudent tongues out at the world. I felt as if I had gone to sleep and awakened in another galaxy.

Next on the list was to get an answering service, then new photos (lobbies), and to transfer from Madison to Local 47. Again, Jimmy's friendships paid off. He contacted Clyde Reasinger, a great first-trumpet player, who had a crack big band in New York in which Jimmy played trombone, and who recorded Jimmy's arrangement of our song "Homeward Bound." Clyde had a lady friend who owned an answering service.

"I'll recommend you guys for some good gigs when people call for piano or trombone." She was really swell and invited us to her home. She also turned me on to a good photographer.

The days flew by—filled with looking for an apartment we could afford and going to the union to pass out cards and check our leads. The union really was *the* meeting place for all the cats, mainly because they picked up their checks there.

At the union, we met Bill Crump, one of the sax players from the old jazz showcase band in Buffalo. For many years he had played for all the big shows in Las Vegas, and now had resettled in Los Angeles. "Hey, soaks!" Boy, we were glad to see him. Fair-skinned with wavy black hair and a Clark Gable moustache, he still wore a porkpie hat from the Lester Young era. "Come on home with me," he invited, "Marie will be happy to see you two again."

Marie used to be a dancer. In fact, I had played for her act with another dancer in Buffalo. She was tiny and quick, her hair cut into a pixie cap framing her Claudette Colbert face. Her Italian temperament sticking way out front, she cooked a mean pot of spaghetti and meatballs, and we dug in. It felt like old times again, sitting around with our elbows on the table, talking about old friends and enemies, and drinking Bill's Old Crow whiskey.

There came a knock-knocking on the screen door, and in walked Bill and Marie's landlady. We were introduced. "Pleased to meecha," she said, seeming more distracted than pleased, and added, "I'm really upset!" She kicked off her shoes and placed the back of her beautifully manicured hand against her perfectly made-up forehead. "Do you know anyone who's looking for an apartment?" She sighed and sat down at the table and lit up one of Marie's little brown cigarillos. She blew smoke out of her nostrils and shook her chemically straightened hair.

"We are!" Jimmy and I exploded.

The landlady stared at us, "Uh, well, the apartment right over this one is going to be available in one week—the crazy old woman just up and decided five minutes ago she was moving back to Georgia."

Our guardian angel had done a hot-sock dance!

Three blocks over from The Jungle, as the area was called, 5018 Coliseum Street became our new home. We got our stuff from Bekins, but didn't unpack everything. My instinct and a still, small voice told me that this was only a way station.

I enrolled in the California Driving School, learned to drive, and got my license on the first try. "If M'Ma could do it at sixty-five, I certainly could at fifty!" I crowed and waved my driver's license in the air.

"We on a roll, babe!" Jimmy laughed.

* * *

Clyde Reasinger's answering service friend got me a rehearsal with Bill Tole's Big Band. They had been featured in the movie *New York, New York*. When Jimmy and I arrived at the rehearsal, the whole band looked surprised because we were black, and super surprised when Bill Tole greeted Jimmy. Then his *and* the band members' mouths flew open when I took my place at the piano.

Bill Tole had no mercy. He called a fast tune from his repertoire in the key of F, stomped off the tempo, and away we went! I didn't have much time to check for page turns and repeats, but I did note that it had an extended solo for piano. "Run with me, Jesus!" I breathed a little prayer and nailed that music to the wall. When we finished, the musicians all applauded.

"I've got a week at Disneyland, could you make the gig?" Bill inquired.

"You bet." I was happy and excited. Bill became one of my heroes from then on, and the week with his band was wonderful.

But, Lawd, everyone was not so gracious, giving, or good to us. Up jumped the devil!

Jimmy was called to a rehearsal at a supper club. I went along for the ride (in case the piano player didn't show up). I called it riding shotgun. I lurked in a darkened corner of the deserted restaurant and observed what was *really* going on. The restrooms were side by side in a narrow, shadowy hallway. As Jimmy greeted the other musicians, who were pulling out their instruments and milling around, I decided to check out the ladies' room. The old-fashioned fixtures showed neglect, and the water ran cold and rusty. I thought, I wouldn't eat here on a bet! and started to open the door to leave. With my hand hesitant on the door, I heard voices.

"Man, there's too many trombone players here from back East! Specially that Jimmy Cheatham. He and Chico Hamilton practically ran the business in New York. If he gets a chance, he'll take over out here!"

"Yeah, you right!"

"So, he's out—and some of those other hotshots, too."

"Yeah!"

The tar pits on Wilshire Boulevard, oozing primordial darkness, must have spawned those cats. The low-life trombone players slithered back to the bandstand.

"Jesus H. Keerist!" I closed the restroom door and waited until I heard the music begin, then came out and seated myself in the dark. Thoughts buzzed in my brain like angry bees. They not gonna let Jimmy work. They gonna try to freeze him out. We can't make a life here. We gotta get a different plan. But what? Where else could we go? Babs Gonzales was right on the money: New York, for now, was a graveyard. All the shows had moved to Los Angeles, except *The Today Show*. Our unemployment checks had met the halfway mark.

I decided not to tell Jimmy about the ugly plot. I knew he would be furious and heartbroken. Over the years he had hired them all, and this was their way to repay him—with envy and greed. I felt sick. These cats were as phony as the used Mercedes they drove: the engines under the hoods were from Ford. The cats had them put in on the cheap, a real Hollywood trick.

My heart sank low, but I put on a happy face and kept my remarks upbeat. Jimmy did get work copying music for a down-to-earth for-real man named Marion Sherrill. He also played some gigs with Streamline and Bill Crump. And the rehearsals with Grover Mitchell. None of the nefarious trombonists were in Grover's band. Grover instinctively knew whose heart was not as big as a mustard seed.

It was time to get superserious about making some back-up money. Once again I looked in the yellow pages and found an agent. His office was located in Beverly Hills. I figured if he could afford *that* rent, he must have access to good, paying gigs. I showed him my letters from the Sheraton in Madison, and he booked me into the Sheraton downtown on Wilshire Boulevard, playing happy hour from four to seven p.m., five days a week.

When Jimmy and Bill were busy, Marie drove me to work. "I really need this bread to save for an emergency," I told her, "but you're an artist, so you know how I *hate* playing single piano." Marie nodded in sympathy. I continued with a tale. "The room filled up with folks just gettin' off from work. They were wolfing down happy-hour hors d'oeuvres, drinkin', laughin' loud. There I was without even a spotlight. Mr. B, the general manager, came in and stood by the piano . . ."

I paused while Marie made a turn in front of an oncoming truck. The driver blew his horn and shook his fist at us.

". . . I was playin' 'Delta Dawn' and 'Isn't She Lovely' and 'Help Me Make It through the Night,' when Mr. B. barked 'WAKE UP, JEANNIE CHEATHAM!' My head came up with a snap. Sure enough, Marie, I was taking a nap while my fingers played on automatic pilot."

Marie laughed, but I clutched at the passenger door while she made a fast turn to avoid the guy trying to pass us on the right. "Then what?" she asked.

He said, "Awake or asleep, you're a fine pianist."

During the last week at the Los Angeles Sheraton, I didn't feel well at all, but I toughed it out and finished with a flourish. I received another recommendation letter from that Sheraton and extended my unemployment.

Things were brought to a screeching halt. The Valley of Smoke—with air you could see—invaded my lungs, lungs that were used to the pure clean air of Wisconsin, with its pristine lakes and green trees giving off pure oxygen. I succumbed to the smog and was brought to my knees with pneumonia. "Thank God for amoxicillin, and not asafetida bags and red-pepper rub and goose-grease poultices!" I croaked.

Great-Gramma Lizzie's genes, Gramma Hattie's grit, and M'Ma's "git up 'n' git" came to my rescue. I was up on my feet and back in the swing of things in no time at all. I couldn't wait to get back to Grover's rehearsal. I went back and sat on that same rickety chair. Big Bill said, "Hey, I missed you, kid!" I nodded. I still wanted in.

"We're going to play the Monterey Jazz Festival!" Grover grinned as he made the announcement. "We're going to take a chartered bus up and back, and best of all . . ."—he paused for effect—". . . we're taking Stan Kenton's place!" The cats reacted with shouts of glee.

My heart started beating fast. Oh, Lawd, I gotta do something, even if it's wrong! I clenched my fingers. I had only two weeks before the festival to make my move. The very next rehearsal, I sat in that chair, and this time Big Bill brought his tenor sax, just in case someone goofed or didn't show up.

Grover seemed really uptight. He wanted that band perfect for the big day. The little piano player still tip-tapped at the piano keys, and Grover, standing in the middle of the band, his back to the piano, was grumbling. The band was really pumping. Grover let loose a string of obscenities. "That's not it!" He had high blood pressure and anyone could see he was getting worked up.

Suddenly, as if in a trance, I got up from the folding chair and walked over to the piano. "I wanna play," I said quietly into the little cat's ear.

He looked up at me, frowned, and said, "No."

"I wanna play!"

"No!"

I sat down on the piano bench right next to Mr. "accent on one and three" and shifted my hips (quite bony from weight lost due to my pneumonia) and booted him off the bench. Then I began to play where he left off, throwing in the color and the accents that Mr. Basie had birthed and the groove that I knew Grover was yearning for.

"THAT'S IT!" Grover turned with a smile on his face. His mouth dropped open when he saw me sitting on the piano bench and the little cat sitting on the floor. Still, Grover didn't drop a stitch. He kept on conducting while his smile turned into a grin. "That's it. That's *exactly* what I want!"

And that's exactly what *I* wanted.

IN.

* * *

Git on the bus! C'mon git on the bus!
If you wanna make music
Don't fuss—don't cuss!
Just git yo'self together
An' git on the bus!

The chartered bus ride up to Monterey, California, was truly liberating for all the cats. We all felt the adrenaline rush of the promise of things to come. We were "back in the saddle again." Just for a little while, we were free from worry, from the hustle and bustle, from having to tiptoe around civilians who did not know and did not want to know how we really felt about the world and its troubles. We were happily aware of a suspension of pretension and dissension. All of us were pointed toward one thing only— playing the gig.

The bus driver sat behind the wheel wide-eyed and open-eared, his face turning beet red at some of the jokes the cats told. The man was getting a contact high from the weed smoke emanating from the back of the bus, and he sometimes veered alarmingly toward the edge of the highway.

One of the cats was relating a tall tale about the sexual prowess of a one-legged woman who ran a small café in South Bend, Indiana.

I closed my eyes and leaned my head on the high-backed seat. I remembered that M'Ma had boarded a Greyhound bus and traveled ninety miles to South Bend just to see about me. And retraced those ninety miles back home the same day after she found out that I was doing okay.

"Now my kids are far away," I said to myself, "and here I am, hurtlin' down a highway, listenin' to a cat I hardly know talk trash about a woman who befriended me in South Bend so many years ago." I knew she never in her wildest dreams thought that some musician would be putting her business in the street twenty-five years later. I sighed, opened my eyes, and shook my head, but the image of my friend from South Bend clung to the corners of my mind. It felt like I, too, had become a little fuzzy around the edges from the cloud of weed smoke hanging beneath the curved ceiling at the rear of the bus.

Finally, we arrived in Monterey. The bus parked on the crowded festival grounds and we spilled out, needing to refresh ourselves and get ready to perform. We discovered we had to put on our stage clothes in the restrooms. Thank God for pantsuits!

Ours was one of the last acts to go on, and the night air had become cold and penetrating. The chill evening didn't dampen our enthusiasm one bit. I wrapped my long, red wool scarf twice around my neck. Onstage, as we took our places, tuned up, and looked out at the audience, we could see people laughing and talking and greeting one another, eating out of baskets with bottles of something or other protruding from them. There was a real homecoming feel to the event. "Let's party hearty" was the mantra of the Monterey festival.

All at once the MC came bounding out on stage, grabbed the mike, and cried, "Ladies and gentlemen, I'd like to present—Mr. Stan Kenton!" And suddenly a big screen lit up the night, and there were cheers and whistles. A giant figure of Stan Kenton appeared, and after a little greeting he said, "Ladies and gentlemen, meet the man and the band who have graciously taken my place tonight. Meet Grover Mitchell!" Even more whistles and cheers came from the audience, and the energy leaped up another notch.

Grover stomped off the tempo and away we went, building a fire that heated up the chilly night. After the concert, people came up to the piano and said, "All right! Go on, Miss Basie!" "Does the Count know you're out?" and "Are you from Kansas City?"

I just smiled and basked in an ecstatic glow—God knows how grateful I was to have found the courage to get myself into this band and to be so warmly accepted by its members and the people who loved its music.

* * *

Jimmy and I recorded several records with Grover, the first one called *Meet Grover Mitchell*. He included Jimmy's arrangement of our tune "Homeward Bound" in the album. In fact, Grover invited Jimmy and me over to his condo in Simi Valley, telling us, "I've got the new test record in my hot little hand." He sounded really excited. "Come on over and spend the night and we'll listen to it!"

So we took the long drive out to Simi Valley, and Grover wined and dined us. Then he proudly put on the brand-new record, a big black shiny vinyl disc with our hearts and emotions ingrained in the grooves.

"You MFs are all over this record," he complained to us, but he was grinning. Then Grover became quiet. "You know," he said, "I took this record to Basie, and he listened to it and asked, 'Who's that cat on the piano?' I told him, 'That's no cat, that's Jimmy Cheatham's wife!' He told me to tell you that he was going to break your fingers!" Grover burst into laughter and so did we. I was beside myself. Such a great compliment from one of the masters!

We recorded *The Devil's Waltz* with Grover, and Jimmy's arrangement of our original song "Blues for J. C." was included.

There were plenty of people pipe-dreaming in the Valley of Smoke. Some dreams came true, some did not. But the dream I prayed long and hard for did come true. I wanted in—and in I got! As the Reverend Babs Gonzales preached, "Ev'ry thing is *most* expubident!"

* * *

"If you got the head of a hippopotamus and the behind of a hummingbird, get ready for a bumpy ride!" A cryptic description of the music business.

Every year thousands of musicians tumble out of music schools and thousands more follow the muse all on their own, only to find that they're all dressed up with no place to go. The business of music is mean, hard and, more often than not, treacherous. Talent alone does not guarantee smooth sailing through the rough waters between rehearsal, performance, and getting paid. Music was fast disappearing from the grade schools and high schools. No more village squares with oom-pah-pah bands. Not much live music at parties and celebrations, and "the day the music died" was fast becoming a reality.

The Crumps' dining table became our strategic command center. Heated discussions about the business of making music went on till the wee hours of the morning. Between Marie's cigarillos, Bill's pinch-back bottle of whiskey, black coffee, and delicacies from my kitchen or Marie's, old days and new ways were woven into a fabric that included the eternal question: "Where is the next gig?"

I sat with my elbows on the table, staring at the man who, but for the "fickle finger of fate," could have been my daddy. As the conversation swirled around the table, words mingling with the blue smoke that made patterns around the chandelier above our heads, I watched him drink his coffee, little finger sticking out in a genteel manner. He patted his lips with Marie's napkin, smiled slowly, and turned his elegant head toward whomever he deigned to address. His skin was smooth and burnished like copper, and his hair was jet black.

"You kids could have had straight black hair," M'Ma's dreamy voice echoed in my mind, still passionate despite the flow of time. "He picked me out of the audience, waggled his trombone at me . . ."

I pictured M'Ma in her early, girly days, swaying back and forth in her red silk velvet dress in front of Duke Ellington's orchestra, watching this handsome devil play his golden trombone. His name was Lawrence Brown, or Larry, as Bill and Marie called him. He had retired from playing with the Duke and was now an official at the musician's union.

Now, here he was, sitting across from me, in the flesh. I wondered what M'Ma would have called him. Larry? Honey? Lamb Chop? Sweetheart? Would we really have dined with Mr. Ellington? M'Ma's old dream brought a smile to my lips and a gleam to my eye. I could not resist. "My mother had a real crush on you, Lawrence Brown," I blurted out.

The conversation came to a complete stop. For a moment, Larry became wary, then he squared his shoulders, sat back in his chair, and preened himself. "Your mother? Well, well. Heh, heh, heh! That's very nice indeed!"

"A whole lot of water over that damn dam!" Bill teased. "You and Duke had many a battle over who's woman belonged to whom." Marie laughed. So did Jimmy. Lawrence Brown scowled. He didn't deign to respond. He turned his handsome head away and, with a wave of his hand, dismissed the whole conversation.

I decided not to tell M'Ma. Even a fifty-year-old pipe dream is precious. I didn't want to be the one to spoil her memories.

* * *

Things got rougher than rough. The rent and the threat of the repo man lit a fire under our feet. By day, we checked every lead we could, some suggested by friends, some by the answering service. By night, we talked to the break of day, going over old and new ideas and lists of possible gigs.

Back in the early '50's in Los Angeles, Jimmy's activities in the music community mimicked a squirrel's putting away nuts for the future. "I worked with Lennie Hayton and Lena Horne, copying music and also some arranging." He began to explain the extent of his adventures in LA and Hollywood. "I wrote a tune called 'Nuttye' that was recorded by Chico Hamilton on Pacific Jazz."

"Really? That's some title."

"Yeah, George Duvivier, the same bass player on your record with Jo Jones and Roberta Como, was on it, with Buddy Collette and Jim Hall on guitar."

We lay in the dark, both of us trying to hide our fears for our future, trying not to think about the cats that were now leaving Los Angeles, going back to their hometowns to work in post offices and hospitals and become weekend warriors. Some of them had hurriedly gotten hitched to women who offered security: nurses and teachers and government gals.

Jimmy explained, "I became the test case to merge the black union, Local 767, and the white union, Local 47."

"Politics? You? You *hate* politics!"

"Well, a bunch of us realized that the time had come. Lemme see. There was Marl Young, Les Davis (the president of the black union), John Anderson, Red Callender, Bill Douglass, Buddy Collette, Gerald Wiggins, Gerald Wilson, Bobby Short, the great Benny Carter, Ernie Freeman, Streamline Ewing, and some other cats I can't remember . . . and me."

"Heavy cats!" I was impressed. These same men, at least most of them, were still Jimmy's good friends, and we were about to enter the '80s.

"It was a great time! I did a string quartet that was premiered at a Paul Robeson concert," Jimmy continued, fueling his future with the triumphs of his past.

"Why . . . ?"

"Why did I leave when I was just beginning to cash in on all my schooling and contacts? You know the answer to that."

I did. Jimmy left LA when his mother became ill. "When we met," he added, "I was trying to get back here." He fell silent. I knew what he was thinking. Had time marched on without him? Could he bridge the gap between his friends' successes and his own reentry into the LA scene? He floated to the top in New York, but to start over here in a declining market? I knew he had had a real dark night of the soul over his decision to go back to Buffalo.

I wanted to cheer him up, so I whispered, "If you hadn't come back to Buffalo, you might not have met me."

"That's right! You *my* baby!"

"I know one thing. All those cats in Duke's band and Basie's band and Woody Herman's band and Lionel Hampton's band better pray their leaders keep breathin', or they'll all be out of a job!" We giggled and soon fell into fitful sleep.

* * *

Talk about weird coincidences! My old friend Rose, Bob the booking agent, and his friend Tamara came out west and took up residence in LA, all at about the same time. So did little Mattie Fields and all her kids. They drove all the way from Buffalo to live with and take care of Big Mama Thornton. Jo Jones even came to stay a week with us. "I came out here because I have to give my ex-wife away in marriage. She wouldn't have it any other way!" He beamed. It felt great to hang with him again.

The beautiful Miss M arrived—not to stay, but to get a face-lift. Heavens!

It seemed as if they brought us renewed energy—a new sense of who we were and what we were really about. I could have played alone at the Sheraton at any time, but I knew that was a trap, a gilded cage. Then an agent, a small middle-aged woman, called me to rehearse with a group and prepare a vocalist for Las Vegas.

Good googly-moogly! That group was a weird mix! The drummer was a Mormon, the bass guitar player was Israeli, the lead vocalist was Sicilian— and me.

The gig was like quenching our thirst from the well of Zem Zem. Our luck had begun to change, and we were about to embark on a grand new adventure. Our dreams were beginning to come true.

I felt certain of one thing: long before all the people came across the Great Divide, looking for a brand-new life, the Indians named the area around Los Angeles the Valley of Smoke. I knew deep down in my heart that their "Great Spirit" was still hanging around, checking all of us out. Glory!

A Standing O in San Diego

. . . .

Just drew a line in the sand—
Put the chip back on my shoulder!
Gotta lay a claim to my life—
Before I git one moment older!

"Who you? The FBI or somethin'?"

I was sitting at the old baby grand piano on the stage at the Sheraton Hotel on Harbor Island in San Diego, waiting for Richard, the star vocalist (a younger version of the movie star James Garner). His debut show was slated for eight p.m. that night, and we planned to do a sound check.

"Well, are you?" I glared at the little man standing at the lip of the stage. Blond hair cut close to his head, his gray-green eyes narrowed as he tilted his face up at me.

"No, I'm *not* the FBI. I'm the assistant manager here, and the policy is NO BLACK PEOPLE ON HARBOR ISLAND!" I took a sharp breath and closed my eyes. I could not believe my ears. "Do you have any relatives or friends in San Diego?" He rocked back and forth on his heels as he pursued his interrogation.

All the old rage came bubbling to the surface, like subterranean water boiling from a geyser. Words echoed in my head, ghost voices from the past, mean and meaning to terrify: "Ain't no nigger gonna ride on no roly-coaster today!" "Gimme all the money you-all made to-night and I'll let you niggers go home." "If y'all didn't steal those instruments, git out the car an' play me a ditty!" I felt faint. Once, long ago, I promised myself that I would never play music in the South. I had broken my vow. I was in the South—Southern California.

Just then Richard bounded into the showroom, closely followed by his manager, a small, nervous woman. Richard's perfect teeth flashed pearly white in his handsome, suntanned face, and his dark hair lay thick and shiny with just a hint of curl. He picked up on the poisonous atmosphere and asked, "What's going on?"

"This person wants to know why I'm on Harbor Island, and since I seem to be here, why I am *black!*"

"What? That's a crock of . . . Jesus! The drummer's Mormon, the bass player's Israeli, and my manager, she's Jewish, and I'm Sicilian!" His voice rose with each new description of the motley bunch, his beautiful face turning cherry red. "All right, if Jeannie leaves, we're all leaving!"

I put out my hands and ran a blues pattern on the black and white keys of the piano, thinking to myself, Fight or run? Cha-cha-cha! In an instant my mind was made up. "Listen, Richard. We were sent here by the 'big boys' of Las Vegas. They paid to get you ready for their showroom. And that's what we're gonna do." Alerted to the contretemps in the showroom, the general manager rushed up, then stood silent, watching the proceedings. I continued nonchalantly, "But maybe you should call the big boys and tell them there's a little problem here."

The assistant manager's jaw jutted at a belligerent angle, and he opened his mouth to say something, but the general manager hurried to overrule his underling. "Er, that *is* true . . . we would not wish any, ah, problems with the Las Vegas people, er, she can stay!"

Richard's tanned brow furrowed and his dark eyes glistened, probing mine. He murmured, "Do you *want* to stay?"

"Look, this is a job. We didn't come here to *colonize* Harbor Island. We'll be history in a couple weeks."

Richard's manager sighed in relief. The general manager and his assistant also looked relieved. The rehearsal began, but I felt so upset that I could hardly breathe. The incident had been so unexpected — racism in all its ugliness in such a pretty place. Then again, if you look at a map and run your finger across in a straight line east from San Diego, you bump right into Birmingham, Alabama.

That night, just before showtime, Richard's manager sidled up to the table in the back of the darkened showroom, where I sat sipping from a snifter of cognac. She seemed jittery and twittery. First she asked, "Where did you get that outfit?"

I wore a red chiffon by Chloe, fluttery and feminine. "I found it at Saks in Beverly Hills." The dress had been marked down to the bottom line, but I sure didn't tell her that. I spoke off-handedly because I sensed that she had something else on her mind.

"Um-m, you know, Richard is the star of the show." I said nothing. She rushed into the silence. "Since he is the star, I want the band to play something for an opener and you to sing. Then, after that, you announce Richard."

"You really don't want me to do that," I told her. She had no idea what she was asking.

She dropped into the chair across from me, and her expression turned steely. "Listen, you're getting paid to do this show . . . handsomely, I might add!"

Intent on saving her from herself, I said, "I'm not getting paid to sing, only to play the piano and accompany Richard."

Silence. "I'll pay extra," squeezed out like the last toothpaste from the tube. Money wasn't the issue, but she thought it was.

I sighed. "Okay, but I'm warning you, you really don't want me to open the show."

"Nonsense! You'll do fine. Of course, I've never heard your voice, but most all you people sing . . ." She paused, then added, "and dance . . ."

I interrupted wearily, "Whatever you want." I turned away.

The room started filling up with people from a teachers' convention from all over the United States and Puerto Rico, and then it was showtime. I gave the musicians short instructions, took my place at the old baby grand, closed my eyes, and called on the spirits of St. Paul's Baptist Church and the ghosts of past generations—riding the wings of simmering, righteous anger—to magnify the sounds pouring from my throat. I made my presence known. W. C. Handy was a man, but he had had a mama, and when he wrote "St. Louis Blues," he wrote the universal lament for *every* woman.

When I finished the ancient tune, there was one beat of silence, then came a roar, people standing, applauding, whistling, stomping. Those middle-aged middle-class white people knew that they had received the real deal from the real source.

Richard's manager tugged on my arm, reaching up from the floor beside the stage and screaming, "Stop this! Stop them! What have you *done!*"

The bass player, drummer, and I went right into Richard's opener, Barry Manilow's "I Write the Songs," while I announced his name. He bounded up the steps on the stage, grabbed his mike, and, to his everlasting credit, smiled at the cheering audience and said, "Wasn't that great? And we didn't even know she could sing! Take another bow, kid!"

He sang really well, a grand baritone voice, and he looked even better than he sang. He wore specially made shirts with scalloped edges down the front—no buttons at all—the shirt opened down to his waist, exposing his tanned chest, muscles sculpted like an urban Tarzan's. Oh, he was a shining example of male eye candy, but most of all he was a nice man whose number-one asset was honesty.

After the show, the general manager came over to the table where I was winding down and asked, "Is the piano alright? If not, would you help select a new one?"

I told him the truth. "This piano shouldn't be replaced. It's a Steinway. It only needs a few pads and a tune-up and cleaning."

His eyes were respectful and his face was solemn. "You know, you can work here *any*time you want . . . after you finish with Richard, just let me know."

"Thanks. I appreciate that."

I received extra money for singing that night. The next evening, before showtime, Richard's twittery manager again sidled up to my table. "Umm . . . Jeannie, dear . . . I've thought about it . . . um . . . I don't want you to open the show . . ." She paused. I said nothing, just looked at the lovely amber color of the cognac in my snifter, then gave the liquor a swirl and watched how it seemed to glow in the subdued light. "All right, all right!" she continued. "I'll pay you *not* to sing!"

"Done." I reached out and shook her bony little, blue-veined hand.

That night we opened the show with the bass player's great arrangement of an instrumental called "Classical Gas." I challenged myself nightly by trying to do the intricate tune using octaves.

Change is so liberating and the best revenge is sweet success!

* * *

We flew into Las Vegas after the stint at the Sheraton. The audition was a success, and the "five-o'clock shadow at noon" men seemed quite taken with Richard's performance. They put him on hold, though, and I could tell that waiting for Wayne Newton to quit was not Richard's cup of tea.

We were booked into a resort in the hills near Palm Springs, where well-preserved women with blue hair and gold wedgies played tennis in the blazing noonday sun. We each had a little cabin, and Jimmy drove over between his gigs and assignments to hang out with us.

After a month at the resort, the inevitable happened. "I'm quitting show business," Richard declared. His manager failed to get him an opening in Vegas, and his career was going nowhere. His announcement didn't surprise us at all. "I'm not sitting around waiting for some gangster to call!" His white teeth flashed, his dark eyes sparkled. Richard and his girl were giving up the fool's gold of the entertainment business for the real thing. They planned to mine gold. "I'm working for myself from now on!"

"Me, too!" The Israeli had been making plans also. "Me and my fiancée are gonna marry and raise babies and build houses."

The little Mormon drummer had tried unsuccessfully to convince me about the merits of his faith. "They don't allow black people in heaven," I said dryly.

"I know, but maybe someday." He was so sincere.

Soon after, I found an article in the paper indicating that the Mormon leader had taken a new stand and, in his advanced age, had decided that all men could enter the pearly gates. Black people could hang out in heaven with the rest of the folks. The announcement really rattled the drummer. "I'm studying to be a priest in the Temple. Now, I'm so mixed up, I don't know *what* to think!"

The band broke up, it's members caught somewhere between deep uncertainty and high hopes. For my part, I disliked spending all that time separated from Jimmy. The break-up, while disappointing, also came as a relief.

Richard asked, "What are you going to do, Jeannie?"

"I've always been a musician, and I'll always be a musician!" And so we said our farewells.

It had been a short run, but a good one. It led me to San Diego and the Sheraton on Harbor Island. And it was to play a major part in our lives— beyond our wildest dreams.

* * *

One morning, the mailman brought me a lovely letter from Jonathan, our prodigal son. To his credit, he did stay in touch with us after his release from the halfway house, even though most of his phone calls were collect.

Dear Mom
I found a poem I wrote when I was a tween-ager. I'm doing pretty well up here.
The ladies are nice and I'm trying to be a disc-jockey. Hello and love to Dad.

Jon

The trials and tribulations of a
Black woman (courage)

Listen all you black women—you are
the insides of the Black Civilization
you are the Heart
you are the Spine
you are the Brain
But most of all you are the
Spirit of the Black Civilization
You have always found the strength
when it appears that all is
about to end
you have always had a smile when
there was nothing to smile at
You've always had the courage
when all seemed lost
For without you many a black man
may not have survived
But there is one thing that you all
are deprived of and
That is the "recognition"—
Those are the
Trials & the Tribulation
of a Black woman
—Jonathan Cheatham
14 years old

* * *

Dear Jon

We are really glad to hear from you! I am using your new grown-up moniker "Jon" (smile). I'm writing this letter to tell you how deeply moved I am by your lovely tribute to Black women. Your letter didn't have a return address, but I'm writing to you just the same. When you get settled, let us know where you are and I will send this letter straight to you.

Meanwhile, remember I taught you that "Thoughts are things and GOOD thoughts have wings!" So I know you'll receive this letter in spirit. I'll keep your poem always. Your Dad says "Take good care of your good self!"

We love you madly!

Mom and Dad

Take It!

. . . .

"Take it!" The words exploded from my lips. After a dry spell that seemed to last forever, the offer seemed like manna from heaven.

Cecil Lytle, our old friend from Madison, the man who strode across the campus in his wide-brimmed leather hat, who played both jazz and classical music with a masterful touch, had called and offered Jimmy a position as visiting professor at the University of California–San Diego, located on the hill above the seaside village of La Jolla. Cecil had received his degree, ditched his dashiki, and donned a dashing "move on up a little higher" three-piece suit.

"But it's only for a year." Jimmy was excited, but cautious.

"How could you not be chosen, with letters of recommendation from Duke Ellington and Lena Horne." My heart soared like an eagle. "We gotta have *faith*."

"I'll have to commute. I would be teaching two, three days in San Diego, then motoring back here to L.A."

"Ummm . . ." My brain turned like a whirling dervish. It spun spirals for a hundred miles, all the way down to San Diego, as we drove to the UCSD campus.

While Jimmy negotiated his contract, Cecil's wife, Becky, drove me around the area. We weren't sightseeing. I wanted to look at houses and apartments. My mind whirled even faster as I contemplated the move to San Diego and sincerely hoped that the racial atmosphere on Harbor Island didn't reflect the attitudes of the rest of the city. I kept these thoughts to myself, and said out loud to Becky, "Jimmy's talkin' about commuting, but I'm not stayin' in LA by myself, especially without a car! Even if this appointment is only for a year, we gonna do it together." My mind was made up and my heart was set.

Becky agreed.

None of the apartments were satisfactory. Oh, they were pretty, but the rent was sky high, almost as much as in New York, but with more space and swimming pools. Jimmy and I could never afford the cost. The situation seemed very discouraging, and my heart grew heavy.

We drove back toward the university. Suddenly, something began to register despite my gloom. In some of the front yards, signs mounted on wooden stakes stood where the lawns bordered the street. The signs, each printed with an arrow, announced "Condos for rent." Almost in a trance, I pointed the way down first one street, then another, following the signs. At last, we arrived at the correct street, or "camino" in a city influenced by nearby Mexico. Framed by beautiful tall trees reaching for the sky, their branches covered with oak-like leaves that were just beginning to turn the colors of fall, the camino called to me. My heart leaped. "Becky," I breathed, "this area makes me think of Ohio! This looks like home!" Hampered as I was by a limited budget, I tried not to get too excited or too hopeful on such a lovely street, but I said, "Stop here."

Becky laughed and pulled the car over to the curb. She stopped by a sign with an arrow that pointed down the walk. This sign said "4 rent." At the end of the walkway, the front door of a condo stood wide open.

"Becky, let's knock."

"Okay," she looked around. Nobody else seemed to be in sight.

"Hello! Anybody home?" I called out and knocked rap-rap-a-rap-rap on the door.

The woman who answered my knock came to the door wiping her hands on a towel. Dressed in blue jeans, a casual shirt, and white sneakers, her round face was flushed and covered with perspiration. Her glasses had slipped down her nose, and she blew her gray hair out of her eyes as she looked us over. "You come to rent this place? I've been here all day long, cleaning. I just finished scrubbing the kitchen floor. I live up north, and I want to leave here and go home." She took a deep breath and rushed on. "Come in, come in! My son's in the navy, and he's stationed back east now. He's got me renting out this condo for him. Just got rid of the last tenants. The kid knocked holes in the walls!"

We followed her through the rooms—a gorgeous little place with off-white walls and rust-colored wall-to-wall carpet. A white wrought-iron railing guarded the stairs. The condo contained three small bedrooms and one and a half baths. We returned to the living room and sat on the floor. We can have a music room, I said to myself. Heaven!

Becky explained that Jimmy was going to teach at UCSD. The woman seemed properly impressed. Then things happened so fast it made my head spin all over again. She named a price that was half the going rate. I hesitated. She said quickly, "Look, I know people. I trust you. My son and I don't want to leave the place empty. Here's my address and phone number. Give me yours. Here are the keys. I'm driving home before the rush hour begins. Take it!"

I did.

Jimmy and I drove to the woman's home in order to pay her the first and last month's rent, and we signed a year's lease. We hired movers this time, since none of Jimmy's students were around. In one week we were installed in our new condo. Jimmy and I unpacked all the boxes in a hurry. He would begin teaching in the fall, but we didn't stop to rest. I went straight to the Sheraton on Harbor Island to see about a gig.

"There is a possibility." The manager smiled and seemed happy to see me. "There is this 'mad' Mexican with an all-girl group who needs a new piano player. They're in Las Vegas right now, but they'll be here in a month. They usually stay a couple of months 'cause they're very popular here with the convention crowds." Then he said wryly, "Their regular piano player's having a baby."

I backed away. "Ummm . . ." I shook my head, east-west-east-west.

He looked at me, his eyes crinkling at the corners. "Look, it's a good job, and it gives you time to look around and get your own group together. Take it!" I did. In my head, the Reverend Uncle Frank's high tenor voice sang down through time, "The big wheel run by faith!"

Jimmy and I didn't have a chance to play house for even another week. We got a call from Donald Cook to play in his big band for none other than Mr. Cab Calloway. At Disneyland, no less! Oh, happy day!

* * *

It was dark, but Jimmy and I spotted Cab Calloway sitting way back in the rear of the rehearsal room near an exit. When you spend most of your life on the road, you learn to sit where you can leave in a hurry — in case a fight breaks out or someone decides to shoot at somebody.

We had retraced our route through the beach towns of Southern California, this time moving toward LA, not away. Jimmy and I checked into the Disneyland Hotel, then sought out the rehearsal room.

Other musicians milled around. Trumpet players engaged in a contest to see who could hit the highest note. Saxophone players limbered their fingers up and down the scales. Trombonists played long, quiet tones, stopping to squirt liquid on their slides and then flick them in and out. The bass player bowed long sonorous sounds while the drummer punched out his trap set with a vengeance. A cacophony of sound met us as we stepped through the door.

I checked out the piano. The keys all worked and it was in tune. Cab Calloway undraped himself from his seat and walked up behind me. I turned, looked up at him, and smiled. He did not smile back. He dropped some sheet music on the piano and said gruffly, "Play that." It was a test. I played and he sang.

Thank God, I had been playing for vocalists all my life and knew just what he wanted. We connected right from the start. He sang and I followed. I led him and he followed. It was the verse of the song, and he was ad-libbing, half singing, half talking—real dramatic. We finished the little duet, and before he took his elegant self back to his corner, he barked, "You played that better than Bill!"

He meant Count Basie. I felt elated by his praise. Cab Calloway's signature phrase was hi-de-ho! Hi-de-ho, indeed!

Count Basie himself had validated my work with a message conveyed to me by Grover Mitchell. Now here was praise from a man who was born when Teddy Roosevelt was president, who had hired musicians like Ben Webster and Dizzy Gillespie, starred in movies like *Stormy Weather* with Lena Horne, and appeared with Pearl Bailey on Broadway in *Hello Dolly!* My mind raced through the list of his accomplishments, thinking at last that the zoot suit with the drape shape was as much his invention as anybody else's. Wow wee, wow, wow!

Now the president was Jimmy Carter, and Cab Calloway still attracted huge crowds wherever he performed, and this night seemed no different. The show opened with the band, playing a tune written and arranged by Leslie Drayton called "A Greasy Brown Paper Sack." Jimmy took the stage as the featured soloist. He stood up and wielded his plunger, holding his big bass trombone with a black-leather-gloved hand, lights from the spotlight gleaming on the gold bell, and talked to the crowd like a "nat'chall" man. He cajoled, wheedled, and finally exploded with sharp barks and bursts of emotion like a man *born* burning up with the *blues*. When he finished his solo, the audience cheered and applauded long and loud. Jimmy took a bow and grinned with appreciation. He looked over at me and I mouthed the words, "Kill 'em, kid!"

Chris Calloway, Cab's baby girl, was up next. She burst onto the stage

—long, lithe, and lovely, her body poured into a skintight, showstopping gown—and more than held her own. You can bet *all* your brand-new money it took a lot of backbone to open for a legend, especially if he's your daddy. She had a good voice and didn't take any guff from the old guy.

Calloway was one of the greatest pranksters on the planet. He played all kinds of tricks on Chris while she was performing, mugging behind her and indulging in other showtime no-nos. She called him on it. Between tender love lyrics, she hissed through clenched teeth, "You blankety-blank-blank son of a blankety-blank!"

The audience never noticed anything amiss as she smiled and took her bows and acknowledged their wild applause. Cab just grinned like a jackal.

He did not stop there. When the MC called his name, he bounded out onstage—dazzling in a high-draped white tuxedo, white shoes, and white top hat—to sing his opening song. In the midst of his performance, he danced over and, in between lyrics, put some new music on the piano. "This is next!" He tossed his white hair from his eyes and danced away.

I scrambled. I had barely time to check out the piano part, and quickly found out the piano had the introduction and—Oh, Lawd! What is this? I felt myself beginning to panic. I said to myself, "Jesus!"

The intro contained a devil run from *hell!* Written by someone who never had any knowledge of correct fingering, the run had an ascending bunch of thirty-second notes from the middle of the piano to the very top. You had to have eight fingers on both hands to play it or, better still, use Lionel Hampton's two-finger xylophone method.

Cab brought his arm down for the downbeat and—Oh, Lawd!—the games began. I knew I couldn't play that run, so I turned it into a gliss and ran it the same amount of time as the run, then hit the top note with a flourish.

Cab turned around and, with the whole world watching, picked up the piano part, looked at it in mock astonishment, then placed it back on the piano. The band was rushing along. Without missing a beat, he grabbed the mike and jumped into his vocal with aplomb. I struggled, trying to find the correct place to reenter. Total humiliation!

He turned to me while the sax solo took over and said, "What's the matter, kid? Ev'rything all right?" Furious, I stuck my tongue out at Cab Calloway. He doubled over with laughter and continued the show until the final "Hi-de-ho!" He danced off the stage and returned for bow after bow, all the time grinning saucily at me.

The show was over. Never had I felt gladder to see an audience depart after a performance. It had been a real bring-down for me. I prided myself on my ability to nail any music put before me. I had failed.

The next night I checked in early so I could have another shot at deciphering that part. The run from hell was still there, myriad thirty-second notes building a virtual Tower of Babel. I tried it with right hand, left hand over right hand, right hand again. Still, I ran out of fingers.

That whole week at Disneyland the show went on with Cab yanking the music off the piano after I missed that run. It turned into a real contest.

"Jimmy," I finally said, "I'm gonna fix that old cat tonight!" Jimmy just smiled. He had no suggestions. Onstage it was every man for himself—even if you *wasn't a man!*

That night, I turned the tables on Cab Calloway. When the time came to articulate that run, I didn't play it at all! I waited. At the last moment, I hit that top note hard, just in the nick of time for him to come in with his vocal. It tripped him up all right. Glory! A grudging respect came into his impudent eyes, and he tipped his white top hat to me.

I realized that the man stayed alive by challenging himself and everyone around him. The words of Ben Jonson sprang to mind: "He was not of an age, but for all time!" Cab was a grand old guy, and I got a great lesson in humility. Hi-de-hi, hi-de-*low!*

The next week, the whole show traveled down to our new hometown, San Diego, to kick off the Summer Jazz Series at the San Diego Zoo. It was grand for Jimmy and me to be introduced to San Diego at large by appearing with none other than the great Cab Calloway.

Hi-de-ho! Hi-de-*high!*

Beelzebub and the Mad Mexican

. . . .

"Beelzebub?"

The Mad Mexican was sounding off about his escapades in the realm of the netherworld. "Yes!" He pulled at his coal black moustache, his hooded eyes glittering behind his glasses. "I met him face to face during a séance high up in a cave in the Sierra Mountains."

I didn't care where he met the Evil One. I was really getting fed up with Beelzebub *and* "Blue Eyes Crying in the Rain." Only one of the girls was a fine musician. She played with the San Diego Symphony. In the group, she doubled on bass and oboe. The other two women were nice-looking and smiled a lot.

All of them squabbled every night over what skimpy costume to wear. "Listen," I told the Mad Mexican, "you can call a halt to all this 'skiggle-dee' if you want."

He threw up his hands in mock horror. "How?" His eyes closed in pretended torment and cried plaintively, "Why me?"

"You got one girl almost six feet, one barely five feet, and one bordering on chubby. The same style just don't cut it! Let 'em choose their own costume, but make sure it's the same color. Red one night, blue one night, white the next. In rotation. No more fights. Chubby can choose a princess line with sleeves covering her fat arms. Teeny can ruffle it up like a Barbie doll, and Stretch can do an empire waist and an A-line. The fights are really hurting the music. Too much pouting and backstabbing onstage."

"Ay-yi-yi!" he cried. "That won't work, Jazz Lady!" (That was my title in the group.) I knew then this cat actually enjoyed the clatter and chatter. I looked at him from head to toe, then walked away, muttering, "Jesus, why am I here?"

The answer came soon enough, with the appearance of two bald-headed gentlemen, one black, one white.

Bradley Smith, the white gentleman, came to see the show one evening, and at intermission came over to my table. He introduced himself, and we began a lively conversation about jazz. Graceful and courtly, he reminded me of Fred Astaire, except for his lack of hair. He sported a fisherman's cap. Beneath it, his eyes were wise and knowing, but he kept them hooded for the most part. He spoke with a New Orleans accent and bought me a cognac. He said, "My dear, I am a photographer. I once was a staff photographer for *Life* magazine. I'd like to photograph you for one of the San Diego magazines."

I felt flattered, but thought I should be cautious.

"What would you do if you had one wish?" he inquired.

"Well," I hesitated, "I always dreamed of a salon—in Paris—peopled by artists, musicians, dancers, poets, and writers. Where we could have jam sessions and string quartets and eat great food and discuss interesting events."

"Hum-m-m." His eyes opened, then hooded again.

"In fact," I continued, "I would like a sort of society—a jazz society. Let's see: a society for the pursuit and study of jazz music."

"I'll see what I can do, my dear," he murmured.

In a flash, I realized, we were rootless no longer. We now lived in San Diego. We needed good friends and neighbors and all that goes with it.

And so, the Jazz Society of Lower Southern California was born, consisting of Bradley Smith's friends, artists, psychiatrists, physicians, lawyers, Pulitzer Prize–winning authors, scientists, provosts, engineers, musicians, and dentists—all lovers of jazz music.

I was elected the first president. It was a wonderful social outlet for Jimmy and me, light-years away from hanging out with hard-ankle musicians and ladies who lunch.

The other bald-headed gentleman was black—none other than Papa Jo Jones, who came to visit us in our new home. "I'll just smoke out here on the patio," he said pointedly, then grinned. It broke my heart to see how frail he had become.

I invited him to watch me play. "C'mon to the Sheraton with me. I want you to check out this chick drummer."

He sat through one set and noted that she had good hands and no feet. "If she hit that bass drum on one and three one more time, I'm gonna cut her foot off with my knife!" he threatened.

"I been tryin' to show her for over two weeks—goes in one ear and out the other!" I felt only too happy to confide in someone who knew the agony I had been forced to endure.

I corralled the Mad Mexican and introduced Papa Jo to him. He seemed pleased and was very respectful. He knew who Papa Jo was, and he conspired with him to pull a trick on the little drummer.

The very next set, Papa Jo came up on stage behind the drummer and said, "Give me your drumsticks and go sit down somewhere."

She had no idea who Papa Jo was, and cried to the Mad Mexican, "What'll I do? Who is this guy?"

"Do what he says," the Mexican replied.

She climbed down off the stage and stared up at Papa Jo.

Her drums were introduced to some real drumming. Her bass drum woke up; her cymbals started singing! We played "C Jam Blues," the same Ellington tune we played every night for my spot as the Jazz Lady—and what a difference! The audience knew there was a "presence" onstage, and when Papa Jo took a solo, they cheered.

I almost cried, playing real music again with Papa Jo. Those few minutes jump-started my resolve. I thought, It's way past time to move on down the line. Fate was shoving me, full steam ahead.

The Mad Mexican came to me two weeks later with the news that his next gig was in Lake Tahoe. To save money, he said, everyone would have to live in a motor home. There was no way I would share my days and my nights with these giddy females. I knew that as far as I was concerned, the gig had ended. The Mad Mexican confirmed my opinion.

He said, "I can't afford a hotel for you, and besides," his eyes glittered, "I found a young blonde, a cute little gal to play piano cheap. So I'm letting you go." His hands made figure eights in the air. "She has a nice little body."

"What, no notice?" I asked dryly.

"Ah . . . er . . ." Silence.

"The words 'blonde' and 'young' gonna cost you some greenbacks," I went on, in a pleasant tone of voice.

"What?" The Mad Mexican pushed his chair back in astonishment.

"I'm gonna sue you for no notice, age discrimination, and racial discrimination."

"What!" he repeated, his eyes grew wide. Then they narrowed. "What'll it take for you to go away quietly?" I named a figure. The corners of his mouth turned down, and his face grew dark. For several minutes he said nothing. Then he stood up. "All right, but you have to sign a release."

"Done!"

I met him the next day, signed a release for the ageism and the racism and no two-week notice. He gave me a check. Smiling engagingly, as casual as can be, he said, "Don't cash the check for three days."

"Done!"

As soon as I left the hotel, Jimmy drove me straight to the Mad Mexican's bank, where I cashed the check and went home. Papa Jo grinned and nodded in agreement when I told him what went down. "Well," he said, "you sure showed him whosit and whatsit!"

The phone rang early the next morning. "You've ruined me!" Screams emanated from the receiver. "I was gonna use that money for the down payment on the motor home!"

"I'm hip!" I spit back. "And leave me with a check marked 'insufficient funds,' I take it?" Through gritted teeth, I added, "Maybe you can't teach an old dog new tricks, but you can't trick an old dog, either!" I bayed like a hound dog, and he slammed the phone down.

His buddy, Beelzebub, had to be mighty grieved at this turn of events. I smiled as I imagined them playing duets in a place described in song by Cab Calloway as "ten times hotter than it oughta be"!

Next morning, Papa Jo said to me, "Jennie, I don't want you and Jimmy to come to my funeral."

"What?"

"You heard me." I opened my mouth, but he barked, "Don't talk back! You two are not to come to my funeral, 'cause I'm not goin' to be there, either!"

I understood. Too full of emotion to speak, knowing that Jo didn't want me to speak, I walked away. In the kitchen I fixed his pork-chop sandwiches for the last time and sent him on his way.

*   *   *

My friend, the manager of the Sheraton Hotel, sent me next door to the little Sheraton, where I consented to start working for Mr. H., who was a friend of Peanuts Hucko, a great jazz musician. Mr. H. was from Kansas City and had absorbed the music with his mama's milk.

I picked a bass player, Dennis Woodrich, from a "Bass Summit" held at UCSD. Not only a good arranger, Dennis also knew where all the skeletons were buried in San Diego. We played as a duo five nights a week. Then I persuaded Mr. H. to let Jimmy and me hold a jam session on Sundays.

There ain't nothin' as powerful as an idea whose time has come! Halleloo!

Make a Joyful Noise!

. . . .

*T*he master drummer had strange powers. He played one Sunday evening and something happened that we can't explain. He and his men started drumming, and all at once three women sitting at a front table closed their eyes and stood up and started leaping into the air. Higher and higher they went until the master drummer changed his beat, and the women's leaping decreased, lower and lower, until, at last, they sank back into their seats. Their eyes opened, and they looked around in a daze. The crowd exhaled and started applauding and whistling. Lawdy! It was a sight we had never seen before and never saw after.

"You both play spirit music!" The master drummer from Senegal took both our hands in his. "I'll sorely miss you. I put on these special robes to honor the spirit of your music."

He was splendid. His robes shimmered, even though most of the lights had been switched off in the room where we had just finished another scorching jam session. Most of the crowd had disappeared. Only a few die-hards laughed and talked quietly at the long low wooden bar. Some of them had gathered outside around the circular fountain in the courtyard, calling to each other, "See you next Sunday!"

The master drummer raised his hand and touched his robe above his heart, "My father is ill, and I must go home to Senegal to take up my duties, but I shall never forget you or your music." He walked to the doorway, raised his right arm, his long robe rippling with light, turned, then disappeared into the night. We never saw him again.

The master drummer and his men had been playing at the Wild Animal Park, in northern San Diego County, and had thrilled all of us with their many memorable performances. They would be missed at the jam sessions.

That was saying a lot, since the jam sessions had attracted top musicians from all over. We had been jamming with Curtis Peagler, my old friend from Cincinnati. He led his own group, the Jazz Disciples, had played with Ray Charles, and Count Basie for seven years, and now became almost a regular with us. The list of great musicians who arrived on Sundays was long: Calvin Jackson, who had his own show commissioned by the CBC in Canada; Billy Taylor, pianist, educator, and inventor of the jazzmobile; Rufus Reid, bassist; Charles McPherson, a Charlie Mingus alumnus; Vi Redd, a great woman and a great alto player; a whole band from Russia, none of whom spoke English, but who all spoke excellent Ellington.

Local musicians joined us, as well: Patty Padden, girl drummer extraordinaire, who could sing like an angel; Frank LaMarca; Hal White; Teddy Picou; Jimmy Noone, Jr., son of the great Jimmy Noone; Dinky Morris; Jimmy Zollar; Gunnar Biggs; Oliver Luck; Rick James; Rickey Woodard and Alfred Jackson, both from the Ray Charles band; and John "Ironman" Harris, who became our regular drummer and all-around good friend. He had played with both Carmen McRae and Horace Silver.

Jam sessions, or little bits of heaven? I was all kinds of happy, playing my beloved bebop again. I felt as if I had been let out of jail or, at least, given a parole from purgatory.

"The jam session is carefully crafted," Jimmy would explain to the many people who marveled at and interviewed us. "First, the session is not in anybody's neighborhood. It is held in a hotel 'cause the revenues aren't dependent on just the bar."

"Yes," I chimed in, "we know from experience that women drive any long-term event. Men follow women. We set the time for Sunday between 6:00 and 10:30 p.m., so it's well after church, but ends early enough so women won't be afraid to go home after the session."

We explained that Rose-Marie Butler, my good friend from New Orleans, made finger-lickin'-good chicken and that we found another jazz lover, who was a chef at a Veterans Administration hospital, who brought huge pans of banana pudding. With his helper and plenty of paper plates, napkins, and plastic forks, they served the whole crowd.

"Nobody has to go home and cook," Jimmy smiled.

"The women have their special seats," I continued, "an' they come early to make sure no one else sits in them."

"The really great kicker," Jimmy waxed eloquent, "is the fact that this Sheraton houses all the airline pilots and stewardesses between runs. They announce our jam session on the plane just before landing, so we get people and musicians from all over the world. The pilots sit at the bar and listen until it's time for them to hit the sack!"

I laughed. "The women have a motto: We can't make Monday without our Sunday."

* * *

I was asked to bring a trio into the penthouse bar at the top of the Sheraton Harbor Island. Patty Padden played drums, I was on piano, and we brought in a bass player from Long Beach. The gig was for six nights a week, and Jimmy and I still hosted the jam session next door every Sunday. I ate, drank, and slept music. I followed the old edict with all my might and main to "make a joyful noise!"

New Mule Kickin' in Our Stall

· · · · · · · · · · · · · · · · · · ·

Let me tell you people
Don't care how long or short or tall
There's a new day dawnin'—
A new mule kickin' in our stall!

"Huzzah! Huzzah!" Jimmy received tenure as a senior lecturer at UCSD, with security of employment. For the first time since 1955, we didn't have to sleep with one eye open, suitcases at the ready, and our emotions always set somewhere between flight or fight. Good news!

A few years before, in 1979, we had also had good news. Jimmy and I went back east for Shirley's graduation from Harvard Law School. *Cum laude*, I must add! We joined the whole Evans clan, occupying a whole floor of the Holiday Inn, and celebrated. M'Da came also. Now in a wheelchair, he seemed truly happy to be the patriarch of the clan. When Shirley's name was called and she received her "passport to an upper room," tears ran down his face like rain. We had all come such a long way.

After Jimmy received tenure, I made a major decision. "I'm not gonna play six nights a week anymore," I announced. "Except for the Bronx years, I've been doing that all my adult life. I wanna do something else—move on up a little higher, if possible." Jimmy nodded.

The jam session roared along. Mr. Evans, from the Bahia Hotel and Resort, set on its own manmade island in Mission Bay, made us an offer we could not refuse. He came to the Little Sheraton, his Panama hat slanted over one eye, checked out the room overflowing with musicians and jazzophiles, and said, "Come on over to my place. We'll treat you right."

Jimmy and I declined, out of loyalty to Mr. H., but left the offer open. Sure enough, the time rolled around sooner than later. Mr. H. decided to retire and move to Michigan, so we moved to the Bahia without missing a Sunday. Our opening theme, "Blue Monk," wafted through the new venue, and the games began.

Jimmy, through the auspices of the Black Arts Program, started bringing giants of jazz to UCSD as artists-in-residence. Next, the Jazz Society would host them for an evening, and the third leg of the stool would be their participation in the jam session.

Thad Jones, Cleanhead Vinson, and Papa John Creach all glorified our community. Then came the day I'd been waiting for nearly half my life. "Baby doll!" Mr. Jay McShann came to town as artist-in-residence at UCSD. He was still my idol! "Baby doll!" he exclaimed again, as we met face-to-face again after thirty years. Still a big brown buddha with gold teeth, he climbed in the white limo we had arranged to meet him, and Jimmy whisked him off to the university to check out his room and the place where he would perform.

Rose-Marie Butler (provider of great pans of succulent chicken at the jam sessions) helped me prepare dinner for Jay and Charles McPherson, who was from Joplin and would be good company for a fellow Missourian.

Everything was going perfectly according to plan until some wayward hot grease from the frying chicken popped from the big black skillet and landed on my left cheek. "Oh, Lawd, Rosie! I better get to the emergency room quick. I don't want my face scarred all up for life—even for Jay McShann!"

We put the chicken in the refrigerator, put ice on my face, and put the pedal to the metal. Rosie drove to Scripps Hospital at breakneck speed. There, the doctors took care of business—a white bandage on my face. We took care of business, too, speeding back to the condo to finish cooking the chicken.

When Jimmy, Charles, and Jay McShann arrived, we were ready. Rose-Marie piled up a plate and said, "See you folks later," leaving us musicians to our own devices—Alabama chicken, greens, corn bread, sweet potatoes (candied, of course), and peach cobbler. A great time was had by all.

After dinner, we really got down to business—drinking whiskey and telling lies: tales of legendary musicians and long-ago shoot-outs, barbequed pig-ear sandwiches in East St. Louis and jamming in Kansas City's out-of-the-way after-hours clubs, albino blues men, wicked men, and wild, wild women.

"It feels like Eighteenth and Vine is right here in this room!" Jay grinned from ear to ear. "Or Twelfth Street and Vine!" It was almost worth being wounded by wayward hot chicken grease, the time we had.

Jay got "tore up" and kept saying, "Fool! Fool! Fool!" until Jimmy and Charles took him to his hotel and poured him into his room.

The next evening, he was as good as new. Amazing man!

The concert was marvelous. Jimmy, Charles, Ironman Harris, and all the other cats picked to play with Jay set the house on fire. Then it was duet time — white-bandaged face and all.

Funny thing. When Pete Johnson and I played duets, it was seamless: ideas and counterideas and polyrhythms swirled around and melted into one another. When Jay McShann and I played duets, it was as if we were playing tag, or as if he were trying to outrun me. It made for some exciting, challenging music. We confessed the blues all over that piano, and one of my most precious dreams finally had come true. There we were, Jimmy and I, new job status, new venue for the jam session, new life changes for our family. Good news! There was a new mule kickin' in our stall!

Blues on the Omnibus

. . . .

Big Mama Thornton was throwing a typhoon of a tantrum in her dressing room at the taping of *Omnibus*, hosted by Hal Holbrook, the respected actor.

Little Mattie, Big Mama's sister-mama-agent-nurse-friend, had called us up to Los Angeles to play for her. We were always happy to accompany Big Mama, and this time was no exception. We had phoned each other often, but we hadn't seen each other for quite awhile. And, boy, were we shocked at Big Mama's appearance!

Still six feet tall, she used to weigh over two hundred pounds and sport a generous, rounded body and a shiny, happy face, but was now as thin as a rail, even thinner than she had been in Buffalo, if that was possible. Her face seemed sunken in upon itself, and though her lovely smile remained intact, her lips pulled back from her teeth in an alarming manner.

"I ain't goin' *out* there! I just ain't gonna sing with *her* here!" Big Mama stomped up and down the dressing room.

"Her" was Aretha Franklin.

"I didn't tell her Aretha was gonna be on the show." Mattie said calmly. "Big Mama wouldn't have come."

"It's almost taping time. Whatcha gonna do?" I whispered. "Big Mama is a diva! She doesn't take too kindly to other females singing on her show."

The producer poked his head in the dressing-room door and asked, "Ev'rything okay in here?"

"Yep, we'll be ready in a few minutes." Little Mattie was smooth. The producer disappeared.

Just then Big Mama spied Jimmy in the hall. She stopped in the middle of her tantrum, like the sun suddenly shining through a dark cloud. "Well, hello there, you handsome devil you!" she cooed. Jimmy stepped into the dressing room, gave her a bow and kissed her outstretched hand. She calmed down enough to see reason.

"You want your money, don't you?" Mattie was matter-of-fact.

Big Mama drew her frail body up tall and straight. Dressed in a man's black pinstriped suit, a man's shirt and tie, shiny black cowboy boots, and a big white cowboy hat, she was as sharp as a tack. "It's not the money an' you know it," she declared. "She hollers, an' I don't wanna be on *no* stage with anybody who hollers!" Mattie and I looked at each other, turned away, and smiled. We knew Big Mama was just jealous of Aretha—and insecure.

Her failing health was so very obvious. She was supposed to have died ten years ago of liver problems. She had stopped eating altogether. She drank only gin and milk—breakfast, lunch, dinner, and between-meal snacks. Nothing but gin and milk.

"Showtime!" The call to arms came over the intercom. Big Mama drew herself up and marched out the dressing room and onto the stage. Jimmy settled himself into the trombone section, and I took my place at the piano. We thought we were in for a rough ride, but as soon as I played the blues opening, she became the consummate pro. She broke hearts with her rendition of "Ball and Chain." Jimmy played a tearjerker of a bass trombone solo. Aretha came on next and tore up the stage. Everything was all right again.

On the long drive back to San Diego, I said to Jimmy, "You know, Big Mama don't look good at all! We have to get some kind of record of how she really looks when she sings: how she lights up the stage, her facial expressions, her command of the audience . . ."

Jimmy interrupted, "You're right. People all over the world have heard her voice on records, but not much stuff is on video or film."

This conversation, carried on while we hurtled along in the dark down Route 5 South, set the stage for *Three Generations of the Blues.*

* * *

I did not tell Jimmy until the next morning about Mattie's kids. The day before, I had said, "Hey, it's so good to see you, Mattie. How are the kids? Jonathan's still roamin' around, as footloose and fancy-free as ever!"

She looked away, then with her usual stoic manner said in a low steady voice, "Stevie's in Sing Sing."

"What? What did he do?"

"He came out here and got in with the wrong crowd, set himself up as a so-called pimp, and shot a woman in the head."

"No!"

"Yes, and my daughter was beheaded in a car wreck."

"Oh, Mattie! What?" These were the worst things imaginable for a mother to suffer. "You are the bravest woman I ever knew!"

I felt helpless. I just put my arms around her and we rocked back and forth for a little while—just a little while. The question burned in my gut—which was worse? Childbirth or child death? Childbirth, with all its pain and fear, was forgotten as soon as you held this little bit of squirming humanity in your arms. Child death? I could not answer. I had experienced only the former.

Little Mattie, an exquisite agony shining naked for a nanosecond in her beautiful dark eyes, her throat roughened by too many tears swallowed whole, finally murmured, "I must go and see about Big Mama."

* * *

Little Mattie had mapped out her soul's journey a long time ago in Buffalo, with the awkward penning of the words to a song of self-fulfilling prophecy. We were present at Rudy Van Geller's famous studio in New Jersey when the song was recorded by Dodo Greene and Ike Quebec on the Blue Note label. The album was called *My Hour of Need*. The song was also recorded by Big Mama Thornton on a disc called *Sassy Mama*. The song was "Everybody's Happy But Me."

Blow Out at the Belly Up Tavern and the Birth of Three Generations of the Blues

· · · · · · · · · · · · · · · · · · ·

Big Mama Thornton:	*I'm comin' to git cha!*
	An' I'm gonna kick you out
	Yo' own back door!
Sippie Wallace:	*You may think I like you*
	But I be hatin' you all the time!

Sippie Wallace, ninety-two-year-old vocalist who represented the first generation, and Big Mama, who represented the second generation, staged a real vocal battle at the finale of the filming of our project, *Three Generations of the Blues*. If words were bullets, the stage would have been littered with dead musicians—or at least two severely wounded divas!

They had disliked each other on sight, and in the trailer provided for us outside the Belly Up Tavern in Solana Beach, California, they bickered and taunted each other unmercifully.

Sippie, a short woman, one gold tooth gleaming in her mouth, sequined cocktail hat tilted rakishly on her head, her pouter-pigeon chest puffed out with pride, said, "My feet so small, my chil'ren cain't hardly find shoes to fit. So my little feet really hurt bad!"

Big Mama, sitting way on the other side of the trailer, tried to tuck her size twelves out of sight under her seat and replied venomously, "You oughta be glad you *got* feet!"

"Whoa!" I said to myself, "What is this?" We had driven through a violent rainstorm, straight from the jam session to the Belly Up, for the taping. My nerves were already zinging. Now, visions of disaster danced in my head.

Anasa Briggs, our producer, Jimmy, and I had fought hard for this project. KPBS at San Diego State University was sponsoring the project, but had no idea what was in store. We set the whole project up for three hours with a live audience. Anasa took care of all the details, large and small. She also warmed up the crowd, and it was on. Showtime, show folks!

The first hour featured Sippie Wallace with her accompanist. The second hour showcased Big Mama Thornton with musicians Jimmy and I had handpicked to play in her particular style: Jack Pollack on piano, Patty Padden on drums, Guy Gonzales on guitar, and Big Mama brought her own bass player.

The musicians for my set included John "Ironman" Harris on drums, Gunnar Biggs playing bass, Mike Price's trumpet, and Jimmy on bass trombone.

"We better not tell either Sippie or Big Mama that we gonna do a finale," I confided to Jimmy.

He agreed. "They both'll balk like Georgia mules!"

"Um-hm, and neither one of them have *ever* heard me sing. They only know I'm the piano player."

When I started my portion of the show, representing the third generation, both divas came out and stood at the stairs to the stage while I performed. Both seemed shocked, I must say, and as soon as I finished, I immediately thanked the audience and then called out on the mike, "Now, ladies and gentlemen, we gonna have a really great treat! We gonna have a good old-fashioned finale! Ladies, come on up on this stage and show all these good people how to perform a finale!" I started playing a blues in the key of C.

My heart was in my mouth. I didn't know whether they would refuse to appear onstage with each other, or with me! But, wonder of wonders! Like old-time firehouse horses, when they heard that bell, they both sprang into action. Those rickety old women climbed those stairs so fast that they hardly needed *any* help.

And it happened. Lawd! They started trading verse after verse of made-up-on-the-spot lyrics—insulting each other and each other's men and their mamas! I was so caught up with watching them perform that I kept playing the piano for them, forgetting that I was supposed to be singing to represent the third generation. Jimmy, my ever-aware companion, took his horn down from his lips and said sternly to me, "You better get on in there!"

I played one more blues passage while I hurriedly made up some words to fit the situation, took a deep breath, and sang as loud as I could:

Ladies! Ladies!
You don't have to fuss and fight!
Let's all get together—
An' ev'rything will be all right!

They both turned to me and smiled, and we began to sing together, "Bye, baby, bye! Bye, baby, bye!" as they slowly marched off stage. The audience roared.

Paul Marshall, executive producer, did a great job of reducing three hours down to one—an embarrassment of riches, I know. In our contract, we insisted that the words "Concept by the Cheathams" be on each video. Like the Good Book says, don't hide your light beneath a bushel.

That film won the New York Film Critics Bronze Award. The station would not pay to send it in for consideration, so some of our good friends contributed the funds and Anasa Briggs sent it in. When it won, everybody at KPBS was very nice, and surprised.

It also won the CEBA (Communicating Excellence to Black Audiences) award; the Silver Award in 1989 from the Houston International Film Festival; first place in San Diego from the National Conference of Christians and Jews; three Emmy nominations; and, finally, it was placed in the Library of Congress's Sound Division. The best reward of all was that the artistry of two grand ladies was preserved on film for the whole wide world to see.

Sippie Wallace died in her nineties in England, still performing until the end.

Big Mama Thornton and Elvis Presley wrestled over the song "(You Ain't Nothin' But a) Hound Dog." She was disappointed sometimes about the way things turned out; she had really struggled in her life while Elvis was making lots of greenbacks.

But at the last, Elvis ended up on his bathroom floor, and Big Mama took her final breath at a party in her honor, sitting on a couch between two gentleman friends, sipping gin and milk.

Mr. Jefferson Comes to Town

. . . .

The beautiful, pastel-colored Bahia Hotel, with its tropical-tinged ambiance and lovely, emerald green, manicured grounds, rose up beside the sparkling blue waters of Mission Bay. Rows of tall palms, their trunks rough and gray-brown, reminded me of the line drawings in the Bible I carried to the old church where the Reverend Uncle Frank waxed eloquent every Sunday morning. I swear I could hear the faint strains of Wayne Shorter's exotic "Footprints" and Duke Ellington's colorful "Caravan" as I gazed up at the splayed fronds swaying in the breeze.

Floating nearby at a dock jutting into the bay was a white double-decker riverboat. Reminiscent of the vessels that chugged up and down the mighty Mississippi in days long gone by, the small side-wheeler was called the *Bahia Belle*.

The "keepers at the gate," a family of seals, cavorted in a pool surrounded by huge stones, at the beginning of the path that led up to the jam-session showroom. As we walked up the path, I thought about the "hit" song that King Solomon had sung to the Queen of Sheba, something along the lines of: "Thou art dark, but comely, O my love." The seals were not only dark and comely, but also sleek and shiny, and possessed distinct personalities. I named them Solomon and Sheba.

"You know," I said to Jimmy, "I can tell in advance just what kind of a session we gonna have by checking out Solomon."

"Really?" Jimmy raised his eyebrows.

We were testing the mikes for the jam session. "Testing, 1-2-3," I said. Then I sang into the vocal mike:

> *If he's lounging on top of his royal rock*
> *And greets us as we pass*

> *By preening himself and barking*
> *I know the session will be a blast!*

The impromptu song made Jimmy laugh.

"Testing, 1-2. Testing, 1-2." I checked the horn mikes next. Then I sang in a low, mournful voice:

> *If Solomon sulks beneath the waves*
> *And won't look at the sky*
> *It's tough-titty time up on that stage*
> *Don't care how hard you try!*

Jimmy mused, "Ev'rything is ev'rything. We're all connected. An' you, you're a real griot." He meant an African storyteller, a keeper of tales and oral traditions who could relate a tribe's history without missing a syllable. Jimmy smiled, "That's what you are—a griot!"

After a while, Solomon and Sheba had a baby. I named him Sideman. Cute as a button, Sideman splish-splashed in the pool without a care, full of piss and vinegar, until Solomon gave him a nip or a warning bark to let the rowdy youngster know, in no uncertain terms, who really was the boss.

The Bahia became the new bottle into which we poured the heady mixture of old wine: bebop, boogie, ballads, and blues. There were some changes made from the nights at the Sheraton. Rose-Marie's great pans of chicken gave way to a hotel-sponsored late-happy-hour spread of delicacies, but our mantra remained the same: You don't have to go home and cook, just come on over and join the fun! And come they did!

Mr. Count Basie came to town.

"Basie will never fill Mandeville Auditorium," the naysayers at UCSD were adamant.

"He's too old-style!" neighed the ninnies of negativity.

But Jimmy stayed firm and committed. He telephoned Basie himself with a personal invite. The Count replied, "I'd be honored to give *you* a play, Jim." And play he did!

Mandeville Auditorium was filled to overflowing. Seats had to be placed onstage in the wings. Some of the upper-echelon folks called in vain. "Please get me a seat." "Where can I get tickets?" But the coveted tickets were all sold out.

Jimmy presented the Count with an award from a grateful community.

"My dear," Brad Smith of the Jazz Society said with his soft New Orleans accent, "it is a monument to Jimmy's good judgment. This band shows the real meaning of the real music."

* * *

Doc Cheatham came to town, also.

A long tall drink of water, handsome and suave, Doc wore his coal black hair combed down around his tan face in the style of a Franciscan friar. Black horn-rims accented his smiling eyes. He and Jimmy traced the Cheatham name back to Jamestown, Virginia, and besides music had a couple of other things in common. They were both born in June, and trusted each other to send back royalty checks mistakenly mailed to the wrong Cheatham.

At the jam session, Doc played his trumpet and sang sweet love songs to the ladies. Later, sitting at the bar, sipping and telling stories, we learned that Doc was nearly eighty years old.

"You know," he told us, "I was scared all my life. Scared of ev'ry single thing till I reached the age of sixty-five." He paused, and his calm sunny smile lit up his face. "Then I decided one day that I just wouldn't be scared anymore!"

Funny thing, M'Da did the same thing at the same age. He quit drinking cold turkey. Maybe sixty-five is the age of epiphany for men. I'd been impressed by M'Da's act of courage. Now, I was impressed by Doc's.

He had played lead trumpet for years, with Benny Carter, Billie Holiday, Fletcher Henderson, Benny Goodman, Bessie Smith, had played for the Tony Award–winning musical *Two Gentlemen of Verona*, and, in the end, his greatest triumph was overcoming crippling anxiety and fear.

Halleloo!

* * *

Notwithstanding all the visits by the venerable jazz giants, Jimmy and I made a visit of our own. We drove up to Los Angeles to meet with Don Cooke, the contractor who had hired us for the Cab Calloway Band.

I had written a slew of new blues tunes that I sang between the blistering battles of the jazz instrumentalists. It dawned on me after awhile that people had begun to request these songs over and over again.

"Jimmy, maybe it's time to bring the blues back to the people," I said as we packed up the equipment after another midsummer night's soiree.

After a moment's thought, Jimmy suggested, "Let's make a test tape with rhythm and bass trombone and take it up to Don. He's a well-known producer, too."

"Yeah. He oughta be able to tell us what's what."

Don Cooke's office was located in the Wilshire district of Los Angeles—very nice indeed. Onyx and dark grey complemented plush carpets. A big brown bear of a man, Don was loaded with quiet confidence.

He greeted us warmly, then settled back in his seat to listen to the tape. When the music concluded, silence settled over us. Don hooked his hands behind his head and declared, "This stuff will never fly! You have to bring it up to date. Add a funk beat. Maybe some electronics, and . . ." He peered at me quizzically, head cocked to one side, his big hands now locked together on his desk. He pushed the tape toward us. He stared at me. "You get on some time with your makeup. You need some false eyelashes . . ." He looked at my hands, the no-nonsense nails colored only with clear polish, cut straight across so I could jump on any piano without leaving chunks of fractured red polish up and down the keyboard. ". . . and some fake nails . . ." He droned on.

Then he looked at my chest. Before he could utter another word, I stood up and grabbed the tape. I could feel heat rising from my toes to the top of my head, and I glared at him past my natural eyelashes. How dare this cat sit in his dark cocoon of an office and ignore the fact that he hadn't played in a nightclub in *eons* and knew nothing about what real folks felt—just knew trends! I tried not to snarl. "Let's go, Jimmy!"

Don Cooke leaned his head to the other side and smiled in a friendly manner. "Well, you asked me what I thought." He hauled his big body out of the chair. "Let me know what happens."

* * *

Mr. Carl Jefferson was what happened. He flew down from Concord, California, with Chris Long, one of Jimmy's former trombone students. That rare bird, the sole owner of Concord Jazz, Inc., Jefferson came to the jam session to check us out in person. No one noticed his and Long's arrival.

People were packed in wall-to-wall, and a long line of cats waited to jam. This particular Sunday was extra special because Freddie Green, a veteran guitarist with the Count Basie band, sat in the audience. He dropped by to say hello whenever he visited his son, and he brought greetings from the cats in the Basie band and from the Count himself. "You so strong!" he always hugged me and laughed. Amidst an audience of jazz fans, he caused quite a stir.

Extreme excitement seized those on the bandstand also. Illinois Jacquet, the current artist in residence at UCSD, fingered his tenor saxophone, getting ready to let loose with his famous solo on "Flying Home." He smiled at the audience members who were applauding before he even hit a note. He grinned at the musicians standing behind him, eager to set riffs, until his eyes fell on our bass player, who was white. Illinois stopped smiling, began to scowl, and said pointedly, "Oh, you got one of *those* in your rhythm section, eh?"

I kept playing the introduction, but motioned to Illinois to come closer. I hissed at him, "Illinois, don't start that stuff here! We gotta live here after you long gone. There ain't no place for no Jim Crow or Crow Jim! You not gonna start the Civil War all over again on *this* bandstand! The cat can really play—so leave it alone!"

Illinois started grinning. Exactly like Cab Calloway, he loved to stir things up, and no doubt, just like the rest of us, had suffered throughout his life with problems of race.

But now it was showtime, show folks! I always believed that as long as the musicians didn't throw up on my shoes, everything was copacetic.

Illinois started blowing and tore up the house. In the middle of all this, Chris Long inched his way up to the piano and whispered in my ear, "Mr. Jefferson would like to speak with you and Jimmy about recording for Concord Records."

"Chris," I was trying to concentrate, "I just cannot talk now!"

He replied, "I understand . . . but . . . well, we have to catch the plane back to Concord. I'll call you from the office."

"Okay, okay. Thanks for comin' down!" I didn't even know what Mr. Carl Jefferson looked like! I glanced out at the audience anyway. One of those anonymous faces wanted to record our music.

Illinois seemed to like our playing. In fact, he said, "I'd sure like it if you and Jimmy would come to New York to play in my band. Jeannie, you can sing and play!"

Boy, were we flattered. "Thanks, but no thanks," we told him. "We wanna develop our own band." Still, we said goodbye to him on very good terms.

The whole conversation felt like peering into a crystal ball. We made a deal with Carl Jefferson and Concord Jazz, Inc., stating that we could choose whom we wanted to record with us, choose our own tunes, and retain our own publishing rights, but would be willing to share them with Concord.

* * *

It is a long time comin'
From a place where we have been
Cain't tell nobody how, Lawd!
Cain't tell nobody when!

We felt delirious with anticipation. What was promised beyond the veil of the unknown? Would we be able to pull off the challenge of rebirthing the blues? Was there an audience beyond the safe harbor of the Bahia on the bay? Was the great big wide world out there willing to accept the humble offerings of two dedicated down-the-decades way-of-life musicians? I could not answer the questions, but over and over again I clothed myself in the mantle of my old mantra: "We are whole, perfect, strong, powerful, loving, harmonious, and happy . . . we are whole, perfect, strong, powerful, loving, harmonious, and happy!"

Glory!

Left to right: me, Grover Mitchell (trombonist), and Jimmy.
Jimmy and I recorded *Meet Grover Mitchell* (1978) and *The
Devil's Waltz* (1980) with him.

Cab Calloway with Jimmy and me at Disneyland, about 1984. From left to right:
(*front*) Jeannie Cheatham, piano; Louis Spears, bass vl.; Jimmy Cheatham,
bass trombone; Donald Cooke, contractor trombone; Buster Cooper, trombone;
Herman Riley, reeds; Fred Jackson, reeds; (*rear*) Paul Humphries, drums; Ray Brown,
trumpet; Snooky Young, trumpet; Leslie Drayton, trumpet.

Cab Calloway and me on tour at the San Diego Zoo Jazz Series, 1984.
Photo by Lea Rudee.

Buddy Collette, *left*, and Calvin Jackson, *right*, at the Cheatham jam session on Harbor Island, San Diego, about 1983.

Illinois Jacquet and me at the Cheatham jam session on Harbor Island, about 1985. Photo by Larry Okmin.

Nat Adderly, Jimmy, Marshall Hawkins, and me at the Cheatham jam session on Harbor Island, around 1985.

Thad Jones and me at a concert for the Jazz Society of Lower Southern California, University of California–San Diego, La Jolla, about 1984.

Jimmy presenting an award to Count Basie at a UCSD concert, around 1982.

Jimmy
conducting his
UCSD Jazz
Ensemble.
Photo by
Grace Bell.

Jimmy Cheatham–UCSD Jazz Band

Three Generations of the Blues. Left to right: me, Sippie Wallace, and
Big Mama Thornton. In July 1983, the video, a Cheatham con-
cept, won an award from the New York Film Critics Circle.
Photo by Grace Bell.

Artist-in-residence Jay McShann and me, playing duets, around 1991. My bandaged lip is from an injury sustained while frying chicken for Jay. Photo courtesy Larry Okmin.

JEANNIE CHEATHAM - JAY McSHANN
FLYIN' FRYIN' CHICKEN BLUES
PHOTO LARRY OKMIN

Jay McShann and me, playing duets at an event put on by the Jazz Society of Lower Southern California, with Jimmy on bass trombone and Marshall Hawkins on bass, about 1992. Photo courtesy Sylvia Gordon.

The Birth of the Sweet Baby Blues Band

. . . .

It was stomp-off time at Ocean Way Studios in Los Angeles. The clock on the wall showed 8:00 a.m., and in two hours we would be recording our first record for Concord Jazz, Inc. The month: September. The year: 1984.

The sound engineer led us into the little studio. The place was dark and dusty, and I could hardly see the piano hiding behind the baffles put up to separate the instruments. I lay the valise that held the charts for the recording on top of the heavy quilted cover of the piano, sat on the piano stool, lifted the lid, and ran my fingers across the keyboard.

"Whoa!" My heart beat faster. This was one of the best pianos I had ever touched. The keys leaped up to meet my fingers halfway and produced a warm, rich, clear sound from the bottom to the top "Hey, you guys!" I exclaimed, "This piano is magic!"

Jimmy stood in a far corner, holding his trombone and flicking the slide. Ironman Harris, who had driven north with us from San Diego, was busy setting up his drums. Both smiled. "That's cool."

We had chosen our little group of musicians with painstaking care. The jam sessions gave us deep insight into the temperament, sound, and style of each and every one of them. Loyalty and respect for the music were assets that could not be bought. It was in their bones.

Chris Long, Jimmy's former student, acted as our producer. At the moment, his long lean frame hovered over the board while he spoke to the engineer. He seemed calm as I watched him through the window of the control booth, but I knew he had to be anxious because he had no idea what we were going to record or how we would sound. Oh, we had discussed the tunes over the phone, but that was all. Not one note had yet reached the expert ear of Chris Long. He nodded and smiled at the engineer and knew absolutely nothing about what to expect.

Neither did the band! But never you mind. We knew they could play great jazz solos and deep-feeling blues, make up riffs on the spot, and read and interpret the arrangements Jimmy had so meticulously prepared. Above all, they knew how to swing!

Everybody came from somewhere else. Red Callender, our chosen bass and tuba player, was born in Haynesville, Virginia, in 1916. Early in his life he had played in bands in Cleveland and won a place with Louis Armstrong while still only twenty. The first African American on staff at NBC, Red wrote the hit "Primrose Lane" and had taught Charles Mingus.

Eugene "Snooky" Young, born in Dayton in 1919, had played first trumpet with Fletcher Henderson's band when he was only fifteen. He had also played first trumpet for the Count Basie band, the Thad Jones–Mel Lewis Band, and Benny Goodman. Now he was performing with Doc Severinsen and the *Tonight Show* band. He played his plunger with a fiery passion—a primal scream pushing its way out of his mute.

Curtis Peagler, alto, tenor, and baritone saxes, was born in Cincinnati in 1930, grew up there, and performed with his own band, the Jazz Disciples. He also worked with the Ray Charles and Count Basie bands.

John "Ironman" Harris, drums, was born in Bridgeport, Connecticut, in 1935. He played with Horace Silver, Blue Mitchell, Carmen McCrae, Phineas Newborn, and Johnny "Hammond" Smith, among others.

Jimmy Noone, Jr., born in Chicago in 1938, was a complete surprise to the world of music. Not many knew that Jimmy Noone, Sr., the famous New Orleans clarinetist, even had a musical son. He worked at the San Diego post office. Jimmy persuaded him to come out of musical semiretirement to play in the jam session, and we included him in many of our casual gigs. He had played with Teddy Picou and Daniel Jackson and led his own band, the New Orleans Good Time Society Band. He drank in his father's New Orleans sound with his mother's milk.

Charles McPherson, our first guest artist, was born in Joplin, Missouri, in 1939. He had performed with Charles Mingus, Barry Harris, Lionel Hampton, Dizzy Gillespie, and Art Farmer, among others.

We came together at Ocean Way Studios from different states, different eras, and different styles with one thing in common: the *soul of music*.

"I hope all the cats get here on time!" I looked at the white-gloved hands of my Mickey Mouse watch, rested my arms on the piano, and lay my head on them. My mind raced back over the past three weeks.

Getting ready for the "Great Gittin' Up Morning" had been a wild experience, full of angst and exploration, full of plain old hard work. I chose a very simple mode to trigger my muse—the plain old bus. I rode the city buses of San Diego, at first hopping aboard and riding randomly from neighborhood to central city to suburbs, then back again. The bus is a great leveler, a gold mine of emotions from people who are not afraid to express themselves. Everybody on a bus has a story—everyday facts from everyday folks.

Two drivers in particular became my favorites, so I picked their runs to ride on purpose. I told Jimmy, "One is a lean mean drivin' machine. A black cat who wears dark wraparound glasses and cocks his driver's cap over one eye. He hurls the bus at least ten feet past each stop and makes all the people run and jump on as fast as their legs can carry them."

"He sounds crazy." Jimmy was concerned.

"Naw, just eccentric. He always hollers, 'All right, all right! Let's get this show on the road!' Then he takes off in a cloud of carbon monoxide and dust, leavin' latecomers to run behind the bus. But it ain't no use. He never stops to let them on." I named him "Bat Cat." Bat was cruel, but he was fair. Crippled or old people fared very well with him. He would get off the bus and help them board, then get back into his Bat Seat and—hold on to your hats!—down the road we'd roar.

"Roll 'em Pete!" I wrote on my little yellow notepad. The fast boogie-woogie that I had played with Pete Johnson as a duet reminded me of Bat Cat. That tune had to be in the new album

"The other bus driver is a woman I really admire," I said in my daily reports to Jimmy. "She's this really huge black woman—not fat—just massive! She drives that bus with distinction, an' she don't smile at nobody. She grabs that wheel an' subdues it an' ev'rybody on the bus." Her run began around three p.m., when all the kids poured out of the schools. The yelling, screaming, punching, and pushing stopped at the first step into her bus. The kids took one look at her glowering, scowling face and order was restored in an instant.

There was only one youngster that Ms. Big, Black, an' Bad spoke to. Tall, blond, and neatly dressed in a shirt, tie, jacket, and slacks, his mind worked slower than the other kids'. He carried a briefcase containing only a peanut butter sandwich. He always got on the bus at 3:30 p.m., looked around the whole busload of folks, and before he dropped his fare in the box, would declare in a loud voice, "I'm a person too, you know!"

The formidable woman at the wheel would always answer, "Yes, Person, you are a brand-new person ever' mornin'—and don't let nobody tell you dif'rent!" He would smile, drop his fare in the box, sit in the seat right behind her, open his briefcase, and eat his sandwich.

The little drama with Person jogged my memory. The song that began in my brain so long ago during a lonely ride on the Greyhound to Columbus under such sad circumstances now was being reborn. Only this time, it was with joy and anticipation of a brand new beginning.

That's when I took out my yellow pad and wrote "Brand New Blues."

> *I gotta brand new blues, this mornin'*
> *Cause my old blues don't fit no mo'*
> *Gonna change my way of livin'*
> *Ain't nothin' like it was befo'—*
> *I gotta new disposition, got me a new routine*
> *Got me a brand new washer—*
> *To keep my laundry clean.*
> *Gonna buy me a hatchet*
> *Cut down my weepin' willow tree!*
> *No mo' bendin' over backwards—*
> *No bitter tears for me!*
> *Don't wanna be no play girl—*
> *Don't need no diamond ring—*
> *Just gimme plenty room to*
> *Do my brand new—ev'rything!*

My love song to my roommate was a gentle little six-eight blues with a gospel tinge.

"Let's put Red Callender on his tuba on this solo part," Jimmy suggested during one of the long nights spent choosing and arranging the music. The tune in question was called "Sweet Baby Blues."

> *I gotta sweet baby*
> *Knows how to rock and roll!*
> *He ain't no mid-night creepah—*
> *And he satisfy—my soul*
> *When the moon shine on the water*
> *An' rise up over the hill—*
> *He tells me that he loves me—*

An' he swear he always will!
Then he rocks me, rocks me —
Till the broad daylight —
An' he whispers "Baby, Baby —
Ev'rything go' be all right!"

"Yeah, that'll be a gas!" I exclaimed. Then I started playing with the song title, "Sweet Baby Blues." I murmured it. I repeated it. I chanted it. "Sweet Baby . . . Blues . . . Band! Hey, that rolls trippingly off the tongue!"

"It feels good in my mouth," Jimmy laughed. Then he grew thoughtful and said, "That's just what we'll call the band. We better name it our own selves, or some 'mo-fo' PR person will misname it for us!"

We laughed and slapped each other's hand.

"Better ground this album with some traditional blues," he said, and I agreed. "I Got a Mind to Ramble" and "Ain't Nobody's Business If I Do" and "Muddy Water Blues" were traditional blues that fit the bill just right.

"Cherry Red," another Pete Johnson blues, was far from traditional: it sat on an eight-bar frame instead of the usual twelve bars. Pete, who was born in 1904, was way ahead of his time with this chord structure.

On the last night before the recording session, we were bleary eyed and bone weary. Jimmy did all the arranging and copying. I lent a hand on the piano parts and bass parts. We worked like two souls in one body. There were eight tunes, eight parts, with an average of three pages each — at least 192 pages of music.

"Jimmy, you're a lot like Duke Ellington — you write for the soloist," I noted with admiration.

He nodded, too tired to talk. The background riffs were worked out for each soloist. Cats that played buckets of notes were given smooth spare riffs. Cats that spoke with lots of space were given more intricate and rhythmic riffs, carefully crafted with plenty of good room for the artist to express himself. At last, just as the midnight hour rolled around, proofreading the charts was done.

"How's it layin'?" Jimmy asked, rubbing his eyes.

"Okay. It's now or never. You can meet me in the mornin' cause I'm turnin' in."

"Yeah, I'll meet you in the mornin', all right!" We started laughing, giddy with fatigue.

"How you gonna meet me, Babe?" I asked.

"Why don'cha meet my mule Monday mornin', mo-fo!" We cracked up at the old joke.

I blurted, "How about I meecha with my black drawers on!" We stopped laughing and stared at each other. It was a lightbulb moment.

I hurriedly dashed off a few verses and checked the key on the piano (key of C), then we added the refrain:

I woke up this mornin', Babe
Reached for the telephone!
Woke up this mornin'—
Reached for the telephone—
I got your message, Baby, to—
Meet you with my black drawers on!

You know I love you, Baby—
You know how to keep me hangin' on!
You know I love you, Babe—
Know how to keep me hangin' on!
All you have to do, Babe, is
Meet me with your black drawers on!

You never have to worry—
I'll never leave you all a-lone!
Never have to worry—
I won't leave you all alone!
All you got to do, Babe, is
Meet me with your black drawers on!

Baby, meet me with your black drawers on!
Baby, meet me with your black drawers on.
Baby, meet me with your black drawers on!

* * *

"A-one-two . . . You know what to do!" Stomp-off time was at hand!

We recorded the whole album in just two days. Most of the songs were done in one take. That was admirable in and of itself, since the cats didn't see the charts until we had passed them out in the studio. It gave a real on-the-spot, live-performance edge to the album. The cup of intuition ran over. We requested that the studio be darkened, only the music stands lighted, so we didn't have to dig too far down to feel that it was 'round midnight in some roadhouse way out on the outskirts of town. The little studio crackled with electricity and high energy.

I sang and played at the same time. No overdubbing (singing over a recorded track) for this kid!

Jimmy told Chris, "We got one more blues we wanna try, since we finished early." Chris nodded. "Just keep the tape rollin', no matter what happens," Jimmy instructed. And we went into "Meet Me with Your Black Drawers On."

We had no written music, except for a few barely penciled-in guide riffs. But we did what we do best—we made music!

We all cheered when we heard the playback. It sounded good! "Now," I looked at the clock, "can we overdub all our voices, like a gospel choir?"

"Why not?" The engineer quickly set up a row of vocal mikes, and we sang to the tape played back into the studio.

Everybody sang with gusto, "Baby! Meet me with yo' black drawers on!" At the very end, Snooky Young, who was enjoying himself immensely, declared in a very suggestive tone, "Baby, you can meet me with no drawers at all!"

It was 1984, the year that George Orwell had used to symbolize an inhumane future. Not for us! We had triplets that year: the Black Drawers Glee Club directed by Snooky Young was born; the Sweet Baby Blues Band was born; and last but not least, the blues song "Meet Me with Your Black Drawers On" was born.

It was a very good year.

Hot Bulbs and Hot Flashes

. . . .

*C*oncord Records arranged a photo shoot for the album cover of *Sweet Baby Blues* in Los Angeles.

"We gotta wear outrageous red!" I insisted. "Red means good luck and good energy."

"And good vibes," Jimmy agreed.

But in between the recording of the album and the photo shoot came one of the most important steps in producing a good product. The mix! It was so important that we paid our own way up to San Francisco. Chris Long picked us up at the airport and drove us to Hayward, a small town nearby, to the studio of Phil Edwards, a pleasant person with phenomenal pitch and a perfectionist streak two miles wide.

Jimmy's years on Madison Avenue, arranging, contracting, and recording with Chico Hamilton and Frank Como, paid off in spades. "Bring up the bass," he insisted. "All these cats came from some place else, and I know it's hard to reconcile the different timbres and attacks, but it was the same in New York. Unless a band is on the road performing with each other night in and night out, it's not gonna meld together overnight!"

Phil Edwards had not won a wall full of awards for nothing! He rode his rolling chair from console to tape machine and back again, and knitted up "that raveled sleeve" with care.

After two days, with breaks only for lunch, we were all happy with the result. "Solid!" Jimmy exclaimed.

"We've got the order of the tunes all ready." I smiled at Chris. "We built it like one of our performance sets, beginning, middle, and closer, with drama in between. We paid strict attention to the psychic shift that happens when you change keys."

"Psychic shift?" Phil's eyebrow went up into his sandy hair. "Have you heard this joke . . ." He really was a delightful character, full of endless puns and stories.

The photo shoot was held the next week in an empty room, the only prop a gleaming, ebony, baby grand piano.

"*Formidable!*" Four little cats with cameras surrounded us. Every time they came near Jimmy, one or another of them spoke that word as though voicing a magic incantation. Their eyes shined with zeal as they made him point his big golden bass trombone straight up into the air in the style of an old 1920s photo.

"What do you want me to do?" I had asked the question several times as I sat at the piano, rearranging my red suede fringed scarf. Soft, sensuous red suede covered me from chin to toes. Jimmy wore a red suede bomber jacket with his customary black cap.

Every once in a while one of them would look at me and run over with a great raggedy powder puff and hit me squarely over my eyes, nose, and mouth. I had my doubts about that big funky powder puff—who knew where it had been? Each time one of those cats smacked me, I had to reapply my lipstick, lip gloss, and mascara.

I wanted the whole thing over. I was going through the valley of the shadow of "men-o-pause," and perspiring a lot. I had been fortunate, and had managed to play it cool through all the hot flashes. I didn't quit show business, as lots of ladies had. On the bandstand, whenever I felt a flood coming on, I would announce, "Ladies and gentlemen, we're gonna play one of our hottest tunes. It's gonna be so fast that we really gonna sweat up here! I mean romp an' stomp an' sweat!" Then I'd set the tempo for "Cherokee" or "Perdido" and off we'd go! The hot flashes flashed, and I brought thunder and lightning out of that piano while my body was assailed by torrential rains. A major storm!

On M'Ma's sage advice, there were no hormones for this woman. The audience would say, "Boy! You really play the *mess* out that piano. Nobody can say you don't play hard, girl, 'cause you really sweat!" I'd mop my brow and grin, fan myself furiously with my gospel fan, and sip my gin and tonic.

"Gin is made outta juniper berries," M'Ma advised. "Gramma Hattie an' Great-Gramma Lizzie said juniper berries are *good* for women of a certain age."

With a little bit of gin and a whole lotta showmanship, I handled the problem pretty well. But I did cut my hair shorter. Oh, Lawd, I *had* to cut that hair!

The four photographers retreated into a corner for a conference, then bounded out, hot flashbulbs blinding us. It took over four hours to finish the photo shoot, which ended only after Jimmy lost his temper and declared, "That's it! No more!"

The little men, still enamored with Jimmy, breathed a final *"Formidable!"*

We carefully packed up our gear and, with our emotions erratically sliding up and down like the Sandusky, Ohio, roller coaster, took the scenic Highway 101 back down to San Diego. The die was cast, and *Sweet Baby Blues*, love it or leave it, was ready to be released and, we hoped, to be well received by blues and jazz lovers of the whole wide world.

> *Gonna live the life I sing about*
> *Ev'ry note—chapter and verse—*
> *'Cause there's one thing that I'm sure of,*
> *Lawd, ain't no luggage on no hearse!*

* * *

Early on a Monday morning the phone rang and a soft voice sang, "Lawd, Lawd, Lawd!" It was the voice of Frank McGrath, a member of the Jazz Society. He had heard the newly released record on the radio, and was the very first person to contact us with the news. "Lawd, Lawd, Lawd," he sang again. "Jeannie! I love the way you sing that song, and the record is a winner!"

The next call came from San Francisco. It was Jerome Richardson, the sax player who had performed with Lucky Millender, Lionel Hampton, Quincy Jones, Thad Jones, and Mel Lewis, and had done commercials with Jimmy and Chico Hamilton. "Cheathams! I fell outta my bed when I heard 'Black Drawers'! I got up, got dressed, and drove all the way into town to the record shop and copped a copy of you-all's record!" He was cracking up. "I never heard anything quite like it. I'm going to call all the cats and tell them about this record. By the way," he added, "if you ever need a tenor player, I'm available. I know how to play the blues!"

Leonard Feather, the noted jazz critic brought to America by Stanley Dance, wrote: "A curious mix! A New Orleans style clarinetist (slightly out of tune), two be-bop sax players, a swing era trumpet player, a blues-drenched vocalist playing piano and a *bass* trombone, playing blues . . . a curious mix!"

Things were rushing along so fast that we could hardly catch our breath.

The calls poured in, each one a thrill, as members of the music industry let us know how much they liked the album.

Like a couple of teenagers, we sped around checking out the record stores, pulling out our records, looking at our photos, glorying in our names being right next to Doc Cheatham's on the display shelves. We dropped in at Tower Records, not far from our house. "Jimmy," I exclaimed, "look at this!" The distributor had set up an eye-catching display of our records near the store's entrance, where customers could check out our album as soon as they walked in.

Our feet did not touch the floor as we headed past shelves full of rock 'n' roll toward the back of the store. "Look, Jeannie," Jimmy nearly burst with excitement, "they have our records in both the blues and the jazz categories!" We bought cassettes to send out to friends, radio stations, and disc jockeys.

The next important call came a few months later from Stanley Dance, informing us that we had won the Grande Prix du Disque from the Hot Club of France. It was the French Grammy.

Lawd, Lawd, Lawd! Let the good times roll!

Then — glory! — we received a call from George Wein's office. George Wein, a legendary impresario, had opened a club called Storyville in Boston, gone on from there to produce the Newport festivals, and finally produced festivals all over the world. He invited us to play the Grande Parade du Jazz in Nice, France. *Formidable!*

We had arrived!

* * *

We did arrive — in Paris, France, at daybreak, with thirty-two pieces of luggage, and not a single soul met us. With Jimmy and I were Jimmy Noone, Jr., Curtis Peagler, Dinky Morris, John "Ironman" Harris, and a woman trumpet player named Clora Bryant, who replaced Snooky Young, since he was committed to Doc Severinsen and *The Tonight Show*.

Clora was a nice-looking woman with clear, bright skin and shiny black hair worn in a chignon that she adorned with a flower, Billie Holiday style. She had performed with the Prairie View Co-Eds and the International Sweethearts of Rhythm, all-girl bands. She played with Eric Dolphy and Johnny Otis. The woman could play world-class trumpet. There's a movie clip of Clora standing toe-to-toe with Harry James; high note for high note she did not give an inch!

Red Callender was already in Europe, playing a tribute to Louis Armstrong with Freddie Hubbard, so we had enlisted Jimmy Woode, a Duke Ellington alumnus, to do the first play date with us. Red would rejoin us on the next.

We walked down the airport ramp looking for signs saying "Welcome, Sweet Baby Blues Band." There were none. We entered the terminal proper and kept looking around for someone from the festival. All we could see were cops carrying huge guns, hundreds of travelers, and thousands of dogs. The French really love their dogs. We stepped out and around the dogs, disentangled ourselves from their leashes, and made our way to one of the ticket windows.

"Ma'am, where do we change planes for Montauban?" We showed her the tickets. She looked down her Gallic nose at us and said in French, "X? X!" and "Non!" And slammed down the cover of the window.

Jimmy Noone went to change his money into francs. Curtis and Ironman went sightseeing. Dinky, Clora, Jimmy, and I were still going from one window to another, trying to get our questions answered.

None of our big red travel-instrument trunks were to be seen anywhere. We tried to use sign language and pantomime, playing trombones and trumpets and pianos. The more we tried, the more people crowded around us, smiling, applauding, and exclaiming "*Formidable!*" The dogs started barking and yipping and running around, sniffing at us and licking our legs.

Finally, some good soul, who was traveling to the festival, said, "You have to change planes at Orly airfield. Just go out that door and catch the shuttle. It'll take you across the way to the bus that goes to Orly."

We grabbed our luggage and sped toward the shuttle that was just getting ready to take off. But where were Curtis and Ironman? Clora spoke up. They had gone to check out the liquor in the duty-free zone.

"Jesus Christ!" It could have been a prayer, honest. Not only did we not have our instruments, we didn't have our instrumentalists! "It's like trying to herd cats," I said through gritted teeth.

"Just keep movin'! There's nothin' else we can do." Dinky sounded testy. He worked as an upper-echelon boss at AT&T and was used to giving orders and having them obeyed.

We jumped on the shuttle bus—Clora, Dinky, Jimmy Noone, Jimmy, and I—our hearts in our mouths. As the shuttle was pulling off, we looked back, and whom did we see running, waving their arms, and yelling, "Stop! Stop!" The shuttle slowed down just long enough for Curtis and John to leap on. We made it onto the bus going to Orly with nary a nanosecond to spare.

Jimmy Noone had just enough francs in his pocket to pay the fare for all of us, and off we went on a wild ride through the streets of Paris. Then we piled off the bus and onto the plane just in the nick of time. Nobody said anything. We were too busy breathing hard and sweating.

We landed in Montauban after a brief flight. Dinky, always the official, said, "Let's go find the luggage office and ask about our axes." He meant our missing instruments.

We didn't have to go far. In the middle of the terminal building, stacked like an Egyptian pyramid in the middle of the floor, we discovered our big red instrument trunks. Perched on top of the trunks were four Frenchmen holding up a sign that read "Welcome, Sweet Baby Blues Band."

You could hear us exhale all over that airport.

The four Frenchmen hustled us into several automobiles and took off with a roar, almost losing Dinky, whose door still hung open. If Jimmy hadn't grabbed him, we would have lost our baritone player and, perish the thought, held a jazz funeral in France for him.

It was a long, long ride, past field after field of sunflowers, their faces following the afternoon sun. The air was suffused with the same weird soft light portrayed in the paintings of French masters. "It takes my breath away," I whispered to Jimmy, "I never thought I'd ever see such beauty in person."

Finally, we arrived at the quaint little hotel in Montauban and found the kitchen closed. To our travel-strained minds, the environment offered both too little and too much. There was no food, but our bathrooms seemed to have two toilets each. One of them was a bidet. Way too European for the cats to appreciate, and the source of joking speculation about the condition of French behinds.

We had feather beds and bathrooms with bidets, but not a bite to eat in a country known for its cuisine. God bless Papa Jo Jones! He had tipped us off to the food crises in Europe and warned us to line our suitcases with Vienna sausages and similar travel-proof chow. We passed out crackers and sardines to everyone.

The next day we were rushed off to the local performance hall for a run-through. Jimmy Woode, the bassist subbing for Red Callender, met us there, and—surprise, surprise!—Sam Woodyard pulled up in his Mercedes and said, "I've come a long way to see you-all!"

He looked dapper in a black suit, white shirt, and dark tie, shoes spit-shined, his small frame as straight as an arrow. One of Duke Ellington's prize drummers, he had been living in Europe for many years.

Hugs all around, and we went to get some food at a nearby combination eatery and bar. When Clora and I walked in with the rest of the band, every man in the place stopped eating, drinking, or talking. They had never seen two black women before.

"Dare we go to the bathroom alone?"

Clora whispered to me, "Not on your life! We go together."

"These mountain cats lookin' at us like we a pig-ear sandwich!" I whispered back. Clora giggled.

Eyes followed our every move—to the bathroom and back. Tongues licked lips as we ate our food. The intense interest reminded me of the redbone country high in the hills of West Virginia—men and women so isolated that they drank in a fresh new face. I knew we would be the subject of many a conversation long after we had gone.

That night we performed. Jimmy Woode fit right in, seamless and smooth. The little hall was packed shoulder-to-shoulder with people. We blew our behinds off, and they sat there with their hands in their laps or with their arms folded. We played tune after tune and got the same response— no response. We ended with a flourish and began to take our bows to dead silence. Jimmy Woode grinned at our puzzled faces, stifling laughter. We were used to standing ovations.

As soon as we finished bowing, a thunderous stomp! stomp! stomp! filled the auditorium. Feet pounding all at once, shaking the very foundation of the building. Stomp! Stomp! Stomp! A sea of smiling faces gazed up at us. Jimmy Woode instructed, "Keep bowing. This is the way these people applaud. *After* the music is over. With their feet!"

Completely shaken by the whole scene, we packed up our gear as fast as we could and headed out to the vans. The drivers were so drunk they could not stand. "Let's leave ev'rything in one van and park it in front of the police station," the more sober of the two suggested.

"Oh, no you won't!" Jimmy retorted, his voice like steel. "Our instruments go right back to the hotel with us. You understand? We got a plane to catch in the morning, and we don't want *any* problems."

When the other cats in the band joined in, the drunken red faces stopped grinning. We packed the vans ourselves so nothing would be broken or missing. Then we made the two drivers, drunk and surly, steer us through the dark empty streets back to the hotel. Fortunately, they didn't hit anything.

Lawd, it was good to get back to the hotel! There we said goodbye to Jimmy Woode, who was taking an earlier flight. Then we unloaded our instruments and ate some more sardines and crackers.

Exhausted, I fell into bed, to dream of sitting at a table in a small café on the Rue De Palais, listening to some French cat in a tight striped top jamming on an accordion.

Sturm und Drang Blues: Vienne, France

. . . .

"Hi there, soaks! Hi there, babe!" Cab Calloway leaned out of an upstairs window of the tiny old hotel in Vienne, France. "Are you following me around?"

"We followin' you around, all right!" Red Callender declared in his deep bass voice, "You under arrest!"

We had arrived in Vienne from Montauban around noon, met Red and his wife, Mary Lou, and the stage crew. There were no vans to be seen, and we had to follow the crew with our instruments on foot. We marched through the cobblestone streets of the ancient city, through passages so narrow you could stretch your arms out and almost touch the buildings on both sides. We climbed the hill toward the outdoor arena stage, where we intended to prepare for the performance that night.

The whole caravan halted when Cab called out to us. Grateful for the brief rest, we waited, huffing and puffing, for him to come down to the street. "Mr. Calloway," I asked, "did anybody *ever* play that piano run in your music?" I tried to sound casual and offhand.

He tossed his silvery hair and said in an ominous voice, "Who know what evil lurks in the hearts of men . . . the Shadow do! My little friend," he continued, "that's for me to know and you to find out!" Then he laughed like a hyena, his many teeth gleaming in the suffused sunlight. I scowled at him.

He quickly began a history of the place. "This arena was built by the Romans," he intoned. "They used to throw the Christians to the lions here."

"Well," cracked Jimmy Noone, "I'm sure glad I didn't get here any earlier."

When we stumbled through the entrance to the arena at last, we felt like ancient Christians who'd gotten pardons, since we could lay our burdens down. Flexing our aching arms, we looked around. The arena was shaped like a giant bowl made of stones set carefully one upon the other. It had perfect acoustics.

"Friends, Romans, countrymen . . .!" We couldn't resist. Each of us stood in the center of the stage and listened to our voices projecting out, out, over the seats of the patrons, and continuing on to the stony back of the arena. We needed no mikes, except for my vocals and for Cab Calloway's songs.

That night, with the perfect acoustic sound and a full moon rising up behind the audience, I floated, suspended between two eras. Then and now. Eerie!

Clora began playing her feature, "I Can't Get Started," with her beautiful clear full sound, when all of a sudden the sky opened up and rain pelted down. Fortunately, the stage was covered, and although some wires were exposed, we kept on playing.

We looked out at the audience, and suddenly the whole arena was wall-to-wall big black bumbershoots. Pop! Pop! Pop! Our music competed with the sound of umbrellas opening until all the people were completely covered. Surreal!

Clora finished up the song with a grand cadenza reminiscent of Louis Armstrong, and as the last high note shimmered in the stormy night air, the rains stopped as suddenly as they had begun. The audience gasped, then cheered and cheered. No foot stomping here!

Cab Calloway rushed out from the back of the stage and called to the audience, "How can I follow that?" He cleverly took our applause and annexed it for his own, and with the full moon once more shining in all its glory, he "hi-de-ho'd" to a new triumph. Being just as stage savvy as the old cat, we ran back out and took more bows . . . with him!

Oh, what a grand game! We threw kisses at the audience, at each other, and at the sky. Finally, we skipped off stage, feeling good! Feeling *formidable!*

Next morning, Mary Lou called our room. "Red can't get out of bed!" she said, her voice small and shaky. Red's condition had to be serious because this petite attractive woman feared nothing. Habitually cheerful and optimistic, Mary Lou had a great sense of humor. She also held a pilot's license. "He can't get up," she repeated.

"I'll be right over."

Jimmy and I suspected that Red had "oversported" himself, dashing around Europe playing for Freddie Hubbard *and* the Sweet Baby Blues Band.

We were booked on a plane to Nice that afternoon. We had to give up our rooms at the hotel and couldn't change our tickets for another flight. What to do? My mind raced. Jimmy Woode could meet us in Nice. We had a whole day off, so we had a little time to make arrangements.

"Well, Red," I took his pulse. It felt strong and even, but his skin was clammy and cold. "Maybe we could call an ambulance to take you to a hospital."

"No! No!" He sat up straight. "I'm not goin' to no hospital. I don't want any strange doctor pokin' at me!"

It occurred to me that he might need some food. There was no breakfast in the hotel. "We have some sardines and crackers. And apricot nectar."

Red's eyes lit up. "Yeah, I like little girls!"

Mary Lou laughed. "That's what he calls sardines."

I rushed back with the food. One bite and Red declared, "Okay, little mama, I'll be ready to leave on time."

Much to my relief, we all made it to the airport and on to Nice on schedule.

* * *

The hotel in Nice teemed with famous musicians: Dizzy Gillespie's whole big band, Richie Cole's band, Marshall Hawkins, Emily Remler, and many, many others. We were so excited that even though this was our first day off, resting was not an option. We parked our gear and hurried back down to the bar to watch new arrivals, sit and sip and tell lies all night long.

We woke up the next morning, and it felt like fifty of the great unwashed had been walking around in our mouths barefoot. Jet lag and gin do not a wedding make.

After a room-service breakfast of croissants, butter, jam, and a huge pot of coffee, to which we added Vienna sausages and apricot juice from our private stash, we felt alive again. I called Red's room. "How's it goin'?"

"Ready for Freddie!" was the reply.

Our hotel room sported a small balcony with two chairs and a table. We took our second cups of coffee outside and gazed at the scene below. The morning was balmy, the sky periwinkle blue. The sounds of Nice were hushed.

Striding along the path below us we spied Ironman and Curtis heading for the topless beach. Jimmy gave them the New York "street" whistle, and they stopped dead in their tracks, looking for the source. That whistle meant "look out!" They tipped their heads back and saw us five stories above them, shaking "naughty, naughty" fingers at them and laughing. They grinned, shrugged their shoulders, and continued their pursuit.

"Four o'clock in the lobby!" we called. "Tell Jimmy Noone, Dinky, and Clora. Okay?"

"Okay!" Their steps quickened, as if they were afraid they would miss something.

Jimmy and I ambled inside and went back to sleep. Later for sightseeing.

We woke up ready to play, and called room service for some of their excellent pasta with fresh-shaved Parmesan cheese. We had the chef's schedule down pat; we never wanted to be caught foodless in France again.

Our excitement began to build as we dressed for our debut in Nice. "Outrageous red" was the color of choice for my stage outfits. I had hunted high and low for travel-ready materials. I found red silk separates that didn't wrinkle, could be cold-water washed, and dried in less than two hours. Heaven! They were very expensive, but they did the trick. Donna Karan red bodysuits and a pair of black patent-leather polka-dot ankle-tie Anne Klein wedge shoes, which defied cobblestones and rain, completed my ensembles.

The band wore black shirts and pants with individual red touches: hats, caps, belts, neckerchiefs, shoes and, last but not least, Jimmy's black leather gloves for a vibrant nonconformity and a "take no prisoners" appearance.

We boarded a large bus along with several other bands, all our instruments, and various and sundry hangers-on. As we rode toward the festival grounds, the sense of excitement grew more and more intense and electrified the air. I felt myself getting caught up in the heightened anticipation. This was it! We were really here on the French Riviera—ready to romp and stomp in a place I had only seen in the movies!

Down girl, I told myself, save the trip-hammer heartbeats and drama for the stage!

We all piled off the bus and spied Doc Cheatham standing at a food concession near the entrance of the grounds, the better to watch new arrivals. In his right hand he held what appeared to be a twelve-inch hoagy; tucked under his left arm was his leather trumpet bag.

"Cheathams!" he called, and his smiling face lit up even more than usual when he saw us. "Hey!" He lifted one foot from the ground and showed us the Birkenstocks he had purchased in La Jolla. "I got 'em on! Lotsa walkin' 'round these grounds. You gotta have some big 'n' easies on your feet to last all evenin'!" he warned.

We all hugged him, then off we went to find our stage, calling over our shoulders, "See you tonight at the hotel bar!"

The area reminded me of a county fair. There were four stages. The bands would rotate among them. By the end of the festival, each band would have performed in every venue.

Richie Cole, aka "Alto Madness," our jam session bassist Marshall Hawkins, and Emily Remler, a wonderful and sensitive guitar player, were on one stage. Doc Cheatham, featured with the Dirty Dozen Brass Band from New Orleans (who later recorded our song "Meet Me with Your Black Drawers On"), appeared on another stage. Dizzy Gillespie and his big band stretched out across stage three, and we, the Sweet Baby Blues Band, were on the fourth and last stage.

We strolled by stage three during our short intermission to say hello to the cats in Dizzy's band. He spied us and came over. "Cheathams," he said, "you cats are *crazy!*"

In the middle of all these performance areas, George Wein's wife supervised a group of New Orleans chefs who prepared red beans and rice, fried chicken, gumbo, and barbeque. It drove me nuts, smelling all that goodness. The problem stemmed from the fact that I could not perform or sing on a full stomach. With all those fabulous scents wafting through the air, I had to make do with the food I had eaten at the hotel. To most of the cats, however, a tummy full of yummy and great jazz music made for a real celebration.

People flocked to this festival from all over the world. The different languages, costumes, and energies of the fans swirled around and followed us from stage to stage. More than a few, without words, placed their hands over their hearts to let us know that we had truly moved them. This simple communication, straight from the heart, was as heady as fine French wine!

Some of the musicians followed us as well. Nat Pierce and Gerry Wiggins, both great pianists, stood on the ground behind me as we romped through "Roll 'Em, Pete." I looked down and they smiled. So when we finished, I joined them.

"We were checking you out," Nat Pierce growled. "We don't know how you do what you do. How do you play boogie-woogie that fast and sing at the same time?" My heart swelled. To hear such praise from these two jazz greats was sweet.

Nat smiled. "I see why Basie wants to break your fingers." He had taken Basie's place in the band when Basie had suffered health problems. "Oh yeah, Basie told me all about you. Now I see for myself just what he means."

A man pushed himself through the crowd. "Where is Curtis Peagler?" I looked around. Curtis was talking to a bunch of women, his tall frame sticking up above the people, his head covered with a red floppy hat. I called him and he ambled over.

The man asked, "Can you autograph this record?"

Curtis was always gracious and mannerly with folks, earning him the nickname "Bourgeois." "Of course," he said. Then he took the obviously old record in his hands and stared at it in disbelief. "Hey," he exclaimed, "this is the very first record I ever recorded! How did it get to Europe?"

Not waiting for an answer to his question, he launched into a story. "There was this record company in Cincinnati when I was a teenager. I told the owner I could play alto sax, but he wouldn't listen to me. Told me I could hang around if I painted the outside of the studio. I told him I would." Curtis closed his eyes, as if he were seeing that paint go onto the walls. "One day while I was painting, and straining to listen to the music inside, the owner came running out. He said one of the sax players hadn't shown up and would I bring my horn in and play with the group."

We waited in anticipation. "Go on!" said Dinky.

"Well, I took my alto in there and tore it up! I knew this was my big chance." He stared at the record again. "I was just a kid. I never had a chance to see or hear this record."

"Wow, man, that's heavy," exclaimed Jimmy Noone. "This is your lucky day."

Curtis signed the cover. You could tell he was really overcome. He'd had a quadruple bypass operation earlier that year, and I knew that this record signing was precious to him.

"*Every* day is my lucky day!" Curtis was always philosophical and humorous. We all laughed. C'est si bon!

Shoofly Pie with Shafafa in The Hague

. . . .

"Boy, oh boy! Look at all that food!" We couldn't believe our eyes. After we played all four of the festival stages, the promoters had scheduled us for a very early flight to the Netherlands. When we arrived at The Hague, sleepy and hungry, for the North Sea Festival, we sped through the lobby of our hotel before checking in and headed straight for the dining room.

The place was one giant buffet. We crowded through the door, dropped our luggage in a corner, and began to question the three men dressed in white who were wearing large floppy chef's hats and hovering over the tables laden with culinary delights.

"Who is all this food for? Can we buy some?"

"Yes, you may!" The chefs grinned and waved their hands, beckoned us toward the food.

I never saw anything like it before or since. One whole area of the room offered all kinds of seafood: shrimp, oysters, lobster, smoked fish, salmon, sardines, and trout. Another area featured ham: smoked, fresh, Dutch, sliced, and diced. Beef—roasted, basted, sliced, cold, hot, or in wine—dominated another table. There were platters of chicken and turkey. The gospel bird was glorified: roasted, fried, smoked, broiled, boiled, and baked. Salads, aspics, gelatins, foie gras, duck, champagne. Cheeses: blue, cheddar, Swiss, Liederkranz. Vegetables: a fantastic display of sliced carrots, leeks, beets, pickled onions, green beans, wax beans, asparagus. Fruit: melons sliced, cubed, and slivered; pears; baked apples and applesauce; berries; oranges. Desserts: chocolate cakes, white cakes, coconut cakes, cheesecakes, ladyfingers, donuts, pies, petit fours, and fruit-filled tarts.

We fell on that food like locusts! In fact three more chefs came out from the kitchen to watch. They laughed and cheered and brought more food. We ate some of everything. But not the sardines. Nobody touched the sardines!

We rested at the tables, then started all over again. After almost two weeks of eating hit-or-miss, we were famished. Every one of us had lost weight, and our stomachs thought our throats had been cut! We finally pushed away from the tables and huffed and puffed up to our rooms. "Hey, cats," I cautioned, "we're scheduled to hit at midnight, so we meet in the lobby at 10:30."

"You got it!"

Later that night it seemed as if the Low Countries were high on something. We were guided toward the stage past people hugging poles and sliding down walls—high and happy.

"Ever'body here is on somethin'," Dinky remarked. "Maybe it's the water."

Curtis wanted to give everyone the benefit of the doubt. "Do you think it's catchin'?"

Jimmy Noone stepped aside as a young girl with long, swinging hair tried to embrace him. "I think I like it here," he chuckled.

We hugged the wall to avoid three chicks with flowers in their hair; they were trying to dance "Ring around the Rosy" with us in the middle.

"Is ever'body happy?" Red Callender grinned at Mary Lou.

Whatever they were on, it sure wasn't gin. And it sure wasn't whiskey. People started cheering before we even reached the stage. And it went up from there. It was insane—delirious and happy.

One of our fans was rolled in to see us in his hospital bed, his IV bottle carried by his attendants. On the last tune, as the whole crowd sang "Meet Me with Your Black Drawers On," the invalid was carried away, smiling, his raised arm giving us the peace sign.

Halleloo!

The next day we flew back to Nice, picking our teeth and grinning. There, we packed our gear again and bid farewell to all the festival musicians. Some we knew we'd never see again.

We loved playing for the French and the Dutch. They really appreciated our music and the fact that we let them look into our hearts for just a little while. Nice was really nice, but there's no place like home, and that's where we were headed.

Lawd, we played some high-class joints
Kings and Queens and all the best!
But when I git home, baby
Please let me lay down—an' rest!

* * *

"You what?" I almost dropped the phone. We had barely been home a week, and we were still recovering from our European adventure.

"Andrew and I are back together again." The sweet lilting voice was that of Jimmy's little mama in Buffalo, New York. She had raised Jimmy and his sister alone.

"Back what?" I stuttered.

"Yes," Jimmy's mama went on, "he called me on the phone early one Sunday morning and said, 'Belle, I'm coming home.' And I said, 'Well, come on! What took you so long?'" She tittered.

"You mean he's in Buffalo? In your house?"

"Our house, now," came the reply.

I handed the phone to Jimmy. "What's up," he asked and put the phone to his ear. "Hello?" Then, silence, as he listened intently to the voice on the other end.

I watched his face change from a sixty-three-year-old man's to a six-year-old boy's. His eyes got wider and wider, his mouth hung open, his breath came faster and faster. "You what?" He finally spoke, the words bursting out of his mouth. Then another long silence. "Whew! Alright, Mudda. We love you, too. Madly! Take care! Bye, bye!"

He hung up the phone and turned to me, his hands nervously running over his face. He cleared his throat. "Dad and Mudda are back together . . ."

"Geez! How long they been separated?"

"Sixty years."

He sat down hard on the wicker rocking chair. "Ooo . . . weee!"

I had a sudden flash. Those two people did not feel the passing of sixty years. I think that by falling in love all over again, they were thrust back to a time when she was eighteen and he was twenty. Be still my heart!

I had scarcely digested this bombshell when I received another call. This time it was from my sister Charlotte in Akron. "The new LP is really nice." She never overpraised anything. She had a kind of dry wit. Four years in the air force and now picking them up and laying them down as a nurse at Akron General hadn't changed anything.

"I'm glad you like it . . ." I began.

She interrupted. "But brother Jerry is heartless mad at you for leavin' him behind."

My breath caught in my throat. I felt tears gathering behind my eyelids. "But Charlotte, I didn't leave him. He left us . . . for Red the Terrible!"

"I know he did," she said, "but I think he always thought you were gonna come back for him after a while. You know, rescue him. You always used to."

I said nothing for a long time, just stood there listening to the empty distance stretching between us. "Thanks for telling me. I'm gonna try to fix it." I didn't know how or where to begin, but I knew I must try.

The next morning I called Jerry. At first he seemed distant, and spoke in short syllables. I asked him about his life, although Charlotte had already filled me in. He drove a city bus and played a few gigs on borrowed basses. (He had never been able to buy another one of his own.) Best news of all, he had finally divorced Red.

"I bought a house with my GI Bill," he said with pride.

"I know. M'Ma told me!"

He laughed, "She would! She's the glue that sticks us all together." The ice was broken. "I have your new record," he said. I waited. "It's pretty good. You got some heavyweights on it."

"Well, thanks. There's only one thing missin'."

"What's that?"

"You!"

"Me?"

"Yes, you! Jimmy an' I are waitin' for you to play bass with this band. Red's gettin' up there, an' you the only cat that can take his place."

"What?" His voice went up an octave. Then the floodgates opened. "All right! I'll get myself together." He paused. "It'll take a little while . . ."

"Whenever you ready, we ready."

"I heard you-all booked to play Rochester, New York. I might drop in on you."

"We'll be waitin'."

"Hey, Sis."

"Yeah?"

"You make my liver quiver and my gall crawl!"

I laughed heartily at that old chestnut and hung up. My heart was full. In fact, it was breaking. But for a long time I didn't tell anyone what else Charlotte had revealed to me.

Jerry, the kid whose diapers I had changed way back on Bina Avenue, whom I took to his first day of school, who was one of the best musicians I had ever played with, had bone cancer, and he never, ever would be ready to play bass with us again.

* * *

The Sweet Baby Blues Band stretched across the stage in Rochester. The evening sun was sinking in the west as I watched the crowd arrive for the concert. I suddenly saw my brother Jerry, as tall as a pine tree, leading two little old people down the steps.

"Jimmy!" I called from the piano, "Look who's here!"

Jimmy stopped flicking his trombone slide and gazed in the direction I was pointing. Then he stared, and his eyes almost jumped out his head. His mama and his daddy, holding hands, looked up at him. His mama gave a little wave. They smiled. Not since Jimmy had been two and a half years old had he seen his parents holding hands. And they, as a couple, had never seen him perform!

Jimmy's lip trembled, and he had a hard time bringing his trombone up to his lips as I stomped off the tempo for the band to open with "Brand New Blues." Our eyes were filled with tears. Jimmy's tears were of disbelief and joy. Mine were of resignation and sorrow. Jerry was my baby, after all.

Be still, my heart!

Chickenshit or Chicken Salad?

· · · · · · · · · · · · · · · · · · · ·

*P*apa Jo Jones always warned Jimmy and me, "Some folks don't know the dif'rence between chickenshit and chicken salad. Either way, you has to have a chicken!"

The song "Meet Me with Your Black Drawers On" was the chicken. It seemed to go into the world in waves—first small, then wider and wider, like the ripples on the water when you send a flat stone skipping across Summit Lake.

"It's taken Chicago by storm. Folks are demanding that the disc jockeys spin it over an' over ever' day," friends reported to us, especially Bill Lee of Chicago, Bubba Jackson and Helen Borgers of KLON in Long Beach, and a cat named "T" at KSDS in San Diego. Chicken salad!

At long last, we finally met the president of Concord Jazz, Inc., Mr. Carl Jefferson, in person! We had been invited up to the Bay Area to do some radio interviews, and Chris Long, our producer, took us over to Mr. Jefferson's office.

Jefferson, a gruff grizzled man with graying hair and beard, used to be an automobile dealer. We had heard through the grapevine all kinds of stories about the man, about his bad temper and explosive outbursts, about how he allegedly ran roughshod over people who worked for him and humiliated them and brought them down low.

Jimmy and I had no trouble with Jefferson, not at all. He shook hands firmly, and his eyes twinkled behind his glasses. Furthermore, he seemed a little shy. His eyes constantly searched our facial expressions for validation of his own opinion of himself. In fact, he was just like the Reverend Uncle Frank—a self-made man who did nothing that did not further his chosen goals. Still, he knew whom to bully and whom *not* to bully. We had learned from our informants that he played the record over and over, even calling friends to come to his office to listen to it.

Even so, he did not know what to do with our runaway record. People were calling us from all over creation with deals for "Black Drawers." Proposals came from record stores, a factory owner in North Carolina who wanted to put out a line of clothing—jeans and underwear—called Black Drawers, a man who owned a slew of dance studios who wanted permission to spin off a dance record and name a dance craze the Black Drawers Shag. We referred all these entrepreneurs to Jefferson. And he did not return their calls! It pissed us off.

Carl Jefferson sat in his office like a mule that Gramma Hattie had on her farm. With two bales of hay in front of him, he nearly starved to death because he couldn't make up his mind which one to eat.

Record sales are only a small part of the business. Movie sound tracks, commercials, and side deals for use of the music or artist bring in the big money. Jefferson did not like other people using "his artists." Under contract, we had to get his permission for other deals.

Ms. Merrilee Trost, a vibrant, "take no prisoners" Detroit native who was raising a family of girls by herself, worked for Concord Records, Inc. Merrilee turned out to be our guardian angel. She maneuvered around and snagged *The Tonight Show* and *The Today Show* for us, along with the Great American Music Hall, where Stanley Dance made sure that we received the Grand Prix du Disc plaque and document from the Hot Club of France in person. Of course, Jefferson insisted that he present the award to us, with photographers firmly in place.

Merrilee put together a nice bio for our publicity package. She kept our band and our publicity going, and we knew that she had to go around the bend to get some things done. Chicken salad!

Lurking on the dark side of the music business—the cut-throat, competitive, jealous side—some Los Angeles musicians did not relish the idea of the rebirth of the blues at all. "The Cheathams are tryin' to set music back forty years!" they complained. Chickenshit!

Opening the Concord Jazz Festival with Count Basie's Band, headed up by Thad Jones, was a real winner. The Sweet Baby Blues Band performed with the whole Basie band standing in the wings, smiling and applauding. As we ran off the stage to a thunderous standing ovation, Thad Jones grabbed Jimmy and me, picked us up off the floor with a bear hug, and cried, "Thank you! Thank you for bringing us back to the truth!"

Gourmet chicken salad!

There was a second printing of the record in Chicago because of the demand. Carl Jefferson never told us, though. We heard about it much later through the ever-present grapevine. Chickenshit!

We phoned disc jockeys all over the country, on our own dime, and did interviews. We flew over the Midwest, rented a car, and drove from Cincinnati to Cleveland, stopping at record stores all along the way, meeting and greeting customers and owners. Sister Charlotte traveled with us. She could ballyhoo with the best!

Enter WBGO, a radio station in New Jersey, where Becca Pulliam and Bob Porter proved to be invaluable in propelling the record onward and upward along the East Coast. Chicken salad.

We gladly worked our behinds off to keep the momentum going. But many opportunities came to our attention too late for us to take advantage of them. Meanwhile, Jefferson put together a band of musicians. The new group was an exact copy of our instrumentation—a five-man horn front with a rhythm section. Off they went to the recording studio in an attempt to produce another hit record—a hit record intended to compete with ours! Competition from our own record company? But I guess it was no dice. The secret of our music lay not in the notes, but in the spirit *in* the notes.

Chickenshit or chicken salad? First you has to have a chicken!

* * *

Papa Jo—Jonathan Samuel David Jones—went home to glory in the fall of 1985. Jimmy's beloved student, Sipho Kunene, who had snagged a long-standing gig playing drums for Harry Belafonte, hung out with Papa Jo until he crossed over.

We did exactly as Papa Jo requested. We did not attend his funeral. We knew he wasn't there, either.

* * *

Who's that woman, dressed in black
She mean an' evil—that's a fact!

"She gotta gun!"

"How you know that?"

"She told me!"

"Aw-w-w shit!" Dinky always cussed.

The setting: New York City, the Blue Note club at the end of a torrid evening of performing. Charles Brown and his band shared the bill with us.

Dressed all in black, her hair like a raven's wing sweeping down across one pale cheek, her red lips fixed in a serious pout, she came in for the last show. She paid for a table right down front and ordered herself a bottle of champagne nestled in a bucket of ice. The waiter placed one fluted champagne glass on the table before her. At the Blue Note, those few things amounted to a whole heap of money!

She gave the Sweet Baby Blues Band token applause. Then Curtis Peagler, or Mr. C. P., as we called him, began playing his showstopper, "Misty." (We called it "Musty"!) He strolled through the audience, his alto sax dripping blues phrases and drowning in emotion. He teased all the ladies, finally stopping at the table where the mystery woman sat.

Now, Curtis had a *note!* When he played the note, it never failed to make all the females cry out and say, "Yes, yes! Um-hum!" In every country, in every town he played, he received the same response when he played the note. But this woman didn't bat an eyelash. So he played his way back on the stage, and, passing the piano, he said to me, "Trouble!" I guess he thought if he couldn't get to her, something had to be wrong with her. Curtis was right.

Charles Brown and his band came on to close the show, and she seemed enraptured by his performance. She didn't move, lingering after the show and after the last customer had straggled out into the night. Then she too was gone.

We all gathered at the bar with Charles Brown, told the bartender to "run 'em 'round!" and had just settled down to drink and wind down a little when the woman, who must have stashed herself in the ladies' room, came up to Charles Brown and said, "All right! Let's go!"

Charles looked startled. "Go? Go where?"

She said, "I came to see you. I bought champagne, and I come to take you home with me, this mornin'!" She had placed herself between me and Charles. She turned and looked at me and said, "I got a gun! He is goin' home with *me!*"

I slid off the bar stool. So did everybody else. The bartender's hand shook as he took a swipe at the bar with a stained towel. We all started backing away.

Curtis leaped into the breach. "Honey," he said, "why don't you wait outside for Charles while he gets his money. We don't have our money yet." He smiled his sweetest smile. "Then he can take you to breakfast."

She looked at Curtis, then back to Charles, and then said, "All right. But I'll be waiting!"

The bartender ran around the bar and let her out, then locked the door and hurried over to where we were huddled. We could see her standing outside the glass door, waiting for Charles.

We all moved out of the line of fire, still bunched up, Jimmy and me out in front. I don't know how we got there. Charles Brown, a very tall man, was trying to hide behind me. "What are you doing behind me?" I hissed at him. "*You* the one she wants!" I didn't feel quite so incensed when I noticed he had tears in his eyes.

The bartender called 911, and soon New York City's finest came and began to question the woman. We watched through the glass door as they hustled her into a patrol car.

Then we got out of there. Big Red Callender walked on one side of Charles Brown, Curtis Peagler on the other, and Ironman, Dinky, Jimmy, and I brought up the rear.

We made our escape in slow motion. Curtis had a gimpy leg because he'd had an artery removed as part of his heart bypass. Red was slow because of his age and because he insisted on eating bad seafood. I always carried a first aid kit full of Pepto-Bismol to counteract his chronic indigestion.

When we reached the hotel, you can bet we were one happy group of musicians. Live musicians!

Would you believe, the woman was released and came back the very next night with the very same gun! Once again, she held us hostage for several nerve-wracking hours after the gig was over. Once again, the cops arrived and hauled her away.

We were only too glad to leave New York City. A city so bad they named it twice! Oh, what a city! Diddy-wah-diddy!

Stay away from that woman
Dressed in black—
She take yo' life—
Cain't get it back!

How Long?

· · · · · · · · · · · · · · · · · ·

Winging our way west, traveling coach, Jimmy, Ironman, Dinky, and I settled in for the long flight back to San Diego. We laughed and talked about the events of the past week, especially about the woman dressed in black. There was plenty of humorous speculation about what might have happened if she had managed to abduct Charles Brown at gunpoint. Would he have taken her to a restaurant, ordered almost everything on the menu, and loitered over breakfast, or would he have climbed out the men's-room window? Would Charles Brown have been up to the task of jumping on the bones of a woman holding a gun on him?

Later, the conversation veered to the making of our new record, *Midnight Mama*.

"Boy! It was colder than a well digger's bee-hind in that studio!" Dinky shook his head.

"It was colder than *that!*" Jimmy snapped.

All too true. *Midnight Mama* was recorded on one of the coldest days in memory in Los Angeles, in a building that used to be RCA Studios, a huge barn of a place. We could see our breaths in the musty air.

I was very unhappy that Chris had booked us into *any* new studio. I mean, why mess with success? We won the Grand Prix du Disque with our first record, put together in Ocean Way Studios. We all loved the intimacy of the former studio, Red Callender in particular. He announced to Chris, "You know, I recorded with Art Tatum in this studio." Wow! No wonder we had felt so grand making music there. The vibes were in the very woodwork, whispering "Play on, play on!"

Shivering in the new studio, Big Red Callender barked, "Where's the heat? My strings are not gonna stay tuned in this barn!" Jimmy Noone pulled his coat collar up around his ears and plunged his hands deep into his pockets. The other cats were especially peeved because they had to cradle their mouthpieces under their armpits to keep them warm. "Can't make music with cold hard steel pressing on your chops!" grumbled Snooky Young.

"We usually turn the lights down low for a 'middle of the night' atmosphere. This time we gonna have to turn 'em up high so we can pretend they givin' off heat!" I croaked to Jimmy.

I could feel my throat begin to constrict from the damp cold. I tried not to clear my throat—that only makes the voice raspy. I just swallowed instead, a neat trick I picked up from Big Maybelle.

Dinky's asthma began to kick up, and he took a few long breaths from his inhaler. I don't know how on earth he could play the biggest wind instrument in the band—baritone sax—*and* the smallest, a dinky little curved, silver soprano. That's why everybody called him Dinky.

Not only was it freezing in RCA Studios, but there was an eclipse of the sun. Even birds don't sing during an eclipse. They hide their heads under their wings and wait until the sun shines again. And here I stood, expected to sing a whole album in two sessions.

Curtis saved the day. He dove into the secret compartment specially built into his leather saxophone bag and—hey, hey!—brought out a whole bottle of cognac. A few belts of the beautiful, strong dark potion chased away some of the cold, clammy, ghost-ridden shadows in the studio. And thanks to the caliber of the men of the Sweet Baby Blues Band, the mood remained festive and their spirits high.

I sang:

> *Oh, this ol' place so*
> *Chilly an' cold*
> *Chill the body*
> *But not the soul—*

As usual, Jimmy and I had kept secret from the band the identity of the guest artist, creating a highly charged atmosphere in the recording studio. Anticipation!

So when the guest artist did arrive, and stood in the doorway with one hand on his hip, grinning, Curtis exclaimed, "Jaws!" and rushed toward the small man holding a tenor sax case. The rest of the cats hurried over to him. They crowded around trying to shake hands with Lockjaw Davis, long the straw boss of the Count Basie band and a member of the Stanley Turrentine–Shirley Scott group.

Jimmy and I knew him from our New York City days, from hanging out at the Copper Rail, where we sat for hours, eating late lunch, listening to the jukebox, and letting Lockjaw vent about the hectic duties involved in running the Basie band. He'd complain, "This job gonna kill me! I have ulcers from it!"

And now, here he was in person again.

The recording went off without a hitch, mostly one-takes, with really great feeling on tunes like "C. C. Rider" and "Big Fat Daddy," a fast, torrid tune that showed off our jazz chops.

Afterward, we gathered in the control room to give a listen back. There were smiles all around until we got to "How Long Blues." It grew quiet in the booth—everyone's head down or thrown back, eyes closed, honing in on the mournful tune.

> *How long—*
> *Has that evening train been gone?*

Snooky Young whispered to me, "Girl, you reached *way* back for this one!"

All of a sudden, sobs filled the little room. It was Red Callender. Tears streaming, shoulders shaking, he stood there until Ironman put his arms around the big guy and held on for dear life. We all gathered 'round and embraced Red—a tight, full circle.

The song, plaintive at first, snaked its way out of the surround-sound speakers. Then, growing from plaintive to powerful, like the wind howling through tall pine trees on the dark side of the mountain, it enveloped the little studio.

Soon his sobs began to subside, and the song came to the end. No one asked why the tears. Nobody had to ask why.

We filed back into the other room and began packing up our gear. Jaws hugged us all. He had to catch a plane back to Las Vegas. "See you-all on the late watch!" he said. Lockjaw did a *job* on that record! A brilliant, original player.

"Jaws was really something else!" Jimmy sighed. "Let's order something long and cool." We decided on something short and warm, cognac, and the stewardess took our order.

With a sense of satisfaction, Ironman, Jimmy, Dinky, and I settled into our seats to enjoy the rest of the flight. I looked out the window at the clouds, so beautiful, so white and billowy. You might step out of the plane and lay down on them as if they were an old-fashioned feather bed.

The stewardess returned, not with cognac, but with a bottle of champagne. "Compliments of the captain," she smiled.

We were completely surprised. "Tell him thanks!" We all grinned. We *loved* freebies! When we finished that bottle, she brought another. Wow! This was a *nice* trip home.

Suddenly, over the intercom came a deep voice, "This is your captain speaking. Ladies and gentlemen, we are indeed honored to have a very famous musician on board this plane." We looked around and over the seats in front of us. The stewardess came up the aisle and stood beside our row and pointed to Jimmy.

He looked startled. "The captain must have seen us perform at the Blue Note," he said out the side of his mouth.

"Ladies and gentlemen," the deep voice continued, "Mr. Duke Ellington is with us. I have all his records, and he is the greatest musician alive today!"

All the wind went out of us. We nearly dropped our champagne glasses as the passengers started applauding and cheering. Jimmy raised his arm, but did not stand up.

"Lawd," I whispered, "how could he think you Duke Ellington? You don't even look like him!"

Ironman snickered, "Well, they say we all look alike."

Dinky sneered, "Don't even go there! Let's just keep our sunglasses and hats on, and when we land we'll wait till ev'rybody gets off." And so we did.

When the plane landed, people came by our seats and declared, "We love your music!" Soon the cabin was empty. We sprinted off the plane, rushing past the captain and crew, who were smiling proudly.

The captain said, "It's an honor, sir, to have you on my plane." Jimmy smiled weakly and gave a slight bow, then stepped on my heels trying to move quickly up the ramp. We were so unnerved that we had to go to the bar in the airport before we went to the luggage carousel.

Then we had a good laugh, but still it was a little sad.

Duke Ellington had been dead for over ten years!

How long—how long—baby, how long?

* * *

Going up the *up* side of the mountain, performing in the bands of our youth, was positively euphoric. We grabbed that goblet filled to the brim with good fun, grand adventures, and great music, grabbed it with both hands, tipped it up, drank it down to the dregs, wiped our mouths on the backs of our hands, and looked around for more.

Now, after most of our friends had quit the music business, here we were going up the *down* side of the mountain!

Now we took the goblet in both hands and sipped and savored and slowly rolled the essence of the new band, the new adventures, the new music around in our mouths like fine old wine.

The bands of our youth were ruled by decree. This new band, full of bandleaders in their own right, had to be ruled by consent. What a challenge it was, and what characters they were!

"If Clora answers the phone, we're in big trouble!" Ironman, our venerable drummer, said in a solemn voice.

We had gathered at the Los Angeles airport en route to play Joe Siegel's jazz showcase in Chicago. We were on a roll, having played Monterey, Catalina, the Vine Street Bar and Grille, the Long Beach Festival, and other venues. The plane was almost ready for boarding, but Clora Bryant had not appeared. All the rest of the cats were present and accounted for.

I was in a phone booth dialing Clora's number to see if one of her sons could tell me if she was on her way to LAX. If she was, I planned to leave her ticket with an agent so she could catch the next flight.

"Hello?" came the voice on the phone.

"Clora! Where the hell are you? We're 'posed to take off in thirty minutes!"

Ironman and Dinky rolled their eyes and threw up their hands. "We're in trouble *now!*" Dinky muttered.

"I'm tryin' to cash a check," Clora declared. "I have to leave some money for my boys! I'll be there soon as I cash it."

I gritted my teeth. Her boys were grown. "Jesus, Clora! One of us could have swung by your house on the way to LAX and *given* you cash money!" My mind raced like a greyhound with a rabbit swinging in front of its nose. I took a deep breath and attempted to keep my voice matter-of-fact. "Are you comin' or not?"

"I'll catch another plane," she replied meekly.

"You could have paged me here in the airport," I scolded.

"Yeah, I know. I know." She hung up.

Disappointed and angry, I dove into my travel bag and pulled out my address book. I called Burgess Gardner in Chicago and asked him to meet us at 7:30 that night at Joe's place.

"Okay, I'll be only too happy." Burgess, a great trumpet player, had come off the road and was teaching school in Chicago. He was an alumnus of our jam sessions at the Sheraton in San Diego.

Jimmy and I had access to musicians whom we could call on all over the United States—from the jam sessions and from our years in New York, from Jimmy's salad days performing with Duke Ellington and Maynard Ferguson, and from contracting and playing with and for Chico Hamilton.

Needless to say, opening night opened without Clora. Still, the gig went off without a hitch. Burgess was superb—fire and fury. About three o'clock in the morning the phone rang, and a wee voice woke me up. "I'm here!"

"All right, Clora. Glad you could make it." I went back to sleep. No, I did not pay the huge amount Clora had racked up for a last-minute ticket to Chicago.

In the old days, all the times the cats were hanging upside down out of hotel windows and getting the clap three times and other misadventures, they had always made the gig on time. Clora was a great trumpet player, and had performed with Harry James and Dizzy Gillespie, but that was then and this was now. Long before, I had learned to draw a line and teach people how to treat me.

"Bottom line," I mused to Jimmy, "Clora always puts her kids first. You have to admire that fact. But to jeopardize seven other people's livelihoods is not the name of the game."

Jimmy was adamant. "There are correct ways to do things. It ain't whacha do, it's the way how ya do it!" One look at his face and I knew the subject was closed.

* * *

Jimmy Noone faced another problem. He had worked at the post office for many years, but when he started getting publicity and newspaper write-ups for being in the Sweet Baby Blues Band, some of his supervisors began acting strange. His eyes filled with tears and his voice quavered with anger as he reported how his success had been greeted.

"Oh, you think you're famous," one said. "Well, when we're done with you, we'll see just how famous you get!"

Jimmy Noone always played by the book. He never took time off from his job; he used sick days and vacation time when he joined the band for gigs and recording sessions. Out of spite, his supervisors sent him to Los Angeles to take extra classes, claiming he needed to update his job skills. He complied because he was afraid to take early retirement and rely on his music for additional income.

"Girl," he told me, "I'd quit these jokers in a minute if I thought I could make it."

Stanley Dance knew Jimmy Noone's father. "Jimmy Noone plays *better* than his father," Stanley declared. "All Europe is waiting for Jimmy Noone, Jr.! I can help him attain international fame."

Meanwhile, the Sweet Baby Blues Band did a video for KPBS, the public broadcasting station in San Diego. The film was for the station's *Club Date* series. Jimmy Noone and Rickey Woodard traded fours on clarinets on "Ain't Nobody's Business." Magic moments. But on film, Jimmy Noone looked almost opaque, his face pale and wan. My heart fell when we viewed the video. Still, I didn't say a word to anyone.

The *Sweet Baby Blues Special* turned out to be really special! In that year, 1992, in the Entertainment category, it was the only program originating in the United States to be nominated for an Emmy.

In the midst of Jimmy Noone's struggle with his post office superiors, New Orleans called us to play the Jazz and Heritage Festival to be held in April. We were thrilled by the exciting news. Then came appalling news: Jimmy Noone had died of a massive heart attack in the post office.

Fragile as he had appeared on our video, we could hardly believe this disastrous turn of events. My mind filled with bitter thoughts. The post office bosses had made it so difficult for Jimmy to get away from work to play New Orleans that it broke my heart to know they had broken his heart by hassling him. Jimmy Noone, Jr., on the day that he died, was only fifty-three.

We musicians gave Jimmy Noone a great send-off. The little church resounded with praise of him and with jazz musicians playing "When the Saints Go Marching In." After the service we all crowded into his favorite bar for a final toast to his safe journey home.

Rickey Woodard, the Young Lion who had jammed with us so many times at the Bahia Hotel, fresh from the Ray Charles Band, had filled in for Jimmy Noone whenever he had been hijacked by the post office. Now Rickey joined us as a permanent member and performed in New Orleans in Jimmy Noone's place.

Rickey started playing the clarinet solo that Jimmy Noone always featured on "Ain't Nobody's Business" and something happened to Rickey's clarinet. The audience gasped and so did we. That clarinet put out sounds that were pure old New Orleans! Low, at first, then all at once soaring up into the very top of the big brown tent and out into the hot, blue New Orleans sky. It made the hair rise up on my neck. The whole band and I knew that Jimmy Noone was with us. Our eyes got larger and larger as Rickey's clarinet took on a life of its own.

Sweet and mellow, it warmed our hearts and filled our souls. When the solo was done, Rickey looked at his clarinet in amazement while the crowd roared. To us, it seemed as if Jimmy Noone had officially handed over his place in the band to Rickey Woodard. Scary—but beautiful.

* * *

Clora Bryant dropped out of the group.

"I'm not gettin' anywhere in the Sweet Baby Blues Band," she declared. "I've written a letter to Gorbachev in Russia, and I'm gonna go over there to play."

I was amazed—but practical. "That's great, girl, but whatcha gonna do after that?" No answer.

Young, slender, and handsome, Nolan "Cat-Daddy" Shaheed, who had played first trumpet with Count Basie, joined the Sweet Baby Blues Band. He told us, "I caught the interview you guys did on Helen Borgers's show, on KLON in Long Beach, and I said to myself, that's the band I want to play with!"

Nolan is one of the very few musicians who, at his age, can read, play lead, play blues and jazz, and light up a stage. A world-class runner, he won many awards in track.

The Sweet Baby Blues Band took on a new luster as the two young players joined veterans Curtis Peagler, Dinky Morris, Red Callender, Ironman Harris, and us two Cheathams.

Leaping from crag to crag up the down side of the mountain suddenly became easier, as youthful energy arced to meet maturity and experience.

Let the games begin!

" THE ORIGINAL SWEET BABY BLUES BAND "

JOHN "IRONMAN" HARRIS
JIMMY NOONE JR.

"SNOOKY" YOUNG
CURTIS PEAGLER

The original Sweet Baby Blues Band. *Clockwise from top left:* John "Ironman" Harris, drums; Eugene "Snooky" Young, trumpet; Curtis Peagler, alto, tenor, and baritone sax; Jimmy Noone, Jr., tenor sax.

GEORGE "RED" CALLENDER

ED "DINKY" MORRIS

CLORA BRYANT

" THE ORIGINAL SWEET BABY BLUES BAND "

More of the original Sweet Baby Blues Band. *Clockwise from top left:* George "Red" Callender, bass; Ed "Dinky" Morris, baritone sax; Clora Bryant, trumpet.

Jimmy and Jeannie Cheatham receiving the Grand Prix du Disque de Jazz award for "Jazz Record of the Year 1985" from the Hot Club de France. Carl Jefferson, president of Concord Records, presenting. Photo courtesy Rochelle Metcalf.

Sweet Baby Blues (1985), our first album for Concord Records. It included the hit song "Meet Me with Your Black Drawers On."

CHARLES McPHERSON

COURTESY CTS IMAGES: Lockjaw Davis

"MR. CREACH" "PAPA" JOHN CREACH
COURTESY GRACE BELL

MR. CLEANHEAD EDDIE "CLEANHEAD" VINSON
COURTESY GRACE BELL

Sweet Baby Blues Band
Guest Artists

Guest artists with the Sweet Baby Blues Band. *Clockwise from top left:* Charles McPherson, alto sax; Eddie "Lockjaw" Davis, tenor sax (photo courtesy CTS Images); Eddie "Cleanhead" Vinson, alto sax (photo courtesy Grace Bell); "Papa" John Creach, violin (photo courtesy Grace Bell).

GATEMOUTH BROWN
COURTESY GTSIMAGES

FRANK WESS

"HANK" CRAWFORD

Photo by GD Funk

"PLAS" JOHNSON

Guest artists with the Sweet Baby Blues Band. *Clockwise from top left:* Clarence "Gatemouth" Brown, guitar (photo courtesy CTS Images); Frank Wess, clarinet; Plas Johnson, sax (photo by GD Funk); Hank Crawford, sax.

The Sweet Baby Blues Band at the New Orleans Jazz and Heritage Festival, around 1990. *From left:* Rickey Woodard, tenor sax; Nolan Shaheed, trumpet; John Harris, drums; Dinky Morris, baritone sax; Curtis Peagler, alto sax; Jeannie Cheatham, piano and vocals; Jimmy Cheatham, bass trombone; George "Red" Callender, bass. Photo by Mike Gourrier.

Me and Gene Harris at the tribute to Carl Jefferson in Concord, California, around 1996.

Effluvia and Euphoria

. . . .

*T*he games began in earnest. Without a business manager, an influential agent, a road runner, a tax advisor, and all the usual infrastructure that underpins any successful group, the Sweet Baby Blues Band ventured forth.

The agent who booked us into the Blue Note in New York arranged for us to play there a second time. We were set to share the bill with Bobby "Blue" Bland and his band. Our agent found herself confronted by the agent hierarchy. The influential agents were mostly men. The club owners did not relish dealing with a woman agent. So the money offered to the Sweet Baby Blues Band was never enough. It paid for airfare and salaries, but not hotels. We used Jimmy's teacher salary to subsidize the band.

Week by week, I sweated bullets, trying to come up with money for hotel rooms. The deadline to leave for New York loomed closer, and still no money. Then the phone rang. "Hello, Mrs. Cheatham. I'm calling to see if I can interest you in a new Visa card." Just what I needed, a telemarketer!

"No," I replied, "the cards I have are at the limit." Some impulse prompted me to explain further. "We have a band, and subsidizing it is gettin' to be a bit more than we can handle." I sighed.

"You gotta band?" A new tone crept into her polished voice.

My ears perked up. I recognized that particular sound. "Yeah," I said, "we have a hit tune, 'Meet Me With Your Black Drawers On.'"

"That's my song! Lawd-a-mercy!" she shrieked. "Is it really you?"

"Yes! We're booked into the Blue Note in New York. Gonna be there with Bobby 'Blue' Bland . . ."

"Say no mo', sistah!" she intoned, "Say no mo'! Let the *church* roll on!"

The very next morning, Mr. Fed Ex knocked at our condo door. I opened the envelope, and out fell a new Visa card. It had a $5,000 limit. Eureka!

* * *

A young trumpet player, Jimmy Zollar, who had graced our jam-session stage, now worked at the huge New York Tower Records store. He took it upon himself to create a colorful display of our albums during our appearance at the Blue Note. Meanwhile, the cat who was supposed to take care of this type of thing finally showed up at the Blue Note near the end of our week-long gig. With him came a bunch of his friends from Long Island. They trooped into the club and wanted us to buy them a drink! Carl Jefferson's publicity department was paying this cat to cover the New York area, but we had to publicize ourselves. Effluvia!

Thanks to Jimmy Zollar, we succeeded in a modest way. He went on to star in Mercer Ellington's big band, among other stellar groups.

The Sweet Baby Blues Band stayed at a little hotel in the Village run by an African gentleman. "I know your music," he informed us. "I know you play *spirit* music." Jimmy and I looked at each other in wonder. The master drummer, fresh from his gig at the San Diego Wild Animal Park, had spoken those same words. The hotel manager continued, "I'll charge you the minimum amount that I can—in homage to your music."

We were overjoyed. And quite mystified by the whole sequence of events. Euphoria!

* * *

Al Williams, a fine drummer, ran a club called Birdland West, in Long Beach. The Sweet Baby Blues Band was set to play there on New Year's Eve. The show would be broadcast, coast-to-coast and farther off, by WBGO out of New Jersey. Becca Pulliam, a friend from Madison, headed up the coast-to-coast hook-up for the station's New Year's Eve jazz show.

"Baby Doll!" Jay McShann cried when we entered the club. There were hugs and smiles and handshakes all around. His group went on stage first, and we could tell he was having a little trouble with the young rhythm section. They had been hired to play with him, but had no idea how to play Kansas City style.

Our mentor, Papa Jo Jones, often complained to us in his latter years, "I can play with everybody, but can't *nobody* play with me!"

We used to wonder what he meant. After witnessing McShann's rhythm section, we were beginning to understand. In our time, we were expected to play all kinds of music and styles. In the 1980s and '90s, younger musicians proved to be narrowly focused. It was like the difference between being a good general-practice doctor and specializing in gnat's knees.

Jay, pro that he was, plowed relentlessly through his hits, dragging them along. They played "Confessin' the Blues" and others, and closed the show amid thunderous applause.

We took the stage and hit it hard right off with "Brand New Blues," and then went on down through our repertoire. Then, inspired, I started playing "After Hours," the piano solo composed by Avery Parrish, the pianist with Erskine Hawkins. The audience recognized the opening phrase and started applauding.

I was in the middle of the intricate solo, my head down, eyes closed, when all of a sudden a huge body came hurtling through the crowd. He shoved Jimmy aside, elbowed past Cat Daddy, our trumpet player, then threw his big butt on the piano stool beside me and began playing the upper register of the keyboard. Who else, but Mr. Jay McShann? He wanted some of that song—and he wanted it coast-to-coast! I couldn't hiss at him to get off the piano stool or cuss at him for interrupting my prize solo, because the eyes and the ears of the world were upon us. Good manners might have muzzled me, but my mind had plenty to say—all of it silent, but very nasty.

The band finally came in with the out chorus, and I kept trying to recapture the upper register, but Jay's big hands were busy plunking away. Finally, we ended the song.

The crowd went wild. A duet between Jeannie Cheatham and Jay McShann? Wow, what a show! They whistled and stomped. We went right into "Auld Lang Syne." It was midnight on the bandstand, and around the broadcast world. Jay grinned at me. "Baby Doll!" he cried, his gold tooth gleaming in the spotlight.

I said dryly, "Happy New Year, Jay McShann."

* * *

An avalanche of activity transpired between composing, arranging, recording, and playing festivals all over the United States. In fact, we had hardly any down time. Jimmy was still teaching at UCSD, and fortunately most festivals took place on weekends and during the summer months.

But there were offbeat forays into other areas that challenged and tantalized us.

Murder She Wrote, a popular television show starring Angela Lansbury, gave me a call. Jimmy's old trombone buddy, Streamline Ewing, was on the show and had recommended me. Since Jimmy was deep into his teaching schedule, I took the train up to Pasadena, where Stream and Vivian, his very attractive wife, picked me up and drove me to their home in Altadena, where I spent the night.

Early the next morning, Stream and I arrived on the set. Nervous and excited, I stood in an out-of-the-way spot and stared at all the activity swirling around us. Cameras, lights, costumed actors, equipment being moved from one place to another—a cacophony of sound made the tweeters in my ears retreat. I fantasized. Perhaps I'd be discovered and add to my career as a big-time movie piano player, like Hoagie Carmichael, Hazel Scott, or Oscar Levant, George Gershwin's friend. Soon I'd be sought after by bigwigs everywhere. I hugged myself at the thought.

Stream introduced me to some of the other musicians, among them Jake Porter and Billy Hadnot, who were obviously disturbed about being asked to play pallbearers in the scene.

"I'm not riding in that coffin!" was the consensus opinion upon our discovery of the long wooden box set up prominently beneath the lights, on a set that looked like a rustic old New Orleans church.

"Me neither!"

"Whoever weighs the least!"

We all laughed.

A slew of black actors milled around, getting ready to play mourners. I discovered that I had been hired as Olivia Cole's double. Now, Olivia, tall, slim and very light-skinned, was supposed to play the piano for the funeral service. Since she couldn't play a lick of piano, enter Jeannie Cheatham!

I looked at Streamline and exclaimed, "Either she gonna wear a whole lotta *very dark* Max Factor makeup, or I'm gonna wear a whole lotta *very light* Max Factor makeup!" I grinned at him. Streamline rubbed his hand over his mouth to muffle a snicker.

I soon received an answer to the color question. My fingers, hands, and arms up to my elbows were slathered in very light tan makeup. All day long I had to hold out my arms and walk around like a zombie. I got a retouch at lunchtime and also after I went to the john. The cameraman carefully avoided the rest of me as I played piano in my one big scene. So much for dreams of newfound fame in the world of film!

* * *

"Ev'rybody says you gotta lotta nerve, writing your own songs!" Chris Long complained to us as we prepared for our third album, *Homeward Bound*.

"Jesus, Chris, we wouldn't be here if we hadn't written 'Black Drawers'!"

"Oh . . ." His voice trailed off. He had a real dim idea of timing and the temperament of artists. This was not the first time he had called me long distance, completely nervous and negative, the night before we were to record.

Jimmy said it was due to his youth, that Chris was being pressured by other people. Right! Okay. But, no matter the reason, the result was the same. I got up on my hind legs and declared, "Look, don't call me at all if you don't have something good to say. That's it!"

Chris demurred. "Okay."

I wasn't done yet. I said, "Thank God for Ronn Gilbert! He sends me all kinds of material from Madison. As for the rest, it's mighty slim pickin's. That's why I write my own songs. Besides, why should we have to pay to use somebody else's songs when we can publish our own? Nobody in their right mind could argue against that!"

I was adamant. I felt powerful. I had finally sailed through menopause and there were no more sweats or sleeplessness or weakness. Only a surge of energy that I had never felt before! Unending energy and grit and single-mindedness and determination. Flexing the muscles of my mentality became pure joy.

We had called Mr. Eddie "Cleanhead" Vinson to be our guest artist on *Homeward Bound.* Texas-born, Cleanhead had the earthy, gritty personality that we loved. He was famous for having a big hit with Pete Johnson's "Cherry Red"; for "Cleanhead Blues," in which he made fun of his shiny bald head; for "Tune Up" and "Four," rollicking jazz tunes that we jammed on back at the old Sheraton sessions; and for a raunchy blues called "Kidney Stew." He played a brilliant bebop alto.

Cleanhead was an avid golfer. His wife complained, "I really believe he'd rather play golf than do anything else. Tho' he does love to garden."

"I should take some of that golf time an' maybe luck upon another hit," Cleanhead would ruefully admit. But then, off he would go to the closest golf course. Between tee times, Cleanhead and I recorded a duet on Duke Ellington's tune "Hello, Little Boy."

"Homeward Bound," the title tune of our third album, was composed in Buffalo during an intermission at a USO dance. It was the last gig Jimmy and I played with brother Jerry in the late '50s.

The glee club song was "Sometimes It Be's That Way." I wrote this tune because I always felt that the blues were as old as dirt and as new as tomorrow.

You hear young yuppies yellin'
"The blues just ain't for me!"
But if you drivin' a taxi
An' you got a PhD,
You got the blues, young yuppie—
Sometimes you have 'em ev'ry day!
There ain't no doubt about it—
Sometimes it be's that way!

* * *

We moved around the planet and passed through so many different time zones that often I would wake up with a start in the dark in a strange hotel room and not remember where I was.

My heart would pound, and my eyes would search for Jimmy and then finally fix on the TV screen. Most musicians keep the TV or radio on all night long. The familiar sounds keep us grounded and keep us from the frightful feeling of complete disembodiment, like floating somewhere in space, like a compass momentarily pointing in the wrong direction. Scary!

Then, whoosh! Reality would set in and I would mutter, "Oh, we're in Chicago—or Minneapolis—or Memphis." Then I'd roll myself into a ball and finally fall into a fitful sleep.

Many a musician has collided with a piece of hotel furniture and hurt something while going to the john in the middle of the night, thinking it was the hotel from the night before.

* * *

Papa John Creach was our choice for the next record, *Back to the Neighborhood*. He stood six feet tall and wore a newsboy cap at a rakish angle. His wiry frame with its stiff, gimpy leg would vibrate as he pulled music from his violin. He could bring tears to every eye, as he did on a beautiful ballad we recorded, "Call Me Darling." Papa John opened for the rock group Jefferson Airplane for years—young people adored him.

Papa John represented the prominence of the black fiddler throughout American history—especially during the era of slavery. Great-Gramma Lizzie filled our childish heads with tales of the slaves on the plantation of her youth, fiddlers who played minuets and reels, for weddings and at funerals—for slave and master alike.

"Stuff" Smith, Claude "Fiddler" Williams, and "Gatemouth" Brown are modern-day cats who fiddle.

Papa John wasn't the only star to contribute to *Back to the Neighborhood*.

Herman Riley played reeds and rose to great heights on this LP. He usually worked with Jimmy Smith, the famous jazz organist.

Clora Bryant, returning only for this recording, played a lovely flügelhorn solo on "In the Dark." Jimmy and I thought it only fair to include Clora because she had done lots of hard work on the road with the band, and deserved to be on this record. Snooky Young sat in as first trumpet.

Becca Pulliam of WBGO in New Jersey transcribed my piano solo on "Big Bubba's Back Rub Boogie Blues" for *Piano Stylist* magazine.

Bells!

I wrote a rousing treatise on a modern lament:

> *You work hard all yo' life, babe!*
> *Saved up all yo' loot—*
> *But now, you need a doctor to*
> *Take the wrinkles out yo' birthday suit!*

As for Cleanhead and Papa John, their biggest fans were their loyal and understanding wives. These women sat at a front table in each club, watching their husbands perform night after night, year after year. Their faces were always shiny and smiley, as if they were watching their men for the very first time. Doing what they love, loving what they do, they were always guaranteed one loyal fan—their loving wives.

Cleanhead and Papa John were part of a growing number of cats who gave up their bands and chose to go it alone from gig to gig, attaching themselves to local rhythm sections—for good or ill.

Papa John said, "He travels fastest who travels alone!"

Cleanhead commented wryly, "He maketh more money and getteth more gigs withouteth a band!"

Was this wit, or warning?

* * *

Sometimes musicians are their own worst enemies, but musicians who become booking agents often are the worst enemy of working musicians.

We always gave our all in our performances, priding ourselves on always bringing the people out of their seats. For us, a standing ovation became an exclamation point at the end of a joyful musical event. We enjoyed an excellent reputation, always on stage on time (and off!), no junkies or wine heads—everyone on their best behavior.

But we ran into a couple of club bookers who really broke tradition *and* taboo. One, especially weird, tried to poke holes of dissent in our little tight-knit group by showing some of the cats my payroll check and declaring that the weekly check was a nightly check, making the cats think that Jimmy and I were raking in dough. Despicable!

And then there was the one who kept trying to get hold of the deposit for the band and keep it as a commission. I always caught that booker before the plan could succeed.

Those times when former musicians tried to take advantage of us made me think of calling on Raunchy Rita and her black-cat bone! Or maybe making the culprit drink a cup of hot lard. Or even that punishment of punishments, Big Mama Thornton's be-all and end-all, a Mississippi camp beating! Aargh!

From Slavery to the White House

· · · · · · · · · · · · · · · · · ·

*W*hen a black family rises from slavery to the White House, it's enough to make you weep for joy. And we did.

Four people stood on a small stage in the bowels of the Labor Department building in Washington, D.C. The tallest person on the stage was my daughter's father, looking pleased as punch. The other three were barely five feet tall. One was M'Ma, beautifully dressed in one of her designer outfits, holding on to a Bible with both hands. The third person was Secretary of Labor Robert Reich, looking a little perplexed, tugging at the other end of the same Bible. The last was our daughter, Shirley, standing in the center, waiting to be sworn in as deputy assistant secretary of labor, Office of Federal Contracts and Compliances.

Robert Reich tugged at the Bible once more, trying to get M'Ma to release it so Shirley could place her hand on it. M'Ma was equally firm about holding on to this moment in history. Her chin was thrust forward, her lips had disappeared, clamped tight in determination, and her body had stiffened.

Reich sighed and turned to the assembled folks, smiled and announced, "Well, it looks like I'm going to have to swear in the whole family!" We, the whole family, stretched across one whole row of seats, cracked up with laughter. So did the other people there: colleagues, friends, senators, cousins, all there to witness this great event.

Mr. Reich turned to Shirley, took his end of the Bible bridge he shared with M'Ma, and said, "Will you place your hand on the Bible and raise your right hand?"

My mind raced back in time to a beautiful fall day over twenty years before when M'Ma, who had acquired her driver's license at over sixty years of age, drove Shirley and me out to visit Gramma Hattie in Springfield.

Harvest time was over, and all the farms were getting ready for the long winter's rest.

When we arrived at the old farmhouse, Gramma Hattie met us at the door, blue-gray eyes shining. She exclaimed, "Well, I thought you-all were in jail!" We all laughed as we trooped into her old-fashioned parlor with its patterned wallpaper and comfortable old chairs.

We sipped Alabama lemonade and munched cookies made from the 1-2-3-4 cake recipe and talked about the old days. Being there felt wonderful. My mind kept snapping photos to cherish and remember. Four generations of women in one room! Gramma Hattie, M'Ma, Shirley, and me.

Gramma seemed frail, but you could see the fire still burning in her eyes. She still sat up straight as an arrow! We talked about the white chickens, ducks, and geese, Gramma's big ol' gun, and Great-Gramma Lizzie's many adventures with Mr. Lincoln's Yankee white-trash soldiers. We laughed and laughed until M'Ma stood up abruptly and said, "Well, Mom, we have to go . . . but we'll be back soon!"

I was startled, and little Shirley didn't want to leave right then, but there was an urgency in M'Ma's voice. Then, looking down at Gramma Hattie, I realized that her shoulders had slumped and she seemed very fatigued. So we hugged her one last time and waved good-bye.

M'Ma kept her head turned as we drove away, but I saw the glint of tears in her eyes and knew in a flash that I would never see Gramma Hattie alive again. She went home to Jesus at the age of ninety-nine.

And now, here we were!

Shirley began her acceptance speech. "I am your policeman!" Her voice was strong and clear. She had worked so hard to earn the right to stand on that stage with the secretary of labor: Mount Holyoke, Harvard Law School (*cum laude*), National Women's Law Center, and, now, deputy assistant secretary of labor!

We all gathered on the roof of the Labor Department building for a reception. M'Ma shook as many hands in the reception line as did Shirley. My heart was so full I could hardly talk. My eyes glistened with unshed tears of joy.

Shirley's new office was decorated with photos of her in the White House meeting with President Clinton. Gazing at those photos, I felt great pride in Shirley, but more than pride was the realization of the long, long family journey from slavery to the White House.

Hush! Hush! Somebody callin' our names . . .

From slavery to the White House. My daughter, Shirley Jean Wilcher: "I am your policeman . . ." Washington, D.C., January 1994.

Tears of Sorrow

. . . .

Ms. Jeannie Cheatham, President
Jazz Society of Lower Southern California

Dear Jeannie:

I have just received word of the Jazz Society's generous gift for the Jazz Society Scholarship Fund in the Department of Music. Your activities through the years have enabled the department to enhance its jazz program in ways that otherwise would not have been possible. For that, and for this most recent manifestation of your support, we are most grateful.

Please convey my appreciation to the Board and to the members-at-large of the Jazz Society of Lower Southern California.

Sincerely,
Richard C. Atkinson
Chancellor

We were on the road with the Sweet Baby Blues Band so much that we decided to disband the Jazz Society of Lower Southern California. Provost and friend, John Stewart, helped us set up a permanent jazz scholarship for students at UCSD with the money in our treasury and matching funds from the university.

We were all so very proud. I was especially elated that the little jazz society, begun from a chance meeting with Brad Smith at the Sheraton where I was performing with the Mad Mexican, came to fruition with a gift that keeps on giving. Glory!

* * *

You need a permanent solution
To yo' temporary love affairs—
This live-in light housekeepin'
Ain't gonna get you any where!

The Sweet Baby Blues Band was sweet! We had so much fun in spite of the heavy hustle and bustle of life on the road and the struggle to maintain the needs of the band. Standing ovations became our trademark.

"Fooled 'em again!" Cat Daddy would exclaim as we ran off-stage to thunderous applause.

Rickey always chewed gum when he blew his horns. We never knew where he stowed it or why it never stuck to his mouthpiece. He'd slip off his shoes during his solos.

Curtis, whose feet were twice as long as Rickey's, snuck behind and exchanged his shoes for Rickey's. When Rickey finished his solo, he stepped back and slipped on Curtis's shoes. Rickey's face reflected total disbelief, as if his shoes had grown. We cracked up and struggled to keep playing.

Now, Red, that sly fox, would go from one to the other of us and collect small sums of money. "Hey," he would say, "let me have a quarter for a phone call." Pretty soon he had garnered quite a tidy sum. He would grin wickedly and the next day start all over again.

Cat Daddy kept up his share of pranks on stage, and he was really a good morale booster, standing behind the soloists, urging them on to greater heights. His own solos often included notes that were so high that they could be called stratospheric!

Dinky, on the other hand, was our band's penny-pincher. The other cats in the band would spend big bucks on their tuxedos and other attire. In fact, they tried to upstage each other in sartorial splendor. Dinky sent away to some warehouse in Chicago that sold tuxedos with all the trimmings for fifteen dollars!

"You cheap," the cats teased. "You sing like a canary! Cheep! Cheep!"

"No," Dinky replied. "Not cheap, frugal! The word is 'frugal'!"

Ironman was the most helpful and giving person in the band. He had his drums to hustle, but when we played big festivals, drums were supplied, so he needed only his drumsticks and cymbals. Freed of heavy burdens, Ironman would help the others with their things.

Of course, everything was not smooth sailing all of the time. I had to lecture the women hanging around the band. "Listen! I don't take sides between you and whomever. But I am *not* going to lose a good player for no *temporary* love affair! Okay?" They would nod, their eyes solemn.

Not one word registered with a certain young lady. In fact, one of the players, who shall remain nameless, contemplated throwing her over the ship's rail during a jazz cruise. Why she would choose the middle of an ocean as the ideal location to inform the cat that she was pregnant is a mystery. Maybe she imagined that a proposal would be immediate, followed by a romantic shipboard wedding performed by the captain.

We invited her to sit at our table—partly out of sympathy for her plight, partly because we didn't want her noising her troubles around the ship.

I wrote the tune "Permanent Solution to These Temporary Love Affairs" because of the pregnant lover who might have met her maker in the midst of a jazz cruise. We included the song on the record *Homeward Bound*.

The dynamics of the band didn't always go smoothly, either. Red had a habit of fiddling around when it was time to start the show. Now, I have never been late for a gig, or late to hit on time, in my entire life. It's a pride thing and a money thing.

We had taken our places on stage, the audience already silent in anticipation. "Red, it's time to hit. Are you ready?" I inquired. He kept fiddling with his music. "C'mon, we play the same opening song all the time," I whispered urgently. "Blues in the key of C . . ." He ignored me altogether.

I smiled to myself. Ahhh, I thought, Red's tryin' to pull a power train on Jeannie! Looks to me like old Reverend Uncle Frank is now standing in Red's shoes. It's his generation, old attitudes coming out in spite of everything we had accomplished together. "Red," I raised my voice, "are you ready?"

He looked up and looked at the cats who were staring at him, then out to the crowd. Then he turned to me, his face like thunder. "You bringin' me down in front of all these people? You a mutha-fucka!"

I couldn't believe my ears, but stayed cool. I said quietly, "But Red, I really can't be *that!*"

He stared at me, then slowly smiled. "You right, little mama! You really can't *be* or *do* that!" I immediately started playing the opening song. All the cats were laughing so hard they could hardly make their entrances.

Despite our differences, we always had big fun on the bandstand. Our motto became "Nobody goes home feelin' bad!"

* * *

The volatile relationship between Chris Long and Carl Jefferson came to a head, and Chris resigned. He was a good producer for our first four albums, and we are eternally grateful to him for bringing Jefferson down to the Sheraton to check us out.

Enter Nick Phillips, a working jazz musician.

As soon as Chris resigned, Carl Jefferson decided that he would personally produce our next record. He flew down to Los Angeles with Nick as his assistant. He was a nice-looking young man and really knew how to schmooze.

"He has a great temperament for our freewheeling, unorthodox style of recording," Jimmy declared.

"Yeah, he's pretty cool, calm, and collected. And he plays good trumpet," I replied. Nick had studied Snooky's style.

During the recording session, Carl seemed real jumpy and abrupt. He kept coming out of the recording booth while we were working on a fast boogie called "Messin' Round with the Boogie."

The band had its own method of recording fast tunes. We played it, then pushed the tempo up faster and faster until it was smoking. Then we told the sound engineer, "We ready. Roll tape!"

Carl popped out of the booth and marched over to the piano in the middle of this pushing-up-the-tempo and said, "Uh, Jeannie, I think the tempo is too fast." The band exchanged amazed looks. We were only halfway there. I didn't say a word, just counted off again, a little faster. "Uh . . . uh . . ." He became more insistent, and repeated, "I think it's too fast. Nobody can play it any faster."

I stopped playing, tipped my head back, and stared at the ceiling. I informed him, "I think I'm beginning to get a headache. When I get a headache, I just don't know *what's* gonna happen! I usually go *crazy!*"

Carl Jefferson took one look at me and fled back to his hotel, leaving the recording session in Nick's capable hands. The song went off without a hitch.

Gatemouth Brown joined us as guest artist. Born in Louisiana, he had played guitar with Jay McShann and T-Bone Walker and had made many award-winning records. He and I traded fiery fours between guitar and piano with the whole band galloping along behind us. Fire and smoke! Gatemouth said wistfully, "I used to have a good band just like this . . ."

Jimmy, as usual, tailored wonderful arrangements for all the songs, and the glee club sang with great gusto on "Raunchy Rita," a song I wrote as a tribute to a red-headed ex–street walker who changed her lifestyle and ended up as a maid in our hotel in Seattle.

Rita always sat on Curtis's bed when she made up his room, pushing her hotel uniform up high on her thighs as she crossed her legs, smoked a cigarette, and told tales of her past life and of her one true love, Dirty Red, a pimp of dubious character. She was from New Orleans and offered to hoodoo any of the band's enemies.

We finished up the recording date with Nick at the helm, and *Luv in the Afternoon* was born. Then we all went to the Spaghetti House to celebrate. The wrap party included Buddy Collette, Stanley Dance, and his wife, Helen, who often came to our recording sessions. Good food! Good drinks! Good music! Good friends!

* * *

Our strange relationship with Carl Jefferson continued. Sometimes he would call our home, or even our hotel when we were the road, and I would pretend not to know who he was.

"This is your pal," he would announce.

"Who?"

"Your pal, Carl!"

"Carl who?"

"Carl Jefferson!" The voice began to sound testy.

"Oh, hey! What's happenin', Mr. Jefferson?"

"I *told* you to call me *Carl.*" He always laughed at the exchange and it was great fun for me.

But make no mistake! Jefferson and the Reverend Uncle Frank were brothers under the skin—profound plutocrats! They believed in the natural order of things. And for Carl Jefferson, that natural order went like this:

Record Executive
Producer
Engineer
Dog
Cat
Musician

In the "Brave New World," it all will be reversed.

* * *

M'Ma taught us how to live. M'Da taught us how to die.

He quit drinking cold turkey. He became the father of my earliest years —caring, gentle, funny, and warm. He even started singing again: "My

Bonnie Lies over the Ocean," "Red Sails in the Sunset," and "I'm Thinking Tonight of My Blue Eyes."

But the time came when he could no longer sing. He lay in the hospital with throat cancer and still whispered to M'Ma, "Lizzie, don't spend all the money on me. Make sure you have enough for yo'self."

He received an award from the State of Ohio for giving more blood to the Red Cross than anybody else.

Before M'Da was admitted to the hospital for the last time, Jimmy and I traveled back to Akron for a family conference. We all agreed that M'Da should not receive heroic resuscitation.

As Jimmy and I got ready to leave for the airport, M'Da gave me a hug and said, "So long, doll! Don't forget to take your pap smear and mammogram." He had given me the same advice before he became ill. As our taxi pulled away slowly, he walked beside it and said through the open window, "Well, I'm going in the house now. I have to see what my bride is doing!" He was eighty-seven years old.

* * *

My sister Charlotte's husband, a grand fellow, gentle and handsome, died shortly after M'Da. Considerably older than Charlotte, I guess his death was no surprise to her. Jimmy and I came off the road for his funeral, and M'Ma reminded us, "You know things happen in threes for good or ill!"

We all nodded solemnly and crossed our fingers behind our backs.

* * *

"I am the Alfalfa and the Omega!"

The tears dried up in our eyes as we looked in amazement at the small figure of the preacher standing in front of us with the Bible upside down in his brown hands.

His dark suit was ill-fitting and wrinkled, the too short pants showing white socks drooping down his ankles and onto unshined, run-over-at-the-heels brown shoes. His wrinkled white shirt was too large, and the collar fought the constraints of his black string tie.

"I said," he intoned once more, "I am the Alfalfa *and* the Omega!"

The whole family had gathered in a small musty funeral parlor in Buffalo for the last performance of my brother Jerry.

He had had bone cancer, but—thank God!—had taken himself home to Jesus in his sleep at the Veterans Administration Hospital and did not have to go through the pain and ravages of the full run of the disease.

His wife (the successor to Red the Terrible) insisted on making all the arrangements. She told us that she had a fifty-voice choir and a dynamic preacher at her beck and call. But upon our arrival in Buffalo it became obvious that none of this was true.

In fact, my sister Jo-Anne (who had inherited Mr. Riley, my first piano teacher) drafted herself to play piano and my brother Ricky to sing, in his beautiful baritone voice, "His Eye Is on the Sparrow" so that all would not be lost.

Afterward, we all felt that Jerry would have enjoyed the service, having been in show business and all, and having played behind Redd Foxx and Scatman Crothers.

Looks like things really do happen in threes. Way down in my deepest sorrow, part of me remembered that even the lowly blues song expresses itself in threes.

Lawd! Lawd! Lawd!

Blues like Jay McShann

. . . .

Jo-Anne's husband, after years of misbehaving, finally left for parts unknown. So, M'Ma said, "Well, looks like we are merry widows."

Charlotte agreed, "At least, two merry widows and one grass widow." A grass widow is one whose man is missing but still on *top* of the ground.

Stoicism and resilience runs through the veins of all the women in the family. After a while, M'Ma, Charlotte, and Jo-Anne started traveling all over. They came to Chicago when we played the jazz festival, opening for Miles Davis. They were so smartly dressed that when we returned to the hotel, there they were on the evening news!

The Sweet Baby Blues Band was invited to play the Floating Jazz Festival aboard the SS *Norway*. I hated all the paperwork, passports, schedules, and lists of musicians' names, but I accepted. The promoter told me, "Jay McShann is going to be on the bill. You two could play duets!"

Those were magic words—a whole week with my idol! A whole week with great musicians such as Toshiko Akyoshi's big band, Lew Tabackin, Al Grey's group, Bobby Durham, Terry Gibbs, Buddy DeFranco, Milt Hinton, Red Norvo, Jon Faddis, Keter Betts, Jackie Williams, and pianists Junior Mance, Kenny Baron, Derek Smith, John Campbell, Ralph Sutton, Jay McShann—and me, Jeannie Cheatham! Huzzah!

And M'Ma, Charlotte, and Jo-Anne! Along with two thousand other passengers. Heaven!

The crowds coming to see the Sweet Baby Blues Band were overflowing. We were one of the hits of the festival.

We moved around the ship after hours, sitting in on jam sessions and eating. "This food reminds me of the North Sea Festival in Holland!" Jimmy exclaimed.

M'Ma went around telling everyone who would listen, "I taught her everything she knows!" People took hundreds of photos of M'Ma and her three daughters, all dressed in outrageous red.

Daytime on the deck, the musicians had to sit at tables and sign autographs and sell records. Jo-Anne and Charlotte helped us sell beaucoup records.

I kept trying to pin Jay McShann down as to when we would play duets, but he just grinned, his gold tooth gleaming, and looked away. Finally, we ended up in one of the little theaters where the piano summit was about to begin. I said to him, "All right, Jay, when do we play?"

He was sitting beside Ralph Sutton, the last of the whorehouse piano players, a really great musician. "We ain't gonna play together!" Jay's gold tooth disappeared along with his smile, "I'm gonna play with Ralph." Ralph looked away.

I was stunned. I had been promised this event, and I felt totally betrayed. Besides, didn't that big buddha invade my space and my solo without my permission—on a coast-to-coast radio broadcast? I walked away as the piano summit began. My mind was filled with mayhem and murder.

One by one, the giants of piano played duets and solos. My turn came, and I said to myself, So far nobody has played any blues, and I'm playing *before* Jay McShann. As I sat down at the baby grand piano, I felt the adrenaline running wild, doubly so because of the world-class pianists sitting in the audience and because I was still furious with Jay Hootie McShann.

I checked out the audience. In the back of the hall and filling the balcony was a big crowd of people from the jazz societies of Chicago and Detroit. I sensed they were restless, and right then I knew what to play. When I started the trill in the key of G, the audience grew silent. I played "After Hours" as I had never played it before.

I heard one of the pianists near the front of the audience exclaim, "How does she *do* that?" The answer, "I don't know, man!"

When I finished the song, I took a long time sitting at the piano, head bowed, before I got up and faced the audience. The folks in the Chicago and Detroit seats went berserk. Shouted comments, cheers, and applause came in waves up to the stage.

I stared at Jay McShann as I walked off the stage and thought, "Take that!" I knew whatever he played he wouldn't be able to top it. And I was right!

* * *

Our next record was called *Basket Full of Blues*, and Frank Wess was our special guest. Frank was born in Kansas City, so he knew just what to do on the record. He had done it all, played with Josephine Baker, Count Basie, Toshiko's band, Nat Cole, Frank Sinatra, Dizzy Gillespie, and many, many more. On top of talent, he had a great sense of humor.

On this album, the glee club sang the sequel to "Black Drawers," an admonition not to boogie with yo' black drawers *off!*

I also wrote a heartfelt song: "All I Wanna Do Is Play the Blues like Jay McShann." It was nominated for song of the year by the W. C. Handy Blues Music Award committee, and the record was picked by the Jazz Scene of Oregon's critics' poll.

Best of all, Jay McShann's daughter called me from Kansas City. She told me that whenever Jay picked up his granddaughters in his car, he was plagued by this request, "Play your song, Granddaddy! Play your song!" And play it he would—"Blues like Jay McShann" pouring from the tape player in his car, over and over and over again.

The best revenge is sweet success!

* * *

Lord, I cannot tell a lie
Cross my heart, Lawd, hope to die!
But there's been too many goodbyes
In my life—

Basket Full Of Blues was the last record for Red Callender. His tumor came back, and his wife, Mary Lou, threw one last birthday party for him.

I called. They put Red on the phone, and he said, "I wondered when you were gonna call, kid. I'm getting ready to check outta here!"

"All right, Red," I said, a lump growing in my throat.

"I'm gonna miss you, kid." The deep voice faltered.

"Take it easy, Red."

"Goodbye, kid."

Mary Lou gave the most wonderful memorial for him. A marvelous painting formed the backdrop, and Clora read one of her epic poems. Buddy Collette led a group of musicians. They played special music, Red's tunes.

Goodbye, gentle giant.

* * *

Basket Full Of Blues was Curtis Peagler's last album also.

He called me one day in December. "I might not be able to play the gig New Year's Eve."

"Why not?"

"Well, I have to have an operation to repair my bypass. I'm gonna pick up my sister from the airport in a few minutes. She's coming in from Cincinnati." My heart sank. Curtis never complained, so I knew this was serious business. He went on. "There's a guy named Louis Taylor. He'll be a good alto player for the group. He's a good musician and he has a good heart." He gave me Louis's phone number. "Jeannie, I'm gonna tell you something. If I think I can't play my horn after this operation, I'm not comin' out!" He was vehement. "I want you and Jimmy to promise me. If I don't come out, I don't want nobody to do a benefit for me!"

"Don't worry!" I replied, my steady voice belying the tears in my eyes. "You can bet that Jimmy and I will never be part of any benefit, and the Sweet Baby Blues Band won't either!"

At around midafternoon of December 19, 1992, Curtis Peagler's sister called. "He's gone . . ."

At his memorial, his wife came up to me. I hugged her, wordless. Finally she said, "Jeannie, whatever are you going to do without him?"

I had no idea. Curtis had been as much a brother to me as brother Jerry. We knew each other from the old Ohio days. We exchanged recipes. He loved Jimmy and always sat beside him at the bar after the gigs. More than a drinking buddy, he would inquire, "Are you all right, boss?"

We both had played for Britain's queen—Toronto for me and London for Curtis, with the Basie band. I felt numb. I had no tears. A block of ice had formed around my heart. At midnight, the ice melted and the tears came at last.

> *A broken heart can make you cry,*
> *But keep on beating,*
> *Lawd, till you die—*
> *You know there's been too many goodbyes*
> *In my life!*

Their music will live forever.

* * *

There was trouble in the lowlands! I know the angel Gabriel was only too glad to greet his new musical guests in heaven, but it left a huge hole in the Sweet Baby Blues Band.

We had Nolan Smith (Shaheed), the venerable Snooky Young, Ironman Harris, Dinky Morris, and Charles Owens, tenor and baritone saxes.

Richard Reid took Red's place on bass. I promptly nicknamed Richard

"Roughhouse," because he was a huge cat and an ex-marine. I'd look out at the audience and say, "If you-all don't behave, I'll let Roughhouse *fall* on all of you." Roughhouse plays more in tune than almost any bass player presently on the scene.

Louis Taylor took Curtis's chair. Rickey Woodard had already replaced Jimmy Noone. Louis was a good player, brash and brilliant and young. He played all the reeds and the flute.

Herman Riley rescued us many times. He could play any style and many different instruments. Most of all, he was a world-class musician with a code of honor. If he said he would be there, he would be there!

"We've got a new record to make," Jimmy said, "but we have a *real* problem. We have to figure out how not to call too much attention to the line between the old band and the new band."

"Yeah," I agreed, "it sure wouldn't be fair to the new cats to be compared by some critic. And it sure won't help to remind people that so many of the cats have died. All our gigs might turn into memorial services."

Cat Daddy, his mischievous eyes wide with mock horror, cracked, "Well, I wonder who's next?"

Weeks went by. The deadline for the new record grew closer and closer. We kept working on the material. Jimmy stayed up nights, arranging. He had to revamp the open, freewheeling style we used before, tighten up the music, and write more ensembles, since some of the younger musicians were not yet used to making up riffs on the spot in the recording studio.

Riffs are a very important part of the Kansas City style. Riffs set up the call-and-response magic of the music, mimicking the old-time preachers and their exuberant flocks.

We also kept working on the list of musicians who might be available to play with us. I suggested, "How about Red Holloway? He can play the mess out the blues and play fast jazz. He'd be a great guest artist."

"He's in Europe," Jimmy replied.

"How about Houston Pearson? He plays with Etta James. Remember, they were on the same bill with us at the Blue Note in New York. He's fabulous and certainly knows the ropes." Houston was all booked up.

We needed someone who could set souls on fire. Someone who had hung out in church when he was small and had hung out in joints when he was grown. We looked at each other. "Hank Crawford!" we yelled together. We had played Hank's record "From the Heart" at intermissions all through the Sheraton days.

In response to our call, Hank said, "When do you want me?" A man of few words, he played his alto the same way. Born in Memphis, the home of Beale Street and the blues, his style was not of the scattershot repartee of the city slicker, but reminiscent of the emotion-driven rhetoric of a Martin Luther King.

In the recording studio, listening to the playback, Jimmy and I shared a moment of complete satisfaction. "Hank Crawford is a musician in complete control of an almost forgotten art—communication!" I declared. "He and Fat Head Newman and other Ray Charles alumni have *IT!*"

"He sure brought *IT* to this recording session!" came the reply.

Blues and the Boogiemasters was a good heart-filled CD full of angst and life and love songs, and, most of all, it sure wasn't Stravinsky. It was *soul*.

We waited for the reviews.

In my book, Jeannie and Jimmy Cheatham and the Sweet Baby Blues Band can do no wrong.

—NANCY ANN LEE, *Jazz and Blues Report*

With no imitators in sight, the Sweet Baby Blues Band remains in a class by itself.

—SCOTT YANOW, *Cadence: The Review of Jazz & Blues: Creative Improvised Music*

Run with us, Jesus!

My prayer was answered.

ABC: Around the World, Beyond Betrayal, Celebrations

· · · · · · · · · · · · · · · · · · · ·

*S*enior lecturer with security of employment, emeritus.

That is an impressive title for a little brown boy with great big dark eyes, his football uniform under one arm, trombone case in the other, leaning against the blustery blowing winds and snows of Buffalo, New York, trudging miles to take his music lessons.

This is my roommate, my love, Jimmy, who retired from the University of California–San Diego, located in La Jolla, in 1993, and was immediately called back to active duty. No more lectures. No more faculty meetings. Only his real love: culling music from the young people in the jazz ensemble.

"Now I have more time to write music and travel with you and the Sweet Baby Blues Band," Jimmy declared.

This is my roommate, my man, who still says, "I love you" every day and compliments my cooking, always says "thanks" and "please" and "Baby, you sure look *good!*" Sometimes we still talk until break of day about anything and everything.

Sippie Wallace sang, "Don't Advertise Yo' Man," but I'm not worried. When I sing "Somebody Go' Get Killed!" I am not joking. "Nobody better mess with my man—nobody!"

He is Professor Jimmy Cheatham, senior lecturer with security of employment, emeritus!

* * *

I have a hard time remembering turning sixty in the year of our Lord, 1987. In fact, I still feel a little dim about turning sixty-six in the year of Jimmy's elevation to an emeritus, 1993.

We traveled above the earth in airplanes and performed above people and their problems on elevated stages so much that we were literally living in another world.

Winging our way over the earth, Dinky, Ironman, Jimmy, and I were heading back to San Diego one morning. Ironman observed, "Man, we been a whole lotta places!"

He was right. We'd just been to Canada, from Victoria, British Columbia, over to Toronto for the Du Maurier festivals.

"Do you remember the time in Toronto," Jimmy replied, "when Red Callender stood under that huge mural of Louis Armstrong and himself at eighteen years old? Man, it gave me chills 'cause Red was then almost eighty!" Jimmy had always been aware of history in the making.

"Let's see," I said, counting off the cities on my fingers, "Billings, Montana; the Syracuse, New York, festival; Kansas City Jazz Fest; Las Vegas at the Four Queens; the Heavenly Ski Resort on Lake Tahoe, where Dinky went to the hospital cause his asthma couldn't take the thin air. And the University of Maryland at College Park."

"Playboy!" we all chimed in at once.

"Three times," I added, "with Bill Cosby as MC. And that party at the Playboy Mansion with all those bunnies—even in the afternoon!" I made a face. The men laughed.

"That long, long trip to New Zealand," I continued, "where the sound man drank up all our cognac an' passed out, but we made music anyway."

"Minneapolis," Ironman joined in, "that was mellow."

"Yeah, we each had an apartment with a spiral staircase winding up to the bedrooms." I smacked my lips. "An' the best bacon I ever tasted in my life!"

"Birdland West, Long Beach, and Kimball's East in San Fran," Jimmy rolled his eyes. "They really rushed us around up there."

"Blake Edwards. That was beyond cool!"

"Oh, yeah."

Edwards, movie mogul producer of the *Pink Panther*, heard Jimmy's arrangement for the Sweet Baby Blues Band's rendition of "C. C. Ryder" on the radio and loved it. The night of his birthday party, his wife, Julie Andrews, the star of *The Sound of Music*, surprised him with *us*. Jimmy grinned as we all reminisced about that big-time Hollywood party. "Awesome!"

"How about the Lifetime Achievement Award from the Los Angeles Jazz Society?" Ironman was proud.

"It made my day that Shirley flew out to watch us get that award." I was kinda proud of that award, myself.

"Now, that was a hoot," Jimmy added, "Louis Bellson was the tribute cat. And Billy May got the award for composer-arranger." Jimmy always kept track of other arrangers.

"Best of all," I laughed, "some of those cats that said we set music back forty years were there too. Now ev'rybody an' his *mama* are recording the blues!"

"Well, we played our *asses* off!" Dinky always cussed, even though he had a degree in sociology from Loyola University.

"How about that place where they picked us up in a limo?"

"Utah."

"And we only drove half a block to the gig!" Gales of laughter.

The thought of Utah brought silence after the laughter. Our faces turned grim. The Sweet Baby Blues Band had been invited to give a series of clinics and concerts in Utah. We planned to appear twice a year for five years. The series of clinics would pay really good money. We were excited because a lot of the cats in the band were teachers or had taught school, and we thought the clinics presented an opportunity to expand jazz through the school systems of the western states.

The Los Angeles–based cats met us in Utah with the news: "Rickey didn't show up!" We stood around in the airport, hoping he would be on the next plane, but no dice. We kept calling his number in LA. No answer. Finally, we gave up and went to the school.

We played the concert without the tenor. Even so, the clinic went very well. However, the headmaster was really upset to see only seven musicians when he had expected eight. He demanded some of the money back and insisted that he be reimbursed for Rickey's airfare. Disenchanted and disagreeable, he canceled the proposal for the whole five-year deal!

Rickey never explained his absence. In the midst of our in-flight reminiscences, we were still trying to figure out what had happened.

"Damn if I know! I heard he had another gig."

The other cats in the band were contacted by famous musicians who thought Rickey could succeed on an international basis. "We gotta lotta calls from back East, telling us to help Rickey get hold of his appointment book. That's God's truth!"

Jimmy closed his eyes. "Papa Jo Jones said the talent was always bigger than the person."

"Well, Rickey sure messed up a good deal! Not just for us, but for future jazz groups tryin' hard to open up new venues for the music." I sighed. "I don't wanna think about it . . ."

"I played with junkies who wouldn't have pulled that," Dinky sniffed. We all ordered a cool one, except Dinky, who was a successful recovering alcoholic.

A toast from Jimmy: "Never above you—never below you—always beside you!"

* * *

"It's the end of an era," Jimmy said quietly.

Carl Jefferson went to heaven in 1995. We were honored to be a part of a huge tribute to him along with eighty-three other musicians: Toshiko Akiyoshi, Howard Allen, Ruby Braff, Ray Brown, Kenny Burrell, Charlie Byrd, Frank Capp, Rosemary Clooney, Herb Ellis, the Gene Harris Quartet, Rob McConnell, Red Holloway, Marian McPartland, Pancho Sanchez, Mel Tormé, Frank Wess, Gerry Wiggins, Rickey Woodard, Ken Peplowski, and many others. Boy, what a camp meeting!

It was recorded.

I sang Pete Johnson's "Cherry Red," and Jimmy and Sweets Edison played solos on the song. I wore an outrageous cherry red silk outfit.

Louis Van Taylor

Rickey Woodard

"THE NEW SWEET BABY BLUES BAND"

RICHARD A. REID

CHARLES OWENS

The new Sweet Baby Blues Band. *Clockwise from top left:* Louis Van Taylor, alto sax; Rickey Woodard, tenor sax; Charles Owens, tenor and baritone sax; Richard Reid, bass.

ERNIE FIELDS JR

NOLAN SMITH SHAHEED
TRUMPET

"THE NEW SWEET BABY BLUES BAND"

HERMAN RILEY

MARSHALL HAWKINS

More new Sweet Baby Blues Band. *Clockwise from top left:* Nolan Smith "Cat Daddy" Shaheed, trumpet; Ernie Fields, Jr., clarinet, bass clarinet, and baritone sax; Marshall Hawkins, bass; Herman Riley, tenor sax.

Me and Jimmy with
Tom Bradley, mayor of Los Angeles.
We received the Lifetime Achievement Award from the Los Angeles Jazz
Society, 1995. Photo by Donna Zweig.

Louie Bellson and me at the Los Angeles Jazz Society's Lifetime
Achievement Award ceremony, 1995.

Cover of *Living Blues* magazine, September/October 1990. (Sold out all copies.)

Jimmy and Jeannie Cheatham

Jimmy Witherspoon

Jay McShann

Big Jay McNeely

Count Basie and the Blues

Me and Benny Carter (alto sax) featured in a promo for *Marian McPartland's Piano Jazz*, a prestigious radio series. 1990.

All the Evans women on the SS *Norway* having big fun, around 1995. *Left to right:* M'Ma, Charlotte, Jo-Anne, and me.

Dorothy Donegan, the Duchess. My pal. Photo courtesy Gail R. Jacobson.

Livin' in the Nineties

. . . .

Thirty years we partied!
But, now all the drinkin's done
Lord, we livin' in the nineties, people
What do we do for fun?

"Jeannie Cheatham!" The voice came crackling over the phone. "What *do* we do for fun?" It was the voice of Frank Wess, our guest artist from *Basket Full of Blues*. Frank always amazed me because he was one of a few musicians who truly listened to, remembered, and sang my lyrics. Frank chortled, "And just who *is* the cat so crooked he could sleep in a slide trombone?"

"That's 'Heaven or Hell Blues' an' no, it *ain't* Jimmy!" I retorted.

My love was full of wit and humor, but relentless when it came to re-hearsing a band. We were from the so-called "old school." We just didn't tolerate slackers or sluggards when it came to our way of life or our music. The old-school cats kept tabs on cats who missed a date without sending a competent replacement, or who were late.

Jimmy always explained to his students, "They'd give you a chance to fix things, but after that you are SOL. They pass the word along, and no one ever calls you again!"

Cats were calling us from all over the country. "Hey, Cheathams," each boasted, "I play the blues!" One complained bitterly, "I am the blues." Every one of them wanted to be our guest artist on future records.

Grover Mitchell, our old bandleader from New York City and now leader again of the Count Basie band, called, "Hi, Cheathams!"

"What's happening, Grover?"

"You-all are what's happening, that's what's happening! I hear you cats on radios all across the country."

Chico Hamilton gave sage advice. "Enjoy your fame. It doesn't last."

Merrilee Trost arranged a piano duet with Marian McPartland and me for her *Piano Jazz Series*. "Two piano chicks hanging out in a studio."

I phoned M'Ma and reported, "We melted into each other's styles really easy. Right from the jump!"

M'Ma sounded impressed. "Just think! She came all the way from England to play jazz music." Then my mother summed everything up in her own inimitable fashion. "Well, after all, you took your first piano lessons from an Englishman, so . . ."

"Er, Ma! It's not that easy . . ."

M'Ma stood her ground. "Looks like since you played in church and all those juke places and honky-tonks, she had to lean more your way than you had to lean her way!"

"But, Ma . . ."

"But me no buts!" M'Ma always had the last word.

I truly enjoyed many memorable moments doing that show with Marian McPartland. It was a gas!

* * *

Amid all the ruckus and reviews and running around the world, we found time to write and arrange new tunes for our last record for Concord. The record company now had a new management team, but Nick Phillips guided us through *Gud Nuz Bluz*.

"Boy, oh, boy! When you cats ask somebody to be your guest an' come an' play music, you cats ain't jokin'!" exclaimed Plas Johnson, a handsome gentleman who hailed from Louisiana. "You cats stomp!"

We laid down a steamy version of "Careless Love" and worked it into a medley with an original I wrote called "That Ain't Right." And Plas and the cats took no prisoners.

Plas was the tenor player heard 'round the world playing Henri Mancini's "Pink Panther," the theme from the movie of the same name. Plas also played on the sound track to *Lady Sings the Blues* and worked on staff for Merv Griffin's television show. A quiet, somewhat reserved man until he picked up his horn, he then morphed into a fierce and fiery soloist.

For this record, Jimmy and I wrote a tribute to Curtis Peagler, "Mr. C. P." We wove themes from his special solos together into a soulful tapestry. "I miss him every day!" I told Ironman, who nodded and looked away. Richard Reid looked solemn, also. Richard was rock-steady and always played in tune on his bass.

Charles Owens again played a big part on the CD. And so did Snooky Young and Nolan Shaheed, whose soaring trumpet never missed. Rickey (temporarily back in the fold) always sounded great. Louis Taylor on alto "blew snakes"—so much so that Plas whispered to me, "Who's the cat on the alto?"

"Curtis found him for us before he passed."

"Well, he sure plays great lead alto!"

Dinky was not on the record. The asthma that had plagued him for so much of his life finally took its toll, and he joined Curtis and Red Callender and Jimmy Noone at that great jam session in heaven. There are no words for missing someone who was truly family.

"Gud nuz! Gud nuz!" The glee club sang loud and lustily.

> *We do anything we choose!*
> *Gud nuz! Gud nuz! We*
> *Ain't got nothin' to lose!*

Our guardian angel did not linger long. Ernie Fields, Jr., came into our lives to take Dinky's place, and what a great asset he turned out to be! He played both baritone sax and bass clarinet. A solid-looking man with a permanent smile on his lips, his costumes were always colorful, down to his red high-top sneakers.

"You know," I gleefully informed Jimmy, "he and his father, Ernie Fields, Senior, are the only father and son team inducted into the Hall of Fame."

"Oh, that's impressive." Jimmy looked a little wistful.

I could always tell when he was thinking of our son, Jonathan, so I hurriedly continued, "Ernie conducts for Ray Charles and Aretha Franklin. The same for Lionel Hampton, Mercer Ellington, and Fred Wesley."

Jimmy's mood grew lighter, and he smiled, "Well, one thing, he's from the old school in spite of his age. He's got respect and never complains about bringin' both those giant instruments to the gigs!"

* * *

There is no way on earth to describe the emotion that overcame my whole being when I saw my *own eyes* staring back at me from our very first magazine cover. There we were, sitting side by side, Jimmy's signature cap riding above his usual broad smile, a long silver mesh tie lighting up his black jacket and shirt. There I was in another outrageous, red silk taffeta, mutton-sleeve outfit, a many-ringed hand draped over Jimmy's shoulder. *Living Blues* was the name of the magazine, and Jim Trageser authored the nice minicapsule of our lives.

"There's our names at the top of a list of top cats!" I finally found my voice.

"Oh, my goodness!" Jimmy exclaimed, "There's Jimmy Witherspoon, Big Jay McNeely, Count Basie . . ."

I interrupted. "Look! There's a piece on Jay McShann! How strange that we end up in the same magazine . . ." my voice faltered. "Wonder of wonders."

M'Ma told me, "Ev'ry decade brings its own special problems and its own special joys!" These days of livin' in the nineties were not "salad days," they were the main course.

Good food, good meat, good God, let's eat!

* * *

Dorothy Donegan, Gail Jacobson (my friend from my childhood days in Akron), and I often talked on the phone. But this time, instead of Dorothy laughing and joking and asking me about gigs in San Diego, she said, "Jeannie, I'm not feeling so hot!"

"What's the matter?"

"Well, pal, I'm shittin' all over the house!"

"What?"

"I can't hold my bowels."

"Have you called yo' doctor?"

"He will only want me to go to a hospital, and I don't wanna do that."

When Dorothy hung up I called Gail and told her what Dorothy had said. Gail immediately went into action, and Dorothy was admitted to a hospital.

I called M'Ma and described Dorothy's symptoms. "She's a dead woman." M'Ma's words cut through me like a hot knife. "She needs attention, right now, if only to make her comfortable and get her affairs in order."

After a very short stay, Dorothy insisted on leaving the hospital. I phoned her, "Hey, pal, how ya doin'?"

"I need a gig," she complained petulantly. "I need some action. I told those people at the Smithsonian that I need five thousand dollars to do their interview."

"What!" I exploded. "They usually pay an honorarium, not 5,000 smackers."

"Well, I don't care. That's what I want." Dorothy was not used to taking no for an answer.

I had known Dorothy since the '60s, when Papa Jo Jones introduced us at the Embers in New York. She was one of the world's greatest living pianists. Art Tatum admired *her*. So did Vladimir Horowitz. Dorothy was a prodigy, born in Chicago in the 1920s, but grew up to be given the American Jazz Master award and to lecture at Northeastern University and Harvard.

I became really upset with her attitude. "Listen, you need to be in the record book in the Smithsonian! Not for yourself, but for the people comin' after you—to inspire them to be *better* than you!"

A lightbulb came on in my brain. "Do you want Marian McPartland to be there an' you *not* there?"

"Marian McPartland!" she sputtered, "if *she's* in the Smithsonian, I better do it!"

"You surely should." No longer angry, I aimed to seal the deal.

"You call them for me, okay?" she suggested. Then asked, "You gonna be there at the interview?"

"Yes, I'll be there, pal."

It worked. I knew in my heart of hearts the competitive nature of this woman would take over and propel her into doing the right thing. I called the young man at the Smithsonian who had contacted Dorothy and told him, "If you want Dorothy Donegan's life story, you gonna have to put on yo' runnin' shoes!" I knew she didn't have much time. And so it was.

The man from the Smithsonian flew in from Washington, D.C., and Gale, Jimmy, and I met him in Beverly Hills. For three days he and I wheedled, prodded, and pulled her story from Dorothy.

She had been placed in a skilled nursing center, and we had to stop taping every time someone called a doctor over the intercom. Bells rang, nurses bustled around, and phones chirped. The interview was nerve-wracking.

Dorothy had a steady parade of loyal friends who came to see her, bringing home-cooked food and goodies to her. They lavished her with love. She presided over the whole room, wearing very dramatic scarves, turbans, and robes. Her dark eyes flashed, and her caramel-colored face shown with light. She rose above her illness, turning away now and then to gather her thoughts and marshal her strength. Whenever she strayed and grew silent, I'd call in Jimmy, and he would kiss her hand. Then, up she would perk, like a princess at a ball.

I asked her questions. How had she felt about having to leave her children and hit the road? She replied, "Like hangin' on a cross, bein' split down the middle." I knew only too well what she meant.

The lonely hotel rooms? Her three husbands? "Good, bad, and indifferent!" she hooted. Life in the little leagues and the big leagues? "I did 'em all!"

I asked her a final question. "Any regrets?"

"No!"

She answered them all—honestly and with unfailing humor.

The young man was a skilled interviewer. He asked her specific questions about record dates, performance dates, times, and places. Then he reversed the order so he could cross-check every jot and tittle.

With my questions, I tried to highlight folks, feelings, and femininity. She had performed for paupers and presidents. She was royalty, and could take her place alongside the Duke of Ellington and the Count of Basie. She was the Duchess of Donegan!

QUOTES ABOUT JEANNIE AND JIMMY CHEATHAM AND THE SWEET BABY BLUES BAND

Leonard Feather: "...distilling enough dirty, greasy, nasty, funky blues
L.A. Times   to take us back to Kansas City with their speakeasy beat."

Jon Pareles: "Mrs. Cheatham plinks out easygoing Count Basie-style piano
N.Y. Times   parts and sings in a wry velvety alto over the band's plush
                   horn arrangements. She can caress the lines of a ballad,
                   toy with the rhythm of an uptempo song and turn a phrase
                   into a series of curves and quasi yodels."

Chris Yates: "Those (like me) who find the confluence of jazz and blues
Jazz News   one of the most interesting aspects of the music will find
International   this album especially rewarding...by jazz or blues
                   standards, the music simply superb." (Back to the Neighborhood)

Scott Yanow: "The Cheathams' Sweet Baby Blues Band has no real competition
Cadence   today in the field of Kansas City style blues and swing."

Lloyd Sachs: "With Ms. Cheatham's gritty singing and crisply efficient
Chicago   piano playing leading the way, the music is as honest and
Sun-Times   direct as it is colorful and winning."

Joseph Blake: "This is good-time roots music. Enjoy."
Victoria, B.C.
Times-Colonist

The Gavin Report: "Back to the 'Hood puts some necessary humor and
Radio Publication novelty into Jazz Radio."

Lee Jeske: "...loose, limber and saucy."
N.Y. Post

The Hollywood   "They play music that makes for fine nighttime listening,
  Reporter: the kind of music that erases sweat or any problems from
                   the day, music to soothe you after a domestic hassle -
                   you can't stay mad while listening to Jeannie's boogie-woogie."

Philip Elwood: "...the ebullient Jeannie and Jimmy Cheatham and their Sweet
S.F. Examiner   Baby Blues Band...wonderful blues and jazz sounds...absolutely
                   marvelous."

George Varga: "...timeless blues and jazz that should be welcomed with
San Diego Union   open arms and tapping feet in communities everywhere."

Quotes about me and Jimmy from noted jazz critics.

Making History in a Small Hotel

·················

The small hotel in La Jolla, California, was within walking distance to the Pacific Ocean. It was the very same one we had booked for Doc Cheatham and Jay McShann when they came to the University of California at San Diego as Regents' Lecturers. This time, we had reserved a room for Matt Watson, program coordinator for the Smithsonian. He came to the Pacific Coast to capture our whole lives on tape.

We sat around a small table almost knee to knee, laying out our memories like a jigsaw puzzle. I smiled. "We gonna minimize the hellhounds."

"Yeah," Jimmy reflected, "um-m, we believe in angels, human and otherwise."

One whole day was allotted for Jimmy's life experiences. One day for mine. The third day belonged to our experiences after we met in Buffalo. The young man was as skillful with us as he had been with Dorothy Donegan. Gradually, like one of Great-Gramma Lizzie's quilts, everything began to come together.

Matt said, "I'm really excited. I'm using up all my tape and there's more material on how to rehearse bands, read an audience, run a successful jam session, put a good rhythm section together, as well as the special social situations you guys experienced. More than I ever dreamed there would be!" He paused. "And the importance of developing your own identifiable sound! I really feel pleased with this interview. It will be so helpful to musicians long into the future to hear these things from your own lips!"

We said goodbye to Matt that last day and embraced.

George Varga of the *San Diego Union-Tribune* wrote about the interview and noted that I was the only musician who had ever inducted another musician into the Smithsonian.

Jimmy and I are getting near to the top of the down side of the mountain. Halleloo!

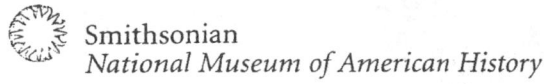

Smithsonian
National Museum of American History

September 15, 1998

Jeannie and Jimmy Cheatham
7836 Camino Raposa
San Diego, CA 92122

Dear Jeannie and Jimmy,

On behalf of the Jazz Oral History Program, I would like to thank you for recording your memories, stories, and reflections for the Smithsonian Institution. Your oral history interviews will provide researchers with insights that have never been documented, and will clarify and correct the written history of jazz. The three days you spent recalling events from your lives will be of tremendous use to jazz enthusiasts, music students, and historians of American music, both today and in future years.

It was truly a pleasure for me to conduct the interviews, as you made it seem like play rather than work. I honestly could not have hoped for better interviews, and I know that your sessions will prove to be among the most useful in the oral history archive. I cannot thank you enough for your generosity and your commitment to passing the music and its traditions on to younger musicians and audiences. I will send you a copy of the interview session (all 18 hours) as soon as it is processed and available for use at the Smithsonian. Again, thank you for sharing your memories and for your support of the Jazz Oral History Program.

Sincerely,

Matt Watson
Program Coordinator

SMITHSONIAN INSTITUTION
National Museum of American History
14th Street and Constitution Avenue NW
Washington DC 20560

Letter from Matt Watson, program coordinator of the Jazz Oral History Project at the Smithsonian Institution. "Jeannie is the only musician who ever inducted another musician into the Smithsonian." George Varga, *San Diego Union-Tribune*.

Me and Jimmy, 1998. Photo by Meredith French.

Back to Bina Avenue

. . . .

"You grew up in a fairyland!" my dear roommate, Jimmy, breathed. Sister Charlotte and I were silent, looking around. We had returned to Akron to celebrate M'Ma's ninetieth birthday. And what fun it was! She sat surrounded by all her children (except Jerry), grandchildren, and great-grandchildren in an ornate dining room at one of the best hotels. A live band played "Satin Doll," and, wonder of wonders, M'Ma danced the Lindy with Jimmy. I don't mean old lady mincing. She threw those tiny feet out, her arms were swinging, and our mouths fell open in amazement.

The next day, Charlotte, Jimmy and I drove across town to Manchester Road, down to Summit Boulevard, and over to Bina Avenue.

As we stood by the blue, blue waters of Summit Lake, my mind was flooded with memories of our little house and the old potbellied stove, the kitchen where we froze our stomachs while we burned our butts whenever we bathed in the round tin tub. I smiled as I recalled the old coal shed where Great-Gramma Lizzie dried her marijuana for her asthma and her eyes.

We strolled across Summit Boulevard and started up the hill along Bina Avenue. Familiar houses still stood there, though the porches where everyone had sat in the evenings were gone. All had been enclosed to make the living rooms larger. The lawns were still green and neatly cut. The tall old trees still loomed over the houses.

We peered past the big house that had once belonged to the Reverend Uncle Frank and down the sidewalk that ran toward the back, and there, nestled in green foliage and huge oak trees, was our little house. "There it is!" I exclaimed. Charlotte seemed a little unsettled and didn't say anything. "Oh, I wish I knew who lived there now!"

Uneasy, Charlotte advised, "Well, don't go walking back there! You don't know what kind of watchdog might be lurking around."

We stood looking all the way to the top of the hill. "Jovie the Eye-talyin's house is still there."

"Yeah," Charlotte started to relax. So was the China-Man's house, and Aunt Catherine and Uncle Sid's neat house, and across the street, cousin Brown's home was still intact, also.

I felt my head go round and round. I closed my eyes and I could almost hear children's voices calling: "C'mon over!" "I can't. M'Ma said we had to stay home." "Forget about what yo' mama said and come on over!"

We turned and walked back down toward the lake, where our car waited. We drove slowly past the old church, the location of so many of my childhood memories. We bumped over the rusted iron tracks where the little boy was struck and killed. We turned and drove back to the foot of Bina Avenue, parked, and strolled down to the lake.

When we had lived there, nearly seventy years before, there had been no hint of television, no man on the moon, no five-hour coast-to-coast airplane rides, no frozen foods, no World War II, no Korean or Vietnam war, no Martin Luther King, and no assassinated young president.

We stood gazing at the lake. It was so quiet we could hear the water lapping as it touched the shore. The weeping willow trees trailed their long green fingers into the blue water. We didn't see any people. I guess they were all working or in school. "This is a fairyland," Jimmy whispered again. "You really grew up in a fairyland!"

Charlotte and I looked at each other and smiled. "Well, we better get goin'," she said.

"Okay," Jimmy said softly.

"One more minute," I pleaded.

I looked at the water once more, clear across the lake. All in a rush my heart squeezed for a moment as I realized Great-Gramma Lizzie, Gramma Hattie, Grampa Mac, Uncle Sid and Aunt Catherine, Aunt Bessie, Uncle James, the Hungarians, the Eye-talyins, the China-Man, Mr. Riley, M'Da, brother Jerry, Aunt Ouidy, and the Reverend Uncle Frank were all gone to glory.

I knew that I had reached three score and eleven—seventy-one years of age—and in a flash I knew that I wanted my last home to be Summit Lake. Just scatter my ashes under the green willow tree, into the cool blue waters, and say a little prayer for me.

But not right now!

There have been 2,000 long years of the blues and there may be 2,000 more. I know I am not running out of tomorrows, because I have two offers to play the blues at two great festivals, one at a ski resort and one in New Orleans. "Boy!" I ask myself, "I wonder which gig to accept? Which one will be the most fun? Which the most meaningful for my career?" I toss a quarter up, up, spinning high in the air, then down it comes. I catch it with my right hand, clap it on the back of my left, and close my eyes. "Heads, we suck on snow cones at Snow Bird. Tails, we gobble up gumbo in New Orleans." I peek under my fingers. Whoa! Tails it is. New Orleans, here we come! I feel that old familiar rush; my breath quickens, my heart races, my fingers begin to play "air" jazz.

So let me gather up my loving roommate, the light of my life, Jimmy and his golden bass trombone, put out a clarion call to all the cats in the Sweet Baby Blues Band to put on the pots and get ready to cook up some great jazz and blues. I'm going to strap on my black patent-leather wedgies covered with many-colored polka dots, wrap myself all up in out-rageous red, and tell "ol' man Gabriel" to "git back, 'cause we goin' down to that freewheelin' city they call the Big Easy," where the tombstones and crypts are aboveground and look like condos and are more spacious than most New York apartments; where a crowd of hundreds of music lovers will be waiting eagerly for my familiar "A-one-a-two! You know what to do!"

Then the horn line will start snaking their way through the rows of applauding folks, second-lining as only the Sweet Baby Blues Band can second-line! Their instruments will gleam and shine like Klondike gold from myriad rainbow-colored spotlights. The rhythm section will stomp out a relentless, foot-tapping head-shaking beat, and the happy notes will soar up to the very tip-top of the huge blues tent—halfway to heaven— then fall back down like soft summer rain on all the people partying in the Garden of Eden. Lawd! We gonna go down there and just do what we born to do—make a joyful noise!

And after all is said and sung, and we're all stretched out across the stage, taking our final bows, sweat streaming into our eyes, receiving our usual standing O, we'll be full of the knowing that "Ain't nobody gonna go home feelin' bad!" And that's a *good* thing.

* * *

A few months ago a good old friend from the good old days phoned me from the East Coast, right after the midnight hour, and queried, "Jeannie Cheatham, I just wanna know one thing. How on God's green earth do you get *all* those men to follow you *all* over the world —*all* these years —playing that crazy song, 'Meet Me with Your Black Drawers On'?"

Glory!

"That's for *me* to know —and *you* to find out!"